TAIWAN

SOUTHEAST ASIA

LUZON

PHILIPPINE ISLANDS

MINDANAO

N

E

D1029608

Celebes
Sea

Pacific

Ocean

SULAWESI
(Celebes)

E   S   I   A

•Makassar

WEST IRIAN

NEW
GUINEA

0   100   200   300   400   500
MILES

TIMOR

AUSTRALIA

TIME OUT OF HAND

Time out of Hand

REVOLUTION AND REACTION IN SOUTHEAST ASIA

by Robert Shaplen

HARPER & ROW, PUBLISHERS NEW YORK,
EVANSTON,
1817   AND LONDON

This book is lovingly dedicated to my
three children, Peter, Kate, and Jason

Contents

7. Laos: The Ugly Duckling   :   342

The Seesaw War
The Struggle in the South
Souvanna and the Americans

.

8. Vietnam: Reaping the Whirlwind   :   371

The Vietnamese and the Americans
The Turning of the Screw
Political Half-Measures
The Failure of Reform
Background to Tet
The Attack—Failure and Success
The Continuing Communist Offensive
Paris and Afterward

9. The United States after Vietnam   :   437

Lessons Learned or Not Learned
Mistakes and Misunderstandings
Faults in the Structure
The Responsibilities of Response

Index   457

Acknowledgments

This book is the product of my most recent period of experience in the Far East, over the decade of the nineteen-sixties, although my first acquaintance with the area dates back to the years immediately following the Second World War. Much of the material has appeared in *The New Yorker*, but there are new sections, particularly the first and last chapters, and extensive revisions and some reformulations have been made in the other sections.

The book is the result of my own research and is based primarily on my own observations and interviews in the various countries of Southeast Asia. I cannot possibly thank all the individuals who have contributed to my knowledge of this part of the world; many of them are my friends, and they are aware of my gratitude for the help they have so unstintingly given me. I do, however, want to particularly express my thanks to Ambassador Soedjatmoko of Indonesia, and to Nguyen Hung Vuong, my long-time friend, of Saigon. I also want to express my very deep gratitude to William Shawn, the editor of *The New Yorker*, who has enabled me to spend so much time in the Far East, and to William Knapp, of the same magazine, for his invaluable editorial help. The help and advice of Cass Canfield and Genevieve Young, of Harper &

Row, are also deeply appreciated. And, finally, as before, my special loving gratitude goes to my wife, June Herman Shaplen, who has shared much of my experience in Asia and whose wisdom and good counsel, and constant encouragement, made the book possible.

Saigon–Hong Kong–New York
January, 1969

TIME OUT OF HAND

SOUTHEAST ASIA

TAIWAN

LUZON

PHILIPPINE ISLANDS

MINDANAO

Celebes Sea

N

W ——— E

Pacific

Ocean

SULAWESI
(Celebes)

E   S   I   A

•Makassar

WEST IRIAN

NEW

GUINEA

TIMOR

0   100   200   300   400   500
—————————————————— MILES

AUSTRALIA

1

Southeast Asia in Context

✻

Hope and Frustration

At the end of the Second World War, having been conquered but not subjugated by the Japanese, Southeast Asia began the slow, snakelike process of shedding its colonial skin. In their own way and time, and with varying degrees of violence, its British-, Dutch-, and French-ruled sections divested themselves of their outworn mother-country coverings and emerged as new nations in the effulgent climate of the postwar world. This revolutionary unfolding, while often painful, was full of early excitement and promise. Much of that promise, however, has since been dissipated. New forms of violence, including Communist insurgency, have swept the subcontinent and have vitiated the normal growth and development of these countries. Violence alone has not been responsible for the disappointing rate of achievement. Other inhibiting factors have included complex social and economic as well as racial and religious conditions and circumstances reaching far back to the precolonial period before the stifling impact of colonial-

[1]

ism and the onrush of Japanese imperialism. Such typical human failings and frailties as earlier beset the more advanced Western nations, including mismanagement, corruption, nepotism, and the desire of those who held authority to cling to it, were frequently more historically endemic in Asian societies. These variant factors, and the angry colonial struggles so soon followed by fresh social upheavals and political strife, combined to retard reform and restrain the revolutionary dynamic that had been so euphorically felt at the outset. By the end of the nineteen-sixties, despite what had been accomplished in some spheres and despite that vast potential for development that remained, the mood of Southeast Asia was one of hesitation, of trepidation, and of more caution than creativity and boldness. Hope and experimentation had not been abandoned, but a gnawing sense of crisis, of irresolution and frustration, had cast a pall over progress.

In the spring of 1966, in a speech to the Socialists' Youth Congress, in Vienna, Sinnathamby Rajaratnam, a lawyer-journalist turned political theoretician in his capacity as Singapore's Foreign Minister, posed the question, "What has gone wrong with the Asian revolution? Why has it not been able to fulfill the great things people expected of it?" In keeping with the role he and the other members of Singapore's small, tight group of social-democratic protagonists have pre-empted for themselves—that of acting as Southeast Asia's almost Calvinistic conscience—Rajaratnam offered his own reasons for the failure of revolutionary movements in Asia since the end of the Second World War. He cited "the deliberate cultivation of petty, pathological emotions" which, added to violence and unrest, "have steadily driven present-day Asia into a state of melancholy bewilderment." Lapsing into a kind of Marxist mnemonics—the Singaporean leaders revel in their Marxist past even as they have relinquished it—Rajaratnam scolded, "Instead of constructive leadership, Asia is saddled with pretentious Messiahs who seek to cover up the growing distress of their people by glittering displays of pomp and flummery in an effort to convey an impression of progress and prosperity." He went on to say that "instead of pressing forward with modernization, they glorify and revive the archaic elements in Asian life." What Asia needs, Rajaratnam asserted, is a strong new breed "of reformers and innovators to assume the hardships and risks of modernization." Such elements, drawn presumably from the younger people in the various nations, would free themselves from the hangover of the old anticolonial struggles and the habit of "defying and destroying authority," whether it was an alien government or their own. "The old nationalist ideologies can no longer provide the ideas and policies which the second phase of the Asian revolution so badly needs," he concluded.

Despite a degree of rhetorical exaggeration, there was more truth than polemics to Rajaratnam's statement. However, applying it alike to all the nations of Southeast Asia, each one with a different revolutionary and/or reactionary orientation, was a risky proposition. Certainly North Vietnam, the one Communist nation in the region, with at least an even chance of extending its influence to South Vietnam if not to Cambodia and Laos as well, would scarcely admit the failure of its national-Communist revolution or its ideology. What Rajaratnam and others like him—among them Foreign Minister Adam Malik, of Indonesia, another ex-Marxist— really meant when they talked about the failure of the Asian revolution was the failure of the non-Communist Asian revolution. Whatever one's sympathies, one could not gainsay the remarkable accomplishments of the North Vietnamese in establishing and maintaining their tough, rigid regime and, despite difficult internal tensions and problems, waging a protracted war against the French and then against the Saigon government backed by the might and money of America. Turning the argument around, one could say that the single greatest failure of the American effort in South Vietnam was that it did not succeed in its original purpose of taking a nationalist revolution away from the Communists. In the process of that sad, mishandled attempt, the United States ended by holding back rather than helping what might have been a southern revolutionary development separate from, and less authoritarian than, that in the north. Yet, partly as a result of Vietnam, one of the healthier manifestations of the soul-searching in Southeast Asia—not only among the youth but among some of the old revolutionary leaders as well—was a growing awareness of the primary need for the area to turn inward and look to its own resources, to begin the "second phase" of the Asian revolution with less dependence on the major powers. To be sure, help and encouragement in the form of economic and social assistance from the United States and Europe would still be drastically needed for many years to come, along with some degree of military protection. But the relationship between givers and receivers, between East and West, had undergone a radical change, psychologically and politically, as well as militarily, and that was probably all to the good.

So far as the United States was concerned, the danger was that in the inevitable re-evaluation of its relations with Southeast Asia the pendulum would swing too far, and that it would find itself back in a mood of isolation, uncommitted to other nations and overreliant on nuclear deterrents. Much would depend on the thoroughness of its own soul-searching. It remained to be seen whether a careful appraisal of the reasons for the failures in Vietnam would coincide with an examination by the Southeast Asian countries of their failure to consolidate their nationalist revolutions. By the end of 1968 the *mea culpa* lamentations and self-effacing or self-serving analyses that were taking place in America seemed to show little awareness of the fundamental problem with which the United States was now confronted, and which were aptly summarized by Henry Kissinger as "more than a failure of policy," rather "a very critical failure of the American philosophy of international relations."

The impact of this larger American crisis, on top of the specific failure in Vietnam, seems certain to be felt indefinitely by the nations of Southeast Asia and will surely help determine the future course of their appraisals and decisions. And since the area may be compared in influence to that of the Balkans on the rest of Europe, what happens in Southeast Asia may determine the political equilibrium of all Asia. Most of the Southeast Asian countries cannot afford simply to sit back and wait for the United States to seek expiation, heal its wounds, and resolve its problems of policy and purpose. During the nineteen-seventies, while taking what help they can get from the Americans, an unknown factor at best in the post-Vietnam atmosphere, these nations will undoubtedly be forced more and more to make their own adjustments and accommodations. They will have to do so both internally and in relation to each other, as well as in relation to the Chinese brand of Communism, to the North Vietnamese variety, to the Russian form, and even to the Eastern European variations, whose compromises may eventually be emulated. This process of adjustment to Communism, in fact, has already begun—beyond the political impact of Vietnam, and of the American decision to de-escalate, there have been other significant manifestations of the willingness of the Asian nations to understand and come to better terms with the Communist countries. For example, welcomes have been extended to trade, cultural, and tourist delegations from Russia and other Communist capitals by non-Communist nations like Singapore, Thailand, and the Philippines. To place Southeast Asia in context, therefore, a number of kinds, or levels, of relationships must be taken into account: first, relationships within Southeast Asia, including the bilateral and multilateral connections and conflicts among the different countries in the region; second, the relationship of Southeast Asia to the several forms and influences of Communism, including domestic rebellions; third, the relationship of Southeast Asia to the other non-Communist nations of Asia, notably Japan and India; and, fourth, the relationship of Southeast Asia to the rest of the world, primarily to Western Europe and the United States. (In time, there might be a fifth relationship to consider, arising from a new attempt to build an Afro-Asian bridge; an earlier effort during the first postwar decade broke down after the Bandung Afro-Asian Conference in 1955, and subsequent attempts to re-create the bridge culminated in the failure of the second Afro-Asian Conference, in Algiers, in 1965. For the time being, at least, there appear to be more differences than similarities between the new nations of the two continents.)

Any discussion of the ten nations of Southeast Asia—Indonesia, Malaysia, Singapore, the Philippines, Burma, Thailand, Cambodia, Laos, South Vietnam, and North Vietnam, with a total population of roughly a quarter of a billion—should begin with a reminder of how different each of these countries is. Racially and religiously, many of their peoples come from separate historical-cultural watersheds—from the Indian west, the Chinese-Tibetan north, the Polynesian south. Animism, Hinduism, Muslimism, and Confucianism arrived in separate waves. The ebb and flow of these multifarious anthropological, historical, and religious tides have had much to do with shaping the course of the precolonial societies in the region and the subsequent evolution of nationalism and nationhood. The significance of these rolling tides is still apparent when

one examines the causes and effects of today's quarrels and accommodations. One need only mention the long-standing conflict
between the dark-skinned Khmers of Cambodia and the yellow-
skinned Vietnamese, between Hindu and Muslim influences in
Indonesia, and between Malays and Chinese in Malaysia and
Singapore, to emphasize the point. Indeed, to change the metaphor,
if ever there was a melting pot, it is Southeast Asia, and the pot
sometimes boils, sometimes simmers, and sometimes sits coldly
in the new nationalist dawn, waiting to be stirred.

The manifold differences among the ten nations are accentuated
by language differences, not only among them but within each—
scores of dialects are spoken in Indonesia, for instance, and the
tongues of the tribal hill peoples of Burma and Vietnam are altogether different from those of the lowlanders, just as those of the
upriver Dyaks in Borneo differ from those of the Malays and Chinese on the coast, and those of the Filipinos differ throughout their
archipelago. Race and custom, family traditions, centuries-old
animistic and religious ceremonies, are other manifestations of
the vast and various social milieus. The wonder is that the dynam-
ism and nationalism proved to be as cohesive a force as it did
after the Second World War and that the new nations came into
being as quickly as they did. Here color must be regarded separately from race. The dark- and yellow-skinned peoples, no matter
what the differences among them, cooperated against the whites,
bearing out the famous late-nineteenth-century warning of W. E. B.
Du Bois that the problem of the twentieth century would be that
of color—of "the relation of the darker to the lighter men in
Asia and Africa, in America, and the islands of the sea." The
impact of both color and race was particularly strong in Asia,
where colonialism was perhaps a stronger force than elsewhere
and where, in a more positive sense, the force of religion, ethics,
tradition, and culture, with concomitant attributes of scholarship
and sophistication, was also stronger. Certainly by the time the
Second World War ended, the Southeast Asian colonies were more
than ready to burst their nationalist seams. When the seams did
burst, the result was a fervor that reached pandemonium. No
one who was in Southeast Asia at the time will ever forget the
explosive exhilaration that accompanied the seizure of power by
native nationalist elements in such far-flung places as Jogjakarta,
Indonesia; Rangoon, Burma; and Hanoi and Saigon in Indochina.

But where such quick seizures occurred, only in one place, Hanoi, was there a slow response by the resurgent colonial powers, and less than a year and a half later, when the Indochina war began, Hanoi, too, was attacked by the French.

Southeast Asian Mosaic

The pattern of nationalist development in the Southeast Asia area after 1945 was highly uneven, and this helps explain the many disparities and some of the conflicts that exist today. From the beginning, time was out of hand, and the unfolding of events was erratic. Each nationalist movement had its own peculiar heritage, its own source of inspiration, its own ideological springboard, and, perhaps above all, its own backlog of bitterness. Under these circumstances, and because the three major colonial powers— Great Britain, France, and Holland—all responded differently to the rebellions they faced, these nationalist movements not only evolved differently but, twenty years later, had created countries that were as different from each other as are England, France, and Holland. This is not to say that the newly independent colonial offsprings were in the image of their respective mother countries, though some attributes were inevitably handed down, such as the qualities of respective civil bureaucracies and of military forms and hierarchies. But, in their own right, the new nations were unalike one another far more than they were alike, and today, aside from the considerable variations in their per capita incomes, national growth rates, populations, and rates of birth and death, among other statistical measurements, their political profiles and characteristics vary greatly. These dissimilarities naturally have affected their manner of dealing with internal problems as well as with each other, and each has formulated its own firm opinion of its regional importance and status. Taking the countries one by one, here is how the mosaic of Southeast Asia looks at the time of writing, in 1969:

Indonesia, with almost half the area's total number of people, can be said, in many respects, to hold the key to the region's future. With its potential of strength and wealth, it is in a position to become the principle stabilizing force in Southeast Asia. Following the abortive Communist coup of September-October, 1965, which led to the gradual downfall of Sukarno, the renewed opportunity for Indonesia to gain leadership was tantamount to a reincarnation. But if it fails to pull itself together and, above all, if it does not succeed in recovering from the economic disasters Sukarno left behind, then its own continued disintegration will have an inevitable effect on the rest of the region. The country's nationalist zeal, so stimulating at the outset, in the mid-forties, flagged as a result of Sukarno's demagoguery and adventurism. Under the more restrained President Suharto and his mixed military-civilian government, the process of political rejuvenation through the remolding of the old parties is bound to be long and difficult; what Indonesia actually seems to need is some new political development, in which the youth of the nation can find an authentic role. Although the Indonesians are aware that they will have to help themselves, their immediate prospects of economic and social recovery, and the likelihood of their achieving a position of stability in as short a time as possible, seem to depend on the continued willingness of the Western nations and Japan to give them enough assistance over the next few critical years. But the failure to put their own house in order, even with outside help, will almost surely encourage new movements on the radical right and radical left. If that happens, the opportunity for democratic development may be irrevocably lost, and the balance of power throughout Southeast Asia will be jeopardized.

Malaysia, consisting of the former British-supervised sultanates of Malaya, and of Sarawak and Sabah, is scarcely a national entity, either politically or economically, and certainly not racially. Though Malaya won its freedom peaceably, economic as well as political conflicts between the Malays and the Chinese continue to pose the threat of communal strife, and left-wing dissidence is again prevalent in the Thai border area and in some other areas as well. The government in Kuala Lumpur organized an effective economic development plan that brought progress to many parts of the country, but its effect among the poorer Malays in the rural regions has been minimal. Falling prices for rubber and tin have also created mounting problems. Furthermore, little has been done to extend the benefits of economic development, which Malaya proper earned through hard work and good organization, to the two Borneo territories, which are far behind in political development, too. Sarawak faces a continuing threat from Chinese Communist insurgents—a threat aggravated by discontent among its various tribal elements. Sabah, which is being claimed by the Philippines as a result of its former occupancy by the Sultans of Sulu, is prospering in its own right, but cannot be said to feel a strong attachment to the concept of Malaysia. In a sense, both Sarawak and Sabah are floating weightlessly in postimperial space. The possibility remains that, sooner or later, the two territories, and the small but oil-rich British protectorate of Brunei, lying between them, will come together to form their own federation. All in all, Malaysia cannot be said to have proved a successful effort in postcolonial racial or political consolidation. It evolved as an expedient more than anything else, the Borneo territories having been incorporated in order to balance the predominantly Chinese population of Singapore. The whole scheme was, at best, premature and too hastily contrived, and posed more questions than answers.

Singapore, which was part of Malaysia in 1963 but separated itself after bitter wrangling three years later under Malayan pressure, is perhaps the most remarkable anomaly in Southeast Asia. The tiny island republic, which is three-fourths Chinese, has managed by sheer force of its own dedication and persuasion, under the leadership of Prime Minister Lee Kuan Yew and his small group of Socialist aides, to sustain itself and prosper against all odds. Without resources of its own, it has successfully started to change from a traditional entrepôt into a small industrial center and trade mart. The Vietnam war benefited it economically, and, politically, as Lee said, has "given us time" to survive and grow. But as much as any nation in the area, Singapore will continue to need, not the charity, but the cooperation of the rest of the world, Communist and non-Communist, if it is to remain viable. In short, this means that it needs the world's business, and that will not be easy to come by in volume. A growing unemployment problem as a result of the plethora of high-school and college graduates, and the loss of jobs as a result of the British withdrawal from the Singapore military base, casts a shadow over the future. Yet there is more reason to have faith in Singapore's "tough and rugged" society than in some other Southeast Asian societies. It is the one place where social democrats have outwitted and outfought the Communists, which in itself is significant. It could be compared, in its harsh and realistic appraisal of itself and of its limited resources, to Israel, and it is no accident that Israeli instructors were hired to teach its paramilitary youth forces.

The Philippines, emotionally roiled by the prosecution of its old claim to Sabah, is also in the throes of endless political contest and confusion, as it has been for two and a half decades. Violent partisanship has become an addiction, and, along with protection of privilege, has made social and economic development all but impossible. Crime is a mounting national problem. New left-wing threats from the once-stifled Hukbalahaps, now as much gangsters as Communists, and from new student and peasant elements, could cause further disruption in the decade ahead. The most hopeful sign, more in the nature of a windfall than anything else, is the development at the International Rice Research Institute of new scientific rice seeds that have boosted production and made the country a rice exporter for the first time; these new seeds, in time, promise to revolutionize rice production throughout Southeast Asia. In many respects, however, the Philippines remains the most disappointing new nation in the region, and this involves an odd historic irony. Having received independence from the United States almost immediately after the war, it has, like a forsaken child, reached back and continued to imitate the worst characteristics of its American parent. Nationalism in the Philippines consequently often seems more like a form of juvenile delinquency than a representation of political maturation and reason.

Burma, having isolated itself since the 1962 military coup led by General Ne Win, shows some signs of emerging from its shell, though it maintains its policy of calculated neutrality, and of caution toward the rest of Southeast Asia. The greatest single factor in Burma's thinking is Communist China, with which it shares a twelve-hundred-mile border. Though Ne Win cracked down in 1967 on local Chinese who took part in Maoist demonstrations, and thereby incurred Peking's wrath, he seems intent on maintaining good relations with China. His reasons are apparent. Beset by some three thousand "White Flag" Communists in lower and central Burma, who have adopted the slogans of the Cultural Revolution in China, Ne Win is worried that the Chinese might try to consolidate these rebels with an estimated fifteen thousand tribal insurgents in the north, members of the Kachin, Karen, and Shan tribes. Ne Win could handle his own Communists, but a combined effort, guided by Peking, would constitute a serious threat. He has been helped by a series of purges due both to ideological disputes and personal animosities within the "White Flag" ranks. These quarrels led, in 1968, to the assassination of Thakin Than Tun, the "White Flag" leader, and numerous other Communists. In the south, some of the Karens have sided with the government, and for the first time in a number of years the famous road to Mandalay has been opened. In the north, however, a hard-core "White Flag" element, trained in China, still seeks to weld together the dissident tribes. Ne Win has responded by introducing some element of self-determination, as well as social benefits, especially among the Nagas and Chins, but the security threat in the area remains serious. In another move to create more national solidarity, Ne Win, since 1966, has been freeing political prisoners, including former Premier U Nu, and he has appointed some of them to a committee to study possible constitutional and administrative reforms. He has also sought to re-establish better relations with neighboring countries and has made a few trips abroad, including a visit in 1966 to the United States, which is still extending him a little aid under the assistance program begun before Burma turned against the West. A few Western foreign correspondents have been allowed to make brief visits to the country for the first time in several years. But Ne Win seems determined to continue walking his neutral tightrope, and this will not be made easier by the failures of his socialist economy, which has been in a state of near-collapse due chiefly to mismanagement. Although much is made of self-reliance and the fact that wages and income have increased for workers and peasants, there are tremendous shortages in the government stores and, consequently, a black market thrives for rice and everything else. Much of Ne Win's economic woes can be attributed to his elimination of Chinese and Indian merchants, who ran the commercial sector, but he remains determined to create a Burmese Socialism for the Burmese, without foreign interference. So long as Burma continues to regard all foreign aid with suspicion, however, the chances for improvement are slight. The Burmese revolution, as a result of the country's self-imposed isolation, is thus still in a state of puberty.

Thailand, the one country in Southeast Asia that has never been under colonial subjection, is facing its own set of ironic dilemmas. Having gone further than they originally intended in openly allying themselves with the United States in Vietnam, by allowing the Americans to use Thai bases for the bombing of North Vietnam and the Ho Chi Minh trail in Laos, and by sending some of their own troops to fight in the war, the Thais are beginning to wonder, in 1969, what the consequences of their actions will be once the Americans start moving out of Vietnam. American assurances of continuing support leave them somewhat skeptical. Faced with their own insurgency problem—Communist terrorists in the north and northeast and in the south constitute a serious potential if not present threat—the Thais seem capable of reversing their position, or modifying it, and adopting a more neutral policy. Their history of adjustment to political trends in Southeast Asia strengthens this suspicion. On the other hand, they are actively pursuing programs of regional cooperation, and, having finally passed a new constitution, are about to undertake a new and hesitant experiment in parliamentary democracy. It seems doubtful that the ruling military group will do anything but change its political clothes, though the influence of the youth of the country and the energetic inspiration of its modern-minded royal family are more salutary factors for the future. Made prosperous by the Vietnam war and the development of its own resources, Thailand is one of the better-off nations in the area, but little of the new-found wealth has reached the poor, and most of the peasants are still scratching the earth for a living. The Asian revolution, by and large, has scarcely touched Thailand, and the prospects that it soon will are dim.

Cambodia, with Prince Norodom Sihanouk as Chief of State, vies with Ne Win's Burma as the nation in Southeast Asia with the closest thing to one-man rule. But Sihanouk, too, is having his problems, with the Vietnamese as well as with the Chinese. A number of his provinces are subject to what he has charged is Vietnamese-inspired Communist insurgency, while the Cultural Revolution has also spilled over among the country's Chinese, who are conducting propaganda among the nation's youth and, to some extent, in its political circles. Furthermore, Sihanouk has finally admitted that the Vietnamese Communists are using Cambodian territory as a sanctuary in the Vietnamese war. As in the case of Ne Win, it seems doubtful that Sihanouk will ever re-establish his former close relations with China, but, while excoriating the Chinese and admitting that if the Communists won out in Southeast Asia he would be the first non-Communist leader to go, he also maintains a policy of placating both Peking and Hanoi. At the same time, while still unwilling to re-establish full relations with the United States, broken off since 1965, and, in fact, while continuing to complain bitterly about American violations of his borders with Vietnam and to threaten reprisals, the Prince has also said he favors American maintenance of a protective military presence in the area. Thus he walks his own tightrope, but he has one advantage over Ne Win, in that Cambodia's essentially agrarian economy, while limited in new development, is still capable of satisfying the country's basic requirements under the program initiated by himself and the Sangkum, the "Socialist Community" that runs the nation. Sihanouk's complete dedication to the preservation of his ancient Khmer kingdom is admirable in its patriotic fervor, and his constant maneuvers, while they often seem mainly designed to gain publicity, do keep world attention focused on his very real problem of survival. His future, and Cambodia's, will obviously largely depend on the outcome and aftermath of the war in Vietnam, and on the nature of regional security guarantees afterward.

   Laos remains an anachronism, its future, even more than Cambodia's, dependent on what happens in Vietnam and on whether Hanoi and Peking will respect its flimsy neutrality after the war. Essentially a "noncountry," belatedly neutralized in 1962 under a tripartite (right-wing, neutral, and left-wing) government, it has endured, in its own fashion, and has even managed, with the help of a foreign financial consortium and economic aid, to prosper— but it is still barely a functioning nation. In a country bifurcated by the war, the Communist Pathet Lao and their forty or fifty thousand North Vietnamese "protectors" hold most of the eastern part and some of the central part, while the government in Vientiane, headed by Souvanna Phouma, tenuously holds the rest, including the vital Mekong River Valley. There are signs, in 1969, that the Communists have abandoned the old tripartite formula and, using the King as a symbol, may seek a Vietnamese-type solution in Laos that would amount to a coalition government which they would hope to control. Despite the violence of war, the Asian revolution, as such, has hardly touched Laos either. There is no indication that its easygoing people really yearn for change; despite the benefits of improved agricultural and marketing methods and new roads, most Lao seem content to remain, in effect, dependents, and to go on enjoying life without working too hard. Whether a new international formula can be found to protect them after the Vietnamese war is doubtful, and they will probably, willy-nilly, go whichever way the wind blows after whatever time it takes to reach a political and military settlement in Vietnam.

In *South Vietnam* sooner or later the war will be brought to a finish or will reach a prolonged hiatus or impasse; but there is no indication, as the year begins, when the Communist policy of "fighting and negotiating at the same time" will change. In an important speech, made public in September, 1968, Truong Chinh, the No. 3 man in the Hanoi Politburo, set forth anew the theory of "protracted war" and made clear the intention of the Communists to guide the Vietnamese revolution to a violent and successful climax. There seems little chance that the United States will continue to fight indefinitely in South Vietnam, though by the same token it is unlikely that all of the American troops will be withdrawn hastily. The capacity of the South Vietnamese to prosecute the fight themselves, militarily if need be but, more importantly, politically, is the key question. Nationalism in South Vietnam is still a debatable factor: it surely exists, if latently, but the government of President Nguyen Van Thieu scarcely represents a national consensus. It remains doubtful, however, whether such a consensus can be found, either as a result of a process of accommodation with elements of the National Liberation Front or by a broadening of the present government's base to include the fragmented political, religious, and social groups of the country. Some such effort, however, seems both necessary and unavoidable. The opportunity for finding an ultimate "southern revolutionary solution" remains, and even for keeping the result independent of the North, at least for a period of years before the issue of reunification is pushed. But for that to happen, and for it to become a real alternative to Communist control, will require far more wisdom and imagination than either the South Vietnamese or the Americans have so far revealed in their long and increasingly touchy relationship. What even seems possible is the rise, in time, of a new "resistance" among the true nationalists of the country, one that would oppose both Communism and the kind of unworkable settlement that could well be imposed.

North Vietnam, about which the outside world knows less than it does about any country in Southeast Asia, despite occasional visits by selected foreign correspondents and carefully chosen political friends, has achieved heroic stature as a result of surviving three years of American bombing. The war has, nevertheless, taken a severe toll. Aside from the damage done, for which the North Vietnamese will undoubtedly demand reparations, the country's economic mechanism has been severely disturbed as a result of the wartime dislocation of the population. Scores of thousands of people have been shifted about, for their own protection from the air raids and to perform production duties and to repair bombed-out factories and communication facilities. There have been some food shortages during the later part of the war, and, while it is difficult to gauge manpower problems, it seems apparent that increasing difficulty was encountered as more and more North Vietnamese were sent south to carry the burden of the fighting. The highly organized and controlled Communist society of the North Vietnamese is showing growing signs of fatigue and strain, and indications of this have come from Truong Chinh and other high-ranking officials, who have warned about corruption, black-marketeering, and additional forms of profiteering, as well as of a slackening of enthusiasm and poor performance by party workers. It seems remarkable, however, that the country has held together as well as it has, that its political hierarchy has remained essentially intact, with virtually no changes in more than two decades, and that Hanoi has managed the delicate business of balancing itself between Moscow and Peking. Whether, after the war, the North Vietnamese will accept American and other offers to take part in regional plans for development, or whether they will prosecute a policy of imperialism of their own throughout the former Indochina area, remains a big question.

Regional Groupings

At the end of the sixties there are many interlocking and separate regional groupings and arrangements that embrace a whole gamut of relationships—economic, technical, social, cultural, military, and political. While undoubted progress has been made in some fields, it cannot be said that these bilateral or multilateral pacts and plans have as yet provided the abiding sense of security or the impetus and capability for the quantum leaps forward their participants have sought. A sense of uneasiness continues to pervade the area, and doubt about the future role of the major powers, particularly the United States, contributes heavily to it. Under the circumstances of sporadic violence and the lack of true common viability, of corruption among the various systems of government and of their mutual suspicions, it is remarkable that there is so much cooperative stirring, and that the nations of Southeast Asia are willing to encourage such efforts, even at the expense of perhaps sacrificing some of their sovereignty.

Stability and security are certainly a long way off, but there is a common, though varied and sometimes contradictory, search for it. In military terms, it seems unlikely, despite American claims to the contrary, that the oldest multilateral pact in the area, the Southeast Asia Treaty Organization (SEATO), which was set up in 1954 at the end of the Indochina war, will endure, at least not without some drastic changes. Although the pact is still regularly cited as the basis of intervention in South Vietnam, two of SEATO's eight members, France and Pakistan, have tended to drift away from it, and the military withdrawal of Great Britain from the Far East has weakened it further. Whatever American military presence is maintained in Asia after the Vietnam war would appear more likely to continue under the ANZUS agreement among the United States, Australia, and New Zealand, and in accordance with American bilateral treaties with Japan, South Korea, Taiwan, and the Philippines. Singapore and Malaysia, with some help from Australia and New Zealand as well as from the retiring British, are seeking through bilateral agreements of their own to fill the British void and provide a new defense system. Eventually, the ten-nation

Asian and Pacific Council (ASPAC), in which Japan plays a leading role, and the five-nation Association of Southeast Asian Nations (ASEAN), or whatever merged group may succeed them, conceivably could play a security role, but the ASEAN members (Thailand, Malaysia, the Philippines, Indonesia, and Singapore) are far more eager to concentrate on economic, social, and cultural matters, as are most of those belonging to ASPAC, whose membership and programs somewhat overlap those of ASEAN.

Differences within these groupings, as between the Philippines and Malaysia over Sabah and between Singapore and Indonesia over reprisals taken by the former in the aftermath of Sukarno's "confrontation" of Malaysia, are holding back cooperation, but both ASEAN and ASPAC have managed to set up a number of subsidiary working groups in such fields as education and linguistics, medicine and science, transportation, trade, and finance. There is still far more discussion than action, but if peace comes to Vietnam, and if relative quiet obtains elsewhere in the region, the prospects for greater progress, despite rivalries and a sense of economic protectionism, will be improved. Such progress is bound to be encouraged by a variety of cooperative government or quasi-government organizations and groups, including the Colombo Plan, the Asian Development Bank, the Mekong Valley Development program, the World Bank and the International Monetary Fund, and such bodies as the Resources Development Company designed to deal with postwar rehabilitation in Vietnam. If anything, however, there are perhaps too many such organizations and too much bureaucracy, overlap, and confusion of purpose among them. What is needed is some synthesis and coordination of effort and programing, but little is being done to achieve it. Perhaps the most hopeful sign is the expressed intention of most of the Southeast Asian nations to work together after Vietnam, as indicated, for example, by Thailand's call for regular foreign ministers' meetings to discuss regional problems, and by the establishment of a regional "brain pool" to share talent in various fields.

The increasing interest of Japan in Southeast Asia, beyond a mere search for profits, is another development at the close of the decade of the sixties. In fact, Japanese diplomats are among the most knowledgeable in several countries. It is ironic that, having lost her war to conquer the region, Japan may in time achieve a political as well as social and economic impact in the area transcending, in point of accomplishment, what she tried to do with her wartime Co-Prosperity Sphere. Some of the nations still retain a backlog of skepticism toward Japanese intentions, but it is apparent that this is diminishing as the benefits of Japanese trade, and, in some cases, of financial support, have their effect. The role of India is less clear, and though Indians on an individual basis continue to play a part in Southeast Asian commerce and trade, that vast and diffuse nation is still too beset by its own problems, and perhaps too inward-looking, to take an active interest in political or security matters in the region, choosing to seek protection for itself through bilateral agreements with the major powers.

One of the most significant developments in the second half of the sixties has been the growing revival of interest in Asia on the part of Soviet Russia. Moscow's representatives, like Japan's, have been in many cases top-flight diplomats, and the Soviets have been finding a receptive audience for their economic and cultural missions. The appearance of the Soviet Pacific Fleet in the Western Pacific area, as well as in the Indian Ocean, has caused some nervousness, particularly since it is unclear how much of an American counterinfluence will be maintained in these seas after the Vietnam war. Talk of an eventual Soviet-American détente that would embrace cooperation in Southeast Asia as well as elsewhere seems premature at best, despite their common desire to contain China. It seems more likely that the Russians and the Americans will engage in some economic competition in the region, and that their military postures will remain sufficiently relaxed to avoid conflict. Diplomatically and politically, the chance remains that Moscow and Washington will reach some sort of agreements for guaranteeing the neutrality of the former Indochina states and perhaps of some other countries, but that this will not happen until the thorny problem of Vietnam is solved.

As for China, that turbulent nation is still so completely in the throes of its own crisis arising out of the Cultural Revolution and its aftermath that foreign adventures and even foreign policy as such have been virtually ignored. With some Southeast Asian countries, particularly post-Sukarno Indonesia, Peking has virtually no relations, while in the case of others, such as Cambodia, ambassadors have been recalled for domestic ideological reasons and have not been replaced. Nevertheless, there are some signs that the Chinese may be starting to re-evaluate their role in Southeast Asia. While there is no indication that the belief in "wars of liberation" has been abandoned, the failure in Indonesia and the opposition to Chinese activities in Burma, Cambodia, and elsewhere have apparently given some pause to the Chinese rulers. There is, further, some reason to believe that, over and above their stated opposition to North Vietnam's willingness to negotiate, the Chinese are not unwilling to accept the advantages of getting the Americans out of Vietnam, if only over a period of years. This, in turn, is prompting some Asian leaders, such as President Ferdinand Marcos of the Philippines, to speak of the advisability of mending fences with China, as well as of establishing relations with Russia and other Communist nations. Such appears to be the likely turn of events in the years ahead, and it will pose a whole new set of policy alternatives for the United States.

All of these uncertain developments contribute to Southeast Asia's sense of uneasiness. It is obvious that considerable changes are bound to take place during the next decade and afterward, and that these will involve many reshapings of old formulas and relationships. The Asian revolution is by no means over, but its "second phase" is beginning, and its unfolding will surely be both difficult and slow. While the various nations, it is hoped, will increase their determination to work out their own solutions and systems of government, the dangers of more Communist aggression cannot be denied. Whatever kind of insurgency occurs is bound to provoke a counterinsurgency, and the result will then be more turbulence. Part of the impetus and direction of events will depend, negatively or positively, on what role the United States assumes after the experience in Vietnam. Unavoidably, the United States and China will ultimately make some adjustment to each other, and, short of establishing full relations, a development that still seems far off, at least seek a *modus vivendi*, if not a *modus operandi*. The resumption, beginning early in 1969, of the Warsaw talks between the two nations, after a lapse of a year, seems a sign that China may be more willing that it has been to explore the conditions for an improved relationship. Perhaps a start may be taken toward solving the knotty problem of Taiwan, although many observers do not feel this will materialize until after the deaths of Mao Tse-tung and Chiang Kai-shek. The Chinese-American relationship is certainly important for the future of Southeast Asia, though the deep moral, psychological, and political impact of Vietnam on the United States is a separate problem that will have to be resolved as a prelude to determining the future role America will play throughout Asia, in its relations with Japan as well as China. It seems unlikely, in any event, that either the United States or China, so engaged in resolving their own crises, will again take the leading parts in the Southeast Asian drama. Their influence henceforth may be more indirect and subdued, and may consequently permit or encourage more native nationalism, revolutionary or reactionary.

2

Indonesia:

SLEEPING BEAUTY

✥

In Search of Identity

Any nationalist revolution, whether violent or peaceful, is as much concerned with a search for identity as with a search for freedom. Freedom, in fact, for the young nations of the world, both Asian and African, has often proved more illusory than real, more tantalizing than tangible. But the demand for it in the post-colonial era has continued to be a matter of pride as well as of patriotism, and the struggle to achieve it, for most new nations, has involved multiple drives and conflicts, subjective and objective. All of these elements are bound up in the larger search for identity, a more complex and more spiritually painful historical quest. Of the many countries engaged in the search during this century, and particularly since the end of the Second World War, Indonesia, a vast archipelago of some three thousand islands stretching across three thousand miles of ocean in Southeast Asia, has had and is still having one of the most painful and difficult experiences. There are a number of reasons why this is so—among them the wide geographic and demographic diversity of the islands; the many social and religious influences to which they have been subjected over the last thousand or so years, including successive and accretive

forms and rituals of Hinduism, Islam, and Christian Dutch colonialism; equally widespread variations in the patterns of agricultural
and commercial development; a peculiarly complex cultural and
class structure, which has been the product of mixed and often
conflicting historical pressures; and, finally, interrelated political
and psychological factors that have marked the long struggle for
independence and the subsequent effort to establish a united and
viable republic.

When, in August, 1950, a united Republic of Indonesia replaced
a brief experiment in federalism called the Republic of the United
States of Indonesia—to which the Dutch had granted independence and recognition in December, 1949—there momentarily
existed, in fetal form, what could be described as the only real
concept of identity modern Indonesia has ever had. True, the
Dutch still managed to hang on to their economic holdings, and
were to do so for seven more years. But at that climactic moment
in 1950 all of Indonesia, except for a few vestigial pockets of
imperial resistance, considered itself one. The government of the
fledgling republic, like that of the Dutch colonial rulers before it,
faced the gigantic task of extending its authority and control across
the whole chain of islands, with their widely varying power structures, social and religious differences, and class distinctions. The
revolutionary struggle had consistently been directed at gaining
independence first and dealing with the challenge of social change
later. It was during the process of confronting the challenge, and
trying to define and unite the republic, that the specific conditions
confounding the search for a stable and permanent Indonesian
identity became apparent. These factors were expressed in an initial conflict between a unique, managerially-minded group of Indonesian reformers and a more typical visionary element addicted to
careless revolutionary rationalizations. The conflict was soon resolved by Sukarno's assumption of fuller Presidential powers. He
subsequently initiated what he called Guided Democracy and
Guided Economy and introduced an ever-expanding panoply of
political and mystic-cultural symbolism, which was designed to
arouse revolutionary fervor but which, in fact, served more as an
excuse for adventurist activities in the foreign field and for postponing a coming to grips with economic and social realities at
home. Finally, Indonesia's irreconcilable conflicts came to a head

as Sukarno's progression from tacit partnership with the military to more than tacit partnership with the Indonesian Communist Party (P.K.I.) culminated in the Communist-led coup attempt of September 30–October 1, 1965, and the bloodbath that followed, a cataclysmic outburst during which possibly 300,000 Indonesians, mostly Communists or Communist sympathizers, were murdered.

Sukarno regarded himself not only as the founder of the Indonesian revolution but as the personification of Indonesia itself— "the tongue of the Indonesian people." When he was finally removed from power in the extended aftermath of the coup's failure, a more sober mood came to prevail in the country, reducing the urge to deal with everything, including the search for national identity, in frenzied emotional terms. As a consequence, the "unity in diversity" Sukarno sought to create out of the former Dutch colonial empire—a new nation of more than a hundred million people that would be the world's fifth largest—and the revolution he proclaimed to realize it were bound to be re-evaluated. There are those who continue to wonder if, in view of its complex geography and conflicting patterns of race, custom, and religion, Indonesia will ever be able to hang together, all the way from Sumatra to West Irian. The Indonesian national personality may remain, like the country's history, in a permanent state of "coexistence"; there may never be such a thing as a single definable national identity—any more than there is an American one.

Indonesian unity has in many respects always been more conceptual than real. Diversity under Sukarno frequently kept the revolution in a state of ferment, and, to a large degree, the perpetuation of the ferment was part of Sukarno's plan and purpose. For twenty years, with a combination of glamour and gall, he sustained the Indonesian revolution in his own image; whenever it flagged or threatened to disintegrate, he managed by sheer bravado or improvisation to piece it together again. The nonstop revolutionary momentum he provided, often in the manner of an interlocutor of an old-time minstrel show, was his unique contribution, and he never seemed to tire of his own performance. The adoption of wild causes, the daring employment of thrust and counterthrust, the dashing forays into the field of foreign policy, were more than method with Sukarno; they were self-generating products of his tremendous ego, and they became part of his life-blood, as necessary to him, in dramatic public terms, as women were to him as a private stimulus. When issues didn't exist, he invented them; he thrived on crisis, and crises permeated his being and ultimately made a caricature of his charisma—which, at its best, was as effective as that of any modern revolutionary figure.

It was inevitable, once Sukarno had been deprived of power, that a vacuum should follow. But if Indonesia no longer needed Sukarno, the country did need a substitute for him, a catalytic force of some kind. While the new military rulers of Indonesia, led by General Suharto, declared their intention of returning to the early, idealistic roots and sources of the revolution, they were more immediately concerned with the need to repair the economic and social wreckage Sukarno left behind and with the job of lifting the country out of political stagnation. These would have been difficult tasks for any group of men, but they were particularly hard for the group of Army officers who had found power virtually thrust upon them. The fact that, as a group, they lacked political sophistication and perspective, and were scarcely qualified to deal expertly with the complicated economic and social problems confronting the nation, was not in itself surprising. What was encouraging, under the circumstances, was that they were capable of enlisting the help of a handful of civilian experts, primarily economists, even though, in the absence of new political leaders able to guide the country toward a workable form of democracy, General Suharto found himself having to supply leadership almost singlehandedly in handling the multiple problems of government.

Politics, in Indonesia, had never had a rational development. From the outset of independence one of its characteristics had been the capacity—often the compulsion—of its countless partisans for engaging in heated polemical discussions and for analyzing and criticizing one another's motives with zest and abandon. While this process had been an integral part of the search for a historical framework in which the Indonesians could place their chaotic and still unresolved national struggle, it had, unfortunately, proved more diverting than decisive. It had, nevertheless, been part of the perpetual search for a national personality. Even in the heyday of Sukarno's dictatorial rule, the search had gone on, if only behind the scenes. Sukarno himself, with all his bluster, had feverishly taken part in it, asking countless rhetorical questions to which he had furnished all the answers as he relentlessly battled his private demons and myths. After he was overthrown, the pursuit of the meaning of the revolution became more complex and more public than at any time since the early days of independence. The accompanying soul-searching, stimulated by the restoration of freedoms of speech and press, served to make apparent the depth of Indonesia's continuing malaise.

Under the circumstances, what sort of prognosis for the country's recovery could reasonably be made? The nation undeniably was suffering severely from chronic economic neglect and stagnation and from prolonged political malnutrition. The symptoms included inflation and a lack of productive development, ideological confusion and a loss of purpose and direction. Yet in spite of its critical condition, it may well be that the future of Asia and of relations between East and West will be determined as much or more by what happens in Indonesia in the next few years as by what takes place in China. The comparison between the Indonesian and Chinese revolutions, in fact, is inescapable. Of the various revolutions in Asia since the end of the Second World War, the Indonesian revolution has probably been the most continuous; the only other one that has been as dramatic and constant has been China's. The two countries' revolutionary goals were similar from the start, in that both sought to forge unity out of unusual diversity and conditions of social chaos. Up to a point, although they applied different methods and ideologies and operated out of different historical contexts, Mao Tse-tung in China and Sukarno in Indonesia succeeded to a considerable degree in achieving their respective aims. Mao, the self-styled leader of world Communism, the presumptive heir of Marx and Lenin, managed, as no Chinese dynastic ruler over two thousand years had before him, to utilize his large peasant army and his tightly organized ubiquitous party to weld together the world's largest nation and even to incorporate such outlying dependencies as Tibet. But Mao's achievement has been threatened by new ideological disputes and draconian excesses, and the unity of Communist China has become subject to all sorts of fresh fissures. The effects of this struggle are being felt in every part of Southeast Asia, including Indonesia. In contrast to Mao, Sukarno created a sense of unity in Indonesia not by dint of dynastic precedent but by the sheer dramatic force of his own evolutionary will. Long before *The Thoughts of Mao Tse-tung* became scripture in China, Sukarno ordered *The Teachings of the Supreme Leader of the Revolution, Bung Karno* to be disseminated throughout Indonesia. However, unlike Mao, Sukarno was never an original thinker or theoretician. He deserves some credit for dramatizing the theory of nonalignment and of the revolutionary struggle between poor and rich nations, but he was always essentially an adapter, a borrower, and a clever synthesizer of other peoples' ideas. And where Mao, though old and ill, is still fighting in 1969 with at least historic justification to preserve his revolution and to deify himself before his death, Sukarno, also old and ill, lost his power as a result of indulging in, among other excesses, excess encouragement of the Peking-aligned Communists in his midst.

It was ironic that the Communist Party, which Sukarno nurtured and sanctioned, and which at the end he apparently regarded as his legitimate heir, was the instrument of his undoing. The irony was compounded by his efforts after the collapse of the coup to save the party, and this helped make his exit from the scene tragicomic and bathetic. Bit by bit, the straw came out of the man, as it had come out of Benito Mussolini, whom he considerably resembled. But, unlike Mussolini, who died quickly and ignominiously, Sukarno was destined to stay on and witness his own slow political demise, and to watch the awful violence that accompanied it. The mass killings that occurred in the wake of the attempted coup may be judged as the almost inevitable excess of a riven nation whose repressed demons and furies were ultimately bound to produce some such cataclysm. The effect of the mass murders was also bound to be sobering, though it was not as much so as the rest of the "rational" world might have supposed. This was mainly because the Indonesians were able to explain the bloodbath, at least to their own satisfaction, in ancient terms of catharsis and the eradication of evil. But the failure of the coup, the brutal aftermath, and the political shocks and re-evaluations that followed, all combined to wreck Sukarno's perpetual-motion machine, and to make Indonesia at last turn inward and begin a belated search for its national soul.

Like a man who had suffered a severe nervous and physical breakdown, and was still engaged in a painful process of self-analysis, the country survived the most difficult initial period of therapy, during which it separated itself from Sukarno, if not altogether from Sukarnoism. Most thoughtful Indonesians soon felt, however, that Suharto's New Order was failing to deal boldly and realistically with the heritage of Sukarnoism; one Indonesian observed that "The New Order is moving ahead to the beat of a slow fox trot." As a result of Sukarno's long mismanagement, the country was not only virtually bankrupt and dependent, for at least several years to come, on foreign aid; it was also shell-shocked. The task of keeping the still-rising inflation within controllable bounds while also balancing the budget was a monumental one, especially when considered in relation to the fact that the population, whose per capita income was only seventy dollars a year, was increasing at the rate of two and a half million annually. To keep pace with this rise, there had to be an economic growth of 2.5 percent annually and a growth of at least 4 percent in food production, which would require a much higher annual investment rate than heretofore, and a particular concentration on more and better rice production, which since 1960 had increased only at the rate of 1.6 percent annually. The long-term economic prognosis indeed seemed bleak. The best hope was Indonesia's tremendous potential of undeveloped or underdeveloped resources—which, after years of antagonism toward Western investors during the Sukarno period, the Indonesians were now eager to have tapped on a profit-sharing basis with foreign companies.

Politically, the Army, under General Suharto, tried to move into the existing vacuum as a temporary force in its own right, but this caused an increasing amount of discontent on the part of those who were seeking to return Indonesia as soon as possible to rule by the old, ineffectual parliamentary parties. Essentially, the opportunity to move ahead could only be grasped if there was strong and imaginative leadership, not only at the top but down through all the echelons of government. Suharto wanted to proceed slowly and build up the country economically before it became involved in new political contests. When, in the spring of 1968, he received a five-year mandate as President from the People's Consultative Congress (M.P.R.S.)—he had prior to that been Acting President—he also succeeded in getting the Congress to postpone elections, originally scheduled to be held in 1968, until July, 1971. He was able to obtain the support of most of the liberal intellectuals and students, who were even more determined than he was to develop new democratic concepts and to create a new and more effective system of parliamentary government built on fresh political movements. While these groups approved of Suharto's personal rule, they and other civilian leaders were considerably less enthusiastic about many of the military men around him and in important posts throughout the country, and there was a growing national sense of mistrust and fear over the Army's becoming too entrenched.

There were some signs during 1968 that new political forces were beginning to emerge. These notably included the P.M.I.—the Indonesian Muslim Party—a "modernist" Islamic group that sought to compete with the old-line Muslim Scholars Party, the Nahdatul Ulama (N.U.), for the large but amorphous Muslim vote. Another new group, with a secular socialist-nationalist orientation and known tentatively as the Development Movement, was hopeful of eventually replacing the old-line Indonesian Nationalist Party (P.N.I.), but it wanted the political dust to settle further before officially launching itself. Many observers felt that Suharto had waited too long to give the go-ahead to these new political movements and had therefore lost the opportunity to create for himself a fresh basis of support. By concentrating too much on economic reforms, and by failing to encourage concomitant political ones, especially among the discontented Muslims, he may have denied himself future support from new elements in Indonesian society if continued delays in economic progress evoked a mass reaction, as could readily happen if the economic crisis did not ease.

In too many respects, the country continued to suffer from a sense of lassitude and a hangover of frustration, reflected in a mood of cynicism and a lack of self-confidence—for which "Doctor Engineer" Sukarno, as he was now called, languishing in almost complete neglect (for him the worst punishment of all) in Djakarta or in nearby Bogor, had still to bear the chief responsibility. With his gradual downfall—there was a feeling on the part of some that Suharto had allowed it to be too gradual—the revolution of which he was so proud threatened to become permanently stalled, in full and squalid public view, on the roadside of history, like the thousands of abandoned vehicles for which there were no spare parts and whose remnants could still be seen along the gutted and pot-holed roads of the sprawling archipelago. The roads were slowly being repaired, and the revolutionary engine was stirring as Suharto and his men tried to crank it, but recharging the battery would obviously take time.

The problem of how much time there was to pull the country together was exacerbated by the fact that President Suharto and those around him were not yet really sure in what direction they wanted to go. They were fully aware that if the national economy did not improve at a sufficient pace to provide new jobs for the three million unemployed and thirteen million underemployed, and if nothing substantial was done about the still-endemic corrup-tion, the political future would remain bleak. In a new climate of discontent there could well be a resurgence of the Communist Party, which at the height of its power claimed three million mem-bers and an additional sixteen million sympathizers and supporters. The P.K.I. was badly shattered as a result of the bloodbath and wholesale arrests in 1965. However, it maintained an underground organization, and during 1968 a number of shadow groups became active, especially in East Java and Kalimantan (Borneo). In react-ing to this threat, Suharto and the military leaders took firm action and, if anything, possibly overemphasized the danger, though it was apparent that the Communists were not prepared to go into voluntary eclipse.

In other respects, however, Suharto was as inherently cautious as Sukarno had been bold, and while he and his aides talked about moving ahead—and took some impressive steps toward doing so —they also thought and talked about going back and starting all over again to redefine the ideals and objectives set forth in the 1945 Constitution, which proclaimed Indonesia's independence from the Dutch, and in the *Pantja Sila,* or Five Principles, Su-karno's official state philosophy, based on belief in God, national-ism, humanity, democracy, and social justice. This moral harking back to the "pure" revolutionary past emphasized the well-inten-tioned motives of the new government and the Army's sense of responsibility toward the revolution, which it had originally fur-nished with shock troops. Negatively, however, this also demon-strated the enduring Indonesian habit of relying on shibboleths, catchwords (there had always been a particular mania for tricky acronyms), and slogans—upon which Sukarno and his followers of the Old Order had depended for so long. All political parties and all mass organizations, including labor and peasant and cultural bodies, paid lip service to the Constitution and the *Pantja Sila*, but no one could or would define what they actually meant in a contemporary sense, or could suggest how these trite words and phrases might be applied to deal with the multiple and confounding problems of getting the country on its feet.

This was not to say that there were not some people who were seeking pragmatically to come to grips with the nation's problems. Notably, for example, among the handful of civilian economists, chiefly professors from the University of Indonesia, was the long-exiled Dr. Sumitro Djojohadikusumo, the Minister of Trade and Commerce, who with his staff was trying to implement a new program of economic and financial austerity while at the same time gradually building up the nation's agricultural and industrial base and restimulating its foreign trade. This group of economists was put in charge of a bold but rational Five-Year Plan for the nation's recovery, to begin in 1969. Meanwhile, Adam Malik, the very able Foreign Minister, had slowly brought Indonesia back into the family of nations, by helping the economic and financial experts negotiate more than $1 billion worth of foreign loans in 1967, 1968, and 1969 from a nine-nation consortium headed by the United States and Japan, while also rescheduling the country's foreign debts, which under Sukarno had reached the staggering total of $2.5 billion. Despite Indonesia's past history of wasting what it had been lent or given and its habit of insulting and even dispossessing its benefactors, it had always had an almost miraculous capacity to draw sympathy and support simultaneously from many nations— Communist and anti-Communist—and some of these, especially the Western ones, were still prepared to give or lend Indonesia several hundred million dollars more of specific project aid over the next few years if there were real signs of effort and progress.

The country, like Rip van Winkle, all in all seemed to have emerged from twenty dormant years into an unrecognizable world. The glossary of acronyms that had made up Sukarno's special Orwellian Newspeak had been dropped. The monuments and buildings Sukarno had erected or begun and had never finished stood in mute and hollow contrast to beautiful old ruins that straightforwardly proclaimed the greatness of earlier empires. Yet the legacies of Sukarnoism lingered in more than crude physical ways. The memory of the last Sukarno years was still too fresh, and the shock of awakening to the disaster he had caused had not yet worn off, nor was it apt to soon. The new sense of reality had not yet penetrated to many people, particularly to those who belonged to the earlier revolutionary generation of two and three decades ago and who still found it hard to believe that Sukarno had been stripped of his power. This element sought consolation in the fact that unofficially he could still be called the Father of His Country, although he had been forced to scrap the official title of "President for Life," along with a dozen other formal titles he had claimed. Father for so long had known best, or had said he did, that with his voice no longer stridently shouting there was a curious emptiness and silence. Even if Suharto acquired an identity of his own, he would never fill the demagogic void Sukarno left—and it remained possible that Indonesia required someone like Sukarno to galvanize it.

The sense of groping and uncertainty prevailing in Indonesia in 1968 was the result of a number of interrelated factors that collectively tended to inhibit response because they were in conflict with certain traditional tensions and restraints. These included habit and custom, and ritualistic elements of Javanese mysticism that had always provoked awe and sometimes fear; while they sometimes had led to violence, as in October, 1965, they more often had tended to hold back reform and postpone what seemed to be practical solutions to problems. Thus, for example, everyone knew that the Army of nearly 400,000 men was too large, as was the bureaucracy of two million civil servants who created less rather than more efficiency, and that together this massive officialdom placed an insurmountable financial burden on a government that was already all but insolvent. These vast numbers of soldiers and administrative employees were another part of the Sukarno heritage; they all belonged to what he had liked to call his "national family," and they all ostensibly worked together under a system Sukarno had called *gotong-royong*, roughly meaning "mutual cooperation and teamwork," which was supposed to extend from cooperative agricultural enterprise in the villages to the conduct of Parliament and the implementation of grandiose but unfeasible economic plans. Sukarno himself defined *gotong-royong* in a famous Independence Day speech of August 17, 1959—the year he had moved toward complete dictatorship, under the guise of Guided Democracy—as "one irresistible wave of heave ho and pull together." This sort of mystique had served to fire people up but had scarcely made them work harder or better, or, for that matter, together. As his unwieldy bureaucracy, lacking scientific and practical guides, had ground to a halt, and the economy had collapsed, while Sukarno had simply printed more money and manipulated the country's political life as he wished, *gotong-royong* became, ultimately, little more than a means for him to compound the confusion he had already wrought.

The new Suharto government, particularly its small team of economic advisers, wanted to re-evaluate the *gotong-royong* principle, retaining its original purpose but eliminating the effects of its malpractice, and they wanted to begin by sizably reducing the ranks of the bureaucracy. But the question was, how? With so many people out of work or without enough work to lift them above a mere subsistence level, the economic experts were naturally leery about demobilizing thousands of soldiers and laying off an even larger number of civil servants. The social restraints that ran so deep in the Indonesian psyche would not permit any such harsh solution. A system of providing a dole for those dismissed while paying better wages to those retained was unfeasible because of a lack of funds, and, anyway, it was not compatible with the idea of sharing what there was. In fact, government salaries were raised in 1967-68 to meet the continuing rise in prices, especially the price of rice, but the inflationary spiral continued, though it began to slow down in the latter part of 1968. Eventually, of course, a solution might be found in providing work for ex-soldiers and retired civil servants in a newly stimulated modern agricultural and industrial economy, but that seemed a long way off in a nation where not only the roads but also the railroads had fallen into total disrepair during the Sukarno era and needed complete overhauling, as did such basic services as the water and electricity systems.

Another factor in the unrest was thoroughly familiar to Westerners—the generation gap. Indonesian students took a major role in overthrowing Sukarno by staging big demonstrations before and during the March, 1967, meeting of the People's Congress which

had formally stripped him of his remaining titles and made Suharto the effective and functioning Acting President, the title he
had held until the 1968 Congress session that made him full President. In any event, the younger men and women of the country—
about 700,000 high-school and college students and graduates
organized into student groups started by Sukarno—seemed destined to become an important new force in Indonesian life for
demographic reasons alone. These young people like to refer to
themselves as the Generation of 1966, and they stood in often open
defiance of the older people, with their residual Sukarnoist sympathies; many members of this older group, some of whom were
officially organized by Sukarno's henchmen into something known
as the Generation of 1945, still suffered from a sense of guilt because they had compromised themselves under the Sukarno
regime. A fair number of these people, in fact, were still engaged
in Sukarnoist activities, both in business and politics. The students
worked together in various so-called action fronts, most of which
were inspired by political parties, but during 1966 and 1967 they
increasingly adopted independent positions within the Congress as
well as outside it, and they impatiently kept prodding the older
political leaders and the military to adopt bold new economic and
social policies and to take firmer steps to eradicate the feudal remnants of Sukarnoism. Where many of the older politicians and
many military men, including a good number around Suharto, had
some sympathy for Sukarno and a lingering admiration for his
earlier accomplishments, the students felt none of this. As one of
the most ardent of the college leaders remarked to me, "Why
should we have pity for Sukarno? If he were an old man under a
bridge, trying to survive in the cold, perhaps we would. But he did
too many bad things. I don't owe him anything. I wasn't around at
the beginning, and history, which is corrupt in itself, was corrupted
by him."

The Meaning of Java

Any assessment of contemporary Indonesia's state of mind must
include an understanding of the dominant influence of Java. This

influence is more than merely demographic, though the fact that Java has two-thirds of the country's population creates a natural imbalance that is reflected in the way the Javanese dominate the Civil Service and other important areas of activity, both military and nonmilitary. This has helped make the people of what the Javanese call the "outer islands" feel not only outer but outcast. While nationalism and national unity have remained the predominant themes under the New Order of Suharto, the elimination of Sukarno was quick to provoke a fresh spirit of independence in several important islands. This burgeoning attitude served to underline the harsh demographic and economic differences among the major regions that have caused more than one observer to doubt the nation's capacity to hold together—at least without the adoption of some greater degree of regional autonomy. The desire for more autonomy, particularly in fiscal terms, has been notably expressed by Sumatra, the third largest island of the archipelago, after West Irian and Kalimantan. Sumatra, which has a population of only twenty-two million compared to Java's seventy million, produces almost two-thirds of Indonesia's export income, and it has felt for a long time that it has not been given its fair share of the returns economically or politically. Again, West Irian and Kalimantan, while in many ways still in the Stone Age, have both been stirring with political activity that has had overtones of separatism. Sulawesi, which lies northwest of Java and southwest of Kalimantan, is rapidly becoming an important trading area and is also asserting itself more politically; Bali, the lovely island just east of Java, is such a tourist attraction that it could become a kind of commercial appendage to Southeast Asia, rather than a part of Indonesia.

It seems almost inevitable that Djakarta, Indonesia's capital, would be in Java. Located in West Java, the area of the island that is at the same time the most sophisticated and modern and also the most steeped in ancient mystic traditions, the city is virtually an island unto itself. A far cry from the quiet colonial capital of Batavia, which is what the Dutch called it, today it is a noisy, dusty, dirty city of three and a half million, the most confused and least charming capital in Southeast Asia—and, although it is a melting pot for people from all over Indonesia, an oddly uncosmopolitan one. In certain respects, it is like a territorial capital in the developing American West, a busy terminus of wagon trails (its wildly miscellaneous collection of dilapidated trucks and other vehicles reinforces the comparison); it is a place where everyone has to come to do business, to make deals and fashion intrigues, to talk politics, but it continues to exist in its own vacuum, and in most respects it represents Indonesia even less than New York and Washington represent America. Holding the strings of power in the country, it still gives the impression of being loosely held together itself by string, which one has the feeling could unravel at any moment. Djakarta is a historical aberration whose importance can easily be underrated or overrated, depending on one's own subjective knowledge and one's judgment of the rest of Indonesia; including the rest of Java, which itself is so diffuse.

The key factors in the Javanese impact on Indonesia are spiritual, ethnic, and social. Behind the tradition of Javanese superiority is the Javanese belief system, a synthesis of native animism and assimilated foreign religion, which the Javanese have fashioned into a philosophical, harmonious method of interpreting nature and society. The method seems simplistic in its application, yet, to anyone but a Javanese, it is highly intricate and complicated in its multifarious formulations. The belief system is dominated by a galaxy of natural and supernatural characters and forces and by religious and mythological figures who ruled the ancient court societies of Java. Ceremonial, allegedly magical acts link the belief system to the rural common people, who have traditionally lived in a hermetically closed, humdrum world. Within that world, removed from the commercial influences that have affected the outer islands and parts of Java itself—including Djakarta and the second-largest city, Surabaya, and several other towns—the belief system offers all the explanations, answers, and rewards a Javanese desires, whether he is a peasant cultivating his terraced ancestral rice fields, or in some way an agent of the ruling classes. This Javanese world-unto-itself neatly integrates all the occult techniques and ingredients of successive religions that have been brought in from the outside, including several Hindu cults, Buddhism, and Mohammedanism. The resulting amalgam is not nearly so dogmatic as most formal religions, including Islam and Christianity, but permissive, pantheistic, humanistic—even humorous. These distinctive qualities are brought out by the traditional

Javanese *wayang*, shadow-play performances employing leather or wooden puppets whose sharply etched shadows are thrown against walls or screens. *Wayang* is still performed all over Java, though economic conditions have made it impossible for average families to follow the tradition of presenting *wayang* as main attractions at weddings and other private ceremonies. Also, where the plays used to last seven or eight hours, they now tend to be much shorter. However, they have been adapted to modern communications, and their dialogues are regularly performed on the radio. Even the peasants nowadays have transistors, and, though in the radio versions the puppets and screens are missing, the plays are so well known that the listeners can imagine what is happening and project shadow fantasies for themselves as the performers' words waft through the warm Javanese night.

The importance of *wayang*, as explained in an excellent monograph by Benedict R. O'G. Anderson, of Cornell, lies in the adaptation of ancient themes to modern patterns of social conduct and morality, and the explanation, in mythological terms, of their relevance to contemporary Javanese life. In thus furnishing a guide to conduct, *wayang*, Anderson says, "like any other metaphysical and ethical 'system,' is concerned to explain the universe, [and man's] relationships to the natural and supernatural order, to his fellow-man—and to himself. In contrast to the great religions of the Near East, however, the religion of *wayang* has no prophet, no message, no Bible, and no Redeemer. . . . It does not offer the ecstasies of the Christian apocalypse, merely the inexorable flux." In reflecting what Anderson calls "the teeming multiplicities" of Javanese life, *wayang*, he says, is permeated with "the ancient Southeast Asian conception of the God-King, by which the temporal ruler represents divine power incarnate and the king's subjects partook of this power in exact proportion to their proximity to the throne." While Java has never had a caste system, Anderson continues,

implicit in an unequal hierarchial social order is the idea that each rank or level has its own peculiar functions within the social structure. Each order is dependent on all the others. If one fails to function, all the others suffer the consequences. Thus, the King communicates with the supernatural powers and secures their benevolence; the *brahmana*, the class of priests, perform the rituals of state and transmit the culture of the community to the next generation; the *satrya*, the upper class of administrators, have the duty of running the government and protecting the state from external attack; the traders maintain economic prosperity, while the artisans construct the material apparatus of the civilization. Out of the concept of function there now emerges the idea of morality. Precisely because all functions are interrelated, and because each order is essential to all the others, special approval for individuals within each order depends on how adequately they fulfill their order's functions.

With the characters of the *wayang* world regarded as appropriate models for daily living, it is no wonder that children grow up playing *wayang* games, pretending to be various heroes and heroines.

The social historian Soedjatmoko, who in 1968 was named Indonesia's Ambassador to the United States, in a series of lectures in 1967 summed up the impact of this tradition on contemporary Indonesian society:

As social hierarchy is seen as a reflection of the cosmic order, one's place in the hierarchy reflects the degree of inner perfection and power one has achieved. At the apex of this hierarchy stands the ruler who rules by divine sanction and whose state of inner development is reflected in the condition of his realm. In this view, territory is not the essential aspect of the state, but the court and the capital are. More than anything else, they stand for the state itself.

Project these ideas and attitudes into the modern state and its mode of operation, and several features of contemporary Indonesian society become comprehensible: the tendency towards paternalistic authoritarianism, the inclination to seek employment in the civil service, the preoccupation with prestige and status rather than function and performance, the unquestioning obedience of authority, the almost exclusive concentration of politics in the capital, and the emphasis on strengthening the national will through indoctrination and revolutionary fervor rather than the solving of practical problems. Moreover, part of this outlook on life is the inclination to view the unfolding of history not as a continuous process in which the present is conditioned by the past and the future shaped by the present, but as a succession of not necessarily inter-related but self-contained situations, periods or times . . . each with its own characteristics, demands and problems to which one should adjust, and opportunities which one should utilize. The perfect state and the perfect society—a constant theme in traditional culture as well as in modern political thought in Indonesia—is therefore not a goal to be achieved through hard work and rational planning but, in analogy with the progression from one mystical state to the other, through the application of a key, a . . . magically loaded formula. The door needs only to be unlocked by the strength of a nation's inner purpose and the application of a key formula or slogan.

By commanding such complete emotional and intellectual adherence, *wayang* serves as an umbrella under which everyone, whatever his religious convictions and whatever his earthly status, lives in an atmosphere of cosmological harmony. In fact, this special mythical world of gods and goddesses and wondrous animals often provides a substitute for formal religion. The belief in *natural* powers, transcending the belief in deities, is a dominant element that guides both spiritual and political life. The political importance of the Javanese belief system is underscored by the fact that it has been directly involved in the decision-making process. Sukarno constantly consulted his gurus and his *dukuns*—wise men, and spiritual advisers and soothsayers versed in or in touch with the natural forces. Suharto, who is even more Javanese in most ways than Sukarno, does likewise, maintaining a major guru in Jogjakarta, on the southern coast of Java, and assistant gurus in Djakarta and Semarang; all his major decisions and actions have depended upon the assurances his spiritual advisers have given him that what he was about to do was in conformity with the incontrovertible laws of nature. In some instances, they have given him what has amounted to instructions. Willard Hanna, a long-time student of Indonesian affairs, has related a story, which I have confirmed, of the extent to which Suharto went to reinforce his magical powers in his long-drawn-out efforts to oust Sukarno. After he had been told by one of his *dukuns* that Sukarno had acquired a mystical total of nine *krises*, which are magical daggers in touch with the natural powers, Suharto was strongly advised by the *dukun* to obtain the mask of Gadjah Madah, an Indonesian warrior-leader of the Hindu-Javanese Madjapahit Empire (A.D. 1295-1525). The mask was in a temple in a Balinese village, and in the summer of 1966 Suharto sent a group of his top aides to get it. At first the aides were too brusque, and the Balinese priests turned them down, but after a second mission, during which Suharto's men were more polite, the priests relented, and some of them accompanied the mask back to Djakarta, where Suharto, in traditional Javanese costume and sitting cross-legged on the floor, received them. After he promised to safeguard the mask for a thousand days, the period the *dukun* had prescribed, Suharto was given the mask, although one of the Balinese priests remained behind to provide it with ceremonial care, including sprinkling it with holy water. Suharto immediately began paying regular homage to the mask, and not long afterward he started to demonstrate a degree of self-assurance he had previously lacked in handling the problem of Sukarno. Thereafter, he obeyed his *dukuns* in other important matters, including the reduction of Sukarno's old Cabinet of one hundred ministers to twenty-four—the six-times-four figure having been suggested by several of his soothsayers (the new Development Cabinet that took over in mid-1968 has twenty-three members, but there has been no indication that this reduction of one was ordered by the *dukuns*, which may mean that Suharto simply became more confident of operating on his own).

Even Javanese who have been trained in the modern Western intellectual disciplines remain true believers, and retain their gurus. Selo Soemarjan, who is on the faculty of the University of Indonesia and who assists the Sultan of Jogjakarta, Hamengku Buwono IX, in supervising economic affairs under the New Order, told me once that until he was well into middle age he did not accept the belief system, and that it was not until he was studying anthropology, sociology, and economics at Cornell University in the late nineteen-fifties that he became a real believer. "It had caused a great frustration in me until I decided that I *had* to believe in it," he said. "There was no logic to it—it was simply unavoidable any longer." Soemarjan, one of the most gentle of men, comes from a family whose oldest son traditionally served the Sultan. "The Sultan is a special person who needs no guru, since he himself is a king," Soemarjan explained. "As such, he can communicate with the cosmological powers, directly or indirectly, through his *kris*, for example, where a guru can only mediate and interpret." Although the Sultan prefers not to regard himself as a king but as a common man, and expects the sultanate to die with him, he still performs his kinglike religious role because his own sense of duty could not allow him to do otherwise. Once a year, for instance, he leads a procession to the sea near Jogjakarta, and leaves offerings of food and cosmetics on the beach for Lora Kidul, the fierce and fickle Queen of the South Seas, a goddess who had a reputation for snatching humans for sacrifice.

It is easy to exaggerate the influence of Javanese culture on the rest of Indonesia, but the fact is that the Javanese domination is traceable not only to direct cultural and religious sway, which is sometimes limited, but more often to ethnic, linguistic, geographic, and political circumstances that have slowly built up and proliferated over the years. Indonesia's size and geographic variation alone, as well as the uneven distribution of its population as a result of the long series of migrations from the Asian mainland, beginning as far back as 2500 B.C., inevitably created fragmentation. Sociologists and anthropologists have listed more than a hundred ethnic groups and subgroups in the archipelago, including a dozen or so major ones, each with its own language and customs. The migratory flux also had its effect on agriculture. Java and Bali, with their rich volcanic soils and heavy rainfalls, long ago built irrigation systems and terraced rice paddies, which they planted intensively—the average holding today is less than two acres— while most of the other islands, notably the large and less populated ones of Kalimantan and Sumatra, followed the system of clearing the jungle and plowing on a rotating basis, while large estates produced rubber and spices. Trade and commerce represented another important influence, especially in the outer islands. In the words of J. D. Legge, an Australian historian:

[One] of the dominant themes of Indonesian history . . . is the interplay between land and sea, between agricultural societies and commercial societies, between kings and merchants, between Java and the outer islands. The fertility and the consequent intensive agriculture of Java has provided the foundation for the pre-eminent role of that island in the past. . . . Such agriculture required cooperation for the maintenance of the irrigation system on which a series of villages depended. Hence the growth of principalities, supported by agricultural tribute and supplying in return a necessary bureaucratic service. Hence the growth of an ordered society, in which rank was important and where it was accompanied by the appropriate material appurtenances, a society in which the court of the prince was not merely a center of government but also of civilization. . . . In the ebb and flow of Indonesian history principalities became kingdoms and kingdoms empires, exercising a unified control over a greater or smaller part of the area.

From time to time, as Legge and other historians have pointed out, the various Javanese kingdoms faced commercial threats from other islands under outside influences, mostly East Asian and Arab. The most successful non-Javan state was the south Sumatran empire of Srivijaya, which dominated Indonesia from the seventh to the thirteenth centuries A.D. But beginning as far back as the eighth century, with the Hindu kingdom of Mataram, the Javanese kingdoms maintained their own separate hegemony, and by the time the Srivijaya started to decline, in the eleventh century, as Legge says, "the island of Java acquired an importance it was never to lose," reaching the apex of its early power with the supremacy of the Madjapahit Empire, which by the fourteenth century controlled virtually the whole archipelago and itself became a commercial as well as agricultural kingdom. By the thirteenth century, however, the influence of Islam had begun to be felt in small Arab trading centers along the coasts of Sumatra and Java, and by the end of the sixteenth century the then Muslim states of Mataram and of Bantam controlled large parts of Java. There evolved here particularly the most sharply defined and most self-contained form of aristocratic rule, in which the nominal Muslim villager, the *abangan*, paid temporal tribute and homage to the *priyayi*, the aristocratic class, and, in a religious sense, deferred to the Muslim teachers, the *ulamas*, and to the *santri*, the devout class of Muslims.

The continuing Javanese supremacy, however, did not go unchallenged. The challenge came not only from the new thrust of Islam but from the new cosmopolitan ports and their commercial influence. One such place, virtually a city-state, was Malacca, on the Malayan peninsula, which, as one of the centers of Muslim activity as well, extended its influence first to the Moluccas, to the Celebes, to the bustling ports of Sumatra, and then to Java. The rivalry between these new commercial centers and the old principalities, mainly those in the interior of Java, thus grew, and the diversity of the archipelago took shape and form.

As the Muslim migration spread, with the added commercial encouragement of the Portuguese, who had arrived early in the sixteenth century, and as the older Hindu kingdoms declined, Islam established strong military as well as religious footholds within the interior of Java. The process of social and cultural interaction, however, was slow and subtle, and Islam proved astonishingly adaptable to Indonesian mores and traditions, and particularly to Javanese animism and mysticism, probably because the Islamic thrust had reached the Far East from Persia via India, where it had acquired its own Hindu-mystic trimmings before it moved on. As a result, the less devout Muslims, the *abangan*, literally "the red ones," or those bound to the earth, blended naturally and easily into the Javanese cultural landscape, and adjusted themselves to the Javanese way of life even as they continued to observe the essential Islamic rituals. While they listened to their *ulamas* and their *kijai*, the village teachers or "white-robed ones," they were ready to accept the native Indonesian, and especially the native Javanese, customs, known as the system of *adat*, as well as Hindu-mystic rituals and beliefs, and they found no difficulty in joining their obligations as nominally monotheistic Muslims with these animistic and basically pantheistic local ways and habits.

There were limits to the blending process, to be sure. Just as Hinduism had been unable to create political and social unity by tying together the aristocratic authority of the Hindu kingdoms with the autonomous authority of the villages, in its turn Islam was unable, as Legge says, "to provide a rationale that could bring village and court and also market into one political and social order." What actually evolved was a new tension between the *abangan* and the devout *santri* elements, and this in turn accentuated the old differences between the villages and the newer trading centers.

Largely because of the uneven nature of the Islamic penetration, two distinct and often competitive political cultures had also developed in Indonesian society, which another Australian historian, Herbert Feith, has defined as "Javanese aristocratic" and "Islamic entrepreneurial." On top of the growing Islamic tensions, Dutch colonialism—centered on Java for most of its three and a half centuries—imposed fresh conflicts. In time, the aristocratic *priyayi*, the administrators under the Dutch colonial dispensation, faced a fresh challenge from the Islamic *santri* and *ulama* elements, who felt their positions threatened, and this competition accounts for the fact that some of the earliest rebellions against Dutch rule, in the first half of the nineteenth century, were Islamic revolts, representing attempts to maintain Muslim identity as much as to define a nationalist cause. As the revolutionary struggle subsequently unfolded, the reformist Muslim groups, which came to Indonesia in the late nineteenth and early twentieth centuries, fostered the Masjumi Party, while the older conservative groups turned to the Nahdatul Ulama Party. The Masjumi became strongest in the other islands, but initially, in Java, it was most active along the coast and in some of the inland trading centers of Central and East Java, where the entrepreneurial class was concentrated. The conservatives of the N.U. Party held sway over many of Java's rural villages, and it was they who, more than any other group, ultimately came into bitter climactic conflict with the nominal Moslem *abangan* elements who had been drawn to the P.N.I., the Nationalist Party; the P.S.I., the Socialist Party; or, especially in Java, to the Communist P.K.I. But even within its own Muslim sphere, the conflict between the reformist elements of the Masjumi, which were the moving force in the broad, evolving modern nationalist movement, and the conservative Muslims, who continued to speak of holy wars and the creation of an Islamic state, did much to inhibit Indonesian unity.

From Colonialism to Independence

The latent social and political conflicts that still exist in Indonesia, which have exploded sporadically in the amorphous post-Sukarno period of the New Order, can only be fully understood against the backdrop of Dutch colonialism and the brief Japanese occupation that followed and immediately preceded independence. When the Dutch consolidated and broadened their Eastern empire in the latter part of the nineteenth century, siphoning off vast fortunes in rubber, tin, and copra to supplement the profits they had all along made from agricultural products, they suffered pangs of conscience over what they were doing, or not doing, to the Indonesian social fabric, particularly at the rural level. The result of this spiritual stocktaking was the so-called Ethical Policy, enunciated by Queen Wilhelmina in 1901, which envisioned nothing less than the ultimate creation of a new mixed "East Indian society" as a happy amalgam of Eastern and Western values and traditions. Although there was a certain missionary note to this benevolent concept, it also was based on a degree of self-interest among Dutch settlers who had come to regard Indonesia as their permanent home and who, looking ahead to retirement, thought of building a vaguely autonomous interracial partnership, a sort of postcolonial nirvana that would permanently check any move for Indonesian independence from Holland.

If this hope was naïve, it did at least denote an affection for the Indonesians that was probably more sincere than anything the British or the French demonstrated for their colonial dependents. In implementing the policy, the Dutch expanded their activities in health, public works, and agriculture in the villages, but instead of laying the groundwork for self-government among the Indonesians by offering them broad educational opportunities, the Dutch concentrated on training a limited number to fit into the colonial administrative service. Subsequently, an even smaller and more carefully selected group of intellectuals and technicians was allowed to go to Europe, mostly to Holland, for study; but these Western-trained scholars were never accepted in the higher echelons of the colonial administration, and ultimately, as what one observer called "emotionally displaced persons," they sought their own outlets for their rootlessness and became the theoreticians—although not the real movers—of the new nationalist movement. In essence, the Ethical Policy was palliative, and in place of gratitude and mutual understanding the Dutch finally reaped rebellion. The failure on their part to encourage the development of a national bourgeoisie that was permitted to think and act for itself aggravated the social and intellectual cleavages in Indonesian life. Such a middle class might have cooperated on a pragmatic basis with the Western-educated elite and worked for firm bonds with the Dutch, but in the absence of a bourgeoisie the elite drifted further away from the masses of the people and were unable to cope with independence when it was, in effect, thrust upon them at the end of the Second World War. As the late Soetan Sjahrir, the Socialist Prime Minister of the new Republic of Indonesia from 1945 to 1947, sorrowfully wrote in his autobiography, after Sukarno had exiled him, "I have been too abstract for my people, too far removed from their 'concepts,' too 'Western.' "

Amid the prevailing cultural and religious tensions and continued urban-rural cleavages, nationalism was bound to grow in fits and starts, without cohesion and without any mass base or systematic group alliances. (Only the Communists, after several false starts, were eventually able to build such a base, but they did so only in Java, and, as events were to show, neither their mass strength nor their tight inner control over their own organization was as effective as they had supposed.) Thus one might say that Sukarnoism, or something like it, was unavoidable—that some sort of revolutionary phenomenon based mainly on slogans and proclaiming a unity and cohesion that didn't exist was bound to evolve in the effort to weld Indonesia together—and was, by its very nature, likely to degenerate into political charlatanism.

Modern Indonesian nationalism can be dated from 1908, when a small group of Javanese medical students formed a society named Boedi Oetomo (High Endeavor) to promote cultural ideas and encourage educational reforms. Significantly, in the same year the Dutch created the first locally elected advisory councils, so Boedi Oetomo's rapid growth to ten thousand members was partly stimulated by the first overt encouragement of political discussion. There were reasons for the Dutch step, for 1908 was also the year that saw the end, after thirty-five years of intermittent fighting, of the so-called Atjeh Rebellion, in Sumatra, which was the last of a series of sporadic anti-Dutch actions dating back to the Java War of 1825-30. Essentially, the outbreaks were Islamic-led efforts to assert religious authority, but they all had in common bitter opposition to the worst features of Dutch colonialism, as epitomized by what was called the Culture System, which set patterns for compulsory cultivation of crops through forced labor and forced deliveries. The several rebellions were costly to the Dutch, in terms of both men and money lost, and the local reforms introduced in 1908, coming on top of the Ethical Policy, announced seven years earlier, indicated a realization on the part of the colonial administration that some ameliorative measures, however mild, were necessary.

The Indonesian response to the new Dutch policy was equally timid at first. In addition to Boedi Oetomo, another group, Sarekat Dagang Islam (Society of Muslim Traders), was formed in 1911 to stimulate Islamic expression and to protect Muslim batik businessmen against the growing incursions of the Chinese. The Sarekat Islam also, to some extent, invoked traditional Javanese belief, and based its appeal on associating its political goals with the advent of a Mahdi or Messiah, known in Javanese as Ratu Adil, or the Just King, who would establish the rule of peace, justice, and prosperity. In 1912 there emerged a third, and ultimately the most important, Muslim group, the Muhammidiah, which was also dedicated to social and educational reforms and the spread of Islamic thought. Muhammidiah still exists today, and, since the fall of Sukarno, has become increasingly active politically—so much so that it may ultimately provide the strongest base of the new reformist Muslim political party. Of the early groups, though, the most politically oriented were the Sarekat Islam and the smaller Indische Party (Indies Party) with which it cooperated. By 1914 the leaders of the Sarekat Islam, notably O. S. Tjokroaminoto, a Western-educated *priyayi* and perhaps the first important Indonesian political activist, were speaking of its members seeking "their rights."

Sarekat Islam included some members who also belonged to the new Marxist-oriented Social Democratic Association, which was the forerunner of the Indonesian Communist Party, organized in 1920. The Communists, notably including a Dutchman named Hendrik Sneevliet—who later played an important role in China as the representative of the Moscow-based Comintern, or Third International—and a European-educated schoolteacher from Sumatra named Tan Malaka, lost no time in moving in to capture Sarekat Islam. The Communists also moved in on the newly formed trade unions, the largest of which was the railway workers' union and the strongest, oddly enough, that of the pawnbrokers. After the Marxists in Sarekat Islam joined the Comintern, the apparent differences between the religious-minded members of the original group and the left-wing activists came into the open, and in 1923 the Communists, led by Tan Malaka, withdrew. Sarekat Islam survived for a time, but, amid the growing fragmentation of the young nationalist movement, it never really recovered. This process of fragmentation was hastened by the defeat of the first Communist coup attempt in Indonesia, which took place in November, 1926, with an attack on the prison and the telephone exchange in the capital city. The effort was badly planned and organized—an effect of the recent violent split between Stalin and Trotsky in Russia, which produced violent factional quarrels among the top Indonesian Communist leaders (including Tan Malaka, who opposed the action and left the party)—and was defeated in a fortnight. Over the next few months thirteen thousand people were arrested, almost half of whom were sent to jails or concentration camps.

The strong reprisals taken against the Communists reflected the attitudes of a new and more conservative government in Holland as well as those of a new group of investors in the islands, especially in Sumatra, who thought more in terms of short-range profits than of settling down permanently and making their accommodations with the Indonesians. The proponents of the Ethical Policy now found themselves in a minority, and the various nationalist movements had to struggle for survival. After the decline of Sarekat Islam, numbers of student groups and study clubs were formed, one of which, in Bandung, was headed by a young East Javanese civil engineer named Sukarno, the son of an East Javanese teacher and a Balinese dancer. At the age of fourteen, Sukarno (who, like many Indonesians, never used a first name) had been sent to live as a foster son in the Surabaya home of Tjokroaminoto, the Sarekat Islam leader, from whom he acquired many of his nationalist ideas (he later married Tjokroaminoto's daughter, who was the first of his five legal wives), and it was these ideas that prompted him to become a student activist during his days at the technical college in Bandung. In 1927, when he was twenty-six years old, he helped found the Nationalist Party of Indonesia. Two years later, after he had failed in efforts to rally other nationalist groups and organizations, the party was banned and Sukarno was arrested. He served two years of a three-year sentence, and in 1933 was arrested again and exiled from Java to the eastern end of Flores Island, and afterward to Sumatra. During this period, hundreds of other nationalists, including Sjahrir and Mohammed Hatta, who later was to become Sukarno's Vice President, were also imprisoned. The other nationalist parties and organizations that existed at this time foundered as the Dutch policy of repression continued. As Louis Fischer wrote in his book *The Story of Indonesia,* "The tragedy was that none of this prepared either side for the future," and as the situation "made understanding and trust, even contact, impossible, Holland lost the Indonesian friends who might have been her bridge to the people's heart." In 1941, on the eve of the Japanese invasion, the Indonesian nationalist movements that were still functioning, including a number of small secular organizations and Muslim groups such as the Muhammidiah and the Nahdatul Ulama, did manage to come together and form a loose Council of the Indonesian People, which demanded the establishment of a parliament and the adoption of a common language, anthem, and flag.

It was, finally, the Japanese, in their doomed quest for a Far Eastern empire, who brought about Indonesian independence, in an ironic way that revealed a confusion of Japanese intentions and a complete misinterpretation on their part of what was taking place in Indonesia. In order to bolster their military rule after they occupied the islands in 1942, the Japanese turned to three groups—the Indonesian civil servants, whom they thought they could keep under firm control; the *santri* class of Muslims, whom they hoped to use as collaborators and as instruments against the nationalists; and, finally, the nationalists themselves, whom they expected to turn actively against the West. That none of their plans worked out was due to a combination of authoritarian harshness and erroneous judgment, and also to the cleverness of the Indonesian leaders, who took full advantage of the new opportunities for maneuver they were given. There has been debate among historians about the degree to which some of the nationalist leaders actually did or did not collaborate, but it is agreed that they used the Japanese far more successfully than the Japanese used them. The key Indonesian figures at the start were Hatta and Sjahrir, both Sumatrans, who were freed from prison soon after the start of the occupation. Hatta worked in seeming cooperation with the occupation officials, pretending to help them in their campaign to win support among the Indonesians but actually serving secretly as the eyes and ears of the underground movement, led by Sjahrir, the more intellectual of the two men. The boyish-looking Sjahrir lived at his sister's house in Tjipanas, near Batavia, and ran a secret radio network that kept him in touch with his own nationalist agents all over the islands; now and then he also traveled around to maintain personal contacts.

One of the first things Hatta did was persuade the Japanese to release Sukarno from jail, and Sukarno thereupon became the third key figure among the nationalists; since he had a charisma the other two men lacked, he soon emerged as the most important of the three. In March, 1943, the Japanese established a party called

Putera (Center of the People's Power), with Sukarno as chairman and Hatta as vice chairman, and six months later they set up a volunteer army named Peta, which eventually grew to a force of 120,000 and became the forerunner of the Indonesian Republican Army. When Putera proved too independent-minded, the Japanese replaced it with Hokokai, a Japanese word meaning People's Loyalty Organization, but this didn't prove much more controllable than its predecessor. Similarly, Japanese efforts to create a single, manipulative Muslim movement simply paved the way for united Muslim political activity, although to some extent the Japanese did succeed in creating dissension between the religious and secular nationalists.

As it became more and more apparent that the Japanese were losing the war, they became desperate and began making firmer promises of independence (*Merdeka*) to the Indonesians. Sjahrir felt that the Indonesians should not wait to be handed their freedom by the Japanese, but should simply announce it themselves. Sukarno and Hatta were more cautious. After meeting with Marshal Terauchi, the Japanese Southeast Asia Commander, in Saigon, on August 11, 1945, they accepted his promise to grant independence on August 24, after the completion of a draft constitution by a newly created Independence Preparatory Committee. Sjahrir, however, kept pushing his two compatriots and had almost persuaded Sukarno to make an independence announcement of his own when, after the bombing of Hiroshima and Nagasaki, the war suddenly ended, on August 15. Two days later, after some hesitation and after conferring with Japanese authorities, who admitted that Japan was no longer in a position to sponsor a declaration of independence, Sukarno declared unilaterally that Indonesia was a free republic.

In fact, Indonesia was as yet neither free nor a republic. Its revolution was only beginning. The next four years saw a nightmare of violence which not only delayed the process of creating an independent state apparatus but set Indonesians against each other and aggravated the social imbalances and dislocations in the archipelago. To a considerable extent, the British were the unfortunate, and admittedly reluctant, instigators of disorder, as they also were initially in the southern part of French Indochina. In both places, British troops were assigned the difficult task of initial occupation before the former colonial masters returned to engage in their benighted and doomed attempts to reassert authority. The allocation of occupation forces was decided on by Roosevelt and Churchill before the Pacific war ended, and those two leaders gave the job of taking Indonesia back from the Japanese to Lord Louis Mountbatten's British Southeast Asian Command instead of to General Douglas MacArthur's American Far East Command. Many Indonesians today still feel that if the Americans, who had more troops available and were more popular at the time than the British, had taken over, the ensuing four-year tragedy might have been averted, or at least ameliorated.

The first British paratroopers were dropped into Batavia, now renamed Djakarta, on September 8, 1945—by which time a constitution had been promulgated by the Indonesians and Sukarno had been installed as President, with Hatta as Vice President. The Constitution provided for a Cabinet responsible to the President, and a representative council to be elected by popular suffrage, but in the meantime Sukarno had appointed a Central Indonesian National Committee (K.N.I.P.) which, in various forms, was to function for ten years. That fall, after Sjahrir and his associates, who had been the strongest anticollaborationists during the war, insisted on a multiparty system, Sukarno and Hatta reluctantly agreed to go along, and in November they accepted Sjahrir as, in effect, a "political" Prime Minister. Sukarno and Hatta remained President and Vice President, respectively. By then fighting had broken out in Java, Sumatra, and Bali between Indonesians and miscellaneous groups trying to restore the prewar system of colonial government. Returning Dutch units had been augmented by former Dutch prisoners of war, but Mountbatten was still short of troops and had to call on the Japanese waiting to be repatriated to help keep order. Although some of the Japanese had turned their weapons over to the Indonesians before the British arrived, most of the Japanese forces still in the country were doing a good part of the fighting against Indonesian paramilitary youth units, the new Republican Army formed from the remnants of the Japanese Peta, and a new territorial home guard.

Because they had by now been caught in the middle in their attempts to restore order, the British were already being accused of bad faith by both the Dutch and the Indonesians, but they succeeded in getting some negotiations started. The need to compromise was recognized most clearly by Sjahrir, who realized that the new republic, which really only controlled parts of Java and Sumatra, was facing a twofold internal threat: On the one side, it was confronted by what he described as elements of "feudalism and supernationalism"—by which he meant terrorist and rabble elements who had "sold themselves and their honor to Japanese fascism"; on the other side, as a democratic Socialist, he saw the dangers of militant revolutionary groups, such as the paramilitary youth formations, being infiltrated by opportunistic rivals of the new Indonesian government, especially the Communists. Sjahrir's fears were justified; in March, 1946, the organizers of a new National Front, who were opposed to any compromise with the Dutch, met in Madiun, in central Java, and, under the leadership of Tan Malaka, the former Communist who had now established his own radical party, planned a *coup d'état*. The coup attempt failed, though the conspirators succeeded in temporarily forcing Sjahrir's resignation. When they could not agree among themselves, however, this left-wing opposition fell apart and Tan Malaka and a number of his aides were arrested.

Negotiations between the Dutch and the nationalists dragged on, amid growing mutual charges of bad faith, but eventually, in March, 1947, at Linggadjati, a hill station in northeastern Java, an agreement was signed under which the Dutch and the Indonesians agreed "to cooperate in the rapid formation of a sovereign state on a federal basis to be called the United States of Indonesia." The Dutch recognized the republic's *de facto* control of Java, Sumatra, and Madura, and agreed on a program of broad economic development throughout the islands. But the fact that the Dutch delayed signing the agreement for several months because of opposition in Holland vitiated its chances of success and undermined Sjahrir's position politically. Although some Dutch troops had begun going home, others still in Indonesia initiated a brief "police action" that weakened the control of the Republican forces in Java. The Dutch action was widely criticized abroad, however, and the United Nations entered the picture when the Security Council appointed a Committee of Good Offices, whose representatives, in December, 1947, engineered the signing aboard the American naval vessel *Renville*, off Indonesia, of a second agreement establishing a federal republic. Continuing opposition among many Indonesians to the Linggadjati and *Renville* agreements forced the resignations of Sjahrir as Prime Minister and then of his Socialist successor, Amir Sjarifuddin, and an important political realignment followed. A coalition of the Muslim Masjumi Party and of the reorganized Nationalists (P.N.I.) took over and switched from opposition to the *Renville* agreement to support of it. This intensified the developing split on the left; Sjahrir formed a new moderate Indonesian Socialist Party (the P.S.I.), while Sjarifuddin created a new People's Democratic Front, which soon came to be dominated by the Communists. Elements of this front and the Indonesian armed forces engaged in repeated small clashes, which culminated, in September, 1948, in a full-scale effort by the Communists to capture Madiun. This second major Communist effort in Indonesia also failed, ending in the deaths of Sjarifuddin and of a top Indonesian Communist named Musso, who had returned from exile in the Soviet Union to head the uprising.

Two months after this, the Dutch began a second police action, occupying Jogjakarta, then the capital of the republic, and interning Sukarno and other Republican leaders. Once again, world opinion, led by the United States, which brought diplomatic and economic pressure on the Dutch, forced the latter to retreat. A new United Nations Commission for Indonesia supervised a lengthy Round Table Conference at The Hague, as a result of which the Dutch were forced in December, 1949, to surrender sovereignty over all the Dutch East Indies to a new United States of Indonesia, of which the republic was only one of sixteen component members. This compromise on the part of the Dutch was, in effect, a policy of Balkanization aimed at warding off complete independence by creating a series of puppet states—most of which would pay homage to, and be tied economically to, Holland—and rendering the new republic powerless. Following sporadic outbreaks all over the archipelago between nationalist and remnant colonial bands of soldiers, the "federal" experiment collapsed after less than a year when it became apparent that, with the Dutch troops gone, the other fifteen federal states could not hold out against the Republican forces, who moved into the outer islands and gradually caused the collapse of one state after another, an exception being the South Moluccas, where there was a strong Christian element.

In August, 1950, the "unitary" Republic of Indonesia was proclaimed, and the idea of federalism was cast aside.

The long and bitter battle had sapped everyone's energies, and little or nothing had been done to improve social and economic conditions. The Dutch still retained their economic holdings, while the masses of people were as poor as ever. Politically, the fight against the Dutch had caused deep fissures among the Indonesians, but at least a common revolutionary fervor and pride had helped provide a semblance of solidarity. With the support of the Western world, particularly of the United States, the Indonesians had finally defeated their Dutch masters, but their internal revolution and their search for their own national identity were still just beginning.

From Parliamentary Democracy to Sukarno

At the outset of its independence, Indonesia had a predominantly civilian leadership that was one of the most impressive in postwar Asia, and only a bobtail, ragged, motley, revolutionary Army. Although Sukarno remained President, as he had been from the beginning, the most influential figure was Mohammed Hatta. Hatta, a trained economist, who had been Vice President when the Indonesians had first declared their freedom, in 1945, had succeeded Sjahrir as Prime Minister during the short-lived federal republic. The most cosmopolitan of the early Indonesian leaders, and the most practical-minded, he was the man who had written the blueprint for independence, and when it had begun to become a reality had taken charge of it, creating a Civil Service and getting the still Dutch-owned and -operated economy functioning again. When the unitary Republic of Indonesia was set up in August, 1950, Hatta resumed his earlier job as Sukarno's Vice President, and the first parliamentary Prime Minister became Mohammed Natsir, another Sumatran and the head of the predominant Muslim Masjumi Party. A dedicated Socialist and Islamic nationalist leader, the author of eight books about Islam, the forty-two-year-old Natsir was an ardent anti-Communist who believed in cooperation among all religious and political groups in behalf of the creation of a social-democratic state sympathetic to Islam but not dominated by it.

Natsir had worked closely, ever since 1945, with Sjahrir, the secular Socialist Prime Minister in the original revolutionary government. Hatta and Natsir were dedicated to parliamentary rule, and Natsir's program, which was actively supported by four other parties in addition to Sjahrir's Socialists, and was subscribed to at first by the leading oppositionists, the nationalists of the P.N.I., was a model of moderation and common sense. Despite its essentially capitalist orientation, the Natsir government sought a mixed economy that would gradually move toward Socialism as a new managerial class was trained; to this end it promised to extend easy credit to Indonesian entrepreneurs and to agricultural cooperatives, especially to those engaged in rubber production, so they could actively compete with plantations run by the Dutch and other foreigners. These Socialist programs were under the supervision of Natsir's Socialist allies of the P.S.I., including the brilliant young economist, Sumitro Djojohadikusumo, who was then Minister of Commerce. Also in Natsir's Cabinet, as Deputy Prime Minister and Minister for Internal Security, was the then thirty-six-year-old Sultan of Jogjakarta, Hamengku Buwono IX, who had organized the new Army and pioneered many social reforms in his realm during the early years of the revolution, and who, like Sumitro, would, in 1968, serve as one of General Suharto's principal deputies. Indonesian politicians, or at least a good many of them, have always had a tremendous capacity for survival, despite their frequent ups and downs; Natsir himself, at sixty, and Hatta, at sixty-five, would again in 1968 be active in Muslim politics.

There was, thus, no lack of civilian talent in the young republic in 1950, and although there were four Cabinet crises in the first three years, a general continuity of purpose and programs was maintained. However, these early Cabinets enjoyed only moderate success, increasing rice production, restoring communications, and reducing bandit activity, but failing to reduce the swelling ranks of soldiers and Civil Service workers—two major problems that still existed in 1969—and failing to move successfully against the Darul Islam, the extremist Muslim movement that had begun to tighten its hold on sections of West Java and was not to be fully exterminated for thirteen years. There was something lacking: a sense of fervor. When I made my first trip to Indonesia at this time, I remember the feeling of impatience on the part of the younger generation that had been weaned on nationalist passions and the excitement of the revolution. To them, an efficient, rational approach under the mild banner of constitutional democracy was uninspiring and dull. They wanted a fresh cause to which they could dedicate themselves, and, by 1952, many among them had begun to look to President Sukarno. Some factions of the Army at this point also looked to Sukarno to assume a stronger role and, with their support, to get rid of the People's Representative Council, the *ad hoc* appointive parliamentary body that had been created in 1949, which they called a "coffee house." This Army element wanted to run the country itself, with the help of a new, more pliable Parliament. Sukarno, however, was not yet ready to take over. "You do not want me to be a dictator, but if I dissolve the Council I would become a dictator, and I don't want that," he dramatically told a throng that had gathered on the palace lawn in October, 1952, when an Army coup was averted. Sukarno, beginning to head for the center of the stage, took advantage of this crisis to fire several top officers he felt had been disloyal to him —among them Colonel Abdul Haris Nasution, the Chief of Staff. Sukarno now also moved closer to an alliance with the P.N.I., the Nationalist Party, which would remain loyal to him to the end. The party, led by Ali Sastroamidjojo, formed a government in July, 1953, and retained control for two years.

During this time nationalism gained ground as an emotional and popular force. "Indonesianization" became a widely used term in reference to the economy, and some progress was made in getting Indonesian firms to enter the fields of shipping, banking, rice-milling, and other areas that had always been dominated by the Dutch, by Chinese, or by other Westerners. However, less was done than the Hatta and Natsir Cabinets had accomplished in dealing with the drab but important day-by-day administrative and economic problems. The split between secular and religious political elements now began to widen. As shaped by the nationalists, Indonesian foreign policy became more militantly neutral and xenophobic; the assertion of this new outlook, including the demand for West Irian, then Dutch New Guinea, whose future had been left unsettled in the independence agreement, was brought to a noisy and emotional climax at the conference of Asian and African nations held at Bandung, in West Java, in the spring of 1955, which was attended by top leaders from all over the world, including Pandit Nehru of India and Chou En-lai of Communist China. The affairs of government were further neglected during this time because elections had finally been scheduled—for a new Parliament in September, 1955, and for a Constituent Assembly, which was to write a new constitution, in December. As a result, there was a great deal of political jockeying going on, particularly between the Masjumi and the P.N.I.

By this time, too, the P.K.I.—the Communists—after having, like Sukarno, remained in the background at first, had again become an important force. Following the defeat of the Communist revolt in Central Java, in September, 1948, the party had all but disintegrated and its remnants had gone underground. One of its young leaders, Dipa Nusantara Aidit, had fled the country and, with a companion party member, M. H. Lukman, had gone to North Vietnam, where for a short time they joined the ranks of the Vietminh fighting the French; they had also visited Moscow and Peking. In July, 1950, they returned secretly to Indonesia as stowaways on a Dutch ship. After being arrested and held for a short time, Aidit was released and he promptly set about reorganizing the P.K.I., which at the time had perhaps three or four thousand members. One of the first things he did was get rid of old-line party leaders who had been shakily holding the reins and trying to maintain an independent position between Moscow and Peking, whose ideological viewpoints were even then beginning to diverge. Aidit was clearly in Moscow's camp, while a Peking faction gradually came under the influence of Lukman. Aidit, who became the dominant leader, favored cooperation with Sukarno, while Lukman unsuccessfully opposed any collaboration with the President or with the organized "bourgeois parties." Together, however, the two men started a newspaper and began mass appeals that built the party up to 165,000 members by the end of 1954 and to a million by the time of the 1955 parliamentary elections.

Principally under Aidit's dominant tutelage, the party was quick to take advantage of the opportunities it saw, in overcrowded Java particularly, to gather mass support among the peasants, workers, youth, women, and veterans, and it started a series of "movements" and associations to rally these and other elements. From the outset, its radical militancy found a ready response. The other parties had tended to neglect the *kampongs* and villages, which were dominated by the *lurahs*—village heads—and, in the case of the Muslim communities, by the *imams*, the mosque officials, and elementary schoolteachers, and by the *kijai*, the scholars. Life in the countryside was extremely boring, especially after dusk, and the P.K.I. aimed to fill this void with its mass organizations, creating what Aidit described as "a united front, including the national bourgeoisie," and building up its image as a patriotic party, sympathetic to religion and opposed to the use of force.

Arnold Brackman, the American author of *Indonesian Communism*, has pointed out that the political reliability of the new P.K.I. mass organizations, which ultimately grew to a claimed membership of some sixteen million, was open to serious question —something that would be clearly demonstrated when the Communist coup attempt in 1965 failed. But, as Brackman has noted, the real significance of the P.K.I.'s identification with nationalism and with Sukarno in the early and mid-fifties under Aidit's leadership was that "it succeeded in destroying the post-independence opportunities of the Sjahrir Socialists to develop the non-Communist left." In effect, this provided the death knell for parliamentary democracy in Indonesia even in advance of the 1955 elections.

During the election campaign the P.K.I. proved itself the best-financed and best-organized party, and certainly fielded the best propagandists. Communist speakers in roving groups roused the population with ultranationalist slogans and banners and identified the party, wherever possible, with local causes as well as with such proved general ones as land for the landless peasants. In Bali, for example, where cock-fighting was popular, the Communists endorsed it; in some Javanese villages they spread rumors that agents of the Muslim Masjumi Party were poisoning the local wells, and appointed "guards" to protect them. They handed out thousands of kites to children—kite-flying in Indonesia is more than a national pastime, it is a virtual obsession. Everywhere, they loudly praised Sukarno, depicting

"Irian" as his "daughter," whom the Dutch had abducted and the Communists would recover. They also vigorously adopted the *Pantja Sila,* which by now had more or less become the special property of the P.N.I. and the P.K.I. in the growing contest between them and all the Muslims, whether of the reformist Masjumi Party or the more conservative Nahdatul Ulama (N.U.). The 1955 elections—the only ones to be held in Indonesia, as it would turn out, for a decade and a half— were conducted in a high mood of national enthusiasm and were surprisingly fair and orderly. Out of the nearly 38 million votes cast, the P.N.I. won 22.3 percent and the Masjumi 20.9 percent, so that each got fifty-seven seats in the new 257-seat Parliament. The N.U. got 18.4 percent of the total votes and won forty-five seats. These three parties joined in a coalition government. The P.K.I. finished a strong fourth with 16.4 percent and thirty-nine seats. It was a remarkable showing for a party that, only a few years earlier, had been a hunted, bankrupt survivor of Dutch colonial suppression.

The four major parties had received 90 percent of the vote and had won 198 seats in Parliament, while none of the remaining twenty-four parties won more than eight seats. The election, indeed, all but destroyed the Socialist Party of Sjahrir as a political force, and it set the stage for regional conflicts in Indonesia that would soon seriously threaten its very survival. The P.N.I., P.K.I., and N.U. derived almost all their strength from Java, while the Masjumi, though it had some strength among the Sundanese population of West Java, was essentially based in the "outer islands," especially in Sumatra and in Sulawesi.

It quickly became apparent that the political parties, singly or in coalition, could not rule the country or provide the masses with all the good things, including jobs and new consumer goods, they had been promised. Soedjatmoko has observed that

The absence of new national goals soon led to the deterioration of politics into mere bickering among the political parties for a greater share of the spoils of power. It led to a succession of short-lived cabinets, all equally powerless to cope with the real issues. . . . Almost all fell . . . as a result of extra-parliamentary maneuverings of political parties who were combining and recombining in temporary and constantly shifting alliances. . . . Instead of developing into organs mediating between the needs, problems, and wishes of the electorate, and the purposes, limitations, and problems at the level of the national government, the parties became mere instruments in the power play of their leaders.

Above all, Indonesia seemed to lack a focus of power. Herbert Feith, the perceptive Australian social historian, has noted in his book *The Decline of Constitutional Democracy in Indonesia* that the failure of the democratic experiment resulted also from tensions between "the administrators," typified by men like Hatta, and the "solidarity makers," including the early P.N.I. leaders, who looked upon political activity as an end in itself and not as a means of achieving stated objectives. The result, as he sees it, was the development of what, even before the 1955 elections, and to their detriment, he calls "the virtually free-floating clique" as "the principal unit of political competition." Such cliques, within the Army as well as within and around the existing political parties, operated without ideology and sometimes solely on the basis of opportunism and personal ties and loyalties. One of Sukarno's greatest advantages, when he became the leading "solidarity maker," was that he knew intuitively how to play various cliques, as well as individuals, off against each other. This was a vital aspect of what has been described by one Western student of Sukarnoism as his "Jacobin style."

The conflict between the solidarity makers and the administrators was part of the larger cultural conflict between the Javanese "aristocrats" and the more far-flung Islamic entrepreneurs. This found its clearest expression in the mounting differences between the outer-island Masjumi elements, particularly those in prosperous Sumatra, and the Java-based parties and groups. With the exception of the traditional N.U., the other Java parties appealed essentially to those who were only nominally Muslims, the so-called *abangan*. Within the Muslim community, the Masjumi, more modern and commercial-minded, found most of its strength among the shopkeepers and middlemen of the outer-island towns and villages. The N.U., on the other hand, was almost exclusively a village-based organization within Java, and had little or no strength in the outer islands. Some writers have placed more emphasis on the ethnic differences between the Javanese and the non-Javanese. These were aggravated by the Javanese-aristocratic clash with the outer-island entrepreneurial group, as well as by the ever-growing Javanese domination of the Civil Service throughout the islands. Another factor, of course, was Java's control of Parliament by virtue of its large population.

These tensions were further exacerbated by regional military rivalries that came to a head soon after the elections, when elements in the Army began openly to express their discontent with the multiparty bickering and indecisiveness in Djakarta and moved to counteract it. At the time, Indonesia was divided into seven military regions—three in Java, two in Sumatra, one in Kalimantan, and one covering all of the eastern islands. The commanders of these regions, to a considerable extent, ran them as autonomous fiefs; their troops were usually loyal to them on an individual basis, while loyalty to Djakarta was nominal and sporadic. The relationship between the Army commanders and civilian officials in the central government varied greatly. In many cases, it was based on mutual accommodation and on loyalty within cliques. In other cases, there were serious clashes. Thus, for example, in parts of Sumatra and the Celebes, Army officers condoned or themselves organized large smuggling rings with the connivance of local civilian officials; the military men maintained that only by trading illicitly with Singapore and the Philippines were they able to get enough funds to pay their troops.

Shortly after the 1955 elections, Sukarno had made a speech in which he had asked, "Who ever heard of a three-legged horse?" and he had sought to get the P.N.I. to create "a four-legged horse" by taking the Communists into the ill-formed, nonfunctioning coalition of the P.N.I., the N.U., and the Masjumi. Prime Minister Sastroamijojo had balked because he had momentarily come to fear the Communists' rising strength. By the end of October, 1956, Sukarno was no longer interested in any kind of party-coalition "horse." He now had an entirely different idea. Returning from a two-month trip that had taken him through the Iron Curtain countries, to Outer Mongolia, and then to China, where he had been particularly impressed by the new communes and factories, he declared that Indonesia had made a big mistake in ever allowing political parties to be established. Condemning them for their "selfishness," he demanded that they "bury themselves." He spoke with admiration of people in China who "work like ants" and added, meaningfully: "The democracy I would like to have for Indonesia is not like the liberal democracy of Western Europe. . . . What I would like to have for Indonesia is a guided democracy . . . especially if we want to construct it in the way I saw in the Chinese People's Republic." The politicians were, naturally, not interested in digging their own graves, but Sukarno and the Army were rapidly moving toward a consolidation of their partnership which would leave the parties, with the exception of the P.K.I., either in hopeless rebellion or in helpless vacuum.

At the end of 1956 Vice President Hatta and President Sukarno came to the final parting of ways when, in protest against Sukarno's new dictatorial concepts, Hatta resigned. At the same time, the military commanders of North, Central, and South Sumatra and some of their civilian supporters pulled off bloodless coups that overthrew the Djakarta-appointed civilian officials; though a counterrevolt in the northern part of the island re-established Djakarta's rule, the other two regions remained under control of the military, who accused the central government, not without justification, of neglect, of corruption, and of being too lenient toward the Communists. The Masjumi, in sympathy with the rebels, quit the government, accentuating the split between the Java-based parties and the outer-island elements, and sought to bring Hatta back as Prime Minister with a program that would give the outer islands more autonomy, particularly in controlling their own imports and exports. The Java group bitterly and successfully opposed this. The Communists, nominally backing the incumbent P.N.I., watched what was happening with obvious satisfaction and waited for Sukarno's next step.

They did not wait long. At the end of February, 1957, Sukarno gave details of what he called his *konsepsi* (over-all conception), and in so doing revealed, for the first time, what he actually meant by "Guided Democracy." Since Indonesia's levels of literacy and prosperity were too low for it to emulate Western-type democracy, he said, the "experiment" it had been making had to be abandoned. In its place he called for the creation of a new *gotong-royong* (mutual aid) Cabinet, to include the Communists, and, more important, for the establishment of a new advisory council consisting of so-called "functional groups" composed of representatives of labor, youth, peasants, business entrepreneurs, and so on. This council, which he said he would lead and which would give advice to the Cabinet "whether requested or not," would operate by the traditional Indonesian village method of *musjawarah* and *mufakat*—discussion and agreement by consensus. The Communists, some smaller radical parties, and the P.N.I. supported Sukarno's plan, but all the Muslim elements and the more moderate political groups opposed it. The Army, under General Nasution, not wanting to challenge Sukarno directly but seeking more power for itself, moved into the position of arbiter.

After Aidit deployed his P.K.I. mass organizations to promote Guided Democracy, dispatching trucks with loudspeakers around Djakarta and painting slogans on public buildings, the situation began to get out of hand, and Nasution ordered an end to the demonstrations. Meanwhile, in the islands east of Java, another military insurrection took place in four provinces. Amid all these pressures, the Cabinet of Ali Sastroamijojo finally resigned. Sukarno immediately placed the country under martial law, and announced that he would choose a new government—something that had theretofore been left to the party politicians. Djuanda Kartawidjaja, the Minister of Planning, who belonged to no party but had served in several earlier governments, became Prime Minister, and formed a *gotong-royong* Cabinet that included a number of P.N.I. and N.U. members, and one member of the Masjumi, who was promptly thrown out of his party. The new Cabinet contained no members of the P.K.I., but did include two well-known Communist sympathizers. More significantly, a new political organization that called itself the Generation of 1945, headed by a left-wing Sukarno man named Chaerul Saleh and composed mostly of labor, youth, and veterans' groups, held two ministries, though it was not a political party and had no representation in Parliament. This amorphous body was to be the horse that Sukarno would ride to his goal of Guided Democracy, and the P.K.I. was to be its willing groom.

With the formal establishment of the "new-style democracy" early in May, 1957, Sukarno appointed a National Advisory Council of forty-five members, among them a dozen known Communists or sympathizers, a majority of malleable radical nationalists, and the chiefs of the Army, Navy, Air Force, and national police. Sukarno declared that he himself would convey the Council's advice to the Cabinet, and the Council quickly came to hold a considerable veto power over the government. In that same month, Sukarno received a distinguished visitor, Marshal Kliment Y. Voroshilov, the Soviet Union's chief of state, who loudly proclaimed his support for the return of West Irian to Indonesia. Sukarno, proudly shepherding his guest to Bali and elsewhere, constantly spoke of the common bonds between himself and Moscow in the struggle against colonialism and imperialism. In the wake of this triumphal tour, provincial elections were held in Java between June and August, and it was no surprise that the P.K.I. emerged as the strongest party on the island, with 27.4 percent of the total vote; most of the gains had been won at the expense of the P.N.I., and there seemed no doubt as to who was now Sukarno's principal ally.

When the United Nations General Assembly, in November, failed to pass a resolution requesting the Secretary General's assistance in resolving the West Irian problem, Sukarno said he was prepared to adopt "other means" to acquire the territory, and he threatened that they would "startle the world." He was then more than startled himself by an attempt on his life by a band of anti-Communist Muslim youths. Four grenades were tossed at a school Sukarno was visiting, and they killed nine people and wounded 150, but Sukarno miraculously was unhurt. The incident increased the sense of awe with which he had always been regarded by his myth-ridden fellow Javanese and strengthened the belief of his supporters that he was destined to rule Indonesia as a father figure, if not as a God figure, indefinitely.

Early in December, 1957, left-wing employees of the principal Dutch-owned interisland shipping line seized the company's Djakarta office and hoisted a red flag. Prime Minister Djuanda used this pretext to order the immediate expulsion of the Dutch. Within a few days virtually all the Dutch estates, banks, and business firms in the country had been seized, most of them by the P.K.I.-controlled labor union (S.O.B.S.I.). The 46,000 Dutch citizens still in Indonesia hurriedly packed their belongings and prepared to leave. Chief of Staff Nasution tried to reduce the economic chaos in the wake of the seizures by arresting some of the S.O.B.S.I. leaders, but by then there was little that could be done.

Besides, the Army as well as the government obtained major benefits from the overnight nationalization; even if the economy could barely function, there was a wealth of fresh patronage that Sukarno and the Army could happily divide. The Communists wisely laid low, knowing that the outer islands were close to complete rebellion and that the P.K.I.'s chances of achieving control of the whole country under the current confused conditions were small because their party was still almost entirely a Java-bound force. So they supported the Djakarta government publicly but criticized it at the village level, as they went on getting ready for what they realized would someday be a showdown with the Army.

At the beginning of 1958 Indonesia showed signs of becoming a semimilitary police state. Under the conditions of martial law that had been imposed the year before, the Army and the civil police, and to a lesser extent the Navy and the Air Force, controlled virtually the whole state administrative apparatus. Military and police authority included control over customs and all export-import operations; over immigration and alien movements; over transportation and communications; over almost all commercial activity, including the operation, by the Army itself, of the former Dutch estates; over censorship and over most forms of investigation, including that of corruption; and over all aspects of political activity, including public meetings and even some social gatherings. The military's right to requisition almost anything it wanted, from automobiles and gasoline to planes and houses, gave it tremendous economic power and also the opportunity to make tremendous profits. For the most part it took advantage of these privileges at local and regional levels rather than at the top, still having neither the desire nor the capacity to impose its will as a single overriding force, and still being rent by internal feuds and rivalries and by a lack of cohesive discipline.

Sukarno, by the beginning of 1958, had managed to get part but by no means all of his *konsepsi* implemented. The political parties had been subjugated but not "buried," and the Communists, whom he had chosen as his chief allies, were still not in the government though they were *of* it—a flexible position that they momentarily preferred. Within a month or so both Sukarno and the Communists were to be jolted by a serious anti-Djakarta rebellion, which was a reflection of deep-seated resentment against the manner in which the country was being run. The revolt was a cry of despair over the demise of parliamentary democracy, over the entire nationalist revolution gone awry, and for a brief moment it struck the conscience not only of many Indonesians but of much of the rest of the world, including the United States. Outer-island opposition, building up for two years, had started to come to a head in December, 1957, when Natsir, acting out of his own despair and on his enduring religious-socialist convictions, fled from Djakarta, with two other Masjumi leaders, to Padang, in Central Sumatra. Self-styled independent "Councils" at this time already existed in Central and South Sumatra, and in parts of the eastern islands, notably in Sulawesi. In mid-February, 1958, the commanders of these rebellious areas issued an ultimatum to Sukarno, who was vacationing in Japan. The ultimatum, which embodied a "Charter of Struggle" denouncing Sukarno's scheme for Guided Democracy as an attempt to grab personal power with the support of the Communists, described the seizures of Dutch properties as an "irresponsible act" that would play into the hands of the Communists. It demanded that Sukarno "resume his constitutional status" and that a new interim working Cabinet, led by Hatta and the Sultan of Jogjakarta, be established within five days. Sukarno, who had rushed back from Japan, ignored the ultimatum, and on February 15 the rebels proclaimed the Revolutionary Government of the Republic of Indonesia (P.R.R.I.), with headquarters at Bukittingi, Sumatra.

At the head of the rebel government was Sjafruddin Prawianegara, a highly respected intellectual who had briefly been Acting President of the first republic, had often been a Cabinet minister, and had most recently served as governor of the Bank of Indonesia. The rebels' supporters, in addition to six well-known revolutionary officers, included Natsir and Burhannudin Harahap, both former Prime Ministers, and Sumitro Djojohadikusumo, the young economist. The rebels had figured that the Djakarta government was too divided to mount a full-scale counterattack, but, starting in mid-March, the Djakarta forces launched a series of successful sorties on Sumatra and then on Sulawesi, and these, by mid-June, had substantially defeated the uprising, though guerrilla fighting was to continue sporadically for another three years. After the fall of the rebel capital of Bukittingi in May, Sjafruddin found himself hiding in the same Sumatran jungle that had sheltered him from the Dutch a decade before. The rebellion had failed because of fundamental strategic errors, because its military leaders had squabbled among themselves, and because those who ran it never succeeded in establishing any sort of functioning administration that proved any more appealing to the outer-island people than had Djakarta's. Their propaganda was also weak and they soon lost many of the foreign friends they had initially, though (with the assistance of the American Central Intelligence Agency) they did acquire a tiny air force consisting of some Second World War American planes flown by Taiwanese and American pilots. The sympathy and encouragement the rebels had first received from Washington shifted to uncertainty and vacillation, and, after the Russians had furnished Sukarno with Mig-16 jet trainers, the United States began shipping arms to the Djakarta government. With the defeat of the main rebel forces, the Americans apparently decided that the wisest policy was to strengthen the Indonesian Army against the Communists. This worried Aidit and the P.K.I., which trimmed its sails and declared Sukarno's Guided Democracy to be "the most revolutionary policy at the moment."

There was little danger that Sukarno would jeopardize his subtle relationship with the Communists. With the back of the P.R.R.I. rebellion broken, and with constitutional democracy to all intents and purposes a dead issue, the remaining government parties were in limbo. The two real poles of authority were Sukarno and the Army, which had gained a great deal of political strength as a result of the quick defeat of the main rebel elements; but the Army remained divided within itself, and, though it held most of the important economic reins, as it had before, it had to share them with the civilian administrators in many parts of the islands. The Army, though more pro-Islamic and anti-Communist than Sukarno, contained pro-Sukarno elements who countenanced his playing along with the Communists, especially in sections of East and Central Java, where Communist sympathies already existed among some of the troops—a factor which was to prove highly significant later. So, by the end of 1958, the Army and Sukarno had established a tacitly acknowledged political equilibrium, which for the time being was beneficial to both. But Sukarno also needed the P.K.I., if for no other reason than that the Communists, by far the best-organized party on Java, had propaganda machinery, all the way down to the village level. This provided him with the platform he required to maintain his popular strength. Similarly, the P.K.I. needed Sukarno to protect it from the Army, and he responded by permitting it to hold meetings the Army wanted to ban and by appearing from time to time at important Communist rallies himself.

The Heyday of Sukarno

In February, 1959, declaring that Indonesia was on the "abyss of annihilation," that political "obstructionism," military "indiscipline and war-lordism," and "new bourgeois" greed had all combined to create "a process of pauperization," Sukarno called for a "return to the Constitution of 1945"—the initial document of independence, which had been replaced by a later, provisional Constitution in 1950. The Cabinet and the Army at once supported him, but there was some opposition, especially from the Constituent Assembly, which had been dawdling for two years over the writing of a new Constitution. Under the 1945 Constitution, a very flexible one that Sukarno described as "genuinely Indonesian," and that he claimed embodied his principles of "Guided Democracy," a strong executive was provided for, with the power to appoint Cabinet ministers who would remain in office for at least five years, unless the President fired them. A special Supreme Advisory Council chosen by the President was, in effect, a private kitchen cabinet. A People's Consultative Congress was supposed to meet at least once every five years to project policies and programs, and part of it, the People's Representative Council, constituted a legislative, or parliamentary, body that was supposed to meet yearly; the rest of the Congress consisted of regional representatives and of "corporate" representatives chosen from among various groups in the Indonesian society. Actually, the Congress, the only body to which Sukarno was legally responsible, had only met once, and he had made virtually all decisions on his own.

When he asked the Constituent Assembly, late in April, 1959, to forget about a new Constitution and let him further implement his

Guided Democracy under the existing old one, Sukarno felt sure the Assembly would carry out his wishes; but early in June, while he was away on a two-month trip around the world, it rejected his plan. Tensions increased, and General Nasution banned all political activity to assure "public order." Sukarno returned at the end of June, and on July 5, by direct Presidential decree, he dissolved the Constituent Assembly and reinstated the 1945 Constitution. Guided Democracy had come to Indonesia. As Willard Hanna, who became a critical observer of the Indonesian scene after his experience as an American official there in the early days of independence, afterward wrote, Guided Democracy had arrived because the Indonesian people, despite their great abilities and their sense of revolutionary commitment, were nevertheless possessed "of a rather remarkable degree of detachment which makes them inclined . . . to play the role of spectators at their own national collapse rather than that of participants in their national regeneration." As for Sukarno, Hanna cogently observed, he "is what and where he is precisely because he typifies Indonesians both in their strengths and weaknesses. He is susceptible not to the planned focusing but to the random convergence of many influences such as to make him at once . . . a Marxist, a socialist, a capitalist, a democrat, a dictator, a puppet, a playboy, a prophet, and more than a little of an intellectual anarchist."

Sukarno was all these things, and more. He was, perhaps above all, a supreme, compulsive romantic, and he demonstrated this continuously both in his public and private life (in addition to his five "official" wives, he had at least three "unofficial" ones, and a steady procession of mistresses all over the world). "I tell you frankly," he declared, not long after he had begun fully to implement his program for Guided Democracy, "I belong to that group of people who are bound in spiritual longing by the romanticism of the revolution. I am inspired by it. I am fascinated by it. I am completely absorbed by it. I am crazed, I am obsessed by the romanticism of revolution. . . . That is why I, who have been given the topmost leadership in the struggle of the Indonesian nation, never tire of appealing and exhorting: solve our national problems in a revolutionary way, make the revolutionary spirit surge on, see to it that the fire of our revolution does not die or grow dim, not even for a single moment. Come, then, keep fanning the flames of the leaping fire of revolution! Brothers and sisters, let us become logs to feed the flames of revolution!"

While repeatedly calling for "a thoroughgoing and revolutionary overhaul of our state and social system," Sukarno rode his "back to 1945" theme to death, and if he didn't bore people—which, it must be granted, he seldom did—he left them feeling confused, bewildered, and unfulfilled, particularly since most of them did not as yet possess either of the two prime necessities that he kept promising—*sandang-pangan,* food and clothing, primarily rice and cloth, which remained in short supply as prices kept skyrocketing. "I am no holy man or reincarnation of God," Sukarno declaimed. "I am just an ordinary human being like you and you." There was little that was "ordinary" about Sukarno, except, perhaps, his total ignorance of economics, which bored him. Certainly he was an extraordinary political animal, with, among other things, a remarkable sense of timing and an instinctive knowledge of how to use the raw material of history to advantage. His astonishing memory enabled him, for example, to cite passages of Marx by chapter and verse, even if he never could qualify as a thoughtful student of economics; but he did apply his real knowledge and understanding of Indonesian traditions to the problems and crises he dealt with, and he did this in his own dramatic fashion. Though his people had been willing to accept his rationale of government, the more thoughtful ones among them soon realized that the machinery of Guided Democracy in fact represented a thorough betrayal of the liberal principles that had sparked the Indonesian revolution. And, as time passed, combining his Javanese mystical background with his crypto-Marxism and his sense of opportunism, he increasingly removed himself from the Indonesian people the more he insisted he personified them.

The process by which Indonesia, between 1959 and 1962, was transformed from a fumbling parliamentary democracy into a phantasmagoric oligarchy was undoubtedly one of the strangest anywhere during this century. Sukarno's wide use of ritualistic symbols and political incantations derived from mystic Javanese sources, all of them spewed forth in a torrent of fancy acronyms representing a weird blend of French, English, Javanese, and whatever, and amounting to a whole new form of Newspeak, made it easy enough to condemn him purely as a metaphysical charlatan, but there was more to it than that. The cultural revivalism, the constant use of mystical imagery, the creation and prolongation of crises and the manufacture of external enemies as scapegoats all demonstrated more method than madness on Sukarno's part; they were essentially tactics designed to take people's minds off their material deprivation, to mask their abject poverty and to detract from the failure to deal with the economic and social situation in a rational way.

Sukarno, it must be said, was as much the result as the cause of Indonesia's failure to come to grips with the problems of modern nationhood. These problems had simply proved too much for the political elite of the new republic to handle, and when Sukarno moved forcibly onto the scene, he did not even try to handle them. Instead, he built what he thought would be a new unitary governmental structure but what turned out to be another administrative labyrinth. First he created a new ten-man "Inner Cabinet" with himself as Prime Minister. Below this were a new forty-five-member Supreme Advisory Council and a special seventy-seven-member National Planning Council. The latter was headed by Mohammed Yamin, a lawyer and poet who liked to look upon himself as an ideologue, too. Yamin, who was Minister of Social and Cultural Affairs, set about compiling an eight-year plan for economic and social recovery that eventually ran to five thousand pages. Hailed by Sukarno for its "richness of symbolic fantasy," it consisted of 1,945 items divided into eight volumes and seventeen chapters, thus paying cryptic tribute to the day when Indonesian independence was declared, August 17, 1945 (8/17/45). The plan was given to the virtually defunct People's Consultative Congress, which never did anything about it. In September, 1959, Sukarno also reorganized the regional governments, doing away with elected regional councils and making the governors of the regions, which were akin to provinces, directly responsible to him, and second-level officials accountable to the Ministry of the Interior. These moves further served to "bury" the parties, as Sukarno had threatened he would do, and they were also hurt by another Sukarno edict that forbade any government official in the upper ranks from belonging to any political party. The P.K.I. was especially bothered by this decree, and the Communists, although still supporting Sukarno's Guided Democracy, were now edgy. They had gone along with another Presidential regulation prohibiting aliens in rural areas from engaging in retail trade—a move aimed at the many thousands of Chinese small merchants who were the business backbone of the countryside, where they also served as bankers, pawnbrokers, and middlemen. But when the regulation was drastically enforced, and some forty thousand Chinese were "voluntarily" repatriated, the P.K.I. and several other parties moved to oppose the manner in which the regulation was being implemented. The Communist mass organizations also began demonstrating against rising prices.

In this atmosphere of dissension, early in 1960 Soviet Premier Nikita Khrushchev arrived in Indonesia for an eleven-day tour. The trip initially seemed a success for Sukarno and for the P.K.I. —though Khrushchev at first did not seem overly enthusiastic about Sukarno's campaign to make the Dutch give Indonesia West Irian. Typically, also, Khrushchev could not repress an earthy ideological warning to the P.K.I. about mass support being no substitute for militant policy: "The Communist Party is not a grocery store where the more customers you attract, the more soap, rotten herring, or other spoiled goods you sell, the more you gain," he said. The warning would prove a prophetic one. The climax of Khrushchev's trip came when he appeared before Parliament and, as it turned out, delivered a speech that had an unexpected effect on the immediate Indonesian political situation. The deputies, annoyed at Sukarno's new rule-by-decree, sat and listened to Khrushchev in silence, and even when he mentioned West Irian no one but the Communists applauded, and they did so only briefly. Sukarno was incensed, and he was not altogether mollified by a final joint Russian-Indonesian communiqué in which Khrushchev pledged Indonesia a quarter-of-a-million-dollar twelve-year credit at 2.5 percent interest.

A week later, when the four leading parties, the P.N.I., P.K.I., N.U., and Masjumi, jointly opposed a draft budget submitted by Sukarno, he responded by dissolving Parliament, charging it with having failed to live up to "the spirit of Guided Democracy" and to "the Political Manifesto of the Republic." This latter declaration, which he referred to, characteristically, as "Manipol," had evolved from his 1959 Independence Day speech, to which he had later added some expository notes and the extra acronym USDEK. This

was a coinage from the first letters of five of his propaganda tags:
Undang-undang Dasar '45 (Return to the 1945 Constitution);
Socialisme à la Indonesia (Indonesian Socialism); *Demokrasi
Terpimpin* (Guided Democracy); *Ekonomi Terpimpin* (Guided
Economy); and *Kepribadian Indonesia* (Indonesian Identity).
From now on, Manipol-USDEK would be Indonesia's new creed
and catechism.

The acronymic era ushered in by Manipol-USDEK furnished
Sukarno with the cabalistic dialectic he felt he needed to dramatize
the Indonesian revolution. Beyond his acronymania, however, he
did effect, with some success, a revival of the national language
called *bahasa Indonesia,* which he hoped would supersede the two
hundred dialects spoken throughout the archipelago. *Bahasa Indonesia* consisted of some Dutch and English as well as Malay
words. Derived originally from early maritime influences, Islamic
and European, it had gradually become a common commercial and
then, to some extent, an administrative language. Sukarno added
thousands of new items, and *bahasa Indonesia* came to be fairly
widely used among bureaucrats and in schools, but it never had a
real cultural foundation or tradition and was not understood or
spoken widely by the common people.

Riding his new ideological steed, Sukarno moved to win the
battle with Parliament and the political parties. He was obviously
determined, following another attempt on his life when a young
Indonesian pilot bombed his palace from a Mig-17, to make it clear
that Guided Democracy was a permanent fixture. At the end of
June, 1960, he appointed a new *gotong-royong* Parliament of 283
members, divided among nine political parties and a score of functional groups, and in mid-August he added another 326 members,
to form the new People's Consultative Congress, still supposedly
the highest body in the land. At the same time, he declared the
Masjumi and Socialist parties illegal, and a month later he prohibited all parties from engaging in any overt political activities
and placed harsh restrictions on the press. All "foreign influences,"
including the Boy Scouts and the Rotarians, were banned. In the
months that followed, Manipol-USDEK was pushed with a vengeance, not only in the press but also in the high schools and
colleges and throughout the Civil Service and administrative channels of the state-run enterprises. Students going abroad to study,

for example, had to swear that they believed in Manipol-USDEK and that they would not marry while they were out of the country, while all government employees everywhere who were not regarded as loyal to the new precepts of the Sukarno regime were "retooled," that is, demoted or, sometimes, pensioned off. Among the first to suffer from the regime's new policies were teachers, writers, and journalists, who, through fear or through direct threats of loss of jobs and even arrest, found themselves either silenced or faced with the prospect of perjuring themselves in order to go on making a meager living. Actually, there had been earlier cases of repression, one of the most notorious being that of Mochtar Lubis, the editor of a controversial, crusading Djakarta newspaper named *Indonesia Raya*, who was arrested late in 1956 after he had written exposés of the private life of Sukarno and other officials and of corruption in the government, and had also got himself involved, if only indirectly, in some of the anti-Sukarno and outer-island rebel plots. For most of the ten years he was under detention, Lubis lived in relatively comfortable circumstances, and, being a man of many parts and talents, he wrote books, painted, made furniture, and gardened. Two or three other journalists who were arrested were more harshly treated, but most of those who remained free simply lived lives of quiet desperation. As one of them, Taufiq Ismael, a young poet and playwright who also taught at Bogor University, afterward told me, "Even though the air was stifling, we kept on writing. We were not activists politically, though we usually sympathized with the Socialists or the Masjumi. We established a private courier system that extended all over Java and even to Sumatra and Sulawesi, so we were able to exchange criticisms of what we wrote, though it sometimes took months for letters to go back and forth. There was no real censorship of material from abroad, fortunately, so we were able to get books and periodicals from America and elsewhere. We read Yevtushenko, for example, and kept up generally with the literature of revolt. In May, 1964, twenty-five of us issued a manifesto we called 'Indonesia in Travail,' which the Congress for Cultural Freedom distributed around the world, and after that things got tougher. I and others lost our jobs as teachers and were prohibited from going abroad, as several of us had planned. A year later, there were plans, apparently, to arrest about three hundred writers and journalists throughout Indonesia, but this didn't happen because events moved too fast."

A number of the leading political figures to whom youths like Taufiq looked up did not fare so well. In January, 1962, several of the early heroes of the revolution and leaders of the outer-island rebellion, among them Natsir and Sjarifuddin, who had surrendered the year before, as well as Sjahrir and Soebadio Sastrosatomo, another leading Socialist, were arrested. With the exception of Sjahrir, who was later allowed to go abroad for reasons of health—he died in Switzerland in April, 1966—they all remained in prison until after the upheaval in the autumn of 1965. These relatively mild forms of intellectual and political repression under Sukarno—certainly not comparable to what has taken place in most other modern dictatorships—were no doubt restrained in part because of Sukarno's overweening desire to maintain an impressive international façade. By 1962, when he had completed his structure of Guided Democracy and festooned it with some more acronymic catch phrases, he turned almost completely into a showman, both on the national and international stages. Sometimes his efforts to perform on both simultaneously were less than successful, as was the case in the fall of 1962 when Indonesia was host to some twelve hundred athletes from seventeen nations who came to Djakarta for the Fourth Asian Games. Among the stage sets were a huge new sports complex, which cost $17 million, largely paid by the Russians, and the new $8-million Hotel Indonesia (rooms thirty dollars a day), financed by Japanese reparations. Both of these structures were major showpieces of the Sukarno era that stood out (and still do today) amid blocks of surrounding wooden shacks and some diplomatic and residential villas. Despite such panoply, plus a thorough cleansing of the city and the importation of a special fleet of new Mercedes-Benz limousines, Sukarno could not avoid mixing politics with sport, and at the last minute Indonesia refused to issue visas to athletes from two charter members of the Asian Games Federation with whom it had no diplomatic relations, Taiwan and Israel. On top of this, there were several extracurricular scuffles during the competitions and an official attempt by the Indians to discredit the games as propaganda and "non-Olympic" in character. All the athletic events took place, but not in the impressive manner Sukarno had hoped for, and he ended by losing rather than gaining prestige.

Among Sukarno's tangible accomplishments was the resolution of the West Irian crisis, which had been smoldering for thirteen years. Prior to its settlement, however, he only narrowly managed to avert disaster. For years he had whipped up his people over the issue, making the recovery of this sprawling tract of jungle and swamp, inhabited by less than a million aborigines, the major theme of his anti-imperialist crusade. After the failure of numerous efforts to settle the affair bilaterally and with the help of friendly nations, Sukarno, at the end of 1961, flamboyantly ordered the Indonesians to prepare for mobilization, making good on his threat to use "other means" to obtain the all-but-useless territory. At the start of 1962, when this policy of military "confrontation" with the Dutch was consuming nearly three-quarters of the national budget and further raising the soaring national deficit, the Indonesians dropped some "volunteer" paratroopers into West Irian. The Dutch repelled them as small-scale fighting broke out, and what threatened to turn into a larger conflict, possibly involving the Western powers, was averted when the United States and the United Nations together persuaded the Dutch to back down; the settlement briefly turned West Irian over to the United Nations, and in May, 1963, Indonesia received the area outright, with the promise of giving the native Papuans the right of self-determination before January 1, 1970 (a plebiscite was subsequently scheduled for 1969). The Indonesians, as it turned out, were to do even less than the Dutch did with the territory, but Sukarno had won his big battle against "colonialism," a battle second only, he had maintained, to the winning of *Merdeka* (freedom) for Indonesia itself.

There was some expectation, after the West Irian settlement, that Sukarno might finally turn his attention to Indonesia's manifold internal problems. In fact, he announced that economic reform and rehabilitation would now get top priority. The chances that something might be done seemed to be enhanced by a carefully worked-out five-year American assistance plan budgeted at more than $350 million and designed, according to Washington, to deal with Indonesia's "present limited capacity to absorb aid for new capital projects" and to "help the country move into the next stage, when its capacity to absorb new capital will be greater."

Since 1950 the United States had given Indonesia a total of $470 million in aid plus $168 million in surplus foods, while other nations had made contributions worth about $1.5 billion, more than half of it from the Soviet Union in the form of modern planes and old warships.

Notwithstanding this largess, economic conditions were worse than ever. Falling production, rising prices, wild deficit financing, bureaucratic overregulation of some enterprises and underenforcement of laws in regard to others, and general corruption and moral disintegration were all part of the picture. Much of the collapse was traceable to the sudden and poorly timed dispossession of the Dutch and other Europeans in 1957, to the curbing of the Muslim entrepreneurial class after the outer-island rebellion in 1958, and to the campaign against the Chinese that began a year later; these moves not only eliminated key managers and technicians and reduced the ranks of the principal merchants and handlers of goods, but also caused a large flight of capital. Foreign-exchange income, nearly a billion dollars in 1959, plummeted to half that four years later. Foreign aid, properly used, might have filled the vacuum, but most of it was channeled into chauvinistic displays. The further result was a fragmentation of the already diffuse economy and a mood in which almost everyone simply did what he could to fend for himself, the majority to subsist and a minority to get rich. Thus, for example, as the price index rose from a hundred in 1953 to three thousand early in 1963; as rubber production decreased by more than 10 percent in the decade between 1950 and 1960 and kept slipping; as the production of rice in 1963 turned out to be less than it had been fifteen years before, though the country's population had grown by more than a third; as virtually nothing was done to tap the country's rich mineral resources; and as transportation facilities, especially roads and railways, disintegrated; as all these things and many more became manifest, money became all but meaningless and the rupiah, supposedly pegged at forty-five to an American dollar, ultimately fell to ten thousand to a dollar on the black market.

In such an atmosphere, it was impossible any longer to exercise any real controls. Civil servants, who were supposed to work from eight in the morning until two in the afternoon, appeared at their offices for an hour or two and then went off to other jobs as traders, clerks, teachers, translators, and so on. The proliferation of corruption in these circumstances was, of course, inevitable, and it extended from the distribution of scarce goods ("The price of an article is determined not by supply and demand but by the number of officials through whose hands it must pass," was a common saw) to bribery for everything from the procurement of goods and contracts to the privilege of entering children in school or being placed on the already swollen government payroll. Overregulation, epitomized by fantastic numbers of forms to be filled out for everything, and all sorts of other paper work, became a disease in the bureaucracy, where jobs were handed out mostly for political gain. Survival depended on being "part of the system," and the poor people, from college professors to *betjah* (tricycle) drivers, had to scrounge in the mounting atmosphere of corruption to supplement their meager incomes—equivalent to a few dollars a month.

The hope that after the end of the West Irian crisis Indonesia would deal forcefully with its domestic economic problems was blasted within a matter of months. In the fall of 1963, after having given his somewhat reluctant approval to the new stabilization program supported mainly by the United States, Sukarno, stimulated, like a drug addict, by a new opportunity to attack the "imperialist forces," challenged the newly created nation of Malaysia. This marked the beginning of the end for Bung Karno.

The Malaysian affair was a long and complicated one, for Sukarno and for Indonesia as well as for all the other states involved —Malaya, Singapore, and the three British dependencies of Sarawak, Brunei, and Sabah (the five areas that together were originally supposed to constitute Malaysia), and the Philippines. Indonesia's original objections to the creation of Malaysia, which Sukarno characterized as a British imperialist plot, were raised in December, 1962, when a nationalist uprising in tiny Brunei, supported surreptitiously by the Indonesians, failed. A compromise appeared likely in the spring and summer of 1963, when Indonesia and the Philippines, which had an old claim to Sabah, agreed to accept the concept of Malaysia if a United Nations referendum could first demonstrate that the people of Sabah and Sarawak supported it (Brunei had by then indicated its intention not to join). At the same time, the Philippines and Indonesia, with Malaysia's agreement, projected the unique concept of a

loose union among the three, dubbed "Maphilindo," which satisfied Sukarno's yearning for a new regional alliance that would
contain only Asians and would extend Indonesia's role in the
area. The Maphilindo project died when the Malayans announced
prematurely that Malaysia would be officially formed on September 16, 1963, whatever the results of the referendum in
Sabah and Sarawak. Sukarno thus had all the provocation he
needed to launch a new *konfrontasi* policy, and once again, as had
happened during the showdown over West Irian, the country was
roused to fever pitch. Sukarno dramatically called for 21 million
volunteers, while more serious internal matters continued to be
neglected. Ultimately, as had also been the case in the West Irian
affair, words led to actions. Beginning in August, 1964, several
hundred thousand Indonesian guerrillas were landed on the
Malayan Peninsula, and almost all of them were quickly rounded
up by the Malaysian Army and police and imprisoned. More significant clashes occurred in the border areas between Sarawak and
Sabah and Kalimantan. While Sukarno had no intention of starting a full-scale war over Malaysia, he nevertheless indulged to the
full in his own form of brinksmanship. He forced the British and
their Commonwealth allies to dispatch sixty thousand troops to
Singapore, Sarawak, and Sabah and to bolster their Far Eastern
fleet with an aircraft carrier and several other vessels—all of
which cost Great Britain more than she cared to spend in defense
of territories she had thought she was getting rid of once and for
all, and undoubtedly hastened her desire to divest herself permanently of her East-of-Suez responsibilities, which was just what
Sukarno wanted.

By this time Sukarno had moved closer to Peking and further
from Moscow, and had all but broken off with the United States.
The history of Indonesia's relations with China had been one of
ups and downs since the two nations had signed a trade agreement
in 1953. Following Sukarno's trip to China in 1956, which had so
impressed him that he had repeatedly referred to it in his speeches,
relations had been cool during the period when Indonesia took
action against the Chinese merchants in the archipelago. By 1960,
when a treaty on dual nationality was signed and the Chinese
agreed to let citizens of China resident in Indonesia apply for
Indonesian citizenship, the situation improved again, and this was

emphasized by an exchange of visits in 1961 between Sukarno and Foreign Minister Chen Yi. Later that year Aidit, attending the Twenty-second Communist Party Congress in Moscow when the Peking-Moscow feud burst into the open, declared that the Soviet Union and China were both "inspiring examples for the people of Indonesia." When Aidit returned home, however, it became apparent to him that in the P.K.I. the pendulum was swinging to Peking and he would have to adjust. The next year Peking was lavish in its praise for Sukarno's diplomatic victory in West Irian, and early in 1963 Foreign Minister Subandrio, who was to play a vital role in furthering relations with China, traveled to Peking, after which the Chinese, who at first had been somewhat hesitant about supporting Indonesia's anti-Malaysia policy, gave it their full approval. Liu Shao-chi, the No. 2 man in China at the time, visited Djakarta, and a group of Chinese doctors came to Indonesia, where they spent five months treating Sukarno with herbs and acupuncture for a worsening kidney ailment. By then he had further shown which way he was leaning by appointing Njoto, the third-ranking P.K.I. member, who was strongly pro-Peking, to his inner Cabinet (Aidit and Lukman had previously been ex-officio ministers). While Sukarno continued to receive some military aid from the Russians, and although Moscow made an agreement postponing payments on Indonesia's vast debt of more than a billion dollars, one of the principal factors in Sukarno's pro-Peking outlook was Moscow's reluctance to support his anti-Malaysia crusade. Probably even more important was Sukarno's new conception of himself as a pan-Asian leader. Furthermore, the Chinese, as what Sukarno called the "legitimate" leaders of the anti-imperialist cause, had never, unlike the "revisionist" Russians, joined the United Nations, and they had been encouraging Sukarno to quit and become the spearhead of a new international organization comprising all the emerging nations of the world.

The most significant events in the developing Chinese-Indonesian alliance took place at the end of 1964 and early in 1965. In November, 1964, Sukarno, having recognized North Korea and North Vietnam as well as the National Liberation Front of South Vietnam, met with Premier Chou En-lai in Shanghai. That same month, Chen Yi suddenly arrived in Djakarta, where he spent a week in secret talks with Sukarno and with members of the P.K.I., as well as with some of the pro-leftist elements of the Army, Navy, and Air Force. Chen Yi, who had been a general before he became a diplomat, was said to have urged Sukarno to give up his inconclusive guerrilla raids on the Malayan Peninsula and concentrate on the guerrilla war in Sarawak. He promised the Indonesians some aid in building up their guerrilla forces, and was said to have proposed a plan whereby a Sino-Indonesian pincer thrust would be mounted against Malaysia, with the Chinese reactivating the guerrilla war in the northern part of Malaya, where a group of five hundred armed men were still holding out in the jungle—survivors of the decade-long struggle waged in the late forties and the fifties against Malaya and the British. Chen Yi may also have promised to send Chinese arms for the creation of a peasant-and-worker militia within Indonesia, which the P.K.I. had been urging on Sukarno but which he had so far resisted because of pressure from the Indonesian Army.

In the second week of December, 1964, Foreign Minister Subandrio, who was also now First Deputy Prime Minister, met with a group of Indonesian diplomats in New York and secretly outlined to them the larger strategy of the new alliance, which he said was aimed at dividing the British from the Americans and eliminating all remaining "imperialist" bases in Southeast Asia. Subandrio not only spoke of the combined Chinese-Indonesian thrust against Malaysia but also envisaged the cooperation of the Vietcong in South Vietnam, pointing out that they already controlled most of the Mekong Delta and the peninsula to the south of it—which, he explained, would serve as a staging area for an attack against Malaysia across the Gulf of Siam. Then, in January, 1965, Subandrio again journeyed to Peking, where he disclosed that his purpose was "to take up where Chen Yi had left off." Before this journey, Sukarno had withdrawn Indonesia from the United Nations and its affiliated agencies, using as his excuse the seating of Malaysia on the Security Council.

All the plotting between Peking and Djakarta had been matched meanwhile by increasingly close relations between the P.K.I. and Sukarno in Indonesia. After several years of balancing the Communists and the military off against each other, with himself in the middle, Sukarno had started to move openly, and with surprising speed and candor, to the left. While some observers feel that he was still willing to leave the outcome of the Indonesian revolution to the forces of history after his departure from the scene, others believe that, in spite of his apparent balancing act, a firm agreement between Sukarno and the P.K.I. was reached as early as the spring of 1964, and that in return for the support of the Communists in his lifetime Sukarno agreed to designate them as his legitimate revolutionary heirs. There had been a number of indications that this was likely, including Sukarno's 1964 Independence Day speech, in which he had denounced those seeking to impede the P.K.I.'s growth as hypocrites who were thereby sabotaging his own policies. Throughout this period, Sukarno had steadily harped on his old theme of *Nasakom* (*Nasionalisme-Agama-Komunisme*— nationalism, religion, and Communism), insisting on the inclusion of the Communists with nationalist and Islamic elements in the reorganization of Indonesian society and intimating that he regarded the militancy of the Communists as the most important ingredient in this grouping. Indonesian Communism, he maintained, was a bona fide national force which would never be subservient either to Moscow or to Peking, and he would brook no interference with its development. He demonstrated this when he took action against a group that cleverly called itself the Body for the Protection of Sukarnoism, which had been formed early in 1964 by a group of anti-Communist but Marxist-oriented men led by Adam Malik, the Minister of Trade, and Chaerul Saleh, who had become the Third Deputy Prime Minister and Minister for Basic Industries and Mining. The B.P.S.—which had quietly obtained the endorsement of General Nasution, who was now Minister of Defense as well as Chief of Staff of the armed forces, and of several Muslim and Nationalist Party politicians—had launched a broad attack on the P.K.I. in some sixty newspapers, accusing the Communists of having violated the "true teachings" of Sukarno and of disrupting national unity by, among other things, seizing land in Java under the pretext of enforcing land-reform laws. When the movement showed signs of becoming a powerful anti-Communist front, Sukarno began infiltrating it, using agents of Subandrio's private intelligence network. In December, 1964, the B.P.S. was formally banned, and Sukarno closed down a score of newspapers that had supported it and demoted Malik and Saleh; Saleh, long one of his closest aides, had until this time been regarded as Sukarno's likely heir, but now Subandrio became the heir apparent.

Following a similar tack, Sukarno next moved against an ardent anti-Communist Muslim student group known as H.M.I., which had been allowed to remain in existence following the banning of the Masjumi Party in 1960. He did this by simply placing H.M.I. under the control of Subandrio, who promptly neutralized it through infiltration and at the same time enhanced his own position of power by claiming the support of a large number of Muslims. Sukarno's next target was the P.N.I., the Nationalist Party, which by now was thoroughly divided as a result of a bitter battle between right- and left-wing factions. In March, 1965, at a meeting of P.N.I. workers, Sukarno declared that Indonesia was currently "in the national democratic stage" of the revolution and that the duty of all good P.N.I. members was "to crush imperialism, to overturn neocolonialism, to smash feudalism and to pulverize the foreign-capital monopolies" in order "to create Socialism in Indonesia." He attacked the party for having been lax in pushing land-reform measures—one reason for the split in its ranks, because a good many P.N.I. members were landlords themselves. A week after his speech, Sukarno announced a new program of state control and socialization of the economy, and seized most of the remaining foreign-owned enterprises.

Having rejected several attempts to settle the Malaysian issue either with or without the help of the United Nations, Sukarno now moved boldly ahead with a plan to form a new organization to rival the U.N. He called this CONEFO (Conference of the New Emerging Forces), and it was supposed to include "all genuine revolutionary peoples" of Asia, Africa, and the Americas. Designating the current period as *Tavip*, a contraction of a Javanese-Italian coinage, *Tahun Vivere Pericoloso* ("The Year of Living Dangerously"), he summoned a *Dasa Warsa* (Sanskrit for "tenth anniversary") celebration in Bandung in April, 1965, marking a decade since the original Bandung Asian-African conference. To his great displeasure, only thirty-five of the sixty nations invited sent representatives, and only three of the twenty chiefs of state he expected showed up. Although the occasion was pretty much of a failure as a demonstration of renewed Afro-Asian solidarity, Sukarno went all out to pretend otherwise, exalting himself as the leader of the new anti-imperialist alliance in a major speech before a hundred thousand people in Djakarta's Bung Karno stadium. After a gaudy series of parades and fireworks displays, a cornerstone was laid for the new CONEFO headquarters, which the Chinese had half-promised to build and which was never completed. To finance the whole *Dasa Warsa* extravaganza, the Indonesian state bank simply printed thousands of new ten-thousand-rupiah banknotes—a feat hailed as part of a "new revolutionary banking process."

Sukarno's acronyms, having multiplied each year with each new crisis, real or imagined, had by now become increasingly shrill and vituperative. The coinages had moved from such relatively mild combinations as *Nasakom* and *Re-So-Pim* (*Revolusi-Socialisme-Pimpinan-Leadership*—sometimes shortened to *Ril*, which is the Indonesian word for rail, implying the revolution was being "put back on the rails") to such slogans as *Banstir* (*Banting Stir*, meaning "slam the steering wheel"—to the left, as Sukarno used it, indicating more nationalization of foreign properties) and *Berdikari* (*Berdiri di atas kaki sendiri*, literally "to stand on one's own feet," implying the rejection of Western aid, especially American aid). Sukarno, in his creation of Indonesian Newspeak, invariably mixed terms from Javanese and from *bahasa Indonesia* with French and English ones that caught his fancy, so that what emerged was an unintelligible linguistic potpourri. Willard Hanna, in a paper he prepared for the American Universities field staff in April, 1965, began as follows: "At Djakarta's mid-April *Dasa Warsa*, a *Tavip* preview of CONEFO, Bung Karno attempted boldly to marshal *Nefos* for *konfrontasi* of *Oldesfos* and *Nekolim* and by practice of *berdikari* and *banstir*, under the device of 'Forward No Retreat,' to ensure that '*Les flammes de l'âme de Bandung fonderont le monde de nouveau.*'"

Despite the failure of the *Dasa Warsa* powwow to build up the Afro-Asian world anew—it was pretty badly split by now anyway, as attested by such absentees from Sukarno's celebration as Egypt's Nasser, Pakistan's Ayub Khan, Ghana's Nkrumah, and the Philippines' Macapagal—Sukarno left no doubt who the Bandung "flames" were meant to consume. There were posters showing Sukarno, Chou En-lai, and Nasser pushing a fat American capitalist into a bonfire of skyscrapers, of the Vietcong shooting down burning American planes, and of American soldiers throwing vials of smoking poison gas at Vietnamese villagers. One large mural showed an Indonesian decapitating John Bull with a huge sword while a fellow patriot was smashing President Johnson's head with a sledgehammer. Even the American Ambassador, Howard P. Jones, who had served in Indonesia for seven years and had become one of Sukarno's closest personal friends, was not spared in the xenophobic display. Two days before the *Dasa Warsa* party officially began, a special American envoy, Ellsworth Bunker, with the rank of Ambassador, who had conceived the formula that had settled the West Irian crisis to Indonesia's satisfaction, quietly left Djakarta after having failed, during a two-week visit, to persuade Sukarno to call off his anti-American demonstrations. Bunker had not responded to Sukarno's hint that relations might improve if the United States supported Indonesia's position on Malaysia, and about the only concrete result of his mission was an agreement to withdraw the American Peace Corps volunteers (the United States Information Service offices had already been closed following several hostile demonstrations) and to re-evaluate the American aid program, which had dwindled from an average of $120 million a year to a token effort in support of a few university contracts for foreign professors. A year before Bunker's mission, Sukarno, at a meeting attended by Ambassador Jones, had shouted, "To hell with your aid!" and he had repeated the phrase in numerous subsequent speeches. At one point, Ambassador Jones' residence had been invaded by a mob of five hundred students. Beyond the P.K.I.-mounted demonstrations against U.S.I.S. libraries, which had been accused of "poisoning the mind of our youth," Sukarno had condoned Communist assaults against American rubber, oil, and other companies in Indonesia. One by one, he had either taken many of these firms over or restricted their activities by means of so many controls that all but a few had voluntarily closed down. The Americans had been further inconvenienced by having their electricity and their delivery of mail sporadically cut off. A couple of anti-American moves had boomeranged: When American films had been banned, there had been so many complaints that Sukarno had been forced to relent and allow them back again. Despite a well-publicized personal fondness for dancing, Sukarno had banned the cha-cha, the twist, and other Western dances as "crazy" and had ordered them replaced by the *lenso*, a slow-moving blueslike local step, and by traditional Indonesian folk dances, but in this case, too, he had run into opposition; private "clubs" had violated the ban and Indonesian teen-agers, as well as members of the older generation, had openly regarded it as a joke.

Regardless of movies and dances, there was little doubt, in mid-1965, which way Indonesia was moving politically. At the end of May, addressing a huge rally in Djakarta in celebration of the Communists' forty-fifth anniversary, Sukarno referred to Aidit, the P.K.I. leader, as "my brother and my friend." (He was shortly to bestow on Aidit the special title of Great Son of the Revolution.) He had declared further, "It's not strange at all that I embrace the P.K.I. The P.K.I. has always stood in the forefront of the implementation of the policies of the Indonesian revolution." And in his Independence Day speech that year, in which he projected the idea of a "Djakarta–Phnom Penh–Hanoi–Peking–Pyongyang axis," he said, "I am a friend of the Communists because the Communists are *revolutionary* people," adding that he regarded all Communists as "*very revolutionary*," whereas only "some" of Indonesia's nationalist and religious party members were sufficiently revolutionary to deserve his blessing. As for the Army, Sukarno, in the same speech, had made it equally clear that he thought many top officers had lost their old revolutionary zeal. "Those who were progressive yesterday are possibly retrogressive, antiprogressive today," he said. "Those who were revolutionary are possibly counterrevolutionary today."

Despite his pretentious schemes—such as one for erecting a huge air-conditioned National Monument, taller than either the Eiffel Tower or Borobudur, the eighth-century remnant of the Madjapahit Empire in Java, which has been likened to the Angkor Wat in Cambodia, and such extravagances as an ostentatious department store that was filled with imported goods that only the rich could afford to buy and that was named after Sukarno's favorite childhood nurse—Sukarno had begun to reveal an awareness of his own mortality. In the August speech, acknowledging the reports of his physical ailments, he said, "Sukarno is just a man. Like you, sisters and brothers, my age is in the hands of God. . . . I would like to live another thousand years, but that, of course, is not possible. But I pray that my concepts and teachings will live another thousand years." Even though, in alluding for the first time to the possibility of his death, Sukarno now seemed to leave little doubt about his political will and testament, his designated heirs, the Communists, may not themselves have been as ready as he assumed to accept the mantle he wanted to bestow on them. They had convinced him by this time, despite the Army's objections, that the peasants and workers should be armed as a "fifth force." Sukarno claimed this to be his own idea, declaring that "every citizen shall have the right and the duty to participate in the defense of the state," and in September he sent Air Vice Marshal Omar Dhani, the head of the Air Force and an ardent Communist sympathizer, to Peking to negotiate on the shipment of arms for the new people's militia. But the P.K.I. had not succeeded, as it had also hoped to do, in persuading him to introduce a political-commissar system in the armed forces—the Army had so far fought this off—or to give the Communists a full share of the important governmental portfolios. Aidit and other Communist leaders had shown a degree of impatience on these matters. Speaking to a Communist trade-union conference in September, Aidit had said that the people themselves had to choose—"If they do not want to be the anvil, then they should become the hammer"—and that party workers, in taking the lead to get rid of the "bureaucratic capitalists [a euphemism for well-to-do generals], pilferers, and corrupters," should be "daring, daring, and still more daring—take over, take over, and take over again, act, act, and act again." During this period, however, Aidit had continued to point out that all nine legal political parties in Indonesia had accepted Sukarno's dictum of the nation still being in a stage of "democratic revolution" that would gradually evolve into "Socialism." And in paying homage to the Sukarno theory of *Nasakom,* Aidit had said, "We remain Communists, but we have to be tolerant of nationalism and religion."

There is, then, ample evidence that, in spite of their displays of impatience, the Communists still wanted to move slowly. Confident, as they were, of their growing mass strength and of the success of their long-term strategy, they would probably have preferred to take their chances on gradually pushing Sukarno further down the Communist path while invoking the *Nasakom* formula. According to their timetable, as it has been revealed in later-uncovered party documents, 1970 was to be the year of ultimate victory. Two domestic factors upset this schedule and now acted to trigger Communist action prematurely—Sukarno's apparently fast-declining health, and the P.K.I.'s suspicion that the military leaders were preparing to take some sort of counteraction against both Sukarno and the Communists. There was a third, external factor —the war in Vietnam. Had it not been for the American build-up in South Vietnam in the spring and summer of 1965, which averted a probable Vietcong victory and posed a threat of new American power in Southeast Asia, the astonishing Communist coup attempt that autumn might not have taken place so soon, and consequently might not have failed.

The Coup That Failed

As with so much else in Indonesia, so many elements and factors of the complex national personality were involved in the 1965 coup attempt, and all of them were so intricately interwoven, that the pattern of the plot emerges not so much as a single design but as a large tapestry consisting of countless figures and configurations created by separate colored threads, each weaving its own story as part of the whole. While the collapse of the coup sharply altered the long and tortuous course of the Indonesian revolution, both the background and the mechanics of the conspiracy have continued to be the subject of considerable debate among foreign diplomats and scholars, as well as among the Indonesians themselves. The question may be largely one of semantics, but there are those who maintain that what took place was not truly a *coup d'état* at all but merely an effort, on the part of the Communists of the P.K.I. and some radical politicians and ambitious left-wing members of the armed forces, to "preserve the revolution" by forcing a political shift to the left.

If this is so, and there was no intention on the part of the plotters to overthrow the existing government and establish a Communist regime, then the means adopted were, to say the least, hazardous and extreme. They included a plan to eliminate seven of Indonesia's top-ranking generals who were thought to stand in the way of Sukarno's efforts to *Nasakomize* the government—that is, to move more swiftly and concretely to include in important Cabinet posts and other positions the heretofore excluded Communists along with the incumbent nationalists and religious elements. Whatever the ultimate aims of the conspirators, they brutally murdered six of the seven generals, while the seventh, General Nasution, Defense and Security Chief at the time, narrowly escaped. It was his escape, coupled with the failure of the plotters to go after three or four other key figures, notably General Suharto, that caused the breakdown of the coup, or *Putsch*, or whatever one wants to call it. When the generals, led by Suharto, in his capacity as head of Kostrad, the strategic reserve of the Army, quickly rallied their forces, the disorganized and poorly coordinated rebel groups disintegrated within a few hours in Djakarta. When they tried to sustain themselves in a number of other Javanese cities and villages, they failed to rally enough support, and the long-smoldering resentments between the Communists and conservative Muslim and military factions led to the frightful bloodbath throughout heavily populated Java and Bali. What followed resembled a performance of a traditional shadow play, and the principal theme was the physical survival and the political eclipse of President Sukarno. His political demise, in the year and a half following the failed coup, was, if anything, more slow and painful than most physical deaths. In a way, he committed extended political suicide, chiefly by refusing to condemn the perpetrators of the plot, especially the Communists, and by refusing to admit that, if he had not been apprised of all the plot's details, he had known beyond what now seems any reasonable doubt that a coup was going to be attempted and that he would be the central figure in it.

On the eve of the coup attempt, there was little doubt that Indonesia was charged with a variety of peculiarly high tensions. On top of the policy of confrontation with Malaysia Sukarno had adopted, which was eating up most of the country's already inflated and deficit-ridden budget, his ambitions to become a new Asian-type imperialist leader had led him to form a virtual alliance with the Chinese Communists. He had all but broken relations with the West, having completed the seizure of all foreign properties with the exception of some oil wells, and his relations with the Americans, in particular, had disintegrated to the

point where the only Americans of importance in Indonesia were a
new Ambassador, Marshall Green, and his embassy personnel, who
were virtually ostracized by the whole Indonesian community.
Green, a first-rate career officer, in July, 1965, had replaced the
long-incumbent Ambassador Jones. After many years as Sukarno's
close friend, Jones had found himself being cut off from the President officially, though their personal relations had remained pleas-
ant on the surface. Early in 1964 Attorney General Robert F.
Kennedy had failed to persuade Sukarno to call off his confrontation with Malaysia or to ameliorate the growing breach between
Djakarta and Washington. When Green took over the embassy, he
adopted a policy of restraint, protesting against the anti-American
demonstrations that took place, including one in front of his
residence the day he presented his credentials, but he issued no
threats about the possibilities of their leading to a total break between the two nations. On September 7, however, following a series
of fresh outbursts, he told Foreign Minister Subandrio that, unless
the insults and the destruction of American property ceased, a
break was imminent. The Indonesians, not wanting this to happen,
particularly since Sukarno's henchmen were profiting personally
from their consular representation in the United States, took the
cue, and the troubles promptly stopped.

Meanwhile, Sukarno veered more and more toward full support
of the P.K.I., believing as he did, or pretended to, that the party
represented a true nationalist force that would remain independent
of both Moscow and Peking. The Communists, emboldened by
their position as favorites, but wanting to reassure themselves of
their hold on the Javanese masses, had started a campaign of
"unilateral action" in Central and East Java to seize land and distribute it among the propertyless peasants. Under the system of
"shared poverty," land had been traditionally parceled out in increasingly small amounts among families in accordance with the
complicated system of inheritance laws designed to take care of
the ever-increasing population. Because of vested interests or
bureaucratic lapses, the distribution of government-owned land
under the national land reform act had scarcely begun. By urging
the peasants to seize this land or that of absentee landlords, and in
thus choosing to deal in their own way with the Malthusian imperative, the Communists had heightened the tensions, including re-

ligious ones, that already existed in Java, and a considerable number of killings had already taken place involving Muslim landlords and their political supporters and the Communist-inspired peasantry. Once these peasants had been told to take things into their own hands and benefit from "the rising revolutionary situation," as Aidit and the other Communist leaders were advising them, agrarian unrest became a political instrument and the whole traditional social order in Java was threatened. As the Communists became more daring and outspoken, strikes by their workers had also occurred in Java and North Sumatra, and in the period just before the coup, Aidit had reiterated that "the duty of the worker is not only to fight for more rice and dried fish but to fight for political power." The P.K.I. leaders felt that Sukarno's timetable for their ascendancy, which under different circumstances might also have remained their own, was now threatened by the combined fears and ambitions of a group of right-wing military commanders who, the Communists maintained, wanted to take power themselves, or who would at least do their best to impede the growing strength of the P.K.I. in any way they could.

Subsequent investigations revealed that preparations for a coup began sometime in the spring of 1965. At this point, apparently, the P.K.I. decided that its initial timetable for a takeover one way or another by the end of 1970 should be speeded up. Sukarno, it has since been learned, was secretly apprised of this decision almost at once, and he was told that the Communists wanted to arrest a number of leading generals. The key factor in the growing atmosphere of tension and uncertainty then became the President's health. Because he had punished himself for years by devoting equal amounts of time to the twin pursuits of politics and pleasure, his kidney ailment had grown progressively worse, and it seemed beyond the capability of the best doctors of Peking and Vienna to cure. In the spring of 1965 the group of Chinese physicians who had treated him earlier tried a new regimen of herbs and acupuncture—the ancient Chinese practice of sticking needles into the body to draw off pain and poison—but after their return to Peking he continued to feel tired and ill, so much so that he was forced to cancel some speaking engagements. During the summer he suffered two severe attacks, the latter on August 5 at a public ceremony in Djakarta, when he collapsed on the platform. Personal concern became mingled with political worry over what would happen if he suddenly died. Shortly afterward Aidit, who had been abroad, was ordered home by Sukarno, and, having been told of the President's critical condition, he brought the group of doctors back again from Peking. Although Sukarno recovered, the doctors told Aidit that the President was still in danger of another attack that could cause paralysis or death. It may be that the Chinese, anxious to stir up trouble in Indonesia, purposely exaggerated the seriousness of Sukarno's condition. In any event, the reports, which the Chinese Embassy also privately disseminated, stimulated the scheming and counterscheming of the P.K.I. and the generals, and were surely another factor in the timing of the attempted coup.

Aidit now called a series of meetings of the P.K.I. Politburo to analyze the situation. The discussions that took place dealt specifically with Sukarno's deteriorating health, with the reported existence of a so-called Council of Generals which might try a power grab before Sukarno died, and with the existence of another group of "progressive officers" in the Army that was ready to take countermeasures to forestall a *Putsch* by the generals. The role of the Council of Generals would remain one of the most disputed elements of the plot; the Communists and their fellow plotters described the Council as a sinister and secret organization composed of some twenty top Indonesian general officers who planned to take power from Sukarno and, while perhaps retaining him as a symbol of national unity, if he lived, to set up a military government. That some of the generals thought this was a good idea may have been the case, but in their subsequent version of that year's events, the Council—which they did not call it—was just a group of senior officers formed in January, 1965, by General Achmad Yani, the Army Chief of Staff, to meet from time to time in order to discuss "political matters" and some internal Army affairs mainly having to do with the promotion and retirement of senior officers. Its members may have been alarmed by a fear that Sukarno was moving too far and too fast to the left, as indicated by his acquiescence to the Communists' demand for a Chinese militia-type "fifth force" and his listening to their further demand, still rejected by the generals, that he introduce a system of political commissars in the armed forces. It seems unlikely that the loosely formed group of generals had conceived any plot to grab power, particularly since they were intimidated by Sukarno—as one of them afterward said, "We wouldn't dare to discuss the problem of what we would do before he died." However, there may have been a secret set of contingency plans to respond to any Communist power play or to take care of any emergency when Sukarno was no longer around. Whatever the generals discussed, almost from the moment they met as a group, the Communists used the existence of that group to justify their suspicions of a deep military conspiracy against them and as an excuse to mount their own plot.

During his talks with his fellow members of the Politburo during August and September, Aidit made it clear that he was personally in favor of the P.K.I. striking first to avoid a takeover by the generals. This could best be done, he indicated, through the progressive officers who opposed the right-wing generals. Since the generals had support in Djakarta and the P.K.I. was weak in the capital, the right-wing officers could only be foiled, Aidit added, if Sukarno's support for the progressive officers could be obtained. Once it was decided by the Politburo that some "preventive" action should definitely be taken, and taken soon, the planning became the province of what subsequent testimony by Communist participants in the coup effort revealed was a highly secret Special Bureau—*Biro Chusus*—which was directly under Aidit. His two lieutenants in the Special Bureau were a pair of top underground agents known by their aliases, Sjam and Pono, and they, in effect, became the managers of the coup under the over-all direction of Aidit, organizing it not only in Djakarta but throughout Java.

The final planning was done in a series of ten meetings that took place in Djakarta between the middle of August and September 29, 1965. These meetings were attended by members of the Special Bureau and by various P.K.I. sympathizers in the armed forces who, as part of the progressive group, were to execute the plan. Obviously, the most important question was to determine which troops could be used. By the first week of September, the troops the plotters decided could be definitely counted on were a company of the Tjakrabirawa battalion, the President's private guards; two platoons of the 1st Infantry Brigade in Djakarta, and one battalion of Air Force paratroopers, plus about two thousand members of the

Pemuda Rakyat, the P.K.I.-organized People's Youth, and of the Gerekan Wanita Indonesia, or Gerwani for short, the Indonesian Women's Movement. It would not be difficult to train these members of the youth and women's groups for participation in the coup, the Communists figured, because, since the first week of July, a total of 3,700 of them had received training as part of the "fifth force" that Sukarno had authorized. This training had concentrated on the use of light and heavy weapons and on political indoctrination. It was being conducted in a remote and swampy area called Lubang Buaja—which means Crocodile Hole—adjoining Halim air base, fifteen miles south of the city. There had been no accident in the selection of this out-of-the-way site. It had been offered by Air Vice Marshal Omar Dhani, the vain and ambitious Air Force chief whom the Communists had flattered into believing that he might someday, with their backing, succeed Sukarno as President. Dhani had permitted the Air Force to be thoroughly infiltrated by P.K.I. members and sympathizers. One of them, a Major Sujono, directed the training at Lubang Buaja.

Gradually, as the plan for the coup took its ultimate shape and form, it was decided that the seven top generals, headed by General Nasution, should be arrested, abducted, or killed, and that, in order to make it appear that the plot was "only a movement within the Army," Army squads would be used for this part of the operation. Djakarta was to be divided into six operational sectors and a number of key installations, including the President's palace, the government radio station, and the telecommunications center, would be occupied and used to maintain control of the city and the population. A Central Command called Cenko was created, to control three armed task forces. Logistics were carefully planned, particularly the procurement of enough guns and food for the participating elements. Once the coup had attained its primary objective— namely, the elimination of the Army generals—a second, political stage would quickly follow. This entailed the creation of a Revolutionary Council, which would take over from the progressive Army elements which had "solved the internal struggle" in the military, and which would then dismiss the Cabinet and rule the country as the highest representative of Sukarno's *Nasakom* policy, which the right-wing generals had allegedly subverted.

Those in on the Communist scheme busied themselves spreading reports of how the Council of Generals, or other alleged cabals, were plotting against the P.K.I.—or, in at least one case, against Sukarno as well. That case involved the so-called "Gilchrist document," a paper allegedly written by Sir Andrew Gilchrist, the former British Ambassador to Indonesia. Sukarno's No. 2 man, First Deputy Prime Minister and Foreign Minister Subandrio, later testified that in mid-March, 1965, he received an anonymous "blind letter" attached to a copy of the controversial document, which had been "found" by some young Communists in the home near Djakarta of "an American Central Intelligence Agency representative" who had fled the country as he was about to be arrested. The document purported to outline a joint British-American plot, to be executed "together with local Army friends," as Subandrio recalled it, to overthrow the Sukarno regime. Subandrio said that he had also heard of the alleged plotting by the Council of Generals, but when he was asked by the presiding judge at his trial why he had not connected the two, he replied that, as Foreign Minister, he had "only wanted to use the document in the international arena against the British." When he told Sukarno about it, he asked the President not to publish it because he wanted to distribute it during the second Afro-Asian Conference, which was supposed to be held in Algiers in June (the conference, as it turned out, never did meet), and Sukarno agreed. Both men, however, in speeches they made during May and June, 1965, said they had "secured evidence" of an "imperialist plot to destroy Indonesia," and Sukarno, on one occasion, dramatically revealed that the plotters wanted to kill him, Subandrio, and General Yani. Neither Sukarno nor Subandrio ever publicly mentioned the Gilchrist document as such, and they must have been aware that it was a total fabrication. So far as is known, the document was the product of Indonesia's own Central Intelligence Board, which Subandrio also headed. It was probably prepared in collaboration with the Communists, with whom Subandrio, like Omar Dhani, had formed what was at least a tacit alliance and in all likelihood a much firmer one.

Sukarno, on May 26, 1965, in Subandrio's presence, asked General Yani about the supposed Council of Generals. When the Chief of Staff told him it was nothing but a small group that dealt with matters of officer promotions, Sukarno smiled and thanked him and gave him a friendly slap on the back. A year after the coup, in a written statement given under oath, Sukarno said he had not heard about the Council of Generals until early September, 1965, and that when he had asked Yani about it then, the General had replied, "I have them [the other generals] in hand, you can trust me on the matter." Sukarno's convenient lapse of memory about the May confrontation with Yani was part of his unconvincing effort to deny that he had known anything about the coup and to pretend that he had been "completely surprised" when it was sprung. Subandrio, who altogether made a poor showing before the court as an evasive witness trying to protect Sukarno as well as save himself, also testified that he had heard on September 15, 1965, that the Communists were going to pull a coup four days later (the nineteenth and twentieth had, in fact, been tentative dates) but that he had not told this to Sukarno because "I felt other intelligence agencies had reported to the President already."

Certainly, by this time Sukarno knew that both the Communists and the generals were up to something, and he was making it quite clear where his sympathies lay. Testimony at the subsequent trials indicates that he had been told by mid-September and perhaps sooner of the P.K.I. plan to create a Revolutionary Council. Anyone who attempted after that to warn him that the P.K.I. was about to take action was peremptorily dismissed as having "a phobia about the Communists." One of these men was General Sugandhi, who was in an interesting and odd position because he had gone to school with a man named Sudisman, who was one of eight members of the P.K.I. Politburo. The two had managed to remain friends, and Sudisman, as well as Aidit himself, had tried to get Sugandhi to join them in their plot. According to a story Sugandhi later told, Aidit and Sudisman, on September 27, made a final appeal to him, telling him they would start the effort to "improve the revolution" in "about two or three days," and that they could not fail because "we have weighed everything well and we have the initiative." Sugandhi said he told them, as he had before, that he could not go along with them because Communism was against his religion. The three men parted friends, but the fact that Aidit did nothing to silence Sugandhi was either a naïve oversight which is hard to believe—or part of the purposeful war of nerves that the Communists were now confidently waging.

At any rate, Sugandhi later claimed that he went to see Sukarno on the morning of September 30, told the President what was about to happen, and said he had been apprised of the coup plans by none other than Aidit and Sudisman. Sukarno, he said, angrily replied, "Don't pull that P.K.I. phobia on me. Do you know about the Council of Generals? Do you know that the generals are rotten?" He then warned Sugandhi "not to interfere" and reminded the General that, according to classic doctrine, "only in a revolution may a father devour his own children." Sugandhi, peculiarly enough, did not have much more luck in attempting to warn General Yani. When he did so, Yani waved him aside, dismissing the threat of a coup as "Communist psychological warfare." Yani had refused to allow the guard around his house to be increased, even though, a week earlier, General Parman, the head of Army intelligence, had received new evidence of what the Communists were up to. Parman was later reported to have been almost as nonchalant as Yani about the whole thing, and even if the two men —both of whom were among the six generals to be murdered— were simply pretending to be ignorant of what was going on in the interests of masking a generals' plot, they were certainly calm actors at a highly dangerous moment.

Sukarno, for one, either thought they *were* acting, or else he was consciously going along with the Communists' scheme to use the alleged generals' plot as a pretext to launch *their* coup. In view of what has been found out since, the latter seems almost surely the case. At nine o'clock on the morning of September 29, a day before Sugandhi's visit to him, Sukarno had received Marshal Dhani, the pro-Communist Air Force chief, who told him that the Council of Generals planned to stage a coup on October 5, which was Armed Forces Day, and that some twenty thousand soldiers were already gathered at the Senayan compound in Djakarta. Sukarno "seemed to know all about the subject," Dhani later testified. When Dhani told him that the progressive military men in league with another key figure, General Mustafa Sjarif Supardjo, were becoming "restive," Sukarno asked Dhani to come to see him with Supardjo at the palace in Bogor, forty miles from Djakarta, on October 3.

General Supardjo's importance was twofold: he was the leader of the progressive element in the Army and, as such, the main link between the dissident military elements and the Communists. Although one of the nine medals he held was for having helped to quell the Communist rebellion at Madiun, in Java, in 1948, he was in subsequent years regarded by his fellow officers in West Java as pro-Communist. For this reason, he had been "banished" to Kalimantan, where he directed one of the combat commands in the border war against Malaysia. Arrogant and ambitious, Supardjo had only recently been made a general, and he was apparently resentful over this delayed promotion. For this reason, and because of his political convictions, he had helped spread the rumors about the Council of Generals among his friends and supporters in the Army, and had himself fostered the "unrest" that Dhani reported to Sukarno. His principal contact with the Communists was with Sjam, who, with Pono, was masterminding the coup as Aidit's chief deputy of the P.K.I.'s Special Bureau. Sjam and Supardjo had been meeting privately over the past two or three months, during which they had discussed specific measures that might be taken against the Council of Generals, and as the plot moved toward its climax Supardjo had arranged a code with Sjam whereby he would return from Kalimantan when he received a cable telling him that one of his twelve children was ill. On September 27 he got such a cable, and he arrived in Djakarta the next day at four o'clock in the afternoon—incidentally making the trip without permission of his commander in Djakarta, Suharto. Supardjo went directly to Sjam's house, where he found Pono; Colonel Latief, commander of the 1st Infantry Brigade of the Djakarta garrison, who was one of the plotters; and Lieutenant Colonel Untung, who commanded the Tjakrabirawa battalion that served as President Sukarno's palace guard.

Untung, who would be the official leader of the uprising, was a paratrooper who had taken part in the West Irian campaign. He was not overintelligent or imaginative, but he was respected as a good, tough soldier who obeyed orders and worked hard. Untung, like Supardjo, had been known all along for his pro-Communist views. He was said to have taken part in the Madiun rebellion on the Communist side, a fact that Sukarno must have been aware of but that apparently had not been considered in the selection of Untung as the head of the private guard at the palace. At his trial after the coup, Untung, who has since been executed, denied that he was a member of the P.K.I., but he probably was, and if not he was certainly a willing tool of the Communists. In addition to his regular palace duties, he had been assigned by Sukarno to take charge of the arrangements for the forthcoming Armed Forces Day celebration, and, since this would be the Army's twentieth anniversary, Sukarno had ordered a special parade of a full combat brigade. It is not quite clear who selected the units that were to participate, but Untung and Sjam undoubtedly had something to do with it. During September, when all the plotters were careful to sleep in different houses at night, the two men met frequently with Colonel Latief and Major Sujono, who was still in charge of the training of the P.K.I. paramilitary elements, the youth and women's groups, at Lubang Buaja, and by mid-September the conspirators were enthusiastic over the verification of the assignment of the 454th Paratroop Battalion of the Diponegoro Division in Central Java, and the 530th Battalion of the Brawidjaja Division in East Java to take part in the celebration. Both battalions, consisting of a thousand men each, were thoroughly Communist-infiltrated, and many of their officers, who had taken an oath of allegiance to the P.K.I., had been privately indoctrinated by Sjam's Special Bureau. On the evening and early morning of September 29-30, after Untung had coordinated his plans with the commanders of the two newly arrived battalions, the conspirators held the tenth and last of their preparatory meetings. Untung's men of the Tjakrabirawa battalion were given the toughest assignment—to kidnap or assassinate the seven designated generals. The two Javanese battalions were to surround the Presidential palace on Merdeka Square and to occupy the radio station and telecommunications building, on two other sides of the square. The youth and women's elements of the P.K.I. were to be armed with Air Force weapons and held in reserve at Lubang Buaja. The plotters gave each of the contingents code names based on characters in *wayang,* and a system of passwords and auto-horn and auto-light responses was devised so that the various participating units, most of which did not know of each other's involvement in the coup, would be able to acknowledge one another.

How much additional last-minute contact Sukarno had with the conspirators has been part of the mystery that is still being cleared up. There is some evidence that he met, privately, with Supardjo on September 29. If so, such a meeting presumably would have been intended to fill him in not only on the broad outlines of the plan but perhaps on some of its mechanics as well, so that he could better gauge his own responses and make his own plans while still playing the role, if necessary, of a more or less innocent bystander. Sukarno's value to the plotters certainly, at this point, lay more in his basic sympathy with their cause than in his knowing all the details of the plot, or at least in his being sure that whatever he knew would not deprive him of room to maneuver in case the coup failed. However, at this final moment the P.K.I. apparently decided that Sukarno had to be taken into fuller confidence in view of what they had in mind—not only to kidnap the seven generals but to kill them. *According to evidence obtained by Indonesian authorities late in 1968, following the arrest of additional officers who had played a role in the coup, Sukarno was told, on September 30, that the generals would be arrested and might be eliminated, and he raised no objection.*

Subandrio, though he was probably not as fully informed as Sukarno and had calculatedly maneuvered himself into a bystander's role, had for several weeks been making strong political statements and speeches, which were tantamount to calls for violence—he had, for example, urged a gathering of students to "smash the exploiters and capitalist bureaucrats" and had told another meeting that if the Indonesian leaders were "corruptors" then "the people have the right to take over," just as the Communists, using the same terms, had declared that "corruptors, capitalist bureaucrats, pilferers, and charlatans" should be "dragged to the gallows" or "shot in public." There was little doubt that Subandrio knew what was about to happen, but two days before the coup he and eleven other Cabinet officials had flown to Sumatra on an inspection trip. An unusually large number of officers and officials, as a matter of fact, were out of Djakarta when the coup occurred. Most of them were in China, either to celebrate October 1, China's National Day, or on missions of one sort or another that Subandrio and Dhani had arranged. They included a forty-five-man delegation of the Provisional Consultative Assembly, headed by Chaerul Saleh, also a Deputy Prime Minister, once Sukarno's heir to power but lately displaced by Subandrio; a fifty-man group representing the National Defense Institute; three economic teams that included some of the staunchest anti-Communist military advisers, and fifty-seven Air Force pilots, most of whom were also known to be anti-Communist.

At nine o'clock on the relatively cool evening of September 30, Sukarno left Merdeka Palace and drove in his black Chrysler sedan to Senayan, on the city's outskirts, where he was to address one of the so-called "functional" groups that sat as separate entities in Parliament and in the People's Consultative Assembly—in this case his audience was composed of technicians. At ten o'clock Supardjo and Untung left Sjam's house in Djakarta and drove to Halim air base, which had been chosen as headquarters for the coup. Supardjo was wearing civilian clothes, but Untung was in uniform. They were met by Major Sujono, who told them that Communist youth and women's groups had been alerted and that one of the buildings at the air base had been set up as a secret command center. Supardjo ordered Sujono to pick up Aidit, the P.K.I. head, at Sjam's house an hour or so later and to bring him out to Halim, and this was done. Shortly after eleven Sukarno left the meeting at Senayan, where he had made a typically impassioned speech but had actually said nothing new, and drove back to the palace, where he stayed only long enough to change his clothes before going to the Hotel Indonesia; his Japanese wife, Ratna Sari Dewi, had been attending a wedding reception at the hotel, and after picking her up there he drove to her home in the suburb of Slipi, where he spent the night. (Each of Sukarno's five legal wives had her own establishment, so he always had a wide choice of accommodations.)

H-hour for the coup was four o'clock in the morning. By that time Untung's seven murder squads, each consisting of between fifty and a hundred men, were in position around the homes of the seven generals who were scheduled to be killed. According to his later account, General Nasution, the only one of the seven who escaped, was awakened about three-forty-five by mosquitoes, and shortly afterward he heard strange noises. The attackers had already overpowered the guards outside his house and had come inside. Mrs. Nasution, also awake by now, opened the bedroom door and saw a man with a gun moving around in the dark. She quickly slammed the door, but Nasution insisted on reopening it and confronting the invaders, whereupon there was a flurry of shots, all of which missed him. He threw himself on the floor as his wife slammed the door shut again and locked it. In a nearby room, Nasution's sister, awakened by the shots, grabbed the General's five-year-old daughter, Ada, and tried to get out of the house, but as she ran several shots hit the little girl in the spine; she died five days later. In the darkness, Nasution's aide, Lieutenant Pierre Tendean, who resembled him, was seized by the attackers in the garden. Nasution meanwhile dashed out of his bedroom through another door that led to the back of the house and climbed over a six-foot wall to the adjoining garden of the Iraqi Ambassador. He was shot at again but still was not hit, though in dropping to the ground he cut his bare feet badly on some glass and sprained his ankle. He hid behind a water drum and finally heard the troops leave; at six-thirty, when he spied a colonel from his own headquarters searching for him, he came out and was whisked away to safety in a private house in another part of the city.

The other six generals were not so lucky. General Yani was asleep at his home with his children; his wife, with whom he was not on the best of terms, had gone alone to a birthday celebration given her by some friends. Yani was awakened and told that Sukarno wanted to see him. When the Chief of Staff headed back to his bedroom to put on his uniform, he was shot in the back and, after lying in a pool of blood on the living-room floor while trying to embrace his eleven-year-old son, he was dragged out by his feet and thrown into a truck. He died almost immediately. General Harjono, Yani's third assistant, and General Panjaitan, his fourth assistant, were killed in their homes when they resisted their would-be kidnapers, and their bodies were also carted off in trucks. General Parman, Yani's first assistant in charge of intelligence; General Suprapto, second assistant in that branch; and General Sutojo, the director of the Military Law Academy, were taken alive and were brought, along with the three dead generals, to Lubang Buaja—Crocodile Hole. Lieutenant Tendean, Nasution's aide, was also brought there. The trucks arrived at Lubang Buaja about dawn, and waiting for them was a near-hysterical mob, consisting mostly of women belonging to the P.K.I.'s Gerwani. According to subsequent testimony, a very gruesome scene took place. Whipped to a frenzy, probably by drugs, the women began beating the three generals who were still alive and the unfortunate Lieutenant with clubs and rifle butts. The four men, smashed to senseless pulps, were then shot, after which the women, using razor blades, dismembered the seven corpses, slashing away wildly, gouging out eyes and cutting off sexual organs. Finally the seven bloody bodies were dumped into a well and covered with dirt and trash. They were not to be discovered until the evening of October 3.

About the time the orgy at Lubang Buaja was beginning, General Supardjo, who had been helping to direct the coup from Halim, drove by jeep to Merdeka Palace, to tell Sukarno that all the generals except Nasution had been seized. Sjam had told Supardjo to bring Sukarno to Halim, according to the plotters' previous decision. Supardjo, at his subsequent trial, denied that he knew the generals were to be killed—he would have opposed such an act, he said—and it may have been that the murders were ordered by the P.K.I. without his knowledge, though this seems unlikely, since he was working so closely with Sjam. Sukarno was not at the palace when Supardjo got there—he was still at Slipi with his Japanese wife—but Supardjo stayed around for an hour or so, long enough to be seen by General Umar Wiruhadikusuma, the commander of the Djakarta garrison, who was surprised to find him there instead of at his post in Kalimantan. When Umar had got wind of what was happening, he had gone around the city in his car, stopping at the homes of some of the murdered or kidnaped generals, and had then come to the palace to see Sukarno. Since Sukarno was not there, he went to the nearby headquarters of Kostrad, also fronting Merdeka Square.

About the same time, Supardjo left the palace and went back to Halim in a helicopter that Dhani, the Air Force chief, had sent for him (Dhani also sent Supardjo a message that Sukarno would be at Halim later—a fact that, when it came out in the subsequent investigation, tended to indicate Sukarno's complicity). By the time General Umar had reached Kostrad, General Suharto, the Kostrad chief, had arrived. There later were reports that he had been on the list of generals to be murdered that night, but the best available information is that he had not been an immediate target of the killers, though he was to have been eliminated afterward.

The conspirators had blundered in not listing him initially, and they could have killed him. Contrary to subsequent rumors that he had obeyed the advice of one of his *dukuns*, or spiritual guides, and gone fishing that night, he had actually gone to a hospital to visit one of his daughters, who was ill. He had returned home about midnight. Shortly after dawn he had been awakened by neighbors, who told him what had happened, and he had then gone to his headquarters on Merdeka Square and had assumed temporary command of the Army under a standing order that stipulated he was to take charge in the absence of General Yani. Upon talking to General Umar, he obtained a clearer picture of what had happened and telephoned the commanders or deputies of the Navy and the police to coordinate action against the plotters —he was unable to get a satisfactory response from anyone of authority in the Air Force. When Suharto was told that Nasution had escaped, he made sure that all precautions would be taken to hide the defense chief until the situation was under control. During the day, Nasution was moved from one private house to another as the plotters tried to find out where he was in order to kill him —they twice visited the hospital where his daughter had been taken—and it was not until evening that he was brought under guard to Kostrad headquarters.

Sukarno had been awakened at Dewi's house at six in the morning by one of his guards, who had news of some shooting at Nasution's house. The news was confirmed at Merdeka Palace, and about 6:30 A.M. Sukarno headed there in his car. En route, he was advised by officers of the security staff over the radio telephone not to come because some unidentified troops were in the adjacent square and it might not be safe. The President decided to go to the home of another of his wives, Harjati, in Grogol, the Chinese section of Djakarta. According to the official account later given by General Suharto, Sukarno was at Harjati's when his aides came and told him more about what had happened, although apparently not that the murder of the other generals had taken place. Sukarno later professed to have been "absolutely surprised" at the news of the attempt on Nasution's life and to have asked his security officers, "What do you want me to do?" They advised him against either staying at Harjati's or returning to Dewi's place and suggested he take refuge aboard a warship in the harbor or go to

Halim, where his Jetstar airliner was always ready for use. Sukarno decided to go to Halim—"It was the best place for me," he afterward said, in case "unpredictable events" made it advisable for him to leave Djakarta in a hurry—but his critics later cited this decision of his own to go to the very place where the plotters of the coup had their headquarters as another indication of his complicity.

On top of Dhani's earlier message to Supardjo to the effect that Sukarno would be at Halim, what is, of course, significant is that Sukarno's decision was taken *after* an announcement on the radio, at 7:15 A.M., by Colonel Untung, the official leader of the coup. This broadcast, which was a communiqué issued by "the information section of the September 30th Movement [the name the conspirators had given themselves]," said elements of the Army had taken action against "the Council of Generals, a subversive movement sponsored by the [American] Central Intelligence Agency." The Council, it was charged, had "organized a show of force" for Armed Forces Day on October 5, when the generals planned to execute "a military *coup d'état*." His group's actions, Untung said, were "solely a movement within the Army" to forestall the actions of those who had "bad intentions against the Republic of Indonesia and President Sukarno" and who had vainly hoped that "President Sukarno would die of his recent ailments." The President now was safe "under the protection of the September 30th Movement," while "a number of generals have been arrested and important communications and some other vital installations have been put under control," the announcement added. It went on to say that similar action would be taken "throughout Indonesia against the agents and henchmen as well as sympathizers of the 'Council of Generals' in the regions," and that to accomplish this "an Indonesian Revolutionary Council will be formed in the center," with similar councils to be set up in the provinces, districts, and villages. Political parties and all publications would remain unmolested if they swore loyalty to the new councils, the communiqué concluded, but "the generals and officers who were lusting for power, who ignored the poor fate of their men and live in luxury and enjoy a spendthrift life at their expense, and humiliate women and also waste government funds, must be kicked out from the Army and punished accordingly."

The events that took place between the time Sukarno arrived at

Halim, at about nine or nine-thirty on the morning of October 1, and ten-thirty that evening, when he departed for his palace at Bogor, forty miles south of Djakarta, are further evidence that he was giving his active support to the plotters. He appeared at the air base just about the time Omar Dhani, the eager Air Force commander, had taken it upon himself to issue a communiqué similar to Untung's, referring to "an epuration" that had taken place in the Army "against foreign subversive elements" and pledging the Air Force's support "to any progressive revolutionary movement." Dhani admitted at his trial that he had been wrong in what he did, but he denied that he had tried to overthrow the government and said that, in defending the President and his country, he had simply tried to inculcate Sukarno's teachings and turn all his men into "little Sukarnos." His defense attorney declared that "if anyone is responsible for the coup, it is Sukarno," but Dhani, at Halim that October morning, certainly made his own position clear, as did Supardjo. First, Dhani gave Sukarno a broad outline of what had happened, and then Supardjo filled in the details. Sukarno's reaction to Supardjo's report, Supardjo later testified, was to ask how it was possible that Nasution had managed to escape his killers, and when Supardjo explained what had happened, Sukarno agreed it was "quite natural" that such unexpected things "could happen in a revolution," but added that the escape was bound to have "certain effects and consequences." He did not in any way reprimand Supardjo for having helped direct the coup that had taken the lives of six other generals, and nothing he said or did indicated that the whole thing had, indeed, been a surprise to him. In fact, he asked Supardjo for more proof that the Council of Generals existed, and nodded his satisfaction when Supardjo promised to give this to him (which Supardjo never did).

Apparently quite calm about the whole affair, Sukarno then went to the home of one of Dhani's aides and took a nap. At about noon he saw Supardjo again, and if there was any doubt about his not having been told of the murder of the six generals, it was dispelled by his asking Supardjo how the movement could now be stopped "to prevent further bloodshed that could lead to civil war." Supardjo replied that he and his battalion commanders would see that this was done, whereupon Sukarno smiled, slapped Supardjo on the back, and said, in Sundanese, "Mind, if you cannot stop the movement, I will kill you." To those who witnessed this slap, there seemed no doubt that the gesture and the remark were not meant as a rebuke but as a sign of approval. Supardjo himself obviously regarded Sukarno's remark as a joke, for he wrote, in a document that was subsequently seized, that Sukarno told him to be sure some of the troops of the September 30th Movement took part in the Armed Forces Day celebration on October 5.

After this meeting with Sukarno, Supardjo talked things over with Untung, Colonel Latief, and Sjam, the P.K.I. mastermind, who was beginning to get nervous about the way things were going. Supardjo later testified that Untung was willing to accept Sukarno's order to stop the movement of troops but that Sjam was opposed to it. "If we do that, we are not acting according to plan," Sjam said. At 1:30 P.M., Supardjo, of his own accord, went back to see Sukarno and found quite a collection of people in the house, including Dhani, the commanders of the Navy and police, several other left-wing generals and colonels, and Johannes Leimena, the Second Deputy Prime Minister. Leimena, who was not pro-Communist, had just come out to Halim at considerable personal risk to tell Sukarno that the back of the coup had been broken and that Sukarno should leave Halim as soon as possible, before General Suharto attacked it. Leimena had either not yet got his word in, privately, to Sukarno, or Sukarno had not believed him. At any rate, the President, again fully indicating that by now he knew of the death of General Yani, told Supardjo that he wanted to appoint a "caretaker Commander in Chief." He asked Supardjo for suggestions. Although Supardjo denied it at his trial, subsequent reports of those present maintained that Sukarno also asked him, "What do *you* want?" Supardjo suggested several names, one of which was that of General Pranoto Reksosamudro, a left-wing officer who had been General Yani's third assistant at one time and who, according to what has since been learned, may have been a secret member of the P.K.I. Both Sjam and Untung had approved of Pranoto, as apparently Aidit had, too, when Sjam had mentioned the name to him. (During the time Sjam and Aidit were at Halim, they did not see Sukarno, who dealt almost completely with Supardjo.) After a third talk with Supardjo on October 1, Sukarno chose Pranoto as his new Army chief, even though he was quite aware by this time that General Suharto had taken over the command of all the armed forces. Suharto's name, incidentally, had been one of those proposed, but Sukarno had ruled him out as "too stubborn."

While this was going on, those at Halim were listening to a second broadcast of the September 30th Movement from the Djakarta radio, which listed forty-five members of a new top Revolutionary Council. The group included Untung, Supardjo, Dhani, and Subandrio, while most of the remaining members were a hodgepodge of Communist sympathizers and miscellaneous officers and civilians—many, if not most, of whom, as it turned out, had never been consulted about being chosen. The list, which had been drawn up by Sjam, included a dozen or so leftist Army, Navy, and police officers, as well as three known Communists and several representatives of known P.K.I. fronts. A smattering of moderates and even a few anti-Communists had been calculatedly included as window dressing. Untung, who, at his trial later, said the announcement was prepared without his knowledge, even though the broadcast was made in his name by an Army captain who was in charge of the radio station, was designated as chairman of the Council and Supardjo was the first vice chairman. It may have been that Sukarno, whose own name, perhaps at his insistence, was not mentioned, was not at all sure at this point how things were going to turn out and simply didn't want to commit himself, one way or another. However, he expressed no objection to the aims of the Council which, the broadcast said, would temporarily replace the Cabinet as "the source of all authority" in Indonesia. Sukarno did sign his name to another communiqué, which declared that he, as President and Supreme Commander, was "in good sound condition" and continued to "hold the leadership of the State and the Revolution," that General Pranoto had been appointed "temporarily to execute the daily tasks within the Army," that "all members of the armed forces are ordered to enhance their vigilance and remain in their respective posts and move only on [Sukarno's] order," and that "the entire Indonesian people are ordered to remain calm and enhance vigilance and maintain national unity as solidly as possible."

When he heard the Untung broadcast giving the makeup of the Revolutionary Council, General Suharto felt that the "real activities of the September 30th Movement were unmasked" and that he need no longer hesitate in taking counteraction; until then he had been uncertain about who the plotters really were and what they were up to, and he had wanted, if at all possible, to avoid new bloodshed. The rebels, mostly the two Communist-infiltrated battalions that had been brought in from East and Central Java for the Armed Forces Day celebration, held three sides of Merdeka Square: they were guarding the palace on one side, had taken over the radio station on a second, and the telecommunications building on a third; Kostrad headquarters was on the fourth side. Roaming around the city by now, in addition, were between two and three thousand armed members of the Pemuda Rakyat, the Communist youth organization, which meant that the total rebel force was between four and five thousand. Suharto's first step was to try to make some or all of the rebel soldiers defect, and he began shuttling some of his own officers back and forth to talk to them. By midafternoon, two companies of the 530th Battalion from East Java began trickling in small groups into Kostrad, and he eventually used these men for mopping-up operations. In addition to a brigade of his own Kostrad troops, Suharto had under his control some of the Djakarta-garrison elements that had remained loyal, despite the disaffection of their brigade chief, Colonel Latief; a battalion of the crack Siliwangi Division from West Java, which had arrived in town late in the afternoon, and a group of paratroop commandos he had called in from their base near Djakarta. By dusk Suharto was ready to move, but by this time the rebels showed little interest in fighting; they abandoned the radio station and telecommunications building without a fight, some of them withdrawing toward Halim and others just dispersing. By eight o'clock Suharto's men controlled the whole of Merdeka Square, and an announcement was made over the recaptured radio station that the September 30th Movement had been a "counterrevolutionary movement" to "kidnap" some generals, but that the situation was now in hand. This speech, which was broadcast all over Indonesia, proved to be the turning point in the coup attempt, and whatever resistance might have been offered by the rebels in the capital disintegrated. When some of the Pemuda Rakyat youth arrived to take over other buildings around Merdeka Square, they found themselves confronted by members of the 530th Battalion who had forsaken the rebel cause, and, instead of replying to the password the youthful Communists shouted, the soldiers arrested the young men and took away the weapons they had been given during their secret training period at Halim.

In Djakarta, at least, the rebellion was over, but Suharto was still worried about getting Sukarno away from the air base before an attack was mounted against it. He knew Sukarno was still at Halim because the President, late in the afternoon, had sent an aide to Kostrad headquarters to demand that General Pranoto and a number of other high-ranking officers come out to see him. Suharto had peremptorily refused, remarking that he did not "want to lose any more generals." He was determir.ed to take Halim on the night of October 1, before the rebels had a chance to regroup, and before Dhani might send his Air Force swooping down on Djakarta (Dhani, in fact, had already equipped some of his planes with rockets). Consequently, he gave orders to the paratroopers, supported by a company of Kostrad tanks, to move toward Halim as soon as it was completely dark, and he told them to hold their fire as long as they could.

The rebel command at Halim was well aware by now that the coup in the capital had failed. When General Supardjo suggested he use what troops he had left to attack Kostrad headquarters, no one, apparently including Sukarno, was very enthusiastic. Whatever Sukarno now thought about the coup and his own involvement in it, he was mostly anxious to get away from Halim. The question was, where should he go? Some of his aides, including Dhani, wanted him to go to Madiun, in East Java, the scene of the abortive 1948 Communist uprising, where his presence might spur the rebels to continue their resistance. However, Sukarno's wife, Dewi, who had come out to Halim by car, and Deputy Prime Minister Leimena, among others, persuaded the President to go to his country palace at Bogor instead. Dewi had come to the air base because she was worried about Sukarno's safety, even though in a note he had sent to her he had said he was all right and was in the hands of some "children" who had "staged a revolution" to protect him. At 10:30 P.M. Sukarno left for Bogor by car, arriving about midnight; Dewi did not go with him since Bogor was the province of another of his wives, Hartini. As soon as Suharto learned that Sukarno had left Halim, he ordered his troops to seize the base, and it was taken at about three o'clock in the morning of October 2 after a brief fire fight in which one rebel soldier was killed. An hour or so earlier, Aidit, the Communist chief, was flown in a plane supplied by Dhani to Jogjakarta, probably accompanied by the dejected Sjam, who had seen his best plans go awry. Dhani then flew his own plane to Madiun, trying by radio to rally his various Air Force commands to continue supporting the coup; he was unsuccessful and returned late that day or early the next to Bogor, where Sukarno had promised to give refuge to him and his family. About the time when Aidit and Dhani flew off, Supardjo and Untung had a final meeting at Lubang Buaja. According to Supardjo's testimony, he urged Untung to "take over the command" of the remaining rebel forces, but Untung demurred, and with a company of his palace guards flew off at three-thirty in the morning to an air base, near Madiun, using three of Dhani's transports. Supardjo then went to Bogor by car. In Djakarta, at least, the coup had been broken.

The Aftermath of Blood

Though the complete details of the coup attempt may never be known, certain conclusions, based on the subsequent interrogations and trials of captured leaders, and on other information that slowly came to light, can be drawn. That the failure of the *Putsch* represented a tremendous blunder for the P.K.I. was undeniable. Moreover, beyond the technical or tactical errors, the disasters it brought in its wake—the awful bloodbath that swept Indonesia at the end of 1965 and the beginning of 1966—demonstrated that the P.K.I. had vastly misjudged its position and strength in the country, and that its whole strategy of revolution, including its bland dependence on mass support, had been wrong. In due time, the Communists themselves were to admit this. How much the P.K.I. learned from the failure remains a question. Having lost almost all of its top leadership, the party faced the problem of beginning virtually all over again to organize itself. Its support among some of the people, especially in the poorer sections of Java, was not inconsiderable, since much of it reflected approval of Sukarno and resentment of the military men. In the first phase immediately after the coup, the P.K.I. sought to take advantage of this pro-Sukarno sentiment, and of the confusion that prevailed everywhere in Java, to continue its resistance. Afterward, it was hoped, new tactics, based on firsthand observation by P.K.I. members of the success of the Vietcong guerrillas in Vietnam, would be adopted. Poor timing and poor organization were essentially what caused the effort to fail. The attempt was obviously not well planned or well executed. The very list of the principal plotters was an augury of failure. A group that included Aidit and Sjam, Supardjo, Untung, Dhani, and Subandrio was certainly a mixed one, at best. Central direction was something that only the P.K.I. could probably have supplied, *if* the P.K.I. had been the sole instrument, and there is evidence that there were differences within the P.K.I. Politburo, involving even the crucial question of whether Sukarno should be killed or kept on as a puppet President in a new P.K.I. regime. Until only shortly before the coup, it should be re-emphasized, the P.K.I., which had been moving toward power slowly on Sukarno's *Nasakom* coattails, had accepted 1970 as the probable date of its evolutionary ascendancy; the party's appeals in the period from May through September to "act, act, and act again" in a "revolutionary" manner were, in retrospect, a demonstration more of hortatory frenzy than of calculated planning —which would presumably have included at least some steps to have the mass elements of the movement, other than the few thousand women and youths trained at Halim since July, prepared for action at the proper moment.

Why was the P.K.I.'s planning so poor? Aside from the time element, the most important factor was that Sukarno undoubtedly believed, or was made to believe by Supardjo, Dhani, and others, that a plot by the generals really existed. It seems highly likely that Sukarno *wanted* to believe this, not so much because he was eager for a Communist coup but because he probably realized how sick he was (an admission he would only make to himself) and was willing to go to any lengths to make the Communists an integral part of the government before he died. In this sense, Sukarno may unconsciously have driven the Communists to the point where they were hamstrung by his ardor. He *made* them move more quickly than they would have liked, and consequently forced them to accept as allies various sycophants and hangers-on, including some men, such as Untung, who patently were immature and unreliable, and some, such as Dhani, who had their own axes to grind. According to this theory, Sukarno, by accepting the possibility of a generals' coup on or before October 5, deprived the P.K.I. of the latitude the Communists would have preferred. The Communists then did the best they could, which wasn't good enough. They had some legitimate professional allies in men like Supardjo, and some undependable foils, such as Untung and Dhani. But once Sukarno had given either an implied or actual go-ahead, there wasn't time for the P.K.I. to organize things as might otherwise have been done. Ironically, though Sukarno turned out not to be on his deathbed, he may have dealt the P.K.I. a deathblow by seeming to be so.

The other probable factors of significance, so far as the P.K.I.'s involvement is concerned, were Vietnam and Peking. The Chinese Communists were surely worried about the American build-up in Vietnam in the spring and summer of 1965 and about the effect the stemming of the current Vietcong drive might have on the rest of Southeast Asia. Whether Peking actually went so far as to urge the P.K.I. to strike sooner than it had planned, primarily because of what was taking place in Vietnam, is not known. But there are a number of circumstances that point to Peking's being fully aware of what was happening in Indonesia, and approving of the planned P.K.I. action. To sum them up: First, Subandrio had been in constant touch with Peking for many months, and Dhani had been sent by Sukarno in mid-September of 1965 to arrange for some of the scheduled arms shipments for the "fifth force." Second, a large number of important Chinese, including Foreign Minister Chen Yi, were in Djakarta for the Independence Day celebration in August, before the Indonesian delegations went to Peking for the Chinese National Day celebrations. Third, although the Chinese said nothing officially about the Indonesian coup until eighteen days after it took place—a protest was then issued against an attack on the residence of the Chinese commercial attaché in Djakarta and a propaganda barrage was begun against atrocities allegedly committed by the military—Chinese officials in Peking knew about the coup within six hours after it occurred and, furthermore, had a list of *all* the generals who were supposed to be murdered, including Nasution.

There are various other indications that, whatever the influence Peking had exerted on the P.K.I., some elements of the party felt that they had been rushed into the coup under pressure. Concerning this, much depends on what credence is given to an alleged "confession" that Aidit signed late on the night of November 22, 1965, when he was captured near Solo, in East Java, before being peremptorily shot early the next morning. The confession is generally treated with skepticism, mainly because it was too pat and served the interests of the Army too readily, but if indeed it was doctored to suit the military's purposes, there are nevertheless a number of points in it that seem valid and that, even if the confession itself was fabricated, may have represented Aidit's views. For example, Aidit corroborated that 1970 was the original P.K.I. target date and said that because "details of this plan leaked out," it was changed and plans were hastily made "to carry out a coup as soon as possible." An earlier scheme had been drafted, Aidit continued, for a coup to take place on May 1, but his fellow Politburo members had vetoed this, arguing that "it was dangerous since preparations were not completed and the plan would undoubtedly fail." Early in August, Aidit confirmed, he had stopped off in Peking "and discussed the health of President Sukarno with the Communist Chinese leaders." When he returned to Djakarta, in mid-month, he said he talked over the details of the coup with Supardjo, Untung, and two members of the Politburo, Njoto and Lukman. Aidit did not say that the full Politburo had met, under his direction, and that the Special Bureau had planned the coup, but he did claim that, since the P.K.I. had information that the Army was about to attack it and its front organizations in a search for illegal weapons, the date of September 30 was chosen on the twenty-fifth, so that the P.K.I. could move before it was placed on the defensive. "The *coup d'état* failed because it was premature and also because there were not a few—even among the P.K.I. officials—who were opposed. . . . The second reason for the failure was the lack of support of Communist China on which we had placed our hopes." Although he had alluded to it, Aidit might have added a third reason: Sukarno's failure, perhaps until the eleventh hour, to go all-out in support of the effort.

Whatever role Sukarno played in the actual execution of the coup, he clearly demonstrated a sense of responsibility, even of concern, for those who had been involved in it, and he also continued afterward to defend its proclaimed revolutionary goals. In the immediate confusion after the clash, he remained aloof and even gently chastised the party. In an aside to Njoto, who of the three top Communist leaders was probably closest to him personally, he described the bungled coup as "childish," by which he apparently meant that, while it had done nothing criminal, the P.K.I. had acted too precipitantly—which in itself was ironic, since it was he who had, in effect, forced the party's hand. Ultimately, however, as his attitude grew more defensive, his old bravado returned, and this made it impossible for his friends to save him or for his foes to let him down more easily in the interest of preserving national unity. If his intention was to show that he had "known everything and known nothing," as one analyst has put it, his behavior soon belied this, and led inevitably to not only his dismissal as President but also the tarnishing of his earlier revolutionary record.

The Communists' troubles began publicly on the morning of October 2, when, though it was already apparent that the coup had failed, the Communist newspaper *Harian Rakyat* appeared in Djakarta with an editorial supporting the September 30th Movement and a cartoon depicting that movement as a vast fist smashing the face of an Indonesian general wearing dollar signs for epaulets, and a cap with a C.I.A. insignia. Colonel Untung was praised by the paper for his "patriotic action" in defeating the "counterrevolutionary" coup attempt of the Council of Generals and in "safeguarding the person of President Sukarno and the Indonesian Republic." Although the paper described what had happened as "an internal Army affair," it said that "the support and sympathy of the people are certainly on the side of the September 30th Movement." After its appearance the paper was banned under the martial-law decree that had been announced by General Suharto. Three days later the party had some second thoughts, and in an announcement sent to correspondents repeated the theme of the coup having been an internal Army matter but added that the P.K.I. members who had been listed on Untung's Revolutionary Council were "not notified and had not given their approval." The next day, October 6, a letter signed by Aidit and dated October 2 appeared in the Communist newspaper of Surabaya, in East Java. It said the same

thing, and told P.K.I. members throughout the country to go on
carrying out their "urgent tasks" in the cities and the rural areas
and to "uphold and strengthen the unity of the party and strictly
observe discipline." A day or so later, according to evidence later
submitted at the trial of Subandrio, Sukarno received the first of
four secret letters from Aidit in East Java, in which the P.K.I.
leader urged him to take charge of the troubled situation in the
country, to give back to the police the responsibility for maintaining internal security (the police were more Communist-infiltrated
than the Army), and to put an end to mutual recrimination on the
part of both the coup leaders and the generals. Sukarno sent back,
by courier, a letter in which he said that "at the present time I
cannot make any speeches in line with your suggestions. . . . I am
just able to make general speeches and try to change the mind of
the commanders not to focus their attention only on crushing G30S
[the September 30th Movement]. Your other suggestions will receive the best of my attention." Sukarno added that Aidit should
try to return to Djakarta, and offered him assistance in this. (Aidit
never did return to Djakarta, as it turned out.)

So far, Sukarno had not publicly denounced the P.K.I. or the
September 30th Movement in any way. In a brief broadcast on
October 3, he had simply said, in a tired, dull voice, that "I am well
and safe and remain firmly in charge of the state and the leadership of the armed forces." He added that the problems arising from
the September 30th Movement must be solved in an orderly atmosphere and, in what amounted to a compromise following a
meeting with General Suharto at Bogor, he announced that Suharto would be in charge of restoring security and order while
General Pranoto would "discharge day-to-day tasks within the
Army" (it was not until ten days later that Sukarno fired General
Pranoto altogether and named Suharto to be Yani's successor as
Chief of Staff). In a second broadcast later in the day, Sukarno
had denied that the Air Force had been involved in the coup. His
support of Dhani—whom he protected in the palace until he was
finally prevailed upon to dismiss the Air Force commander, on
October 16, whereupon he sent him on a buying mission abroad—
also angered Nasution, Suharto, and the other generals who had
broken the coup. At one point, confronting Dhani in Sukarno's
presence, Suharto ripped the Marshal's epaulets off and slapped his

face with them. The generals were also infuriated by Sukarno's protection and support of Supardjo. On October 2, at Bogor, the President had ordered Supardjo, who by then had already been formally dismissed from the Army, to take charge of "confining" the elements of the two rebel battalions that were still at Halim, and seeing to it that they remained orderly. A day or so later Supardjo disappeared, armed with a letter of protection from Sukarno, and he was not to be captured until more than a year later, in January, 1967—the last of the major coup figures to be caught and brought to trial and sentenced. On October 4 two important events took place. Sukarno held a plenary Cabinet meeting at Bogor, which was attended by two P.K.I. Cabinet members, Njoto and Lukman, and the bodies of the six murdered generals were brought out of the well at Lubang Buaja, after captured coup officers had disclosed their whereabouts. Suharto attended the exhumation and made a brief and angry speech, in which he emphasized that the well was in an area administered by the Air Force, and that members of the Air Force had trained the P.K.I.'s youth and women's groups in that very place. Lubang Buaja became a place of national shame, and the clear involvement of the P.K.I. in the affair led immediately to widespread demands throughout Java that the party be banned.

In a statement read by Subandrio on October 6, after another Cabinet meeting at Bogor, Sukarno, who further riled Generals Suharto and Nasution by referring to what had occurred as "just a very small ripple on the mighty ocean of our great revolution," repeated his opinion that "these things can always happen," and spoke for the first time of seeking "a political solution" to "preserve the Indonesian revolution and the spirit of *Nasakom*." He did not ban the P.K.I., as Suharto and Nasution had urged, but he said that he would not acknowledge the formation of the Revolutionary Council or its subcouncils and that he would take action against anyone supporting them. Subandrio, too, disavowed the Council and said he had not given permission for his name to be included on it. Sukarno appealed to his Cabinet, which still included Njoto and Lukman, to work together "as usual." For the first time, he condemned the murder of the six generals. The day before, however, when instead of the scheduled military parade a mass funeral was held for the dead officers, Sukarno had been conspicuously absent, and this further angered Suharto and Nasution, as did the absence of any Chinese representatives and the refusal of the Chinese Embassy to fly its flag at half-mast in honor of the dead men.

During the fortnight after the coup, even as it became apparent that the Army and Sukarno were moving in different directions, the P.K.I. leaders in the countryside were doing their best to sustain some sort of opposition. The manner in which they operated, half at bay and half on the offensive, indicated further that they had acted without having had enough time to prepare, or that they had hoped that simply by killing the generals they could take over the government in Djakarta and then move ahead more slowly and deliberately to dominate the rest of the country. One of the captured Politburo members, in a written statement, described the situation during the days after the coup as "not yet hopeless," of there being "openings we should have entered at once."

According to an Indonesian intelligence report, Aidit's flight to Central Java after the coup "was under the President's instructions." When Aidit had arrived in Jogjakarta on the morning of October 2, elements of the pro-Communist Diponegoro regiment there were in control of the city and, just before Aidit's arrival, they had murdered the local regimental commander and his chief of staff. Posters denouncing the Council of Generals, the United States, and Malaysia, and hailing the Revolutionary Council, went up all over town. Within forty-eight hours, however, as it became obvious that the coup had been crushed in Djakarta, and that loyal troops were on their way, the Jogjakarta rebellion also collapsed, and within four days the city was calm again. However, Central Java as a whole was not by any means secure. Of the seven government battalions in the region, three, as it turned out, had been wholly committed to the coup through their commanders and two were committed under other officers. But within a few days loyal officers had either regained control or neutralized the rebel elements. Semarang had been seized by the Communists and held for a day before it was retaken, and the same was true of Solo, another large city. In some of the other towns the P.K.I. held out for a week or more. At first, the P.K.I. continued to maintain that the rebellion was an "internal Army affair." On October 5, having traveled by car, disguised as a monk, from Jogjakarta through Semarang to

Solo, conferring en route with Lukman, Sakirman (also a member of the Politburo), and other top Central Java leaders of the party, Aidit failed in efforts to commandeer a plane to take him to Bogor to confer with Sukarno, or, alternatively, to Bali, where he wanted to hide out. He then decided to seclude himself in Central Java, in the vicinity of Mount Merapi, an active volcano that dominates the Jogjakarta-Semarang-Solo plain, in an area that traditionally has been a sanctuary for rebels and bandits.

In Djakarta the Communists' troubles had also been mounting. Mobs of Muslims, mostly adherents of Ansor, the Muslim youth organization, had quietly been given the word by a number of officers to *sikat*, which means "sweep," and on October 7 they burned the P.K.I. headquarters to the ground and rampaged through the city shouting "Kill Aidit!" "Crush the P.K.I." and other anti-Communist slogans. They also burned the homes of Aidit, Lukman, and Njoto. Truckloads of youths drove past the American Embassy, chanting, "Long live America!" One of the few American correspondents who was there at the time, John Hughes of the *Christian Science Monitor*, afterward wrote in his book, *Indonesian Upheaval:*

> It was a historic little moment. For more than a year the embassy of the United States had been the target of an increasing series of hostile demonstrations. If anything was burned in Djakarta, it was a good guess that it was something belonging to the Americans or the British. Now, for the first time in the world as far as anybody could remember, the headquarters of a major Communist party had gone up in smoke at the hands of anti-Communists.

As the mobs, in the days that followed, burned other Communist buildings, including the headquarters of Pemuda Rakyat, the youth group that had helped murder the six generals, and S.O.B.S.I., the pro-Communist labor union, they also began venting their spleen upon the Chinese, demonstrating in front of the Chinese Embassy and attacking a Chinese university and other Chinese institutions. The Foreign Office tried to play down this anti-Chinese reaction, referring to the need for Indonesia and China to continue collaborating against "imperialism and colonialism." In a speech shortly after the demonstrations had started, Subandrio said, "Don't say 'Long live America' just because there is some tension between Indonesia and China. We still cannot say the United States is our friend." And Sukarno warned about campaigns of "hatred" that would only play into the hands of those who wanted to move to the right. Peking had by now lifted its veil of silence on Indonesia and, in a series of notes, protested against the search of official and private Chinese premises all over Indonesia. Despite the efforts of Subandrio and Sukarno, who summoned the Chinese Ambassador for a friendly chat, the anti-Chinese sentiment spread, and Peking responded by cutting off military aid and recalling the Chinese technicians who had been working on Sukarno's ill-fated CONEFO project.

Throughout the country, during October, the Army moved ahead on its own to "suspend temporarily" all P.K.I. activities. Everywhere P.K.I. offices were shut down, Communist and left-wing newspapers were banned, P.K.I. mayors were fired, and the party's deputies were kept from attending regional council meetings. Thousands of P.K.I. members or supporters were arrested, and thousands of other members tore up their party cards, which indicated that many, if not most, rural card-holders were "rice Communists" who had simply joined the party because they thought it would help improve their economic condition or because they had been lured by P.K.I. propaganda. After General Suharto formally was named Army Chief of Staff by a reluctant Sukarno in mid-October, he issued an order "to continue to liquidate the remnants of the counterrevolutionary September 30th Movement" and sent tough paratroopers under General Sarwo Edhy to Central Java to purge the Communist-infiltrated battalions there. The P.K.I., now realizing it could no longer pretend it was not implicated in the coup, ordered its members to accept arms from their supporters in the military and to set up regional commands in the villages, particularly in the Communists' stronghold area, a triangle between the towns of Klaten, Bojolali, and Kartasura. The loyal Army elements, following long-established counterinsurgency formulas, in turn created local People's Defense Units of citizens considered politically reliable. These were mostly Muslim or nationalist youth representatives with some military training. Sukarno was now clearly playing a double game. While he cleverly criticized the coup leaders and the murderers of the six generals and said they should be punished, he also issued a warning about Indonesian "stooges" who were "trying to destroy our fight against imperialism" by establishing foreign military bases and, worse, "foreign mental bases." In an open rebuke to Generals Nasution and Suharto, who were still vainly trying to get him to issue a formal Presidential decree that would clearly denounce the September 30th Movement and the P.K.I., Sukarno issued an order that took mild note of the "so-called" movement's activities and asked for an end to "racialism, burning, and destruction," and "slanders and actions based on revenge," and demanded that all officers and officials work "shoulder to shoulder with the people" to find a "political solution" in dealing with the coup conspirators that would "preserve unity" and "step up revolutionary mass actions constructively in a high spirit of discipline to face *Nekolim* [neocolonialism, colonialism, and imperialism] and foreign subversion." This was just what Aidit, in his letter to the President, had asked him to do, and it demonstrated that Sukarno was still intent on protecting the P.K.I. and its affiliated organizations.

As the differences between Sukarno and the Army became more apparent, with the Army arresting anyone suspected of having supported the September 30th Movement and Sukarno taking no steps at all to punish anyone, the tension, especially in Java and in Bali, began to reach the breaking point. Psychoanalysts and sociologists, as well as historians and journalists, have tried to apply scientific methods of analysis to the murderous bloodbath that occurred in Indonesia between the end of October and the end of December, but there are no simple explanations. Many factors and pressures were involved—racial and religious, economic and social, as well as political. These included tensions and conflicts in the Muslim communities between the devout, or *santri*, elements, and the *abangan*, or nominal Muslims, who were more responsive to the pragmatic political appeals of the P.K.I. Separately or together, these Muslim elements, in their social and religious milieu, came up against the older spiritual challenge of Javanese mysticism. Despite these cultural and religious cleavages, a sense of tolerance, of willingness to live together in unusual harmony had for years maintained a surprisingly effective way of life. Manners and grace, as well as a native passivity, were factors in this, and another reason for the widespread mutual tolerance was the fact that, until the Malthusian imperative began to take over, there had been enough land and food for everyone. Yet the tensions were there, waiting to be sprung. Perhaps the best analysis of what happened late in 1965 was given to me by Soedjatmoko: "Notwithstanding the cultural differences, and what can be termed 'the unfinished Muslimization' of Indonesia—the incomplete adjustment of the Muslims to the older mystic life and pre-existing *adat,* or custom, of interior Java—the social mechanism somehow functioned," he said. "But when the rural unit got to be too imposed upon, when the population pressures grew too strong, when class stresses took over and, finally, when the P.K.I. began to rally the landless laborers and urge them to seize the land, the dam burst. What really took place was a psychological and historical breakdown. Tolerance and consensus vanished overnight, and passion replaced compassion. For the Javanese as a people, what happened was beyond their cosmos and their comprehension. It was incomprehensible to me, too, although, as I look back on it, I realize that, given the developments of the last few years, under Sukarno, as the government condoned the new class stresses the P.K.I. was inducing, the blow-up was inevitable. If it hadn't been the coup that did it, something else would have."

The situation came to a head on the night of October 22, when the Communists began their last concerted stand in Central Java. Gangs of youths belonging to the Pemuda Rakyat, many of them armed only with bamboo spears and knives, attacked a police station and a small Army base in the P.K.I.-dominated towns of Klaten and Bojolali. They were after weapons, and they managed to capture some. During the early morning hours, the *kentongs,* the traditional Javanese drums, were sounded, which was a signal for the P.K.I.-dominated population to rise and join in a rampage of murder, kidnaping, and arson. By noon the next day an estimated three or four hundred people had been killed in the two villages —mostly anti-Communists, who were shot, decapitated, or simply slashed and thrown alive into deep wells. The orgy would have continued indefinitely had it not been for the quick arrival from Jogjakarta of Sarwo Edhy's paratroopers, who restored order and then continued on to nearby Solo, where, with the help of a Communist mayor, rebellious troops of the Diponegoro Division still managed to maintain a tenuous hold in parts of the city and around it. Edhy's mission was highly successful, if highly ruthless.

He ordered his armored-car gunners to shoot any and all Communist demonstrators and anyone else who resisted their entry into villages, especially the pro-Communist ones around Mount Merapi, and by the time he took Solo the core of the P.K.I.'s remaining resistance had been crushed. But the killings were by no means over. Edhy afterward said, "We decided to encourage the anti-Communist civilians to help with the job." In Solo, where a motley local force of anti-Communists had already been organized, Edhy gathered up some additional men, gave them two days of training, and then, as he said, "We sent them out to kill Communists." As other Army officers afterward explained it, in defending such actions, "If we hadn't killed the Communists, they would have killed us."

The pattern of killing took different forms in West and Central Java, and in East Java and Bali. In the former two areas the Army did most of the killing, with some help from the Muslims. In East Java the purge was carried out mostly by anti-P.K.I. members of the P.N.I., the Nationalist Party, many of them small landholders, who had been given weapons by the Army, and who were helped by the armed members of Ansor, the Muslim youth. In Bali the P.N.I., encouraged by the Army, was chiefly responsible for the slaughter. While it started as a "political cleansing," it quickly turned into a wild and indiscriminate outpouring of vengeance based on personal feuds and on mass hysteria among people who were emotionally and psychologically ready to run amok. Chinese merchants and their families were killed wherever they lived, mostly by civilians. Under the circumstances of how the killings took place, and the time span they covered—though the worst was over by the end of December, 1965, they continued after that on a lesser scale—it was virtually impossible to make an estimate of the total number killed. During my travels through Java and Bali, I heard estimates that were as high as a million and as low as fifty thousand, but the average was between 250,000 and 350,000, and this was what most Indonesian officials, as well as American and British and other diplomats, have concluded.

The accounts of murders in West Java were far less lurid than those I heard in Central Java, where almost everywhere I went there were stories, each more gruesome than the last, of nocturnal round-ups of whole families and even of whole villages, of the victims either being made to dig their own graves before they were shot or killed with knives, or of bodies simply being dumped into the many rivers that flow through Java. Weeks later corpses washed up on shore or clogged shallow passages and canals like decaying logs. While there was a considerable reluctance on the part of anyone to admit that he had participated in the murders, there was a general tendency, especially among the more ardent Muslims, to explain them as "the will of Allah." "To kill a Communist became a duty, in accordance with the Koran," one writer and political leader told me. "If you didn't do it, you were *malu*, you felt ashamed." In villages where the Army did not do the killing itself, it assigned anti-Communist informers to do the job, and in these cases, since guns were not always available, the murders usually took the form of beheadings, with the heads of the victims often placed on spikes and paraded around or deposited on fence tops. Sometimes the Army ordered or offered trucks for hauling away villagers who had been fingered as Communists or pro-Communists, and these people were then shot en masse. The Muslim fanatics often commandeered the trucks of Chinese merchants for the same task, and then killed the merchants, too. In some cities bands of vigilantes wearing black clothes operated mostly at night, rousing families out of their beds and killing all the children as well as the parents and servants. In Solo the head of the local vigilante group, a former Army major, told me that at least ten thousand were murdered in and around the city, and he pridefully brought out a collection of trinkets, mostly Chinese Communist buttons and pins, that he had personally taken from the Communist mayor and from others who had been victims of what he jarringly termed "the final solution." Skulls were still being found in the nearby river beds. "Hundreds of bodies were thrown into the Bengawan Solo River alone," the Army major said. "The Dutch and the Japanese used to throw them there, too." In many places members of families informed on each other, as was also true among students and professors in the universities, and there were even cases of a man killing his father or a brother to avoid letting the Army or, worse, the Ansor killer squads do it. In some instances the Communists fought back and killed their Muslim attackers, but by and large they offered little resistance and went to their deaths in white funeral robes with an astonishing passivity, as if they were admitting their guilt and were hoping for a better life next time.

This was particularly true in Bali, where the influence of ancient Hindu mysticism is even greater than it is in Java. The Balinese are highly superstitious people, with a hidden demonic urge that belies their outward gentleness and charm. Their lives and deaths are bound in ritual, and the performance of rites, from their sacred dances to their wedding, circumcision, and burial ceremonies, is packed with spiritual meaning. Unlike most of the rest of Indonesia, Bali was only under direct colonial domination for fifty years prior to the Second World War, and the Hindu mystical influence flourished there unmolested by any significant Muslim invasion. Then came the Japanese occupation, with its special cruelties, and after the war came the Communists, who did not try to convert the two million Balinese directly but simply sought to propagandize among the people of the overcrowded and underdeveloped island with vague promises of land reform and other economic benefits. They made some headway, and various high local officials were pro-P.K.I. men at the time of the 1965 outbreak. However, the P.K.I. and its adherents demonstrated what was essentially a contempt for the religious Balinese, mocking their festivals and customs, and arrogantly taunting them about their special belief system. The Communists also used terror as a means of influencing the population, and when the murders began—they did not start in Bali until early December, after an Army man was killed during a raid on a P.K.I. meeting in the western part of the island—the Balinese reacted with a fury that was almost unbelievable. In avenging themselves against the Communists, who had had the protection of the governor and earlier of a pro-P.K.I. local Army commander, their response assumed the quality of a mass exorcism, "as if they were ridding the soil and their souls of evil and purifying themselves," as one Balinese friend of mine put it. "All the humiliations and tensions that had been submerged burst forth," he added. "The Balinese had been subjected to so many pressures for so long that this had to happen. Colonialism and the Japanese occupation were not forgotten, and then at least sixteen hundred people were killed in the eruption of the volcano Mount Agung in 1963, when families lost all their cattle and saw their fields submerged in lava. When they moved against the Communists, their actions had a ceremonial quality of righteous vindication, over and above simple vengeance."

Here the pattern of killing was clearer than elsewhere. The Army began it, then handed the job over to the Balinese, and finally stopped the bloodletting when some of Sarwo Edhy's roving paratroopers were brought in, but not before an estimated forty thousand people had been murdered. Whole villages were set ablaze, night after night, red flames spouting through the azure Balinese sky as the smell of burning houses overpowered the customary fragrance of the rich island flora. This dreadful period was described to me by one of Bali's best-known artists, Antonio Blanco, a Spanish-Filipino by birth who is an American citizen and who lived with his Balinese wife and his bare-breasted daughters in a magnificent house and studio he had built in the hills of Ubud, which is west of the capital of Denpasar. "Every night we could see one village after another go up in flames," he said. "We were in deathly fear of our own lives—certainly if the P.K.I. had won out, we would have been killed—but I kept on painting, almost obsessively. I did eighteen canvases in two months." Most of the murders in the interior of Bali took place in cemeteries near the villages, while along the coast they were carried out on the fringes of the broad beaches. In some cases, P.K.I. members were brought back to their native villages to be killed by those who knew them best. Other Communists committed suicide, others fled to temples, where they vainly sought sanctuary; still others went to hospitals, where they were hunted down and attempts were made to kill them in their beds. Ironically, leaders of the killer squads, called *tamins*, mostly black-shirted members of the P.N.I., included some who had secretly supported the Communists before and had now turned against them. Other groups of young men, called "avenger squads," roved with their knives from one village in a district to another, killing almost at random. One Dutch woman and her Indonesian husband, who had long been residents of Bali, told me, with a sense of shared shame, "Everyone got the blood lust. At night, sleeping with guns under our pillows, we found ourselves saying, 'Why don't they kill *that* man instead of *this* one?' "

During this period of mass murder, many of the leading Communists throughout Indonesia were either killed or taken into custody. The first of the important figures of the coup to be captured was Colonel Untung. He was seized on October 11, near Tegal, his home town in Central Java, while he was trying to escape to Semarang on a bus. (The bus was named "Untung," which ironically is the Javanese translation of the English word "Lucky.") When Untung was spotted by two soldiers who recognized him, he leaped out of the bus and tried to escape, but he was seized by a group of villagers and brought to Djakarta under heavy guard. He asked to be taken to Sukarno, but the request was never granted. After a trial before a military tribunal in Djakarta, he was sentenced to death and executed. Njono, who had supervised the training of the P.K.I. youth and women at Lubang Buaja, was captured in Djakarta about the same time as Untung; he was also found guilty, sentenced to death, and executed. Lukman, the First Vice Chairman of the P.K.I. and a Politburo member, was caught near Semarang during October and executed almost at once, according to reports, when he refused to answer questions. Njoto, the No. 3 man in the hierarchy and a Politburo member, was arrested in December, in Djakarta, after a Cabinet meeting in Bogor and is also believed to have been shot after refusing to give any information about the coup attempt. Sakirman and Rewang, two other Politburo members, were also shot upon capture. Early in 1967 Sudisman, another important Politburo man, was caught and tried, and his trial, along with that of Sjam, who was not a member of the Politburo, shed the most light on the coup. Both men were sentenced to death—Sudisman was executed late in 1968, and, following further interrogation, Sjam was due to be executed early in 1969. It seemed astonishing to many observers that, in the time that Sjam and Sudisman had still been free, the Chinese Communists had not tried to get them out of the country. Adjitorop, a seventh Politburo member, who was in Peking at the time of the coup, is said to be there still—the only member of the eight-man 1965 Indonesian Politburo still alive. As for Aidit, he was captured at nine o'clock on the evening of November 22, 1965, in a closet in the home of a retired railway worker, a P.K.I. member, in the village of Samben, near Solo. He is said to have been betrayed to Sarwo Edhy's paratroopers the day before by a former comrade. He was questioned for several hours by a military intelligence major and is then said to have signed his alleged confession early on the morning of November 23, after which he asked to be taken back to Djakarta. His captors agreed but said he would first have to go to regional headquarters at Semarang. About 3 A.M., on the way there by jeep, he was reportedly taken out of the car near Bojolali and shot as he kept shouting, "Long live the P.K.I." He is supposed to be buried in an unmarked grave. Indonesian officials will only admit that he is dead but will not say how he was killed. Whatever degree of validity there is to his confession, since he was so close to Sukarno, and since Sukarno was by no means willing to ban the P.K.I., there was ample reason for the Army not to want Aidit martyrized by bringing him back to Djakarta and trying him publicly.

As for other key figures in the coup, Dhani, who while not a P.K.I. member was certainly deeply involved, was tried and sentenced to death, but both his appeal and Subandrio's were still being considered by Suharto at the end of 1968. Supardjo, captured in Bandung in January, 1967, while hiding in the home of an Army lieutenant, has also been sentenced to death, and his clemency appeal was turned down by Suharto in October, 1968. About a score of lesser plotters have been tried and sentenced either to death or to long prison terms, and five of them were executed in 1966-1968. Among the high-level Communists, the two best-known of the old guard who are still free are Rusman, a member of the old fifty-two-man Central Committee, and Pono, Sjam's co-worker in the Special Bureau that planned the coup. Indonesian authorities, as of the end of 1968, did not know who the new head of the P.K.I. was, but they suspected that a younger element, including some of those who had visited the Vietcong in recent years, had taken over.

Suharto vs. Sukarno: A Javanese Shadow Play

The bloodbath, in a psychological as well as physical sense, was the tragic climax of the Sukarno era. The retribution and vengeance it involved, and the sheer horror of the mass killings, can be said to have represented the final failure of "the Sukarno revolution"—perhaps the inevitable outcome of the President's long subversion of the Indonesian revolution. But the killings did not signify the end of the Sukarno regime. After the bloodbath the uneasy coalition that had existed between Sukarno and the Army gave way to a new struggle in which it became increasingly apparent that there would be only one victor. Politically, the battle of 1966-67 between the military leaders and the President, in which the youth of the nation played a vital role, was ultimately more bitter and significant than the coup itself, which simply set the spark.

As 1965 ended, Sukarno resolved to bid for a complete return to power and not to compromise with the generals. His gamble was based on his plans to re-establish his own stature as leader of the revolution, and that in turn depended upon his being able to re-furbish the P.K.I. or to create a new leftist element that could replace it. Had he chosen the alternative course, which would have meant admitting his past mistakes and condemning those who had helped him commit them, he might have been able to survive with his reputation tarnished but still intact. This was probably beyond the capacity of his character and personality.

In the initial period after the coup effort, Sukarno apparently hoped for an interval during which passions would die down. Early in December he adopted a new tack. In an address to the People's Consultative Congress, he went so far as to describe the Communists as "rats which have eaten a big part of the cake and tried to eat the pillar of our house." He added, "Now let's catch these rats, and I will punish them, but in catching the rats we should not burn the house." In a new vein—half pleading, half tough—he again said he would find the proper solution, complained about being "ignored by some groups" who "say they stand behind me and abide by my words but in fact push me and kick me about what to do." "Let me handle things absolutely," Sukarno continued and, wagging his finger, he shouted, threateningly, "If you do not like me any more, tell me. I will quit. God knows I have done well enough for the nation. You may discharge me." Sukarno was, in effect, throwing down the gauntlet. A week later he was saying, "We are all sons of the revolution and these sons should be loyal to their father, otherwise the father will eat his own sons," and that "while the September 30th Movement should be crushed, a thousand angels from heaven won't be able to kill *Nasakom*." He repeated the same theme in several other talks, bemoaning the fact that so many P.K.I. members and sympathizers had been killed and that "no one took care" of their corpses. Communism in Indonesia would survive, he said, "because the teachings of Communism have been the result of an objective atmosphere created within the Indonesian society, just as is the case with nationalism and religion." He even said he might build a monument to the Communists in West Irian to honor their service there, and, as for Malaysia, he served notice on the British, the Americans, and the Malaysians that the war would continue.

Generals Suharto and Nasution chose not to pick up Sukarno's gauntlet. Instead, there now began the year-long shadow play that Suharto, even more of a Javanese than Sukarno, understood better than his adversary. It may be, as some say, that Suharto moved only in careful stages against Sukarno because he believed, or was convinced by his spiritual advisers, that Sukarno was still the chosen wearer of the Presidential mantle and that neither Suharto nor anyone else had as yet been selected to wear it instead. There is considerable evidence that this was the case; but whether it was or not, it soon became apparent that Suharto was determined to proceed in his own way in cutting Sukarno down to size, and that his main reason for moving slowly and carefully was to make sure that the support Sukarno still had in the countryside, especially in Central and East Java, would not flare into active opposition and provoke a real civil conflict that might destroy the nation. The military moved first against Sukarno's flanks, and his most important flank was obviously Subandrio, who, at this juncture, was still the President's top adviser on domestic as well as foreign matters, and among other things was doing his best to salvage the shaken Peking-Djakarta alliance. In mid-December the Army forced the dismissal of Subandrio as Sukarno's deputy in KOTI, the armed forces' supreme operations command, and he also lost his job as head of the Central Intelligence Board, though he remained Foreign Minister and First Deputy Prime Minister.

In the first week of January, 1966, members of KAMI, the Indonesian college students' Action Front, which had been formed with Army inspiration in 1963 to counteract Communist infiltration at the University of Indonesia but had been dormant until the fall of 1965, took to the streets in Djakarta and Bandung to demonstrate against high prices. In the eight years since January, 1958, the price index had risen from a base figure of 100 to 56,000, and it had soared twenty thousand points alone in the previous month, after an unsuccessful government attempt to stem the rise by revaluing the rupiah. The student demonstrators carried posters which said, "The People Are Hungry" and "Long Live the Armed Forces," and for the first time some of their slogans attacked Sukarno personally, mostly over the question of his many wives. When, during a Cabinet meeting at Bogor in mid-January, several hundred students tried to force their way into the palace grounds, guards fired shots in the air to disperse them. Sukarno thereupon scolded them for "heaping abuse on their fathers" and in a nationwide radio address said, "I am sick of the secret campaign being launched against me. I, Sukarno, the Great Leader of the Revolution, the Supreme Commander of the Armed Forces, say whoever is still willing to follow me should rally behind me, defend me, build your strength." The following day Subandrio called for the formation of a Barisan Sukarno, a Sukarno Front, with branches all over the nation, but the Army responded quickly by banning it locally in several places and demanding that all its supporters register with military authorities. Then, in a maneuver worthy of Sukarno himself, the military leaders called for the creation of a new Pantja Sila Front, adopting for their own purposes the most sacred of Sukarno's political-philosophical tenets.

The great political shadow play of 1966 was now fully under way, and for the moment the center of the stage was once again held by Sukarno. Late in February he made his boldest bid since the coup to re-establish himself as Indonesia's supreme leader. He peremptorily dismissed General Nasution as Minister of Defense, abolished the armed forces staff, which Nasution had headed, and appointed a new and unwieldy Cabinet of one hundred ministers and subministers, about a quarter of whom were either pro-Communists or left-wing opportunists—what Indonesians call *plinplan*. The new Minister for Aircraft Industry was none other than Omar Dhani, the former Air Force chief, who had just returned from the vaguely defined mission to Europe on which Sukarno had sent him after the coup, and who had not yet been arrested. Subandrio remained the first of four Deputy Prime Ministers as well as Foreign Minister. Sukarno described the changes collectively as "just a normal reshuffle so my assistants can better help me carry on with the revolution."

Suharto, who had retained his post as Minister of the Army and Chief of Staff, was furious but held back as the student shock troops once more swung into action. Two days after Sukarno's announcement, nearly fifty thousand college and high-school youths stormed Merdeka Palace and ransacked the State Secretariat building next to it. They were dispersed by palace guards using rifle butts and bayonets, but the next day, when the Cabinet was being installed, they were out again in full force. This time they caused a tremendous traffic jam by stopping hundreds of cars and trucks and deflating the tires; the confusion and delays were so great that most of the fourteen top Cabinet members who were about to be sworn in had to be ferried across the stalled cars and the angry student mobs by helicopter. During the ceremony at the palace, as the students kept up their demonstration outside, shouting slogans against the P.K.I. and especially against Subandrio, the palace guards opened fire, and a medical student named Arif Rachman Hakim was killed. KAMI and KAPPI (the latter being the high-school students' front) now had a martyr, and their anger mounted. So did Sukarno's. Following a mass funeral for Hakim, he banned KAMI and declared, "Here I am—Sukarno, President and Great Leader of the Revolution. I will not retreat a step—not even a millimeter." The college students defied the ban on KAMI, and when Sukarno shut down the University of Indonesia, they met secretly and formed a "Hakim Regiment" composed of seven battalions named for the seven officers murdered on October 1. Meanwhile, the KAPPI students kept demonstrating.

Previously, the students had been under the influence and sometimes been the instrument of the various parties or the government, but most of their activities had been confined to campus issues. Now they had suddenly become a force in their own right, and the streets were their parliament. They were often away from their homes for days on end, living an exciting new quasi-underground life in and around the university, but for the most part they had the tacit or even the active support of their parents, who sent them bundles of food and clothing and, in a sense, vicariously lived their own earlier revolutionary experience all over again through their children. Oddly enough, the students did not seem to have any significant leaders other than some natural-born rabblerousers among their ranks whose fiery speeches would suddenly galvanize one group or another into action. They did, however, have their heroes and mentors. They had always looked up to Nasution, who had done much to encourage them originally, but after his dismissal he did as he had done before in a moment of crisis—withdrew into the background to watch and wait. Suharto was also somewhat remote and was moving too slowly, the students felt, although he had earned their respect and they trusted him to guard against the establishment of a military dictatorship. A number of the younger generals, however, were the students' principal sources of advice and encouragement, partly because these officers, too, wanted Suharto to move more dramatically and rapidly against Sukarno. The two most important among them were General Sarwo Edhy, the paratroop chief, and General Kemal Idris, who had become the deputy chief of Kostrad, the strategic reserve.

For a week or so after Sukarno's firing of Nasution and his announcement of the new Cabinet, it seemed as if he had used all his old guile and gall to force his way back into power. However, egged on by Edhy and Idris and other officers who realized that Sukarno was trying to split their ranks with his fresh appeals for unity and for "returning the revolution to its original leftist rails," the students again turned the tide. Despite a dusk-to-dawn curfew, they kept up their demonstrations, and the military looked the other way. Early in March, 1966, a band of KAPPI students seized the capital's Basic Education Office and turned it into their headquarters. On March 8, after hanging Sukarno in effigy in front of the Foreign Ministry, the students made their boldest bid by ransacking the ministry and grabbing large numbers of documents, among them one that purported to be a new secret agreement between Subandrio and Foreign Minister Chen Yi of China, in which Peking promised to support another coup attempt against the generals. During the sacking of the Foreign Ministry, as the rampaging students scrawled anti-Subandrio slogans on the walls and put up posters depicting him as a Pekingese dog, a group of leftist students from Bung Karno University, in Djakarta, counterattacked and there was a series of wild fights, which the police finally broke up with tear gas and by firing shots over the heads of the mob. Two or three hours later, some two hundred Bung Karno students attacked the American Embassy, which is close to the Foreign Ministry. "It was quite a day," one of the American political officers later recalled. "The students climbed over the gates of the embassy grounds and started throwing Molotov cocktails, one of which set fire to our warehouse. They broke some windows, including Ambassador Green's. They pulled down the American flag and hoisted an Indonesian one, and when one of our Indonesian employees climbed up to pull that flag down, the students grabbed him and carted him off. He was back at work the next day, though, just slightly bruised." The pro- and anti-Subandrio demonstrations went on for another two days, and they included attacks on some official Chinese Communist buildings, though not on the Chinese Embassy. A KAMI mob invaded Parliament to make speeches and deliver a petition. Djakarta was in virtual anarchy, and it was obvious that a showdown was imminent.

If there remained some doubt as to Sukarno's participation in the plot of September 30—and much of it was being dispelled by the initial treason trials that were now being held—there was no doubt at all about who was the ringleader this time. It was Sukarno himself, with the help of Subandrio and a few of his other trusted friends. In a final effort to assert his authority, Sukarno had evolved a three-day plan that depended, essentially, on the combined use of charisma and clubs. Only part of Sukarno's plan went off as scheduled. On March 10 he summoned the leaders of the nation's nine political parties and thoroughly cowed them with a histrionic display, reportedly at one point emphasizing his argument by crashing a chair against the wall. The politicians docilely signed a statement deploring the actions of the anti-Communist students as serving the cause of imperialism and colonialism. On the morning of the eleventh Sukarno summoned Cabinet ministers to Merdeka Palace for a similar showdown. Before the meeting, it was reported that Subandrio and his assistants were rounding up "loyal" Army elements and some "irregular" forces to crack down on the students and other anti-Sukarno elements. General Suharto and his aides moved swiftly. General Edhy's paratroopers, wearing no insignia and without their customary red berets, began closing in on the palace. Just before noon, the commander of the palace guard entered the Cabinet room, where the meeting had got under way, and slipped Sukarno a note saying that unidentified troops had the palace surrounded and were advancing. Sukarno leaped to his feet and, followed by Subandrio, who had slipped off his shoes

and didn't even have time to put them back on, and by Chaerul
Saleh, the Third Deputy Prime Minister, rushed out to the palace
lawn and into the Presidential helicopter, which headed for Bogor.
The Cabinet meeting was adjourned five minutes later by Second
Deputy Prime Minister Leimena.

Suharto at once sent three of his generals to Bogor by car. On the
way, on the basis of what Suharto had told them to do, they drafted
an order for Sukarno to sign. They got to Bogor at half-past four
and spent two hours talking to Sukarno, who at one point summoned Subandrio and Saleh and some of his other advisers. At first
Sukarno was furious, but as the three generals continued to talk
he quieted down. The gist of what they told him was that Djakarta
was about to be the scene of violent demonstrations, arson, and
possibly assassinations that could lead to a civil war, and that
unless he gave Suharto sweeping powers to control the situation,
the Army could not guarantee Sukarno's personal safety. It was
probably the last warning that persuaded Sukarno; he signed the
prepared order, giving Suharto authority, in the President's name,
to take "all measures required for the safeguarding of security and
government stability," and to protect "the course of the revolution." Suharto was only required to "report" on his actions to the
President, and, in return, he would "guarantee the personal safety
of the President." The next day, the twelfth, turned out to be a day
of celebration. The paratroopers organized a parade and thousands
of shouting students, waving flags and throwing flowers, rode
around in commandeered trucks and buses, or dashed through the
streets on scooters tooting their horns. Helicopters dropped copies
of the Sukarno order over the city. There were no incidents. In the
morning the three generals went back to Bogor to bring Sukarno to
Djakarta to attend the meeting of regional Army commanders he
had himself summoned. When his helicopter landed, the palace
was surrounded by Edhy's paratroopers. A glum Sukarno climbed
out, told the assembled officers in the palace to carry out their
orders under Suharto's direction, and returned grimly to Bogor.

On the thirteenth Suharto signed a decree banning the P.K.I. He
then began preparing for the next step, the reorganizing of the
Cabinet. Sukarno, who spent most of the week in Bogor, now
claimed that Suharto had no right to ban the Communists and
accused him of having masterminded the students' demonstrations

against Subandrio and the other members of his government. There were indications that he was making a last desperate effort to foster a rebellion against the Army by elements of the Air Force, the Marines, and the police, who had always been loyal to him, but if this was so, the attempt quickly fizzled out. As the week went by, the students again grew restless, and when Sukarno declared that he was still President and had not delegated any of his power to Suharto, they went back to the streets. But Suharto was now ready to act again. He sent the same three generals to Bogor to bring Sukarno back to Djakarta and, early on March 18, with the palace again surrounded by paratroopers, he seized the city's radio and television stations. In midmorning Subandrio was arrested in the palace guesthouse. With tank guns trained on the palace, he had no choice but to surrender meekly, and Sukarno could do nothing for him except to whisper a plea to his captors that he not be killed. Sukarno was allowed to go back to Bogor by car, and Suharto quickly arrested fourteen left-wing Cabinet members. Later that evening he announced a new interim Cabinet, in which the Sultan of Jogjakarta would be First Deputy Prime Minister and Adam Malik, a long-time anti-Sukarnoist, would be Foreign Minister.

The victory, to all intents and purposes, was now complete, but the shadow play concerning the future role of Sukarno continued. Sukarno still refused to bow out gracefully, and Suharto, aware of the prestige of the President's name, was still determined not to rush matters. He worked out a compromise whereby a number of pro-Sukarnoites were added to the Cabinet, but the guiding triumvirate remained Suharto himself, Malik, and the Sultan. Although it was apparent that the confrontation with Malaysia would be ended, the new government moved gradually on this, since Sukarno had made the war such an emotional part of his anti-imperialist crusade. By June 1 Malik had formulated a tentative agreement for a settlement with the Malaysians, but Sukarno's continued anticolonial diatribes threatened to upset the careful negotiations and also to destroy the behind-the-scenes arrangements Malik and the Sultan were making to restore good relations with the United States and other Western nations in order for Indonesia to get some much-needed aid.

Most important, in Suharto's own appraisal, was his deep private conviction that he had to handle Sukarno with dignity and grace. For the sake of the country, he felt, it was important to maintain a properly dignified image of the President and to pay permanent respect to the revolutionary contribution he had made over the years. This had nothing to do with what Suharto thought personally of Sukarno—which, according to those who know him best, was said to have always been very little. From the outset, Suharto insisted on proceeding on the basis of the Constitution and on summoning the People's Consultative Congress, which was still the highest policy-making body and theoretically had full authority over the President, though under Sukarno the Congress had faded far into the background. After a brief postponement when Sukarno balked, the Congress met, late in June. General Nasution was elected chairman. Sukarno made an impassioned speech, in which he demonstrated more humility than had been his custom. He said he would give up his title of President for Life if Congress wanted, and said he was ready to serve "the cause of freedom" and to continue to give "excellent leadership" to the country. The Congress went about its business methodically. It ratified the turning over of powers to Suharto, called for elections within two years, proclaimed a nonaligned foreign policy, stated that Indonesia would rejoin the United Nations, banned the dissemination of Marxism, Leninism, or any other form of Communism anywhere in Indonesia, and ordered Suharto to form a new Cabinet by Independence Day, August 17. Then it solemnly stripped Sukarno of his President-for-Life title, authorizing Suharto to serve as "Acting President" if Sukarno was ill or out of the country. The only title Sukarno retained was the meaningless one of Great Leader of the Revolution. In a speech at the closing session, Sukarno disputed the right of Suharto to appoint a Cabinet, contending it was still his responsibility to do so as President, but he indicated he would accept the Congress' wishes. "I myself feel that I am the tongue of the people," he cried. "The will of the Indonesian people is not the will of the people in Djakarta alone."

This was a not so oblique reminder to the Congress of Sukarno's enduring popularity, and the point was attested by a series of demonstrations in a number of East and Central Java towns, where his picture still hung in most official buildings and private homes. The Army was fully aware of the dangers of a revived Sukarnoist opposition, and a number of skirmishes had already taken place. All of this appeared to justify Suharto's caution, but for the students, and for some of the politicians as well, Suharto's methods still seemed exasperatingly slow. They and others felt that he and his fellow generals had prolonged the drama of Sukarno's exit by their failure immediately after the coup to establish some sort of firm organization in the touchy areas of Central and East Java. Others continued to feel that Suharto was right in not showing an iron fist and in following the quiet course of persuasion, but there seems little doubt, retrospectively, that, while there were risks in moving faster, a somewhat firmer hand would have made it easier to get rid of Sukarno and move on with the business of the nation's recovery. There were various odd manifestations of residual Sukarnoism: his picture remained on all rupiah bills, for instance, because Suharto felt that to remove it too soon would cause a further loss of confidence in the currency (the removal of the picture was finally begun in 1967). Following the Congress meeting of June, 1966, the new Cabinet, though selected by Suharto, still represented a compromise between him and Sukarno. It was dominated by the military but contained an odd mixture of Old Order and New Order politicians; though a quarter the size of Sukarno's previous, unwieldy hundred-man body, it still noticeably lacked good administrators and technicians. The public reaction to it was negative, the general feeling being that Sukarno's imprint was much stronger than it should have been.

By the time Sukarno delivered his traditional Independence Day speech in August—it was to be his last—he was making it abundantly clear that he was hell-bent on returning to full power. He denied that Suharto had been given any real authority in June, insisted he was still Prime Minister, Supreme Commander of the Armed Forces, Great Leader of Indonesia, as well as President, etc., and made clear his disapproval of the decisions of Suharto and Foreign Minister Adam Malik to end the confrontation with Malaysia and return Indonesia to the United Nations. By then the students, who all along had taken the lead in the campaign against Sukarno, had returned to the streets. They openly ridiculed the President, mimicking and mocking him contemptuously. Suharto, to the dismay of those, including several of his own generals, who now urged more drastic action against Sukarno, meanwhile continued on his slow course of moderation, choosing to ignore Sukarno. In a speech to Parliament, he modestly and carefully projected his recovery program, and when none of it proceeded as quickly as he had hoped, the slow momentum, as well as the effects of political drift, played into Sukarno's hands further. In the fall of 1966 Sukarno's old confidence and bravado had started to return. Though Marxism had been banned, he again extolled it—"Marxism is in my heart"—and, in his best hortatory style, demanded, "How could anyone ban me? I cannot be banned!" As O. G. Roeder, the Indonesian correspondent of the *Far Eastern Economic Review*, wrote at the time: "There is a continuous thread in [Sukarno's] behavior, designed to demonstrate that he is still on the stage, 'insulted,' but not defeated."

This analysis, as it turned out, was right on the mark. Already, by then, in several parts of Java, an underground pro-Sukarno movement had begun to gain momentum, and a number of Communist leaders who had not been arrested in the days and weeks after the attempted coup—about half of the fifty-two members of the Central Committee were either still at large at this point or were abroad—were beginning to distribute illegal pamphlets that called for the resurrection of "patriotic and progressive" forces and the creation of a new "anti-Fascist front against the rightist clique of Nasution-Suharto in order to defend Bung Karno." Suharto was by this time convinced that another "final" showdown with Sukarno was unavoidable. Parliament, in a plenary session, demanded that Sukarno stop calling himself a Marxist and cease talking about his old policy of *Nasakom;* he was also requested by the full Congress to explain his knowledge of and role in the coup effort.

By October the students were once more getting out of hand. The Army, while eager to retain their support, was determined not to permit a "Parliament of the streets" to take over. Matters came to a fresh head when, during a demonstration by KAMI and KAPPI students, sixty-two of them were injured by soldiers on guard in front of Merdeka Palace. Sukarno was obviously benefiting from these disorders, but he was also increasingly nervous. Appearing at the graves of the generals who had been murdered during the attempted coup, he broke down in public. The episode was described to me by Claude Cheysson, the French Ambassador: "The cemetery was very quiet, very beautiful. Two bugles played the call of the dead, and then there was silence. All of us passed, in parallel lines, along the edges of the graves, to scatter petals on them, as is the fashion in Indonesia. As it happened, I was just across from Sukarno when we stopped at General Yani's grave. Suddenly, Sukarno started shaking. He could not recover himself, and then he put his hands to his face and kept them there. He was crying, and he used his hands to hide his tears, but they rolled down his cheeks anyway. It was several minutes before he regained his composure and moved on. That was the first time I knew he was really finished. It also made me wonder, of course, how deeply he felt himself responsible for Yani's death." That evening, at a party at the palace, in an apparent counterreaction, "He behaved like a bastard," in the words of one of the people present, ordering his distinguished guests to sing and dance as he desired.

Sukarno was obviously nervous over the forthcoming trials of former Vice Premier and Foreign Minister Subandrio and Air Marshal Omar Dhani, both of whom had played such important parts in the coup. When the Subandrio case began, Sukarno's written testimony that the violence had taken him completely by surprise was scarcely convincing, particularly in the light of other evidence submitted, including some to the effect that Subandrio had ordered the burning of a secret letter sent to Sukarno by Aidit, the P.K.I. chief, from Central Java. This was the letter in which Aidit had made a number of suggestions for ways in which Sukarno ought to handle the situation, at least some of which Sukarno had adopted. The Dhani trial, which was broadcast by radio throughout the nation, implicated Sukarno even more thoroughly, particularly in regard to the mission on which the President had sent Dhani to China shortly before the projected coup in order to obtain weapons for arming the P.K.I.-dominated "fifth force," and in the matter of Sukarno's behavior at Halim air base on the morning of October 1, 1965, when he had taken the news of the murder of the generals with apparent equanimity and had almost nonchalantly accepted the plot's apparent success. Subandrio and Dhani did their best before the military tribunal to shield Sukarno, but they failed. Their pleas that they had simply acted as Sukarno's agents seemed further to indicate the President's own guilt.

Following the trials there were increasing demands for Sukarno to explain fully his own role, and the students, this time with the approbation of the Army, began new demonstrations against him. Sukarno at last simply repeated an earlier declaration to the effect that when the coup occurred "it was a complete bolt out of the blue for me." He refused to take the blame for the nation's moral and economic decline, and said, "If people talk about 'Truth and Justice,' I, too, ask for 'Truth and Justice.'" The statement left everyone as unsatisfied as before, particularly because of its defensive and blustery tone. Suharto, who had remained in the background during this period, now began to take steps to end what almost everyone was decrying as an impossible situation, and he was prodded along this path by Foreign Minister Malik, a tough-minded, high-principled, and independent man who had once been an ardent nationalist Marxist but had for a number of years been strongly anti-Sukarno. After a series of meetings with military chiefs, during which he was alternately defiant and conciliatory, Sukarno began to talk about resigning and taking a trip to join his favorite wife, Ratna Sari Dewi, who was in Japan expecting a baby.

The final act in the long, debilitating drama of Sukarno's downfall took place in February and March, 1967. As students paraded and demonstrated, tearing down pictures of the President and denouncing him, among other things, as "a marriage maniac," he lashed out at Congress, which was about to convene again, asserting that it was "bound hand and foot and castrated." Parliament and Congress had already declared Sukarno to have been negligent in fulfilling his constitutional obligations, and the growing consensus in both legislative bodies was in favor of bringing him to trial. He continued alternately to talk of resigning, of going abroad ("I am going to the moon," he quipped on one occasion), and of staying in office and "continuing to work hard for a socialist society." Suharto was being urged to act on the basis of the earlier Congress resolution, which enabled him to oust Sukarno if the President was "indisposed," but he still wanted to proceed "constitutionally" and "step by step," and by now he was against bringing the President to trial for fear that there was still a danger that this could trigger a civil war. After another painful series of meetings with the military commanders in mid-February, Sukarno, in the interest of "national unity," gave Suharto complete executive powers; this actually just confirmed the situation as it had existed since the previous March, except that there was now a further surrender on Sukarno's part—it was agreed that Suharto simply had to report to the President whenever he, Suharto, deemed it "necessary."

When the 1967 Congress convened, I attended the five-day session, which was held in the Russian-built badminton hall of Djakarta's huge sports complex. The tone of the gathering was somber, in contrast to that of previous Congress meetings, when Sukarno's personality, and his penchant for combining politics and entertainment, had dominated the proceedings. Now, for the first time, Sukarno was not even allowed to be present (his repeated requests had been denied), nor were there any of the usual huge portraits of him, but his spirit still seemed to hover about, and one almost expected a skylight suddenly to be flung open and the Bung to descend from it in his bemedaled white uniform. General Suharto delivered a long opening report that dealt mostly with Sukarno's involvement in the coup. Suharto carefully considered all the evidence against Sukarno, particularly his behavior at Halim air base the morning after the generals' assassination, and then, having presented what sounded to most of his listeners like a convincing summary of the President's complicity, he concluded, almost paradoxically, that Sukarno "could not have known for sure about the planned September 30th Movement, neither about the scheduled period of its happening nor about the form that the event itself would take." Therefore, he added, "we cannot mark Bung Karno down as a direct instigator, or the mastermind, or even an important figure . . . unless there are indeed still facts we haven't been able to find out until this very day." (Such facts were to come to light a year and a half later, when the testimony of newly captured pro-P.K.I. officers directly linked Sukarno to the final plot, indicating that he knew the generals were to be eliminated one way or another.)

Having said this, Suharto set forth on what amounted to a fascinating public psychoanalysis of Sukarno. The trouble, said Suharto, was that Sukarno had become obsessed with his theory of *Nasakom*, and because of this he had betrayed his own earlier and more fundamental revolutionary concept of *Pantja Sila*. He then referred to "the history of the patriotic struggle of Bung Karno," to his many contributions to the nation, and without specifically recommending that Sukarno be let off easily, concluded by saying that "the steps we would take should be those that will most benefit the struggle of the people and the nation, that will offer the smallest risk of creating danger, based on the objective evaluation and calculation of realities. . . ."

During the next three days, as the Congress broke up into various committees and countless speeches were heard on the floor, some defending a policy of leniency toward Sukarno but most calling for harsher measures, the procedure that was followed was in the best Indonesian traditions of *musjawarah* and *mufakat*—discussion and decision by consensus—and the final consensus was what Suharto had asked for, namely, a solution both "authoritative and tactful." In a series of resolutions adopted on the last day, Sukarno was judged to have failed to make a satisfactory explanation of his conduct in accordance with "the hopes of the people," and his mandate as President was consequently revoked. He was, further, prohibited "from conducting any political activities." It was at this meeting that Suharto was officially appointed Acting President in his own right, without any strings, and was given the task of determining what additional legal steps, if any, should be taken against "Doctor Engineer Sukarno," whose title of Great Leader of the Revolution was no longer held to have any special significance. When asked afterward by Western correspondents seeking a logical explanation of what Sukarno's status really was, General Nasution, the Congress chairman, who is a Sumatran, gave a typical Javanese reply: "When an Indonesian meets a tiger in the jungle, he addresses the beast as 'Grandfather.' If he comes across a crocodile, he addresses the reptile as '*Kijai*' [religious scholar]." It remained for Suharto himself to dot the "i"s and cross the "t"s. The Congress' decisions were "very wise and correct for the further course of our history," he said, and "the conflict situation" had been terminated. "For the time being I will regard him [Sukarno] as a President without authority in the political field, in state and government affairs. Aside from the practical and psychological reasons mentioned, I need to explain it to the whole of the Indonesian people that, based on the report of a competent team of doctors

made on oath, the condition of Bung Karno's health has deteriorated . . . so that it is more than proper that as a nation with the
spirit of *Pantja Sila* we shall treat him according to the condition of
his health. . . . So let all of us no longer discuss the problem of the
position of Bung Karno."

Actually, Sukarno's physical health was no worse or no better
than it had been before the whole drama had begun. Emotionally,
however, he was a beaten man. He had found it hard to believe, at
first, that he was really no longer President—reportedly, he had
shaken his head and murmured, "There are still some people in the
Moluccas who support me"—but it was not long before the truth
became apparent to him, that he was a man without a voice, deprived of almost all the former appurtenances of power. His position was somewhat comparable to Khrushchev's in Russia, except
that for the time being he was allowed to remain in his villa on the
grounds of Bogor Palace, where he continued to live with his No. 2
wife, Hartini, and with some of his various children. Early in 1968,
however, he was ordered to move into the equivalent of a *dacha,*
which had been specially built for him nearby. Occasionally he
was permitted to travel, well guarded, in an ordinary Volkswagen
to Djakarta to visit his doctor or dentist, and once or twice he
stayed at Merdeka Palace, where he still had a number of personal
possessions, including his private collection of nude paintings and
statues, but he was soon forced to move those out, too, and thereafter, when in the city, he stayed at the suburban house belonging
to Wife No. 3, Dewi—who, after giving birth to a daughter in
Tokyo, moved to Europe, where she gave every intention of remaining, with or without Sukarno. Since he officially had five living
wives instead of the maximum of four allowed to Muslims, he
divorced Harjati, formally No. 4. Fatmawadi, who is No. 1, continued to live in Djakarta, while the new No. 4, Juriwati Sanger, was
rumored to have gone abroad. (There are said to be two other
wives, both beautiful Kalimantan girls, but their legal status has
remained unclear.)

In Bogor, Sukarno saw only a few friends, and his movements
were thoroughly circumscribed. On a number of occasions he was
seen walking around the local market, chatting informally with the
vendors, and he and Hartini sometimes would turn up at a fashionable restaurant in the hills above Djakarta. One Westerner who

ran into him there once began a conversation, which Sukarno's guards quickly stopped, admonishing the visitor to remove himself because "It will get you into trouble, it will get him into trouble, and it will get us into trouble." According to some of his old friends, Sukarno, in the year or two following his downfall, still genuinely felt that his countrymen, bored by lack of circuses and frustrated by the increasing cost of living, would sooner or later call for his return to power. By the end of 1968 this no longer seemed possible, even to him. In September of that year he was suddenly brought to Djakarta and subjected to intensive questioning about his secret association with some of the conspirators, both military and civilian, who had led a new series of left-wing outbreaks in East Java, which had resulted in the arrest of several hundred officers. He was specifically questioned about his association with a dozen or so officers of the nearby Siliwangi Division in West Java, who had just been arrested. It was during this questioning, and the questioning of some of the suspected left-wing officers from East Java, that Indonesian intelligence experts obtained the further information about Sukarno's involvement in the 1965 coup, and particularly his apparent knowledge, on the eve of the attempt, that the generals were about to be forcibly removed. After being held for four days, he was allowed to return to Bogor, but later he was brought back to Djakarta, where he remained for some time. Though according to the decision of Congress in February, 1967, Suharto was empowered to bring Sukarno to trial "whenever he finds it necessary" for "alleged complicity" in the coup effort, it seemed unlikely that any such trial would ever take place. It was more probable that, having in effect been given another stern warning, Sukarno would simply drift further into political oblivion.

A Tour of the Islands

Not long after the climactic March, 1967, meeting of the Indonesian Congress, I took an extended trip through Java, Bali, Sulawesi, and Sumatra. At that time, the country was still in a state of shock and confusion as a result of the coup attempt, the bloodbath that had followed, and the prolonged and painful political aftermath. My first stop was Bandung, in West Java, which has always been an important center of power because, among other things, it is the site of the Army's Staff and Command School and the home base of the Siliwangi Division, the nation's most prestigious military unit. Indonesian divisions have well-defined regional origins and affiliations, and the Siliwangi has occupied a predominant position not only because of its strategic West Javanese base but because of its size—about forty thousand men out of the Army's total of more than 300,000. Initially formed by students and young revolutionaries after 1945, it was identified from the outset with the views of the more intellectual elements of the revolution; subsequently, the Siliwangi lived up to its reputation as an elite force, and various of its components and sometimes just individual officers were moved around the islands to handle dangerous situations or to take charge of poorly run outfits whose morale was bad. Over the years, the Siliwangi's tradition of intellectual and political enlightenment was influenced particularly by contacts with the Indonesian Socialist Party (P.S.I.), which was finally outlawed under Sukarno. Suharto, who never finished secondary school, became acquainted with some of the P.S.I. leaders while attending the Staff and Command School in 1960-61. A number of P.S.I.-oriented academicians are now part of his economic and political "brain trust."

The Staff and Command School was built into a remarkable military institution by General Suwarto, who died of cancer in 1967. Suwarto, an unusually broad-gauged and politically sophisticated officer, was also close to the P.S.I. When I saw him in Bandung a few months before his death, he was actively engaged in reorienting the Army's thinking after the long years of Sukarno, a process that he described as putting senior officers "through a drier and cleaner" so they could "rediscover their true revolutionary role" and become aware of the necessity of working in partnership with civilian leaders. The officers had been warned against "creeping militarism" during the critical post-Sukarno period and against permitting their role as stabilizers of the shaken Indonesian society to stifle fresh democratic growth. Suwarto said his interest in the civic responsibilities of the military dated back to the immediate postrevolutionary period, in the late nineteen-forties, when the new government's limited control in many areas of the country forced military commanders to run the civil administration. Now, cast in a new role of leadership, the officer corps was being challenged as a result of the vested interests it had slowly developed over the years and because of its often arrogant treatment of civilians. The task of Suwarto and his staff, in the words of Guy Pauker, a RAND Corporation expert in Indonesian affairs and a close friend of Suwarto's, was to convince as many as possible of the Army's 150 general officers and 400 colonels that it was their responsibility to maintain "the delicate balance between the representative democratic principle, which makes parties and policemen a 'necessary evil' in any polity, and the corporative principle which gives the Army the means to participate in the government without creating a military dictatorship." In this, Suwarto had Acting President Suharto's full support, but not necessarily that of other top officers—including, unfortunately, a number of generals on Suharto's personal staff and some of the more independent-minded of the seventeen regional commanders in the country, as well as the generals who were the majority among the twenty-five governors in charge of the civil administration in different areas.

I met Suwarto, a charming and modest man, in his bungalow near Siliwangi headquarters. Launching at once into a discussion of the importance of the military in underdeveloped nations, he came directly to the point of the Army's role in Indonesia's New Order. The chief current task, he said, was to make military men aware that "while in the past the emphasis has been on ideology and politics, it must now be on development." The problem, as he saw it, was to get rid as fast as possible of Sukarno's whole feudal framework, of his habit and practice of dealing with the apparatus of the state as he saw fit, without any rational method, so that the interlocking system of speculation and corruption in which the Army was also involved had come to be cynically condoned. A three-level approach was now necessary, Suwarto said: first, some fast economic and social results had to be achieved; second, "psychological solutions" had to be found to some of the complicated and deep-seated political problems; third, a fresh attempt had to be made to formulate a popular and mass approach, and in this the best elements of the Army could become a unifying force.

During my long trip around the country, I became aware of a

growing gap between those who were impatient for bold new paths to be broken and those who seemed content simply to return to old ways and formulas, with some minor changes. Those most seriously concerned about Indonesia's future were in almost unanimous agreement that there was very little hope if the old parties, the N.U. and the P.N.I., were simply to engage in tired contests to capture the ignorant electorate without consideration for the new forces in the nation and the continuing dangers both on the right and the left. In addition to the possibilities of Communist resurgence, there remained a right-wing threat among Islamic elements, both orthodox and nonorthodox, which played an active part in the brutal mass killing after the coup and now were talking again of an Islamic state. The long delay that had preceded the establishment of the new Indonesian Muslim Party (P.M.I.) in February, 1967, had made the N.U. more determined to hang on and to dominate the rural areas, where its strength had traditionally depended on popular control through the local Muslim teachers and oracles.

The future of the P.N.I. was even more complicated and difficult to forecast, but its leaders were equally determined to hang on. While many supporters of Suharto's New Order believed the party, which was still deeply divided between right- and left-wing elements, should be banned, and that its worthwhile remnants should be incorporated into the new Democratic Movement, Suharto had come out in favor of the P.N.I.'s resurrection and had ordered it to "crystallize" itself by getting rid of its Sukarnoist trappings. On the basis of my own observations, I would say that there seemed little chance of revitalizing the P.N.I., chiefly because it was so much Sukarno's vehicle that without him it would have no driver and no destination. Part of the P.N.I.'s internal struggle had concerned its efforts to "refine"—or redefine—the concept of Marhaenism, a Sukarno doctrine that derived its name from that of a poor Javanese farmer, and which Sukarno had liked to describe as "Marxism adjusted to suit the conditions of Indonesia." Now that Marxism was banned, the P.N.I. had tortuously tried to present "pure Marhaenism" as "belief in an Almighty God, socio-democracy and socio-nationalism." This was a typically Indonesian theoretical accommodation, which, the party leaders maintained, rendered Marhaenism akin to the *Pantja Sila* and, despite the hangover of Marxist terminology, eliminated any overtones of Marxism. These amateur dialectics convinced virtually no one, and although the party had officially renounced the personality cult of Sukarno and his title as "the father of Marhaenism," and had let it be known that it no longer expected the return of Sukarno under any conditions, it was obviously still in a state of disarray. Little had actually been done to get rid of the pro-Sukarno elements within it, mainly because these elements were numerous enough in most areas to withstand the pressure against them or because they had taken refuge in further self-exculpating platitudes. Words and definitions in Indonesia can be twisted and turned to mean, or pretend to mean, almost anything, and the P.N.I., which in fact had never had any real political philosophy of its own, was simply flopping around on the New Order beach and hoping that some new tide would wash it back into its old muddy sea again.

In Bandung I had a long discussion with a lively group of students representing several of the universities in this city of intellectual ferment. Listening to them talk about their role as "watchdogs," of their responsibility for "educating the military" and "giving the people a realization of political and social life based on the rule of law," I had the feeling that these intense young men were playing a game of pretending they were in charge of the government and were explaining how they would run it. It was hard to realize that thirteen students from various parts of the country at that time were actually members of Parliament, and that one of them with whom I was talking, Soegeng Sarjadi, was the same exuberant fellow I had sat with the day before in the Bandung sports stadium, where he and his girl were wildly cheering a parade of their university class teams about to take part in an intramural soccer contest. These Indonesian students were not to be discounted. Although the country had its share of hippies and wild Honda drivers, the majority of students were still deeply involved with current social, economic, and political problems, and their confidence or lack of confidence in the new government was bound to be an important factor for a long time to come.

The outstanding characteristics of the students active in the national KAMI and KAPPI student groups, the majority of them from the urban middle class, were impatience and suspicion. I found them solidly behind Suharto but already wary of many of the military men around him; in the months ahead their dissatisfaction, particularly over rising prices, rice shortages, and corruption, was to lead to some disenchantment with Suharto himself. The letdown was partly because of the decline of the students' hopes of being able to work politically with the democratic elements of the Army against the authoritarian factions; the untimely death of General Suwarto, who was a sort of father-confessor to many of the students, hastened this process of disillusionment. There had been an increasing resentment of the Army's domination of state enterprises, both those taken over after the coup and those that the military had previously run in Sukarno days. On this issue, most businessmen, the majority of politicians, and the leaders of other action groups, such as KASI, the cultural organization to which many teachers and professors belong, supported the students' views. In Bandung, for example, one of the Muslim liberals of the N.U. and a KASI spokesman cited the Army's operation of local sugar, textile, oil, and cement factories, and its domination of the transportation business, as examples of "creeping militarism." They also spoke in worried tones of the Army's control of most of West Java's administrative apparatus, from the regional level down through the *bupatis,* or district leaders, and below them to the village level, where sergeants and ex-sergeants were often in charge. "It is true that the Army is doing many things by default because the civilians are not up to it," the KASI leader told me. "But we're disappointed that the Army is acting so purposefully as a political force. Most of the officers are too dictatorial." The N.U. liberal spoke of the civilians' "sense of inferiority" in their dealings with the Army. "We don't know where we stand, because the real political issues have not yet been clarified," he said. "Consequently, we aren't courageous enough."

The ferment in Bandung seemed in keeping with the rolling green hills of West Java and the lush growth of its multicolored flowers. As I rode into Central Java, I could almost smell as well as see the difference. The countryside became drab, and the *kampongs,* the villages, were often built on barren ground. The roads, which the Army was starting to repair under the new civic-action program, were still full of potholes, and the number of vehicles diminished as we moved eastward. It was a common sight to see two men perched on top of an open hood piecing together a dying engine, and the roadside ditches were littered with the carcasses of abandoned trucks. A motley collection of people, mostly old men and women and young children, skimpily dressed in torn and patched clothing, trudged endlessly along the roads from village to village. Their impassive faces bespoke their calm belief in Allah's will, and they seemed neither despondent nor despairing, only resigned. In the fields, beyond the muddy pools where water buffalo soaked themselves contentedly, with only their luminous and bulbous eyes and the tops of their heads showing, youngsters scampered about with their ubiquitous kites. As we got closer to the city of Semarang, we passed villages and towns where many of the shops that had belonged to Chinese merchants were boarded up—mute signs of the anti-Chinese campaign that had accompanied the bloodletting after the 1965 coup and that would soon lead to a near-total break between Djakarta and Peking. As we crossed several rivers over rickety bridges, my driver, an English-speaking Indian Muslim, dispassionately noted that these were among the streams where thousands of unidentified corpses had formed logjams during the frightful weeks at the end of 1965.

We were now in the heart of the country dominated by the P.N.I. but where the P.K.I., too, had once held sway and Sukarno had ruled supreme. His pictures were still everywhere to be seen, since General Surono, the Central Java military commander, aware of the popular sentiment, had announced that they could remain up if portraits of Suharto were placed alongside them. No official portraits of Suharto had been distributed yet, so most people simply left those of Sukarno hanging, or put up an accompanying Indonesian coat of arms. Later, when the Suharto pictures were sent out, the pro-Sukarnoites, which meant the majority of the population, left both portraits up, or put Sukarno in their bedrooms, if they had two rooms. One man told me that he had placed the two pictures side by side. "I keep lowering Sukarno an inch a day," he said. "Pretty soon he'll drop out of sight altogether." More than one devout Sukarno worshiper insisted that his idol was still President, still the Father of the Revolution, the founder of Marhaenism, etc. "It's different for you, a Westerner," a schoolteacher said sadly. "But for us a dream dies hard."

The Sukarno dream, many observers felt, would disappear in

Central Java if something believable could be substituted for it, but the fact that he was a father image for so long, and that he had served to satisfy the emotional needs of a population spiritually steeped in Hindu and local varieties of mysticism would admittedly make it hard to find anyone or anything to take his place. Sukarno knew his Javanese people well. He knew, for example, as a liberal Catholic priest explained it, that "the people of Central Java, as a whole, are not yet conscious of their place in the world and have no world outlook, that their awareness is limited to suffering, and to being passive, not active." And a law professor said, "Most of us don't believe in democracy—the villagers don't know what it is, and intellectuals don't understand it. Certainly Sukarno gave us no political legacy or legitimacy. There was just his presence, his promises, and his slogans. All we now have left is our strange Javanese accumulation of values. Even those Indonesians who looked to Western teachings and technology found it too rich for their blood. Sukarno knew this, too. It was not just that he neglected us economically and wasted our resources. He knew how to put a check to the revolution of rising expectations." What alone offset the endemic passivity, in the opinion of the rector of a Christian university in a strong P.K.I. area, was, ironically, "the old feudal influence—if you passed in school, you almost automatically became a state official. But even when this produced doctors and lawyers, it did not provide an intelligentsia. What we need now is a crash course in intellectuals, but that's not easy. A reformation of the whole educational system is more important. It will be impossible to find a national identity without more education."

Sukarno did provide widespread education, but too much of it was under the influence of the Muslim village teachers or of the P.N.I. and P.K.I. It was no accident that, of the approximately 120,000 elementary-school teachers in Central Java, a third were among the estimated 250,000 persons arrested throughout the country after the coup attempt for being P.K.I. members or suspected sympathizers (the bulk of these 250,000, including most of the teachers, had, by 1968, been released, leaving between sixty and eighty thousand still in jail; of these, only about five thousand were said to be hard-core P.K.I. members, and another five thousand solid supporters, while the rest remain "unclassified"). The desire for education was still as strong as ever, and the educational structure, physically, remained intact. At the end of 1965 there were forty-five state universities, eighty-five "academies" at the higher-educational level, and more than two hundred private institutions of higher learning in the country. What was lacking was money. Less than 5 percent of the tight national budget was earmarked for education, and there were thousands of schools at the primary and secondary level that needed to be rebuilt, that were without books and equipment, and that were all but empty shells. There were no funds for government officials to travel around and inspect the public schools, and, after all the dismissals for political reasons, there was, naturally, a dearth of teachers. In the private schools most teachers could afford to give only two or three hours a day to their students—then, like almost everyone else, they had to work at other jobs in order to support themselves and their families. This pointed up the need for the country to find economic solutions before it could make real political progress—as one of the former Socialist Party leaders commented, "You can't think about democracy if you have to spend all your time thinking about survival."

An economist in Jogjakarta who was associated with Suharto's brain trust brought home to me the problems the arose from the Army-dominated setup. "The Army, while aware of the need for efficiency in the Western sense, is loath to take advice," he said. "The regional commanders and those below them are often incompetent, and they make things worse by failing to follow Suharto's instructions. If he tells them not to interrupt the flow of goods interregionally, they do it anyway, in order to get money as quickly as they can. If someone wants to export a local product, like seaweed, for example, which you get on the south coast of Java, you have to wait for the commander to grant a license—for which you have to pay, of course. Aside from the hindrance of sheer bureaucratic inefficiency, a lot of money goes under the table. Domestic production remains the real problem, though. We're trying to kill inflation with a tight-money system and a tight-trading system, but that doesn't always help. Very few Army people understand the importance of the flow of goods. There are too many entrepreneurs around who get an allocation of funds to bring in, say, textiles, then go ahead and sell their imports on the black market. The result is that goods are hoarded or used for speculation, and the whole inflationary process continues. So only the

strongest entrepreneurs can produce domestically. In the meantime, those who suffer most from the price increases and from
inflation are the fixed-income groups, as always. If things improve,
particularly if we have some good agricultural crops, the government's stabilization plan should work."

What impressed me most, throughout Central Java, was the
poverty of the people, which was primarily due to overpopulation.
There were twenty million people in the region, and in some areas
more than a thousand per square kilometer, while the average, of
almost six hundred, was the highest in the country. In the volcanic
hill areas, where the soil was poor, the peasants were trying to eke
out a living by utilizing every inch of available ground. Hordes of
them flocked with their families to the already crowded plains,
where even the better land failed to produce enough to feed everyone. So thousands more went into the cities—to Semarang, Jogjakarta, or Solo—where they became part of a floating unemployed
mass. "By all Western standards, people here should be starving," a
businessman in Semarang remarked to me. "Yet, somehow, they
get by. There is not enough rice, and much of what is grown is
smuggled out to West Java and Djakarta, but they manage to live
on less and less. At least we grow our own vegetables and there is
enough beef. One solution, which the government keeps talking
about, is transmigration to other islands, but little has been done
about this yet. On a long-term basis, the answer is light industry
and better transportation, plus improvements in the irrigation system, in the use of fertilizer, and in curbing deforestation, which
causes floods. But to do all that, and other things, we need a lot
more foreign aid than the rest of the world has so far been willing
to give us."

With this abysmal economic background and amid the stale political puppetry of the old parties, it was not surprising that, given
their mystic compulsions and their yearning for the equivalent of
wayang, the people of Central Java had searched for other forms of
emotional release. Religious sects had always been prevalent here
—the fanatic right-wing Darul Islam was active for thirteen years
during the Sukarno period before it was finally suppressed—and
these mystic organizations had blossomed in the postcoup period.
Some two hundred of them were active, many practicing a weird
variety of rites, including sexual ones, and some simply serving as

new underground covers for the Communists. The burgeoning of these sects, whose followers totaled several hundred thousand, prompted the Indonesian Attorney General's office to establish a special section to keep a watch on them and to make arrests when they were considered dangerous to the national security. In the spring of 1967 two of the largest sects were crushed. The first was directed by a small bearded man named Muljono, who was better known as Mbah Suro and who pretended to be the reincarnated grandson of Mohammed as well as the rightful heir of Djojobojo, a twelfth-century Javanese Sanskrit scholar and prophet. Sukarno, who was thoroughly addicted to mysticism, was said to have consulted Mbah Suro in the year after the coup and to have been guided in his stubborn refusal to surrender authority by Mbah Suro's advice. Mbah Suro, who may have been a member of the P.K.I. and was at least a thorough sympathizer, operated in a remote area of Central Java, near the village of Nginggil. When he refused to answer a summons for interrogation, Indonesian paratroopers attacked his headquarters, killed him and more than a hundred of his followers, and arrested another fifteen hundred. Despite the fact that his corpse had since been dug up three times to prove that he was dead, his devout disciples still insisted that he was alive. One month after his death, the paratroopers arrested another mystic leader, Heru Tjokro, who operated with about eighty followers from the village of Sredjiwan, also in Central Java. Tjokro, too, had a close association with the P.K.I., but this did not keep him from leading a sybaritic life surrounded by concubines and scores of servants and guards, who kept all visitors away and permitted messages to be sent to him only on recorded tape.

The success of the sects in Central Java reflected the political as well as the spiritual void that existed in the wake of the coup, the ensuing mass violence, and the collapse of the P.K.I. and the P.N.I. It was also an expression of a general nihilism and despair, the feeling that Central Java, with its tremendous economic and social problems, was beyond redemption; the failure of the New Order to demonstrate that life would really be much different from what it was under Sukarno had, so far, accentuated this feeling. It was no accident that one of the mystical sects, the Manuggal, was envisaging a nirvana wherein one grain of rice would be enough to feed a person for a day. Most of the sects were violently against the organized religions, especially the Muslims of the Old Order as epitomized by the N.U.

The N.U. remained, above all, opportunistic and pragmatic, with a history of accommodation to power, and it had been quick to react to the predicament of the P.N.I., by doing as much proselytizing as it could in the villages among the *abangan*. In further seeking to win as much popularity as possible, the N.U. had restored old mosques and built new ones as well as new universities, and had taken advantage of the fact that religious instruction was now mandatory in the primary and secondary schools. With three million members in Central Java, the party was increasingly demonstrating the dictum that "politics should serve religion," as one of the regional leaders put it. This new feeling of self-confidence on the part of the organized Muslims, despite their discontent over not playing a larger political role in the New Order, reflected their assurance that they were the strongest civilian force in the country. While they continued to campaign for more important posts in Suharto's Cabinet and in the civil administrations throughout Central and East Java, they were also adopting a posture of antimilitarism, objecting to the Army's trying to dominate so many jobs and functions. This policy of continuing opportunism had not been accompanied by any new thinking on the part of the N.U. Its leaders claimed to be indignant about the continued manifestation of Old Order habits and ways, but, like most other politicians and even more than some, they kept repeating the same old slogans of the *Pantja Sila* and belief in the principles of the 1945 Constitution, along with their Muslim prayers. As one of the Djakarta intellectuals observed, "The N.U. is not interested in ideas and ideology—just in power."

There was some fear that if the N.U.'s demands were not reasonably satisfied, fanatical elements within it would sooner or later begin to agitate for the creation of a long-dreamed-of Islamic state. The danger that this could happen, and the desire to avoid it by maintaining some kind of balance, was undoubtedly one of the factors in Suharto's decision to give the P.N.I. a chance to reform itself. The need to solve the Islamic problem is certainly crucial to the future of Indonesia. The difficulties of doing this satisfactorily are enhanced by the fact that Islam remains such a diffuse force in Indonesian society. Because, in Java, it is an overlay on an earlier

Hindu mystic base, and because of the long process of interaction between the two, many observers feel that the Islamic movement is incapable of being "modernized" or of even "digesting the modern process." Soedjatmoko has ably stated the problem:

> Under pressure, Islam tends to respond in fundamentalistic terms, falling back on the inseparability of the State from the Faith, and the need for Islamic forces to score a political victory before the ills of society and of the State can be cured. . . . In the eyes of the orthodox, secularism is not only a danger to Islam but also the source of a variety of social evils, from prostitution to Communism. Hence the constant appeal to intellectuals to abandon their secular concerns and return to the fold. Hence also the inclination to consider as real Moslems only those who have taken the formal act of joining a Moslem political party. . . .

Soedjatmoko's analysis is borne out by the fact that the N.U., like the P.N.I. but for different reasons, is deeply divided between New Order and Old Order factions, and, more importantly, between new and old ways of thinking. Most of the younger and more liberal N.U. members who want to reform the party from the ground up favor a single Muslim political regrouping. Others, including some who belonged to the former Masjumi Party, have begun to turn to the new Indonesian Muslim Party. There is a strong desire on the part of such men as former Prime Minister Natsir, after his years in jail, to have their anti-Sukarno position historically vindicated. When I visited Natsir, a scholarly, reflective man, he maintained that the Masjumi should never have been banned, but he spoke tolerantly of the past. "The important thing is not the party name but to get people moving in the right direction," he said. "We cannot afford the privilege of doing nothing. To allow frustrations to build up, new attitudes of mental isolation to develop, is dangerous." Although the men of Masjumi—Natsir, Mohammed Roem, and the former party chairman, Prawoto, among others—seem likely to remain in the background because of their tangled pasts, they are expected to play advisory roles in the new P.M.I. as well as in the new Development Movement led by Foreign Minister Malik and by Umar Khayam, the head of the Indonesian Radio and Television Authority. Roem, in fact, was named late in 1968 to be chairman of the P.M.I., but when Suharto refused to approve his election, he resumed his advisory capacity.

The P.N.I., the Nationalist Party, is naturally watching all these Islamic maneuvers sharply, and if anything can galvanize the party into taking the necessary steps to cleanse itself, it seems likely to be the fear of big new Muslim gains. One searches in vain, however, for any signs that the current leadership is capable of coping with the problems of purging and reorganization. Typically, the party leader in Jogjakarta, an elderly physician, spoke reverently to me of Sukarno, dogmatically insisted that the elections should be held in 1968, as originally scheduled, and, when asked about a new party platform, smiled wanly and began repeating the litany of Marhaenism, the *Pantja Sila*, etc. A somewhat more imaginative leader, who had tried to conduct a purge in Jogjakarta but had been outmaneuvered, was bitter. "The party has no principles and no clarity of purpose," he said. A realistic businessman in Semarang, who favored an election postponement, thought that by hard work in the villages, and by a tough policy of screening all the ex-left-wing elements, the party "could still be saved and could provide national leadership." But he admitted that the ranks were full of "opportunists, carpetbaggers, and political guerrillas. The trouble is we're like a supermarket."

At his house on the outskirts of Semarang, I visited Hadisubeno, the Central Java chairman and one of the top three P.N.I. men in the country. In this uneasy triumvirate, he represented the mass party groups, while Mohammed Isnaeni spoke for the radical youth and other left-wing elements, and Hardi for the civil servants and scholars. As party chairman, Hardi was theoretically the first among equals, although his influence was mostly confined to Djakarta, where the party as a whole was weak. I had seen Hardi before leaving on my trip, and he had admitted that "we've been ideologically shadowboxing for years, and now we must redefine our position in practical and meaningful ways." He had added that this meant "putting the Sukarno issue in historical perspective, pointing out that he has played an important role in the past but that now this is finished." I had been eager to meet Hadisubeno because he had been making speeches in the last year defending Sukarno and telling his people that their beloved Bung was still President. A tall, heavy man with horn-rimmed glasses and the look of an old-line Tammany Hall politician, he smiled when I brought this up and corroborated what I had also heard—that his defense of Sukarno had been "just tactical," an effort to let the population of Central Java down easily. "Now that we don't have to think about Sukarno any more," he said, "we have to look at the situation as it is—although if Sukarno were to be put on trial, the people would be very upset and there would be more trouble. There is no longer any question of applying his slogans, or of collaboration with the P.K.I. We believe in God, and the Communists don't. But we can still learn from the early Sukarno of 1926 and 1927. We believe in 'pure' Marhaenism, as well as in the *Pantja Sila*. We must work hard to teach what this means, from the primary schools up, and we must help the government in its new economic program or Central Java will become a new breeding ground for the P.K.I."

There was common agreement, among almost all the politicians I spoke with, that the future of the P.N.I. remains the most crucial question in Central Java. Perhaps the gravest challenge it faces is the reconstruction of its mass base. One of the most knowledgeable men I saw, a Jogjakarta Socialist, felt that the P.N.I.'s mass following was still heavily infiltrated by the Communists and that the civil servants, who traditionally had been the party's backbone, "can't control the situation." The Army, he added, had replaced the P.N.I. as the predominant influence among many civil servants, and this had made the party's leaders even more nervous as they sought to "cleanse" the ranks. The Army, this man felt, "needs far more political training and experience," while the Navy and Marines, which were always strongly pro-Sukarno in Central and East Java, were still subject to left-wing influence.

In Solo, a city of half a million that has often been regarded as the political thermometer of Central Java, there had been a heavy influx of unemployed peasants, and the atmosphere was sterile and uneasy, giving added meaning to warnings about the resurgence of the P.K.I. The Mayor, an Army colonel and a Catholic, said it had taken him two months to get the killings under control when he took over in October, 1965. Of fifteen thousand men and women arrested in the area in the weeks after the coup, about half had been screened and released, while the remainder, including about two thousand hard-core party members or known sympathizers, were still awaiting trial and the disposition of their cases in temporary jails in and around Solo, including a school right behind

the Mayor's office, where I saw them hanging out of the windows
and shouting at the passers-by—a fairly typical sight throughout
Central Java. The city seemed full of idle people. Solo has a number of batik factories and some other small industries, but there
was a shortage of raw materials, so most of them were not in
operation, and the inferior goods that were being produced cost
more than cheap imported products, or those smuggled in from
Singapore. The political situation was quiet, the Mayor said. He
was hopeful that small Catholic and Protestant parties would continue to get stronger, as they showed signs of doing, and would
help create a balance between the P.N.I. and the N.U.

As I moved from Central into East Java, the countryside grew
still more barren, and the look of poverty increased. The unre-
strained violence of the killing after the coup was said to have
been greater here than anywhere else—estimates varied, but I was
told that at least a hundred thousand persons were killed in the
region. Perhaps because of this the state of shock, of dullness, was
more perceptible here, and beneath it a residue of latent tension
that was soon to break out in a new spurt of violence. Here, too, the
influence of the P.K.I. had been strong and widespread. Beginning
late in 1964, the P.K.I. had urged landless peasants to seize land
belonging to Muslim owners, including that of the mosques; some
property of rich urban P.N.I. landlords was also taken over. This
had led to some killing prior to the coup, which the Brawidjaja
Division—of which several battalions had been infiltrated by the
Communists—sometimes stopped but at other times had simply
ignored. When the coup occurred, the furies were released, and
Muslim killer squads, encouraged by the predominant anti-Communist elements in the Army, went on their rampage. Some
left-wing non-Communists became victims, along with the Communists, in what had assumed the proportions of a holy war. "It
became a matter of 'I'll kill you before you kill me,'" a businessman in Surabaya told me. The antagonisms between pro-Sukarno
police and Marines and the loyal elements of the Army that had
fanned the violence was still apparent.

Sukarno was born in East Java, and the impact of Sukarnoism
had lasted longer here than in any other part of Indonesia. My
Indian driver was constantly asked questions about what had happened in Djakarta. Was Sukarno still in power? Was he safe? And

so on. A European who had lived in the region many years told me, "We never realized how deeply the Communists had infiltrated. They had got into all the channels of communication, the estates, the schools and universities, and into the ministries and administrative offices, too." The new military commander, General Jasin, who took over at about the time of my visit, had proved firm in his resolve to wipe out the vestiges of Communism, but this would not be easy, or it would be only temporary, unless much more was done to deal with the basic causes of conflict. In East Java, which has a population larger than Central Java's, the pressure on the land is even greater, while the quality of the soil, except at the eastern tip, is generally poor. When I was there, most of the Muslim landowners had recovered their properties, and the old class distinctions had reappeared. Village controls through the Muslim *kijai* and *lurahs* had been re-established, and, as in Central Java, the N.U. had made a much better recovery than the P.N.I. When I spoke with the East Java P.N.I. chairman, a mild-mannered law professor named Soendoro who had been appointed only a year or so before, he was confident that he had subjugated the left-wingers, though he admitted there was still a strong pro-Sukarno feeling in the party. Others, however, including American consular officials and local Europeans as well as Indonesians, said that the party was still deeply affected by left-wing activity, and that, in fact, the leftists still controlled the local party hierarchy and machinery—which the P.K.I. underground was using for its own recovery. One former member of the regional P.N.I. board, a right-winger, claimed that the Communists were obtaining funds from Peking, channeled through local Chinese and through three or four top Indonesian businessmen who had close ties with the left wing of the P.N.I. The independents and intellectuals, including a sprinkling of Socialists and "modernist" Muslims who were worried about the threat of an Islamic takeover, were doing what they could to get some alternative political activity started, but the general atmosphere of frustration and recrimination did not encourage new initiatives. Economically, the region was struggling along, and while the roads had been improved and more goods such as clothing, had become available, the price of rice had doubled in the last two years, and such natural calamities as floods had made the situation worse. "We're still several centuries behind," a

Surabaya leader told me. A political-science professor put it more hopelessly. "On our way it will be a long, long journey," he said. "Please do not forget the difficulties imposed by our mental attitudes. We are what we are."

It was apparent, early in 1967, that the Indonesian Communist Party had not given up. Whatever success it might achieve in reestablishing itself would depend not only on its own abilities but on the degree of economic recovery and on the headway made by non-Communist parties. To some extent, of course, what happened elsewhere in Southeast Asia, particularly in Vietnam and Thailand, and in Singapore and Malaysia, would be a factor, and so would events in China. The outcome of the war in Vietnam would also undoubtedly affect Indonesia's relations with the Russians, who had not yet expressed much interest in the revival of Communism in Indonesia. In their view, the collapse of the coup demonstrated the impracticality of armed uprisings in underdeveloped countries, as advocated by Mao. Moscow had criticized the Suharto government for keeping so many pro-Communist or Communist suspects under detention and for executing the coup leaders, and it had described the new regime in Indonesia as "rightist." However, the Russians had sold the Indonesians some spare parts for the planes and naval vessels it had earlier given the Sukarno regime. These sales, and a partial rescheduling of Indonesia's heavy debts to the Soviet Union, were just about all the assistance the Russians were offering, though, and there was considerable criticism in Indonesia about their reluctance to help out more, on the matter of the debts especially. (In the fall of 1968, following the Soviet invasion of Czechoslovakia, the anti-Soviet criticism increased, and it seemed bound to slow down further any new commercial or cultural relations.)

In its underground statements since the attempted coup, the P.K.I. showed itself to be, if anything, closer to the Peking line. During 1967 and 1968 several underground documents were circulated secretly and published in the *Indonesian Tribune,* a Communist magazine, and in the world Communist press. The most important of these, entitled "Build the P.K.I. Along the Marxist-Leninist Line to Lead the People's Democratic Revolution in Indonesia," appeared in January, 1967, in the *Tribune.* Accusing the

P.K.I. leadership of the past of engaging in "adventurism," by, among other things, putting too much faith in Sukarno's revolutionary intent, the statement cited "subjectivism" as the party's chief ideological weakness and said this derived from "petty bourgeois influences." This led to a consequent failure to stress Marxist-Leninist principles and resulted in "right opportunism that merged with modern revisionism." The party's mass base, the document continued, was badly educated and led and far too loosely organized, and it was allowed to drift along in the belief that Socialism in Indonesia could be achieved "through parliamentary means" and by a "peaceful road." This was an illusion, the new Politburo said, adding: "To achieve its complete victory, the Indonesian revolution must follow the road of the Chinese revolution. This means that the Indonesian revolution must inevitably adopt this main form of struggle, namely, the people's armed struggle against the armed counterrevolution, which, in essence, is the armed agrarian revolution of the peasants under the leadership of the proletariat." Such a policy "requires the Indonesian Marxist-Leninists to establish revolutionary base areas" in the backward villages and remote parts of the country, as was the case in China and Vietnam. Interestingly, the document admitted that "300,000 patriots" were lost in the mass killings after the coup attempt, and it now advocated a "revolutionary united front with all anti-imperialist and antifeudal classes and groups based on the worker-peasant alliance under the leadership of the working class."

Beginning in 1967 and increasing in the first half of 1968, there was renewed rebellious activity in the East Java area, especially in the backward South Blitar region, and, to a lesser extent, in Central and West Java. In Blitar a wave of terrorism was directed by new Communist shadow groups against the Muslims who had led the mass slaughter after the coup. About one hundred Muslims were murdered during 1968 in such recriminatory attacks. Most of the shadow groups operated in small bands of a few men, and the pattern of the new terrorism showed a decided Vietcong influence; even before the coup an unknown number of P.K.I. cadres had been sent to Vietnam for observation and training, and the new bands in Java were adopting typical Vietcong hit-and-run tactics and using underground tunnels and storage areas, like the Vietcong. The groups, which employed various nicknames, had some modern weapons but were also crudely fashioning their own, as the Vietnamese Communists used to do. Their arsenals were strengthened as a result of the defection of members of the armed services over the previous five or six years. By the end of 1968 about four hundred of these pro-Communist military men and officers had been captured, but another four hundred in East Java alone were still free and the majority were believed to be cooperating with the Communist underground. In addition, several hundred alleged pro-leftists in the ranks of the Brawidjaja Division had been dismissed. The Army was said to be shocked at the discovery that many officers and men had pledged allegiance to the P.K.I. even *after* the 1965 coup.

The Army claimed that its coordinated campaign to crush this new Communist rebellion had led, by the end of 1968, to the killing or capture of two thousand P.K.I. members. The government also said it had foiled at least half a dozen plots aimed at murdering Suharto and other top generals and officials and at restoring Sukarno to power; while there were announcements of the arrest of the ringleaders, including, on one occasion, several well-known officers, no details of these alleged conspiracies were made public, and they may have been partly government-inspired campaigns to further discredit Sukarno and discourage any opposition his name might still inspire. By and large, at least for the time being, the random attempts by the Communists to cause fresh trouble had been repelled, although kidnapings and robberies as well as murders continued sporadically. There were indications that, suffering as they had been from communications handicaps and other difficulties in reorganizing themselves, the P.K.I. may again have made the mistake of bad timing in launching an offensive too soon. This was the line taken in mid-September, 1968, by *Pravda,* in Moscow, which, in renewing its attack on Maoist revolutionary theories, said, of the new Indonesian offensive: "Disregarding the Leninist position that an armed revolutionary struggle can be successful only when it has been carefully prepared and is based on broad support of the masses, the [party] officials called on the Communists to go into the jungles and to undertake actions against regular units of the Army and the police." As a result of this premature action, *Pravda* added, "the Communist movement in Indonesia suffered another disaster."

The P.K.I., however, may have felt, even without prodding from Peking, that it had been forced to take some action before the Suharto recovery program got started and economic conditions improved; or Peking may indeed have ordered the new wave of terror to keep the P.K.I. in step with Communist insurgency efforts in Thailand and elsewhere in Southeast Asia, as the war in Vietnam was reaching a climax. Certainly there was no indication that, even if they continued to suffer setbacks, the Communists would stop their attempts to recover their strength in Indonesia and persuade the people in the backward areas that they remain the best revolutionary hope. As serious as the underground activity was the continuing effort of the P.K.I. to infiltrate some of the youth movements and the military, and to maintain a position of influence in the P.N.I.

Another significant avenue of approach the P.K.I. was still adopting was through the indigenous Chinese. Of the approximately three million Chinese in Indonesia, perhaps more than a million and a half had, by 1968, become Indonesian citizens and adopted Indonesian names; another million or so were classified as stateless, and a quarter-million held Chinese Communist papers. All had become the scapegoats under Suharto's New Order. Although they had proved themselves virtually indispensable as skilled workers, merchants, middlemen, and money-handlers, controlling somewhere between 30 and 40 percent of the national economy, they had been pilloried in the wake of the attempted coup because of Peking's suspected involvement in it. The attacks against them, both before and after the suspension of relations between Peking and Djakarta in October, 1967, represented a continuing emotional outlet for the pent-up tensions of the Indonesians, although they had generally accepted the presence of the Chinese in Indonesia as a commercial and financial necessity. It was undoubtedly this latent hostility, which goes back to colonial times and even earlier, as well as the fact that a considerable number of wealthy Chinese supported the Communists, that led to the murder of an estimated twenty thousand Chinese after the coup. In the months that followed, Chinese schools were closed and harsh measures were taken, notably in populous and poverty-stricken East Java, to restrict Chinese influence in business. Chinese nationals and stateless Chinese were banned from trade above the retail level and forbidden to change their place of residence or to communicate with each other in Chinese when doing business; they were forced to register all their personal property, including even such things as kitchen utensils, and they were subject in some areas to special head taxes and exorbitant payments for licenses, utilities, etc. In parts of East Java and Sumatra, and later in Djakarta, they were physically attacked and their homes and business establishments were looted. By the end of 1968 about seventy thousand had voluntarily left the country; another four thousand had been repatriated to China by the Peking government, and sixteen thousand more had registered for repatriation but were still awaiting transportation. Thousands of others had drifted to the cities, leaving their village shops boarded up or in the hands of Indonesian friends.

The break in diplomatic relations between Djakarta and Peking, which was probably inevitable, took place in a nasty fashion following outbreaks of violence in Djakarta in April, 1967, when a Chinese resident known as a pro-Peking Communist, who had been arrested for disseminating pamphlets, committed suicide in jail. Chinese official protests and a mass funeral demonstration by pro-Communist Chinese led to student assaults on the Chinese Embassy, during which some members of the staff there were injured. The Chinese retaliated by making life miserable for the Indonesian diplomats in Peking. Finally, an exchange of diplomatic personnel was arranged, and relations, as Foreign Minister Malik put it, became "frozen." Anti-Chinese demonstrations and riots continued, however, and became serious again in Djakarta in January, 1968, when Chinese shops were ransacked and their owners beaten after the killing of an Indonesian soldier by a group of local Chinese. Thanks largely to Malik, attempts were then made, with Suharto's approval, to formulate some compromise regulations whereby the Chinese would be allowed to resume a role in Indonesian life, although it was largely restricted to the area of retail trade. Although Malik and his liberal friends were aware of the dangers of fresh Chinese Communist political and economic penetration, and warned against it, they were equally aware that Indonesia needed the talents and money of the Chinese, and they remembered the void that had been created in 1960-61 when some 120,000 Chinese fled abroad during a similar period of persecution.

As Malik summed it up when I saw him, "The answer is not to crush the Chinese but to curb their illegal activities, separate the loyal from the disloyal, and allow those who are loyal, even if stateless, to go into business with Indonesians, or even on their own."

The tense situation vis-à-vis the local Chinese was obviously made to order for the P.K.I. There were several cases reported throughout the archipelago of Chinese Communist "patriotic" bands and "revolutionary committees" taking part in the new underground movement, and even of Chinese Communist officers leading them. One group of Chinese captured in the mountains of West Java had military radios and weapons with them. The most serious situation existed in Kalimantan. Here several thousand armed men of the Sarawak People's Guerrilla Force (P.G.R.S.), supported by another thousand guerrillas of the North Kalimantan People's Troops, carried on a rebellion in classic guerrilla surroundings—an unmapped jungle area where there were few roads and only scattered Dyak villages. Nearly seven thousand government troops, including elements of the Army, Navy, Air Force, and police, as well as some crack paratroopers, were committed to the area during 1967 and 1968 in what threatened to become more than just a thorn in Djakarta's side. The P.K.I., aided by other left-wing elements, including some disaffected servicemen, was directing the guerrilla effort, which apparently had Peking's support; there were some reports of Chinese arms smuggled to the guerrillas across the border dividing Kalimantan from Sarawak. This border area had been the scene of the major confrontation between Indonesia and Malaysia between 1963 and 1965. Sukarno ordered the local Indonesian commanders to train about eight hundred Kalimantan guerrillas to take part in that conflict, and when Suharto's New Order ended the confrontation, in mid-1966, about half of them disappeared with their weapons and joined the P.G.R.S. Almost all of them were either Chinese or of mixed blood, and they were joined by other Kalimantan Chinese after July, 1967, when the guerrillas, some of whom carried Mao Tse-tung's little red book of *Thoughts* and wore Mao badges, attacked an Indonesian air base, killed four Air Force men, and wounded several others while making off with 150 semiautomatic weapons.

At first the guerrillas had the support of the local Dyak tribesmen, but after some roving bands of P.G.R.S. men killed twelve Dyaks in raids on villages in west Kalimantan in September, 1967, the tribesmen switched sides. The Dyaks were once headhunters, and their chief weapons are large swords. Reverting to their primitive customs, they went from village to village carrying bowls of pig's blood, a symbolic summons to action. During October and November an estimated five hundred Chinese were murdered by the frenzied Dyaks, who had filled themselves with rice wine, smeared their faces with chicken blood, and gone about beheading Chinese villagers. The headhunting later subsided, but more than fifty thousand Chinese meanwhile fled the interior and sought refuge in coastal cities. With the help of Dyak guides, the government, by the fall of 1968, had killed about five hundred guerrillas, while another three thousand had surrendered or been arrested, including a Chinese described as the Communist commander of the guerrilla operation. The Indonesians obtained the cooperation of the Malaysians, and some of the antiguerrilla units were supplied by air from Kuching, in Sarawak, but logistics problems complicated the campaign. Most of the operations were conducted in high grass or jungle country, where, once on the ground, the Indonesian forces had to forage for themselves in competition with the guerrillas, who knew the area better and frequently laid successful ambushes. There was some contact between the guerrillas and the P.K.I. underground in East Java, and, although by 1969 the backbone of the Kalimantan insurgency had been broken, it was feared that, depending on other political and economic factors, the struggle could be renewed and become a prelude to the P.K.I.'s resurgence in the outer islands as well as in Java.

"Unity in Diversity," in Sukarno's words, had all along been one of the principal themes of the Indonesian revolution, but, to repeat, there seemed a serious question as to whether any permanent unity could be achieved in the face of Indonesia's regional differences. The Dyaks of Kalimantan and some of the wild tribes of West Irian—whose customs also included headhunting— were as far removed from the highly intelligent Batak tribesmen of Central Sumatra as from the Western-educated social scientists and economists in Djakarta. Similarly, the ignorant Javanese peasant, locked in his tiny Muslim village orbit, remained oblivious of the cosmopolitan ferment among the urban-educated students who believed in a socialist society and who wanted to see men like Malik become the future leaders of the country. The chances of synthesizing all these differences were at best problematical. Certainly any solution would have to take into account the special circumstances and conditions that obtained among the many islands and regions, and, in addition to acknowledging the growing demand for more autonomy or self-expression, would in effect, have to reverse Sukarno's slogan and demonstrate that "diversity within unity" was feasible.

In Sulawesi, for example, the crab-shaped island of the Celebes group that lies northeast of Java and east of Kalimantan, the matter of religious variations had become extremely important. The ten million people of the island are known for their independence of mind and action—many of them took part in the separatist rebellion a decade ago—and they were now collectively determined to gain more autonomy for themselves, particularly in developing their economic potential and in trading on their own with the Philippines and other Southeast Asian countries. In contrast to Java, where the population was seven times as large, there was plenty of land for everyone in Sulawesi. The island produced copra, spices, and lumber, and had a surplus of rice, but what it lacked, along with the rest of Indonesia, was transportation facilities, especially ships. It was also rich in minerals—the International Nickel Company, Ltd., of Canada, had successfully signed a multi-million-dollar contract in 1968 to develop some large nickel deposits. Politically, however, under the New Order, the island, like the rest of Indonesia, quickly found itself in a state of ferment, and the underground Communists sought to take advantage of this by stirring up separatist sentiment. The city of Menado, in the north, remained virtually isolated from the rest of the country; a plane came once a week from Djakarta, and a ship came perhaps once a month. A largely Christian community of 200,000 people, Menado retained a frontier look and atmosphere, enhanced by its reputation as a center for smuggling. The Army and police were resented for profiteering in this illegal trade, conducted mostly with the Philippines, and the Javanese were resented for their domination of the Civil Service.

If Djakarta failed to respond to the Sulawesis' demands for self-expression, the submerged P.K.I. and left-wing P.N.I. elements were likely to continue to cause trouble. Furthermore, a religious conflict existed in the south, where the recent growth in influence of the Catholics and Protestants threatened the domination of the Muslims and was especially resented by the fanatic elements that used to support the right-wing Darul Islam. In October, 1967, in Makassar, when a Christian teacher made some slurring remarks about Mohammed's being an adulterer, a Muslim newspaper printed what he had said, and within hours Muslim rioters attacked nineteen Protestant and Catholic churches, damaging six of them severely. One of the more wholesome aspects of the Sukarno regime had been its encouragement of religious tolerance, and the Makassar outbreak, the first of its kind anywhere in Indonesia in many years, caused a national sensation. There was some evidence that the incident may have been provoked by the Communists, but whether it was or not, it also reflected a growing Muslim unrest over the inroads of Christianity. There was a fear on the part of the Christians that, despite Islam's official tolerance toward other religions, the Muslim leaders might foment a national anti-Christian campaign; for this reason, the Christians, though politically conservative, tended to support the efforts of the secular nationalists in the P.N.I. to reform the party. After the disturbances, which fortunately soon subsided, a nationwide interreligious conference was summoned in Djakarta, but it was not particularly successful. The Christians argued for their right to spread the gospel and to proselytize, rights guaranteed in the Indonesian Constitution. However, the Muslims' attitude of tolerance tended not to go that far, and the conference broke up without a compromise being reached.

On the picturesque nearby island of Bali, religion was a less definable factor. The two million Balinese were still predominantly nonpracticing Hindus who nevertheless had come to accept the ceremonial and social rituals of Hinduism and the strictures of the Hindu class hierarchy. Although basically tolerant, the Balinese could be whipped to a frenzy, as happened after the coup, when the killing there had been greater in relation to the size of the population than it was anywhere else. Margaret Mead once described the Balinese as "schizophrenic"; having lived under feudal conditions and resisted change for centuries—they were not colonized by the Dutch until the end of the imperial era—they tended to become psychopathic when exposed too suddenly to the hazards of modern politics. The special impact of Sukarno was another factor. His mother was born in Bali, and his frequent visits to the island provided the population with a new and dynamic living myth. It was not surprising that the P.K.I. and the P.N.I. gained easy adherents among the susceptible population with vague promises of pie in the sky. Nor was it surprising that the Balinese subsequently reacted with religious fervor to the Army's signal to exterminate the P.K.I. The P.N.I. was more fortunate. Most of the Balinese, largely because of Sukarno, were pro-P.N.I., and the party in 1968 was still the strongest on the island, although it was in turmoil, as it was elsewhere, and was still subject to strong left-wing influence. Though there was no strong Muslim influence in Bali and only a small percentage of Christians, the island needed to be developed for something more than tourism if the post-Sukarno void was to be filled. What it needed most of all, as people there emphasized to me, was to be brought rationally into the modern world—by education and the opportunity to work for a living. It had no electricity (except in a few places such as the plush Bali Hotel, run by Pan American Airways) and only a handful of small factories, making such things as soap and cigarettes. In December, 1967, there were signs of progress when the governors of the islands of east Indonesia met in Bali with a group of top Djakarta officials to work out a new system of taxing trade, which would replace the graft that was going to local officials, and to try to arrange for more and better shipping, which Suharto promised. The conference ended with the announcement of a new interisland policy of *Koordinasi* (cooperation), Integration, Synchronization, and Simplification—or KISS, for short, which the romantic Balinese considered wholly appropriate.

One step toward greater self-sufficiency was taken during 1967 when Djakarta agreed to let the regional governments retain an automatic 10 percent of all their export revenues (in the case of most products the individual exporter kept 75 percent of the income in foreign currency, while the central government got 15 percent). This new regulation, and new agreements to conduct barter trade with Singapore and Malaysia which cut down on smuggling, particularly helped the big island of Sumatra, which was responsible for nearly two-thirds of Indonesia's exports, mostly rubber, tea, palm oil, and crude oil. A thousand miles long and nearly 170,000 square miles in area, with a population of twenty-two million, Sumatra is the third-largest island in the archipelago, after West Irian and Kalimantan, yet not only had it been far more developed than the other two politically and economically over the last twenty years, but there was now the opportunity for much more development. Sumatra's relatively small population consisted of various tribal people—some of whom, like the Bataks, were very sophisticated—and of independent-minded Muslims who had less of a strong Hindu and mystic influence to contend with than the Muslims in Java. The Sumatrans had remained aloof from and suspicious of the Javanese; they had sporadically rebelled, survived, and prospered, but they had never felt that they were allowed to attain an identity of their own, within the larger and still undefined Indonesian identity. A number of Sumatrans, among them General Nasution and Adam Malik, had risen to positions of prominence in the central power structure and the bureaucracy, but the island as a whole had always been regarded by the Javanese as a lush possession more or less inherited from the Dutch, and the subjugation of the separatist revolt of 1958-59 had encouraged this attitude of superiority.

The issue of militarism in the New Order seemed more likely to be tested in Sumatra than anywhere else. Since 1965 the Army's record in Sumatra had been both good and bad. Under two top officers, first General Achmad Junus Mokoginta and then General Kusno Utomo, the emphasis was being placed on rebuilding Sumatra's communications, which had been in a state of collapse since the departure of the Dutch. The road system had slowly disintegrated and the harbors were full of silt or of the wrecks of ships left over from the Second World War or from the separatist revolt. Progress at first lagged on the Mokoginta Plan, or Operation Hope, as the reconstruction program came to be called, because money was not forthcoming from Java, but some funds were made available in 1967, and arrangements were also made for the seven Sumatran regions to contribute a share of their export profits. General Mokoginta's original aim was to bring the road system back to its 1952 condition and then to concentrate on getting the dilapidated harbors, inland waterways, power plants, and railways back into shape. Although it was agreed that Mokoginta was doing an excellent job, there was a suspicion in Djakarta that he was also building an empire of his own, and late in 1967 he was dispatched to Cairo as Indonesian Ambassador. Under his successor, General Utomo, the job of renovating essential facilities and of getting the tea, rubber, and copra plantations operating again continued, but the Sumatrans became increasingly suspicious of the military's long-term aims.

More than anywhere else in Indonesia, the Army and the other service branches in Sumatra injected themselves into every sort of activity, from running the plantations to collecting a head tax from every passenger who flew out of Medan (a sergeant in charge set these payments on the basis of his own scrutiny of each passenger). Each service branch had established what amounted to its own trading company, which drained the still shaky economy of between 10 and 20 percent of its profits. The Army dealt in rubber, for example, taking a certain amount of the raw product from the estates at a lower than market price, transporting it in Army vehicles, and making its own marketing arrangements through its own banks and intermediaries. The Navy engaged in smuggling and general export trade, while the police dealt in miscellaneous merchandise. Each service also had its own warehouses, where it stored goods coming in as well as going out for a price, selling licenses and "protection" to ordinary merchants. More than corruption and influence were involved in all this: the service forces, especially the Army, argued that such economic activity was the only way they could get enough money to support their men, who couldn't live on the equivalent of a few-dollars-a-month pay, and that they also had to build up "welfare funds" for future veterans. Many demobilized officers, as well as some still on active duty, were acting as overseers or managers of the estates. The bigger estates, mostly producing rubber and palm oil, were gradually being returned to their former foreign owners under complicated new arrangements worked out in Djakarta, but the foreigners generally accepted the military's continuing management role and were glad of the protection of some guns. Incidents of soldiers barging into shops, especially Chinese-owned ones, and demanding pay-offs or free goods gradually diminished, but they still occurred.

The Chinese situation in Sumatra remained critical. Of more

than ten thousand who had registered for repatriation to China, less than half had left by the end of 1968, because Peking had been slow in sending ships to take them away; the remainder, as well as others who had not registered but also wanted to go back to China, were languishing in camps set up by the Army. In Sumatra, too, as in Sulawesi, there was trouble between the Christians and the Muslims, and since quite a number of Chinese had turned Protestant or Catholic to avoid further persecution, the Chinese question had aspects of both anti-Communist and anti-Christian feeling. A soldier with a gun still had more leverage than anyone else in Sumatra. Civilians complained of having to do things the Army's way or not at all. Many resented the Army's usurpation and its refusal to consult them on economic matters, or to bring them into long-range planning councils. "The military have a vested interest in everything," a university economist told me. "They could achieve more by asking our advice, but they don't."

Politically, Sumatra was still in a state of confusion that threatened to become explosive. The uncertainty mostly revolved around the question of the P.N.I.'s future. As in East Java, a considerable element in the P.N.I. in the island cooperated with the P.K.I. and other radical groups in the past. After the military rooted out these elements, many of the P.N.I. branches were ordered to be disbanded by the Army commanders. Then, in December, 1967, Suharto issued his order for the party to "crystallize" itself. Many Sumatrans, especially students and other action or functional groups, felt that this would be impossible, particularly since the party was already in a stage of disintegration. Suharto, on the other hand, felt that a complete break-up of the P.N.I. in Sumatra might provoke a resurgence of the old Muslim groups with separatist ambitions. The majority of Sumatrans were generally fed up with the performance of all the old parties, and, if anything, there was a general feeling that fresh elements, such as the P.M.I., the new modernist Muslim party, and a possible new secular party, would have a better chance of standing up against the rising influence of the Army. Though reluctant to give the green light to such developments, Suharto proved sensitive to this anti-Army sentiment. In mid-1968, he transferred General Sarwo Edhy, who had been serving as military chief of the key North Sumatra area, to West Irian. Edhy had done a good job but, like Mokoginta, had become too independent and powerful, and he was strongly against any and all political parties. (His talents as a commander were soon applied to deal with the touchy situation in West Irian, where tribesmen, to some extent fed by Communist propaganda, were giving the Indonesians trouble. Edhy got most of the tribal rebels to surrender under amnesty or killed them. Under the terms of the long-scheduled plebiscite due to be held in 1969, 700,000 people of this large and backward island would decide whether they wanted to be part of Indonesia or not. Edhy's pacification, and Indonesia's willingness to develop the island with the help of the United Nations, was expected to keep West Irian in the Indonesian republic.)

Sumatra is an anthropologist's (as well as a zoologist's) dream, and it is full of anachronisms, including human ones. Several months before his death, in 1968, I spent a delightful hour talking with a gentleman who bore the title of the Sultan of Deli, in his broken-down palace on the outskirts of Medan. The palace, a rambling brown wooden building with an endless veranda, resembled a run-down borscht-circuit hotel. It was built in 1888 by the Sultan's grandfather. The contemporary Sultan—he was the last one to be recognized by the central government and there will be no official successor—was a bent man of sixty-eight who wore a loose brown native suit; he was the titular leader of a Mogul Indian family that had its origin in Delhi and had re-established itself three hundred years ago in Atjeh, in Central Sumatra. His unofficial "realm" was now only a portion of what it once had been, but he was philosophic about the sultanate coming to an end. "Why not?" he said. "I have no power anyway." He had been married ten times, he told me proudly, and had had six daughters and four commoner sons, who occasionally visited him, but for the most part he and his present wife lived alone in the vast and empty palace, served by a skeleton staff of ten. He said he was an avid reader of contemporary magazines and newspapers and that he spent a good deal of his time listening to music—as we talked the strains of rock and roll from a radio somewhere inside wafted through the high-ceilinged rooms. The Sultan obviously was lonely and welcomed the chance to talk to someone.

"I'm a federalist," he said. "Twenty-one years of mismanagement under Sukarno have got us nowhere. He was nothing but an orator. Napoleon knew how to pick people to help him, but Sukarno never did. He was an able man, but his trouble was that he wanted to run all of Southeast Asia without putting his own house in order first. I don't believe in revolutions anyway. They're never won and there's no end to them. I'm really feudal and old-fashioned, though I believe in social welfare and social justice, but not in Socialism. You can't be a Muslim and a Marxist at the same time. I don't have many political friends left. General Mokoginta, who was also a prince, you know, of a Sulawesi line, came to visit me once. I liked him. I have to depend on the government to support me now, which is why everything is so run-down. Still, my sons are doing well. In my youth I played soccer and rode horses. I was brought up by a Dutch family in Djakarta, and I had to learn Dutch, English, German, and French. I visited Europe last in 1947, when Queen Wilhelmina was still alive. Terrible winter, 1947. Of all the seasons, I like spring best. I like Europe. The French are very amiable. The English are nice, but they are too gentlemanly—after six glasses of champagne they're still gentlemen. The Germans are too military, but I like German music and Viennese. I hope before I die to get to America. I have many American friends, former businessmen here in Sumatra. I like to read a lot about a country before I go there. What do you think of the moon? Do you think you or the Russians will get there first?"

The New Order Emerges

During a Cabinet meeting in December, 1967, the ordinarily undramatic President Suharto predicted that "the year 1968 may be the year of final hope or the year of the limit of patience of people who have almost lost it." Shortly before Suharto made this observation, he had startled—and momentarily disarmed—a group of student demonstrators who had marched on his office to protest the soaring prices of rice and other commodities by telling them, "I am the one who is responsible for the situation in this country. I am responsible for everything." Whether consciously or unconsciously, Suharto, who had taken to wearing civilian suits or modest tunic-style outfits instead of his general's uniform, had simultaneously evoked the past and sharply distinguished it from the present. His rare use of the personal pronoun, particularly in such a manner, was anachronistically reminiscent of the Sukarno era, when Bapak (Father) Sukarno had constantly and self-glorifyingly proclaimed his responsibility for guiding the destinies of the country by his own revolutionary vision and intuition. Yet, in Suharto's terms and tone, the usage was altogether different. Although some Indonesians had begun to call him "Bapak," or "Pak," Harto, there was something more avuncular than paternal about Indonesia's new leader. Forty-seven years old in 1968, the son of a poor peasant from a suburb of Jogjakarta, he had become a successfully pragmatic soldier-statesman almost by accident. After joining the Army at the age of nineteen, he had risen steadily but unspectacularly through the ranks, first under the Dutch and then with the new Republican Army. His outstanding performances had been as a battalion commander in Jogjakarta during the fight against the Dutch and as a coordinator of the West Irian campaign in 1961-62. When he emerged as the nation's leader after the failure of the coup, it was doubtful that more than a relative handful of Indonesians even knew his name. And even then he chose to stay out of the limelight as much as he could, continuing to live quietly in Djakarta with his wife and his children in an Army villa. Although he subsequently expanded his residence by acquiring some adjacent property, he maintained his modest way of life, using Merdeka Palace only for official ceremonies.

Gradually, however, as he gained confidence in his own abilities, and particularly after he finally solved the Sukarno problem in his own slow Javanese way, his stature perceptibly increased. The respect in which he was held not only was a tribute to his honesty and good intentions—it became the bedrock of the people's faith that he was the country's best hope. This faith was demonstrated when Congress elevated him from Acting President to President early in 1968 and at the same time continued his emergency powers, which were designed, among other things, to wipe out corruption and inefficiency in government agencies and within the military itself. The gulf between the military and the people had, if anything, become wider since the final elimination of Sukarno as military men continued to dominate the administrative apparatus of the country, as well as many business activities, and it was perhaps with this in mind that Congress retained the right to supervise the emergency powers, which also gave Suharto a free hand to foil any fresh efforts by the Communists to create new disturbances and prepare the way for a comeback. To achieve the objectives set forth by Congress, and particularly to deal with the resurgent attempts of the Communist underground in the poorer sections of East and Central Java and on Kalimantan, Suharto necessarily had to depend on the military, which remained the most strongly organized element in the nation. At the same time, he was fully aware, as his remark about the limit of the people's patience had shown, that there was still a widespread feeling of discontent in the country. The common sentiment that not enough had been done quickly enough was evinced by the student demonstrations that continued sporadically in Djakarta, Bandung, and elsewhere, and which were precipitated by the shortage of rice and the fresh wave of price rises late in 1967 and early in 1968.

As a moderate and cautious man by habit and instinct, Suharto became increasingly aware, too, that his success in dealing with Indonesia's multiple problems largely depended on his ability to achieve a better balance between the group of civilian managerial experts and the military. During 1968 he set about doing this. Not only did he give civilians the key jobs in the new Development Cabinet chosen in mid-year—only six of its twenty-three members were military men—but he abolished his private staff, known as SPRI, which downgraded the influence of officers in a position to hand out favors on a personal basis. As the civilian-military partnership grew, and as ordinary government agencies assumed a stronger role, Suharto also gave more of his personal attention to straightening out the military bureaucracy and its spheres of power. He eliminated or curtailed the nonmilitary functions of his service chiefs, except where special circumstances obtained, as in East Java, and took important new steps to clean up the remnants of Sukarnoism in the branches of the armed forces that had been most reluctant to cleanse themselves. This notably included the police, which became a unified element under an efficient officer, General Hugeng, for the first time since Indonesian independence.

The effect of this slow process of establishing more orderly procedures in the government apparatus was manifest in many ways, visible and invisible. No longer, for example, were business deals made under the table as a result of pay-offs to members of SPRI or other officers and officials close to the seat of power. The improvement in implementing legal methods of doing things created greater confidence among both Indonesian and foreign businessmen. To be sure, there were still many problems, notably the overall inefficiency of the top-heavy bureaucracy; in some government agencies more than half the employees were told to stay home, which meant they would still be paid but could try to find other jobs and those who did come to work too often failed to buckle down and improve their slovenly work habits. This was, ironically, the case, for instance, in the ministry specifically charged with improving the government apparatus, where a thousand employees remained at home and the four hundred who reported for work did little or nothing to overhaul their own apparatus, let alone that of other creaky ministries. The improvements that took place at the top, however, had a salutary effect in stabilizing relations between Indonesian officials and foreign embassies, especially those seeking to assist in the nation's recovery—the American Embassy in particular. In the months just after the coup, Ambassador Green had hardly been able to see Suharto because the small, tight group around him had kept Green away. Green did manage to establish quiet and steady contact with men like Foreign Minister Malik and General Nasution, but it was not until mid-1967 that he had his first successful meeting with Suharto, an intimate and frank four-hour session, and it was not until the abolition of SPRI that full freedom of association became possible. Thereafter, American diplomats and others were able to deal openly and even bluntly with members of Suharto's Cabinet and with his special advisers, as well as with all government agencies.

On the political front, Suharto showed himself reluctant to move ahead more forcefully for fear that this would endanger the balance of the new military-civilian government he was seeking to create. As one experienced Indonesian observer put it, while praising the fiscal, economic, and administrative reforms Suharto had initiated, "Our ultimate national renaissance, in psychological and political terms, can only come from Pak Harto, too. Only he can open the door for new faces, but he's not doing it, and the result is that there is still a vacuum that could become dangerous. If it is not filled in a rational fashion, and if economic conditions do not improve quickly enough and jobs are not found for the many unemployed and underemployed, the Communists and the radical Muslims could still attract the large floating groups whose political loyalties remain uncertain and who don't see much practical difference as yet between the Old Order and the New Order."

There were some attempts to renovate the political structure by what was called a "refreshing" of the Parliament and of the larger policy-making Congress of which it was part. This effort, carried out under the government's supervision during 1967 and 1968 by the eight post-Sukarno legal political parties and the various so-called "functional groups" of students, women, intellectuals, etc., and the military—which remained the largest of these groups —involved the elimination of some lingering Sukarnoist elements and other deadwood and the substitution of "cleaner" elements for them. The process resulted in the enlargement of Parliament by the addition of sixty-seven new members appointed by Suharto, including thirty-two military men. This brought the total membership of Parliament to 414, while that of Congress—the M.P.R.S.— which by law must be twice as big, rose proportionately to 828. All this took longer, and proved more difficult and painful, than was expected, and the difficulties were increased by the uncertainty and confusion that marked the prolonged removal of Sukarno from the political scene and by the continued economic and inflationary crisis that contributed so heavily to the lack of national and social confidence.

The "refreshing" procedure actually was an additional factor in holding back new political developments, and it accounted for the fact that it was not until the spring of 1968 that Suharto gave his belated permission for the "modernist" Moslem party, the P.M.I., to launch itself officially as a counterforce to the older, more conservative Nahdatul Ulama. There remained considerable dissatisfaction among the mass of Muslims, who, of varying degrees of orthodoxy or of more nominal belief and practice, felt that they had been neglected by the New Order and had not been given Cabinet and other jobs commensurate with their strength and numbers—about 90 percent of Indonesia's population is still Muslim. In point of fact, Suharto's reluctance to hand out more jobs to Muslim political hacks was justified, since, with rare exceptions, they were solely interested in money and power. His suspicions, however, went much further than that, for essentially he had no faith in political parties, at least as they existed in the light of their historical development. He could not ignore them, but he was determined to let them lie fallow while he maintained the priority of economic recovery and of creating the new managerial balance he sought between civilian experts and the military that he felt could alone, for the time being, provide stability. Democratic institutions in Indonesia had to be strengthened first, Suharto believed, and people's lives improved; after that, political stabilization would be possible, and political parties with specific programs would be able to operate on higher ground and cease being just self-serving cliques.

Both the Muslims and the old-line P.N.I., on the other hand, saw themselves, with equal justification, as being involved in a race against time to survive. The Muslims were also upset by the still unresolved discussion at the March, 1968, meeting of Congress over human rights, specifically over the issue of whether changing one's religion should officially be declared such a right. While fully aware that the Protestants and Catholics had been gathering converts and political strength, partly as a result of financially well-backed missionaries in the country, the Muslims objected to having the right to conversion formalized by law. Despite their large numbers, they felt themselves increasingly isolated politically under Suharto's rule, and, with their power being chipped away at, their rising discontent conceivably could stir the more conservative among them to take radical action. Thus, with a disgruntled Muslim element on the right and the still functioning Communist underground on the left, there remained two potential poles of attraction for the millions of Indonesians who felt themselves caught in the post-Sukarno vacuum. As Soedjatmoko commented during one of the many conversations I had with him, "Much of our political trouble today stems from the fact that there was really no idea of where the country should go after independence. What took place was a struggle for spoils rather than a formulation of new directions and goals. The parties simply became little oligarchies contesting for leadership, and the consequent crisis of nonresponsibility paved the way for Sukarno and Guided Democracy. Unfortunately, the experience under Sukarno does not seem to have sobered the old parties much. They seem primarily to be dreaming of an early restoration of their full 'rights.' One danger is that they will push too hard and that the Army will strike back and push them aside."

Suharto himself was fully aware that there existed in the Army a strong sentiment to do just that. Men such as Sarwo Edhy, if they had their way, would have done away with all parties, officially, and established at least a quasi-permanent Army rule, ostensibly benevolent but practically dangerous. Other generals, such as Dharsono in West Java, basically approved of what Suharto was doing but were perhaps more aware than he of the need to have political developments parallel economic improvements under the Army's aegis (the fact that Dharsono and other "liberal" generals were said to be out of favor early in 1969 was another sign that Suharto still wanted to move ahead slowly politically). Still others were perfectly content to have things go along just as they were, and herein, amid the current contest among the old parties, the new political elements, and the Army, lay the danger of the military's further expanding its influence, of "Parkinsonizing" itself indefinitely and thereby adding a new parallel structure to the already top-heavy civil bureaucracy. This was the cause of the rising apprehension of the students and other civilian elements who were eager to have the New Order prove that it was really new. There was no doubt that, despite Suharto's good intentions, and despite his constant disavowal of any desire to create a military dictatorship, a good many military men throughout the country as well as the center were still intent on carefully consolidating their own positions.

In his 1967 Independence Day address to Parliament, in which he dryly and rather dully set forth the still unrealized objectives of the New Order and defended the ostensibly modest and patriotic aims of the military during what he insisted was just an interregnum, Suharto maintained that the Army was temporarily fulfilling a dual role "as an instrument of the state and as a functional group." But this reference to the Army as a functional group came as a not very reassuring reminder of what had been an important element of Sukarno's Old Order, and Suharto's subsequent permission for military men to participate in politics not as members of parties but as functional-group representatives did little to allay the growing suspicion that the Army was in politics to stay.

Too many Indonesians recalled that Sukarno invented the device of functional groups mainly to give special governmental representation to elements such as labor and the students, but that in fact he had ended up using them, as he had so candidly expressed it, to "bury" the political parties and to control the legislative machine as he wished. The groups that had remained or been added to the list since Sukarno's fall were, with the exception of the Army, weak and amorphous. It was true that they served some useful purpose in provoking discussion of important issues and, in time, they might become significant forces. The students and their allies, for example, had been given a chance through the functional-group arrangement to express their views as members of the "Generation of 1966" as opposed to the older revolutionary Generation of 1945, which, while it included some leaders of the New Order such as General Nasution, was still thoroughly identified with the Sukarno period. For the time being, too, the new Development Movement of Socialist and Nationalist intellectuals, harboring its hopes of eventually replacing the P.N.I. as the leading secular element, had the status of a functional group. Most of the other groups in Parliament and in Congress, however, were so thoroughly engaged in the process of ridding themselves of their Old Order stigma that their capacity for imaginative and projective political activity was limited.

Suharto, with his peculiar Javanese political antenna, seemed aware of the problem of the other functional groups and at the same time defensive in his efforts to explain the Army's new role. In assessing the military's position as the major functional group— and, though he did not say so, as by far the strongest political force in the country—he said, in the 1967 address, "The role taken by the armed services is not due to their thirst for power. If [they] were out for power, they could have achieved it on October 1, 1965 . . . when there was panic and a vacuum in government. . . . There has been no desire on the part of the services to increase the application of military law to set aside human rights and the democratic rights of the people. . . . The armed services do not intend at all to monopolize any positions in the government. . . ." This defense of the military's role, which Suharto afterward repeated on several other occasions, was received politely and respectfully, but it still did not remove the suspicion that the officers around him, and their colleagues and friends throughout the country, would seek to maintain their dominance of every phase of daily life—and to profit therefrom. This suspicion was inevitably reinforced by the long delays in defining the ground rules for reorganizing Parliament and Congress, and in writing new laws for holding the next elections and for the conduct and operation of political parties—at the end of 1968 those laws were still being debated. Further suspicion was engendered by the rising importance of General Ali Murtopo, Suharto's top political adviser, who believed firmly in restraints on political development.

Despite the impact that the cleavages and conflicts of the past have had on the New Order, and despite the conflicts that remain between Djakarta and the various regions and among the various ethnic groups, Soedjatmoko has said that because nationalism "retains its integrative force, it is almost certain that whatever problems still exist will be solved or accommodated within the framework of the unitary state of Indonesia." But he has qualified this with the observation that the problem of building a stable and effective political system "turns on our ability to bring about a relatively stable and effective coalition between elements of the Islamic community and those groups which are openly committed to a secular state—the nationalists, the Socialists, and the Christians." The relatively "low level of tolerable disagreement and conflict in Indonesian society" may prove to be its greatest blessing, he has emphasized, since no one political group can attempt to assert total dominance without tremendous resistance from the others— as the Communists found out.

Virtually everyone was in agreement in 1968 that no political system could achieve stability without an expanding economy. A principal early criticism of the New Order's economic program was that it concentrated too much on conservative fiscal policy and not enough on overhauling the administrative and banking structures in order to stimulate production. Part of this was based on the convictions of Suharto, his academic brain trust, and experts from the International Monetary Fund that the country's financial position was so dreadful in 1966 that all efforts had to be concentrated on creating some degree of solvency. But a year later a European diplomat well versed in economics put it this way: "The Indonesians have used very drastic fiscal measures, including tight credit facilities and a relative minimum of new rupiahs injected into the economy, in order to try to balance the budget and hold down inflation. In the beginning this was fully justified, but they should have switched more rapidly thereafter to a policy of economic expansion. If I were to coin a slogan for this country it would be one word—'production.' In a developing country you cannot expect to balance the budget. If you do, it leads to stagnation."

This criticism seemed valid in view of economic conditions throughout Indonesia. Most factories were producing at between a third and a half of their capacity, if they were functioning at all, and the immediate prospects of significant improvement, beyond emergency measures to get the textile mills operating soon, were slight. In 1968 the prospects had increased somewhat, but textile owners were still complaining about favoritism to foreign concerns. Even if raw materials could be imported, the decay and destruction of the nation's transportation and communications facilities, and the shortage of trained technicians, would make it impossible, they maintained, to get the industrial wheels turning again in a hurry, unless the government undertook an all-out mobilization of existing production equipment already mounted in the country's factories.

The nation's bankrupt condition, and the reluctance of the rest of the world to give Indonesia enough financial aid to enable a rapid production drive, was another major factor. In 1967 and 1968 foreign financial and commodity assistance from a consortium of nine nations, headed by the United States and Japan, had been essentially just enough to help Indonesia pay for necessary imports and achieve some improvement in the flow of exports while keeping the country's balance-of-payments and budget deficits within bounds. In 1967 the total amount of foreign aid was $212 million, and in 1968, including contributions from the International Monetary Fund and the World Bank, it reached $400 million. The nine-nation consortium pledged $500 million for 1969. Some foreign experts who had studied the problem estimated that an advance pledge of $500 million for several years to come would alone allow Indonesia to achieve the desired financial objectives and at the same time enable a faster take-off in production. These experts felt that the international consortium members had perhaps been guilty of letting political considerations outweigh economic realities; by wanting to make sure that the New Order meant business about putting its own fiscal house in order first, they may have risked new political calamities. A more sizable aid package from the outset would undoubtedly have helped Suharto deal with what he frequently referred to as one of his main problems—the transformation of passive public and private institutions into more vigorous instruments of social action. In drawing attention to the problem, Guy Pauker, who had studied economic conditions in Indonesia for many years, found it "difficult to explain why the level of expenditure considered appropriate for Indonesia (by the United States) must be restricted to less than one-half of one percent of the cost of our security expenditures on the mainland of Southeast Asia." Were it not for the Vietnam war, the United States would probably have been willing to give far more toward Indonesia's recovery, but, as things stood, Congressional cuts in foreign aid probably had hurt and would continue to hurt Indonesia more than any other major country.

Another reason for the reluctance of the foreign nations as a group to be more generous was the existence of the $2.5 billion in foreign debts. The government was still trying, late in 1968, to obtain long-term postponements from its many creditors, but whatever arrangements it might eventually make to extend the repayments schedules over ten or twenty years, a good share of the national income for the foreseeable future, partly deriving from new grants and loans, would probably have to be used to pay off the old obligations incurred by Sukarno, who had used the money to build up his military machine for futile foreign adventures or to erect his chauvinistic show projects.

As a consequence of its limited recovery resources, Indonesia was constrained to deal almost exclusively with the problem of food production, aggravated as it was by its demographic chart: to keep pace with the rising population, the experts kept emphasizing, the production of food, especially of rice, had to increase faster than the birth rate. One of the results of the tight-money policy and the overemphasis on fiscal controls, most of the experts agreed, was that the unexpected drop in rice production due to drought was enough, at the end of 1967 and the beginning of 1968, to throw the whole economic picture out of kilter. Because of this, inflation, which was supposed to be held down to a 65 percent increase in

1967 (versus 665 percent in 1966), ended up 115 percent higher. This was still a big improvement, but the steep rise in the price of rice caused rises in other key commodities, too, and produced a near-panic situation that had political overtones, expressed in the new student demonstrations. Another factor was the persecution of the Chinese. Since they had traditionally handled so much of the nation's money and goods, their removal from these normal pursuits threw everything off balance. As the rupiah rate during 1967 rose from a relatively stable figure of about 140 to the dollar to more than 300 to one, the so-called Bonus Export rate, which represented foreign exchange sold by the government to traders at a rate determined solely by the normal market demand, also went way up and became a source of speculation and corruption. All of this helped retard the free flow of goods, which was the essential purpose of the new BE rate.

By its policy of fiscal stringency, the government almost succeeded in balancing its budget of 81 billion rupiahs in 1967, and it hoped to balance the 1968 budget of 97 billion rupiahs by, among other things, reducing military expenditures. Total national exports (including crude oil), which reached $770 million in 1967, an increase of 8 percent over the previous year, were expected to rise considerably more in 1968—they had reached nearly $600 million by the end of August. Oil production, in particular, was zooming. Caltex, the major oil producer, was putting out 450,000 barrels a day in the fall of 1968 versus 300,000 at the beginning of 1967, and the prospects for offshore exploration were good. It would be some time, however, before the development of other extractive industries would begin to show results. The improved tax system was also expected to bring in more income, though this, too, would take time. Like most other Asians, Indonesians had never paid many taxes. Direct taxes, including those on corporations, were expected to account for almost half of the 1968 budget —most of the rest was still dependent on foreign aid. It was hoped that income taxes in 1968 would be collected from 600,000 individuals, almost three times as many as in 1967. However, a number of critics, while commending the new tax aims, pointed out that the continued taxing of exporters would simply hold back the sector of the economy that most needed encouragement.

One of the unpleasant results of the tight-money policy in the first two years of the New Order, and of the continuation of an unsophisticated banking and credit system, was that the poor kept getting poorer and the rich richer. This was partly due to the fact that the government was by far the biggest urban employer, and that the government payroll accounted for two-thirds of budgetary expenditure. The inability of government employees to make ends meet was thus still a basic factor, despite some wage increases for civil servants, and this stimulated continuing unrest and dissatisfaction. Though inflation, by mid-1968, had dropped to a rate of 2 percent a month—from January to September it was half what it had been for 1967—the rupiah had slowly moved to 430 to the dollar, and prices, which went down somewhat after the 1967 year-end crisis, still showed more than a 50 percent increase by the end of the second quarter of 1968—in 1967 they rose 112 percent, and in 1966, 635 percent. Much of the new increase was due to Suharto's fearless effort to put the prices of major commodities realistically in line. In April, 1968, he simultaneously raised the costs of gas, electricity, kerosene, and transportation, all of which had been unrealistically low. This was a bold step that was undoubtedly necessary, and, in the words of one veteran foreign diplomat, "To me, that was the measure of the man—it showed he was ready to make more tough decisions on his own."

Nevertheless, prices of almost everything, including rice, still remained too high for the average wage-earner, who had to moonlight to get along. Rice remained the key, and here the outlook was better. The expectation in mid-year was that the 1968 target of 9.8 million domestically produced tons, an increase of 500,000 tons over 1967, would be surpassed by at least 200,000 tons. The government was making plans to assure a stock of 1.2 million tons in order to avoid another year-end crisis. Half of this was to come from domestic production and half was to be imported, mostly from Thailand and the United States, which also sent Indonesia some wheat and bulgar. Because of the six months' delay that took place in organizing the nine-nation 1968 aid package—the United States stubbornly refused to put up its one-third of the total until Japan did the same—there was some danger in the middle of the year that the necessary rice and wheat would not reach Indonesia in time to avoid another crisis, but by October it appeared that most of what was needed would get there before January, 1969, and if the 1968 rice crop in Indonesia proved to be as good as expected, the crisis would be passed anyway. By 1969, it was hoped, new rice strains developed at the International Rice Research Institute in the Philippines, plus improvements in irrigation and fertilizer distribution, would enable the nation to make large strides in domestic production and preclude permanently any danger of new shortages. A larger domestic crop would enable Indonesia to make important budgetary cuts in rice imports, which accounted for a fifth of the basic budget in 1968.

Nineteen sixty-nine was scheduled to be the first year of the government's carefully conceived Five-Year Development Program. The basic aim of the five-year plan was to double the nation's over-all rate of growth, from 3 to 6 percent. Food production was regarded as the continuing key to both recovery and growth, particularly in overcrowded and unproductive Java. One of the most interesting projects to increase rice production called for vast tidal-irrigation schemes to reclaim swampy areas in Borneo and Sumatra; once drained, and with acidity reduced, these areas were to be planted with new rice strains and then irrigated by high river tides as they backed up. Suharto and his aides planned to use demobilized Army men for this work, and then to settle these veterans in the new areas with their families. As the production of rice and other commodities rose, through such intensive use of labor, the increase of purchasing power on top of money saved by cutting down on food imports would, it was anticipated, enable the development of industry on a rational basis. At first, after the stimulation of textile production and the repair of basic transportation and communications facilities, the stress would be placed on those industries, such as the production of fertilizer and cement and plastics, that would further improve the agricultural sector and stimulate construction, particularly public housing. Subsequently, other sorts of construction and the mining industry would receive attention, and Indonesia's tremendous undeveloped wealth would be tapped.

As Suharto emphasized in his August, 1968, state address, all of this would take time and patience, but he sounded much more optimistic than he had at the end of 1967. "Next year is to be a period of transition, putting an end to the period of stabilization and rehabilitation," he said, "and we shall start with reconstruction in the real sense of the word." He added that the various regions, while justified in their desire to run their own reconstruction drives as much as possible, would have to adhere to the national plan, for reasons of manpower coordination, among others; they would particularly have to improve the economic condition of the estates, including the rubber, palm oil, copra, and tin plantations, which were still run-down through long neglect or abuse. One of the more encouraging signs was the return of foreign investors to Indonesia. By the end of 1968 nearly seventy had agreed to consider investing about $375 million in a variety of projects, mostly mineral developments, and had begun preliminary investigations. One of the largest was the exploratory investment in copper mining of the American Freeport Sulphur Company in West Irian. Although corruption in many areas of business remained a major problem, the fresh climate of opportunity had brought scores of interested corporations to Djakarta. Attractive incentives for investment, including two-to-five-year tax holidays and the right to repatriate profits, were being offered, though other features of the new foreign-capital investment law of 1967 were less encouraging. Nationalization could still take place "in the interest of the state," and permits for investment projects were good for only thirty years, though they could be renewed.

In stressing his aims of "stabilization, development and reconstruction," Suharto let it be known that the word "revolution," as such, was no longer applicable to the Indonesian situation because of its "Marxist connotation." Commendable as the new objectives were, as set forth in the Five-Year Plan that had won the plaudits of such restrained observers as the members of the International Monetary Fund and the World Bank, they scarcely provided the sort of dynamic thrust that many of the regime's critics continued to say was lacking. In his constant trips around the country and his efforts to identify himself more with the people, Suharto seemed to have become increasingly aware that his image, so far, had been more that of the quiet man holding the rudder than the dashing hoister of new sails. Despite the fact that he had gained more confidence in himself and was beginning to act like a President, his leadership continued to be more practical than passionate, and for a people so long used to Sukarno, with all his flair and flamboyance, the Indonesians at the start of 1969 remained uncertain in their judgments of the New Order and unsatisfied over what it had done for them. (It was significant that one of the most popular younger generals was Ali Sadikin, a Marine who was Governor of Djakarta, and whose dash and good looks, on top of his ability, were building up his image as a new political force in the old Sukarno style.) In calling for a new consensus, Suharto had seemingly been aware of the national uneasiness and discontent, but he still often approached the problem negatively, or perhaps too much in the Javanese style. In his August, 1968, address, for example, he declared, almost apologetically, that "it appears as if the people are not patient any more to see the 'slow' progress and improvements we have achieved with so much pain within the last two years." Aware, too, of Indonesia's volatile political history, and maybe because of his own tardiness in allowing new political forces to emerge, he warned that "the realization of sound democracy does not mean that 'politics is to be in command,'" and pointed to the sad consequences of the last twenty years, "when the attention of the whole of society and of every group was focused on political issues only." As a result, he emphasized, "the problem of economic reconstruction was automatically ignored" and everything was measured "by the yardstick of group interest," which led to "the emergence of an abstract and chaotic pattern of thought."

True as this was, and true as it was, also, that Indonesia's immediate future would depend more than anything else on such mundane matters as rice production and distribution, it remained doubtful that either politics or group interests could be subjugated indefinitely. The rumblings before, during, and after the 1968 session of Congress demonstrated this, despite Suharto's elevation to the Presidency for his desired five-year term. His compromise of "refreshing" Parliament and Congress and of resuscitating and "reforming" the older parties instead of allowing the newer ones to create a real political reformation had created an odd new vacuum in which various elements in addition to the Muslims continued to stir uncomfortably in potential opposition. These included the remnants of the old guard, whose views were reflected among some military men, and in the left-wing groups that were still turbulent throughout the islands, especially in Java; followers of General Nasution whose own latent ambitions to be President were subtly expressed in several speeches; and, above all, student groups, who were more and more discontent with the lack of substantive political activity and who, to some extent, and despite the improvements in civil rights and judicial procedure, had been harassed and had had some of their individual members arrested for voicing criticisms of the New Order. There seemed little doubt that one of the chief failures of the Suharto regime so far had been its inability to harness or integrate the so-called Generation of 1966 and give its members a sense of useful participation in the new scheme of things. This group's restlessness was aggravated by the fact that, being both socially mobilized and highly literate, it felt its new alienation all the more keenly for having lent its early support so strongly to the Suharto regime. The danger still existed that the younger generation as a whole might yet be attracted to new extremes of revolution or reaction, as has happened in more sophisticated political climates, such as that of the German Weimar Republic at the end of the First World War. On top of that, there remained the twin problems of inefficiency and corruption. The national board dealing with corruption on a broad national basis had accomplished essentially very little by the end of 1968, and Suharto's decision to abolish his private staff was only one step in the right direction. It seemed unlikely that there would be any real progress until the swollen bureaucracy, which encouraged both inefficiency and corruption, was reduced and reformed. And while the stabilization program was showing considerable success, it was hurting the mercantile class, which normally depends on protective tariffs and easy bank credit; there was a consequent danger of an alliance between this element and certain members of the military hierarchy who were opposed to political reforms.

Unless the larger problems of group reconciliation were dealt with, along with those of improving the economy and instituting wider social justice, and unless the new political elements and parties spearheaded by the youth were allowed greater latitude, there was a further danger that the lassitude that still permeated post-Sukarno Indonesia would be transformed into fresh conflicts before elections occurred in 1971. It was one thing, as Suharto said, to want to avoid a recurrence of the old political styles and formulas, but it was something else to stifle indefinitely the development of new political forms and to seek to contain political activity in the claimed paramount interest of balanced budgets and financial solvency. Indonesia's potential role as the chief stabilizing force in Southeast Asia would depend not only on the nation's production and prosperity, but on its regaining its national *élan* and assuming a role of positive leadership in the area's affairs. This could only come through forceful internal political development, accompanied by and not separate from economic rejuvenation, followed by thorough participation in the regional activities that were already burgeoning. Happily, Indonesia had begun, though with some trepidation, to re-enter the Southeast Asia community via such organizations as ASEAN (Association of Southeast Asia Nations), which already included Singapore, Thailand, Malaysia, and the Philippines. It had re-entered the United Nations and affiliated organizations. It was no longer afraid to speak out against what other nations did or failed to do, and it was as outspokenly critical of the United States in Vietnam as it was of Soviet Russia in Czechoslovakia.

If, after the Vietnam war was finally ended, there would be a "third force" in Asia, and if, as many hoped, such a force would be able to remain both nonaligned and essentially Socialist in orientation, what happened in Indonesia would, in all probability, be increasingly more important than what took place in Vietnam, where events were likely to be indecisive for some time to come. In 1969 there seemed two alternatives in Indonesia: One was an increasingly strong military rule, which, if something should happen to Suharto, could pose a real danger of Army dictatorship, and if that happened, the chances of another Communist resurgence would surely be enhanced. The other, more hopeful alternative was for some form of enlightened and mixed system of authoritarian government continuing indefinitely, accompanied by a gradual approach to normal parliamentary forms subject to some restraints. The importance of foreign aid in encouraging the modernist elements in Indonesian society could not, in this connection, be overestimated. The more that such aid, particularly American aid, could be applied to specific projects that could generate self-help and improve employment opportunities, above all in the agricultural sector, during the initial recovery phase, the more would the position of the modernists—the economic experts and those looking ahead to new political programs that would have more meaning than mystique—be strengthened. This, in turn, would attract more investment from abroad, and would inspire a healthy relationship between Indonesia and other nations, above all with the United States, as it sought to reduce its military role in Southeast Asia without abandoning its friends. Such was the primary challenge the New Order of Suharto faced in 1969, as the Five-Year Plan began. It was a very complicated, very meaningful one, and it was not too much to say that much of the future of Southeast Asia would depend on how it was met.

3

Singapore-Malaysia:

DIVORCE, ASIAN STYLE

Going It Alone

The small island republic of Singapore may be compared to a divorced woman who, having been forced to live in reduced circumstances in a hostile neighborhood, has learned how to fend for herself while still harboring the hope that her alienated ex-husband will someday agree to re-establish amicable relations, at least for the sake of protecting the children's interests. The ex-husband, of course, is the predominantly Muslim nation of Malaysia, which, much in the manner of a Muslim man seeking to shed a wife, abruptly terminated its tempestuous two-year-long union with predominantly Chinese Singapore on August 9, 1965, by simply announcing, in effect, "I divorce you." Left alone in the turbulent anti-Chinese atmosphere of Southeast Asia, Singapore thereafter did its best to cope, and, all things considered, it did remarkably well. Its relations with Malaysia continued to deteriorate for a period after separation, but by the spring of 1968 they had begun to show some signs of improvement. This was due to a number of extenuating circumstances and developments, the most important of which was the sudden decision of Great Britain, in January, 1968, to accelerate its departure from its historic military base in Singapore and to pull out completely from the Far East by the end of 1971 instead of in 1975, as had been planned. Aside from the fresh economic pressures this placed on Singapore, already fighting to maintain itself as a viable separate country, the British decision, which also affected Malaysia, although not as drastically, forced the two nations to re-evaluate their joint problems of security in cooperation with Australia and New Zealand. It was too soon to predict that Singapore and Malaysia might eventually come together again—there were still many differences and sources of mutual annoyance and antagonism—but the possibilities, if not the necessity, of a new approach at least existed, and for the first time since the break, perhaps since the premature merger took place, both parties realized it.

For Singapore, the stepped-up timetable of the British withdrawal from the largest naval base east of Suez posed a series of problems both real and psychological. Its brilliant, impulsive, sometimes irascible Prime Minister, Lee Kuan Yew, was so upset about the announcement, which was brought about by the worsening British financial crisis, that he flew immediately to London to try to talk Prime Minister Harold Wilson into a postponement. Lee actually did manage to get the final and complete withdrawal of some thirty thousand soldiers, sailors, and airmen and the shutting down of the naval base postponed from March to December, 1971, but, more important, he received assurances that the British would help him supplement his small Israeli-trained military force of six battalions plus some special units by selling him a dozen or so jet trainer aircraft and forty or fifty surface-to-air Bloodhound missiles already set up in Singapore, in addition to which the British agreed to make available the necessary ground and support facilities and to assist in the training of the necessary technicians and specialists. The British also agreed to make available to Singapore £50 million, a quarter of it in the form of a grant and the rest in a long-term low-interest loan. Singapore, with part of this money and with funds to be raised by popular subscription, also hoped to increase its militia force, the Vigilante Corps, to 150,000 in ten years' time.

One effect of the British announcement was to bring about immediate talks with Malaysia, whose Deputy Prime Minister, Tun Abdul Razak, said, "We are doing everything possible to cooperate with Singapore for the good of our two peoples and countries." In June, 1968, a five-nation conference was held in Kuala Lumpur among Malaysia, Singapore, Australia, New Zealand, and Great Britain to discuss the impact of British withdrawal. Singapore and Malaysia agreed that their defense was indivisible and "required close and continuous cooperation." Denis Healey, the British Defense Minister, pledged that the British would take part in a major training exercise in 1970, and pointed out that the mobility of British forces would enable them to be used in the Far East after 1971, if necessary, in "the continuing interest of peace and stability in the area." The Australians agreed temporarily to retain an Air Force detachment at Butterworth base in Malaysia, with some units assigned to Tengah Field in Singapore, and to keep some small Army contingents in both Malaysia and Singapore, at least until 1971. But the general tenor of the conference made it clear that after 1971, despite the possibility of a mobile emergency force being set up to include Australia and New Zealand, Singapore and Malaysia would pretty much have to go it alone.

When the conference was over, Prime Minister Lee told his Singaporean audience that he was hopeful of solving the security problem through cooperation, and added, in a typically hortatory fashion, "This is the acid test—have we the will and the grit to be a nation . . . a rugged and robust society?" "Rugged" and "robust" had always been two of Lee's favorite words, exemplifying his whole approach to Singapore's survival as a self-governing state. Even before the ill-starred merger with Malaysia, survival for Lee was more than a goal—it was a crusade. He was determined to prove to his neighbors, and to the great powers, particularly to the United States and the Soviet Union, not only that Singapore could sustain itself economically but that he could maintain his adroit political control over its industrious but highly volatile population of nearly two million, three-quarters of them Chinese and the rest mostly Malay, Hindu, and Tamil. Furthermore, he was intent on proving that he could achieve this without either turning Singapore into a "Third China" or letting it become a sort of Cuba-like appendage to the great Chinese Communist colossus to the north.

Singapore's assets were considerable. Its humming port had become, by 1968, the fourth busiest in the world. It had a well-developed and modern, if limited, industrial plant and economy.

Capitalizing on these resources and on its strategic position between the southernmost tip of Asia and the Indonesian archipelago, Singapore had managed to deal pretty much on its own terms with such disparate capitals as Washington, Moscow, Peking, and Djakarta, and had managed in the process to assert its role as a Southeast Asian linchpin. Many observers felt that it could play an increasingly influential role in furthering the prospects of regional cooperation and the gradual evolution of a neutral group of nations that could deal with, and accept help from, both the Communist and democratic powers; this feeling had been reinforced when, in 1967, Singapore, along with Indonesia, had joined ASEAN.

Despite its tangible assets and its realistic attitude, Singapore faced a stunning economic challenge in the wake of the British withdrawal, particularly since the prospects for ending the Vietnamese war threatened to curtail the economic benefits it had enjoyed from large-scale exports to South Vietnam. It already faced an unemployment rate of almost 10 percent of the total work force of 500,000, and an additional 25,000 young men and women were finishing school and entering the job market every year. The British departure would mean the direct loss of 45,000 jobs, and at least 50,000 more part-time employees would be affected by the withdrawal. The British military presence had been responsible for about a fifth of Singapore's gross national product of slightly more than $3 billion a year in Singapore currency—$1 billion in American dollars—and for 16 percent of the national income. Even to keep the unemployment rate steady, it was estimated that an equal amount would now somehow have to be put into the economy, and, since 1963, in spite of prodigious efforts to create new sources of employment, only about five thousand new jobs a year had been found, about an eighth of what was necessary. The continuing influx of new capital from nations all over the world, especially from Japan, and the pledge of the British to give "significant aid" for more encouragement of industry and tourism were hopeful signs, but the likely flight of British capital investment in the wake of the defense pull-out and the devaluation of the pound partly offset this. The "boom" that Lee Kuan Yew had recently talked about was obviously in jeopardy—despite an 8 percent increase in trade in 1967, a 15 percent increase in goods handled as well as in total tonnage flowing through the port, a rise of nearly one-third in total bank deposits and of two-thirds in construction—all of which had contributed, over a three-year period, to a 9 percent annual rate of growth. The huge 1969 defense budget of more than 330 million Singapore dollars virtually froze all other development funds and threatened this earlier rate of growth. Most of the defense expenditures would be used to create a standing army of some 8,500 men, plus the new militia based on periods of training for all males between eighteen and forty-five; a small navy and air force would also be established.

Singapore's resiliency, and its confidence in its ability for future growth, nevertheless, remained strong points in its favor. It had become accustomed, by 1968, to repeated changes and challenges. Some observers have compared Singapore to a Chinese Israel, isolated and surrounded in a Muslim world. With Malaysia to the north, Indonesia to the south, and another Muslim nation, East Pakistan, not far away in the west, the comparison did seem to have some validity, but it was effectively rejected in a speech delivered in 1967 by Singapore's Foreign Minister, Sinnathamby Rajaratnam, who is a Ceylonese-Tamil educated in England. "Singapore is no Israel," Rajaratnam said. "The Chinese of Singapore are not Israelis or Arabs. Nor are the Indians, or the Eurasians, or the Ceylonese, or the Malays of Singapore. History has brought all these diverse peoples from all over Asia to this little island. They will live here for all time as Singaporeans, and we will see to it that they are tutored to live as good Southeast Asians as well. That is why we don't go about shouting 'Chinese unite!' and 'Malays unite!' and 'Indians unite!' "

Many students of the area, however, remained convinced that Singapore would never succeed in ridding herself of her essential "Chinese-ness." Among its Malay neighbors, these observers maintained, Singapore's multiracial pretensions would always be suspect. It was inevitable, despite Lee Kuan Yew's protestations, that Singapore would be regarded in some quarters as the potential spearhead of a "Third China," apart from either Communist China or Kuomintang Taiwan. The Chinese in Southeast Asia, having for the most part remained aloof from politics, and content with their roles as small merchants and business and banking leaders, were being compelled by events in the late nineteen-sixties to consider themselves as Chinese rather than as integrated residents of their various countries. Even Lee Kuan Yew, preaching multiracialism, had taken note of this problem of Chinese assimilation when he had admitted, in a speech to Chinese university graduates in 1967, "The descendants of the Chinese will be identifiable from the other races even a hundred years from now. . . . They find it very, very difficult to be assimilated completely with the indigenous peoples —not only because of language and culture, but more because of religion, a very important factor." While he drew a distinction between such "descendants" of Chinese, of whom he is one, and the Overseas Chinese, who traditionally sojourned in Southeast Asia and then went back to live and die in China, Lee pointed out that, while relatively few Overseas Chinese voluntarily returned to China any more, "There are many people who think that because you are a Chinese, you will one day become an agent of China or become a subversive element." He warned his listeners, "If you want a Chinese chauvinistic society, failure is assured. Singapore will surely be isolated. But even if you are not isolated and you extend your Chinese chauvinist influence to our neighbor [Malaysia], they will, if they find no way out, join up with another big neighbor [Indonesia] to deal with you."

Lee seemed to be saying that, if the racial problems in the area were not solved, Singapore would be forced to become a Chinese city, politically and socially. In a subsequent speech at the University of Singapore, he quoted an old Chinese proverb: "Big fish eat small fish; small fish eat shrimps." Now that the Europeans had left, the stage was set "for local big fish to settle terms with small fish, small fish with shrimps." The Singaporeans, he said, "having the smallest area in the region, must naturally be concerned." Sounding a note of bravado that was not untypical of him, he added: "There are various types of shrimps. Some shrimps stay alive. Species in nature develop defense mechanisms. Some shrimps are poisonous: they sting. If you eat them, you will get digestive upsets."

Lee's worry that the biggest fish in Asia—China—might someday try to swallow the other fish was based less on his current appraisal of Communist China, of whose severe internal and external difficulties he was well aware, than on his continued concern over how his neighbors, particularly Malaysia and Indonesia, would ultimately adjust to Singapore's independence, and on how the Communists in the region would in turn react. "If we want to play on these racial, ethnic, cultural, and linguistic loyalties, the Malay Peninsula can well become the Balkan peninsula of Asia," he said. While he had faith in the moderating influence of Tunku (Prince) Abdul Rahman, the Prime Minister of Malaysia, who was expected to stay in office at least until 1969, Lee and other Singaporeans were afraid that the people around the Tunku, most notably the Muslim extremists, would unwittingly play into the hands of the Communists. The Communists, in 1967 and 1968, were quite active, either underground in Singapore, in Sarawak, a part of former British Borneo that belonged to Malaysia, or in Malaysia proper, where they were behind a series of riots in the ultra-Malayan areas and were causing renewed trouble on the Malayan-Thailand border, where several hundred remnants of Chin Peng's rebels of the "Emergency" period of Communist guerrilla activity in the late nineteen-forties and fifties were still at large. When I saw Lee late in 1967, he prophetically warned that the Malayan Communists might sooner or later launch a new drive throughout Malaysia that could be far more subtle in its approach than was the case during the decade-long Emergency. Such a Communist attack, he said, would aim at destroying the social and economic fabric on a much wider scale than before and, in the case of Malaysia, at purposefully sowing racial dissension. It was Lee's fear that the Malayan extremists in Malaysia, by pushing too hard on such things as the legalization of Malay as the national language in 1968, would give the Communists an opportunity to build a new common front among discontented liberal and left-wing elements of all races. Lee and his close associates, Socialists of a moderate stripe, were afraid that if the Communists gained new strength in Malaysia, or, for that matter, again in Indonesia, the Communist movement in Singapore would gain new momentum. As Lee saw it, the formation of a "Third China" movement might then be forced on him against his better judgment, but he was not particularly sanguine about being able to hold his ground if he was surrounded by well-organized Communist movements in Western Malaysia (Malaya) and Eastern Malaysia (Sarawak and Sabah).

Some of Lee's fears were expressed in an interview he gave, in April, 1968, to Fred Emery, the capable correspondent of the

Times of London, when, on the assumption that South Vietnam would eventually go its own way and perhaps come under Communist domination, he envisaged "insurrections elsewhere in Southeast Asia." He thought that while the Chinese Communists would not move their own armies across national frontiers to take part in these insurrections, they would give "a lot of assistance in training, in weaponry, in ideology, in morale." While he didn't anticipate a "national liberation war" in Singapore, he did foresee "sorties into Singapore, the kind of terrorism and sabotage which they [the Communists] mounted on Hong Kong. I think we've got to be prepared for that if it happens. . . . Nobody is going to start anything before the British have gone, and therefore I've got to prepare for that position before the British go. If we are able to create a credible alternative defense arrangement, and nobody believes they can take liberties with us and get away with it, then I think we are all right for seven, eight, perhaps more years. Beyond that, of course, it will depend on what happens in Malaysia, what happens in Indonesia. . . . And I do not expect the Russians or the Americans or the Chinese to lose interest in South Asia."

Windfalls and Problems

The Singaporeans, whether they were accepted by the Malays as assimilated Chinese or rejected and forced to fall back on their own devices, obviously would have to apply all their political sagacity in the years ahead to maintain their precarious balance. "Our problem really is this," Lee told me, when I saw him. "First five years, consolidate; next five years, perhaps a regional arrangement. Either the region begins to tick or the region begins to crumble. And if it begins to crumble, then we are all in for a very unhappy time. And if it is going to tick, then I think Singapore can play a very important role in making it tick. It can be the spark plug."

Singapore had certainly been lucky, during the first year and a quarter of its enforced independence after leaving Malaysia, as a result of unexpected developments in Indonesia. The failure of the Communist coup there and the subsequent success of the generals in stripping Sukarno of power had set off a series of intricate chain reactions in which Indonesia's decision to recognize Singapore had ultimately helped bring about a formal end to the "confrontation" between Indonesia and Malaysia. By approaching Singapore, in April, 1967, before they approached Malaysia, the Indonesian successors to Sukarno were initially suspected of seeking to drive a further wedge between the two countries. In Kuala Lumpur, the Malaysian capital, the immediate reaction was an enraged outcry, and despite Singapore's assurances that she would consult Malaysia on all matters affecting Malaysian security and that "no move against Malaysia's interests will ever be made," Tunku Rahman declared that "Singapore as an independent nation may think that she can make friends with whomsoever she likes, but in this instance she must choose between Indonesia and Malaysia." Lee Kuan Yew's asseverations that "I like to be friends of friends and not to be an enemy of friends' enemies," and that "we should not allow the Indonesians to exploit the different styles in which we publicly deal with their moves" failed to mollify the Malaysians, and officials in Kuala Lumpur continued to describe Singapore's willingness to be wooed by Djakarta as "an unfriendly act that would bring the Indonesians to Malaysia's doorstep" and charged, further, that "Singapore is prepared to allow herself to be used for Indonesian hostile purposes." The Singaporeans, who had no more intention than the Malaysians of allowing Indonesian conspirators on their narrow soil, promptly denied that they would in any way allow their territory to be used as a base for further confrontation with Malaysia, but, even so, Kuala Lumpur imposed security checks on all traffic across the Johore Causeway between Singapore and Malaysia and announced that immigration restrictions would also be instituted.

When the Indonesians, not long after approaching Singapore, began making overtures to Malaysia for talks to end confrontation, it became apparent that they were simply using their imminent recognition of Singapore as a lever to prod Malaysia into accepting peace negotiations as soon as possible. Although it might have been surmised that Singapore would have welcomed continued Indonesian-Malaysian friction while herself benefiting from a resumption of relations with Indonesia, particularly in trade, her more earnest desire, if one could believe what her leaders said, was to promote general peace throughout the area. At any rate, by the spring of 1966 the new Indonesian leaders, notably Adam Malik, the astute Foreign Minister, had persuaded Sukarno to start full-dress negotiations with Malaysia to end the confrontation. Discussions finally got under way in Bangkok, Kuala Lumpur, and Djakarta, and when formal recognition of Singapore was announced on June 4, of that year, the peace talks were spurred. Two months later, on August 12, confrontation was officially ended. By having thus used the ploy of Singapore recognition, the new Indonesian rulers had outflanked Sukarno and had at the same time achieved their primary aim of bringing Malaysia to the conference table.

The question of some sort of referendum or elections in Sabah and Sarawak to determine whether or not the populations there wanted to remain in Malaysia was left hanging. While some such poll was part of the rather tenuous agreement between Djakarta and Kuala Lumpur, no one seemed in any hurry to hold it. Ultimately, most observers believed, the two Borneo states might withdraw from Malaysia and, with Brunei, the tiny state between them that had opted out of the Malaysian Federation at the outset, in 1963, might form a new Borneo Federation of their own. Singapore would probably welcome such a step; theoretically, it would create a buffer zone in the area, though the danger of Communist infiltration, especially in Sarawak, would still exist. An even greater threat to Singapore could come from the proposed Maphilindo union of the three nations whose racial heritage is Malayan—Indonesia, Malaysia, and the Philippines. This would undoubtedly increase Singapore's isolation and drive Lee into the "Third China" position he professed to want to avoid. However, there remained some vital differences among the three countries, including, above all, a dispute over an old claim to Sabah between Manila and Kuala Lumpur. Furthermore, as Lee saw it, "Indonesia is so far behind Malaysia in its development that the Malaysians would have to lower their standards too much, and the Indonesians can't pull themselves up that quickly."

The establishment of relations with Djakarta and the end of Indonesian-Malaysian confrontation brought Singapore some much-needed economic benefits. A trade agreement was quickly signed with Indonesia, under which Singapore agreed to extend $150 million of private commercial credit in Singapore currency to private traders over a six-month period, and the Indonesians promised to trade with Singapore on terms "no less favorable than those accorded any other country." Exports of all products, including rubber and tin, were resumed to Singapore, which thus regained its former entrepôt role. By 1968, although the total level of trade with Indonesia remained below the preconfrontation level, imports of rubber for processing were moving ahead of the 1962 figures, and Singapore's exports of manufactured products to Indonesia—wheat, flour, galvanized-iron sheets, cement, etc.—were setting new records. Traditional barter trade, limited to cargoes carried by ships of less than two hundred tons, was also resumed, but illegal smuggling remained a problem. Singapore's suspicions of Indonesia's ability to maintain political stability kept trade relations from being better than they were, and there was still a hangover feeling of a new Sukarno-like threat to Singapore's security. During an official visit in the spring of 1968, Malik sought to reassure the Singaporeans on this score, emphasizing that, while Indonesia wished to remain nonaligned and free of military alliances, it would, as a member of ASEAN, defend its fellow member nations against any Communist threat, "even if it comes from Genghis Khan."

The improved relations with Indonesia was thus one major windfall during Singapore's first year as an independent republic, and another was the boost in trade brought about by the war in Vietnam. Sales totaling $10 million a month in American currency —mostly building equipment and spare metal parts—had made South Vietnam Singapore's best customer, and the city was also being used as a rest and recreation center for American servicemen. It would be crass to suggest that this is what caused Lee Kuan Yew to modify his earlier critical stand on Vietnam and the American position there, though it was perhaps a factor. More compelling political reasons were mainly responsible—above all, Lee's realization, after a trip he made through Western and Eastern Europe in 1966, that Europeans were little concerned with what was happening in Vietnam or elsewhere in Asia, and that the Asians would have to fend for themselves, with the help of the Americans, in resisting Chinese or Vietnamese Communism. Lee's previous anti-Americanism had been mostly the result of personal annoyance over a bribe that was allegedly offered by the Central

Intelligence Agency to forget about a C.I.A. man's unsuccessful effort to buy information from Singapore intelligence officials, and over Washington's refusal to urge a private physician to fly to Singapore to care for Lee's ailing wife. Once he was over his prolonged pique, Lee's position was that South Vietnam had become a big-power battleground and that to denounce the Americans for escalating the war would solve nothing. After his return from Europe, he said that the war was being fought "to decide that Vietnam shall not be repeated" anywhere else in Southeast Asia, and that whatever negotiations were ultimately conducted and whatever solutions were reached would be worthwhile "only if there is a credible formula and a credible undertaking that the same process will not be repeated on the periphery after South Vietnam." The war, therefore, as Lee had come to see it, enabled Singapore and other nations to buy time—"But whilst we buy time," he added, "if we just sit down and believe people are going to buy time forever after for us, then we deserve to perish."

In October, 1967, Lee made a highly successful state visit to the United States, where President Johnson went out of his way to entertain him and praise him as "a patriot, a brilliant political leader, and a statesman of new Asia." Lee, whose talents as a speaker were widely acclaimed, spoke of the need for "patience and perseverance and prudence so that the "superpowers," by which he mostly meant the Americans, would "demonstrate that firmness for a fair peace which can make the world a safer and a better place for all—Asians, Africans, Americans, and Europeans." He declared that Vietnam need never have happened, but that "since the United States had remained in the country, it was committed to stay there . . . to meet force with counterforce and to let the political situation develop behind the protective military shield." If the United States turned its back on Asia, he warned, "we are in for a grievous struggle which cuts across ethnic lines." Until Americans considered Asia as important to them as Europe, he added, they were going to find "a lot of Asians, like me, critical of you," and he expressed the hope for an eventual multilateral support for all of Southeast Asia by the United States, the Soviet Union, and China. On his way back home, Lee stopped off in England and on the continent, where he reiterated these themes and spoke of the "even greater misery that may befall so many more millions of other South and Southeast Asians if this costly effort [in Vietnam] were to end in circumstances that did not lessen the danger of similar trials by ordeal in other adjacent non-Communist states of Asia." In a speech in Zurich he said that "when Singapore was abruptly asked to leave Malaysia, the study of what small countries surrounded by large neighbors with big populations do for their own survival led us to compare three tightly knit and well-organized communities—Switzerland, Finland, and Israel. In the end we opted for the Israeli solution, for in our situation we think that it might be necessary not only to train every boy but also every girl to be a disciplined and effective digit in the defense of their country."

Background of a Bad Marriage

Lee's frequent public and private references to his long ordeal with Malaysia clearly demonstrated that the whole tortuous history of his relationship with Kuala Lumpur was still very much on his mind. The marriage between the two states was, unfortunately, in most respects more of a shotgun ceremony than a love match. Aside from blaming Lee and some of the extremist Malayan leaders for the collapse of the union, there were those who ascribed part of the blame to the British for having rushed the whole idea of federation in the first place, before its component parts, especially the Borneo states, were prepared for it. As a candid British friend of mine, a long-time resident of Singapore, once put it, "We have a good record, I think, of delivering our former possessions their freedom, but there have been cases, including that of the West Indies and Central Africa as well as Malaysia, where in our haste to withdraw from the scene we pushed federation among disparate elements too fast for their own good."

In 1962-63, both Kuala Lumpur, as the husband, and the British, as marriage brokers, felt that a politically tense Singapore could become, if left to herself, a Southeast Asian Cuba, and that the best way to help Lee Kuan Yew maintain his still tenuous control over Communist obstructionists in the port was to make Singapore part of Malaya. Lee, who had long favored such a merger, agreed himself, but Kuala Lumpur was worried that a Malayan-Singapore union would have a Chinese majority, which would be totally unacceptable to the Malays. (At the time, of some seven and a half million people in Malaya itself, about a third were Chinese.) It was for this reason that Sarawak and Sabah were brought into the marriage act, somewhat like two naïve young flower girls. With their admixture of races—Malay, Chinese, and various native tribes—the Bornean states swung the majority around in such a way that the Chinese and Malays would be about equal in numbers in Malaysia but the Malays would remain in political command. The whole relationship was difficult from the outset and was not improved by the fact that none of the participants had a very clear idea of what they were getting into, individually and collectively, or how it would work.

The four partners, with a population of nearly eleven million people of widely diverse racial stock, scattered over 130,000 square miles, not only varied greatly in economic and social development and in political experience and sophistication, but, as it turned out, were never able to establish even a tentative political consensus. The easygoing Tunku saw Malaysia simply as an extension of Malaya, designed primarily to contain the area's Chinese. He frequently said, in his fatherly way, that he looked upon Singapore as Malaysia's "New York." Lee Kuan Yew, scarcely content to be merely a mayor, saw Malaysia, more logically in demographic terms, as a brand-new country, with Malaya just one of its four parts. Furthermore, Lee, who was only forty-one years old then, visualized himself as a national leader, perhaps not yet on a par with the elderly Tunku, who was already in his sixties, but as his potential equal and successor.

Lee, the great-grandson of a Hakka peasant who left China a century ago to seek work in Malaya, liked to point out that he would never have become Prime Minister of Singapore if his great-grandfather, upon returning to China with his savings, had not left a son, Lee's grandfather, behind. The grandfather prospered, and Lee's father, a jewelry merchant, saw to it that Lee received a good secondary education in Singapore and then sent him to Cambridge to study law. There Lee distinguished himself by winning a rare "double first." He also became an ardent Socialist. Somewhat in the manner of the late Jawaharlal Nehru, Lee was always thereafter ambivalently caught between East and West; though he admired the British in many ways, and adopted their language (he learned Mandarin only years later) and many of their customs, he at the same time remained a Chinese, and, as a dedicated Socialist, he was violently anticolonial. In 1954 he and Toh Chin Chye, who was to become his Deputy Prime Minister, were among the founders of the People's Action Party in Singapore. In the late fifties, while the moderate Tunku was patiently negotiating Malaya's independence, Lee, as an intellectual firebrand and a tough pragmatist, applied his knowledge of Marxism and of Communist tactics to the outwitting of Communist opponents of the P.A.P. in Singapore—except on occasions when he found it expedient to cooperate with them. In 1959, when Singapore was granted internal independence by the British (who retained control of foreign affairs and defense), Lee's party took over and at once broke completely with the Communists while working toward union with Malaya.

During the first months after the union had taken place, late in 1963 and early in 1964, increasing racial and political strains, exacerbated by personality differences, emphasized the fundamental differences of approach between the Malays and the Chinese. The Malay leaders were determined to elevate the status of the Malays socially and economically and to maintain their political dominance; Lee and his Singapore associates, on the other hand, felt that a multiracial Malaysia should be just what the phrase denoted —that the Malays, whose average living standard had been far below that of the Chinese, should be encouraged to improve themselves by being given certain privileges, but should not be favored to a point where almost all the political jobs were assigned to them. When I saw Lee in Singapore, shortly after separation, he told me that virtually every new post after merger *had* gone to a Malay, and he brought out a 1961 speech of the Tunku's, which he said he now could reread "with knowing eyes" because "it clearly showed that, from the very start, the Tunku had looked upon Singapore as a junior partner in any proposed federation, a naughty girl that had to be controlled."

Perhaps even more important than these basic differences in approach between the Malays and the Singapore Chinese was the clash between the conservative Chinese element in Kuala Lumpur

and the highly sophisticated and ambitious Chinese in the cosmopolitan port. The battle lines, in fact, had been sharply drawn,
even before the creation of Malaysia, between the Malayan Chinese Association in Malaya—which with the United Malay National Organization and the Malayan Indian Congress formed the
ruling Alliance Party in Malaya—and Lee's ruling P.A.P. in Singapore. To Lee, the Secretary-General of the Malayan Chinese Association, Tan Siew Sin, who was also Finance Minister of the new
Malaysia, was the archetype of the rich and compromising Chinese
who was willing to continue making money without making any
real political demands on the Malays. Consequently, Lee felt that
the M.C.A. had little or no appeal for the politically maturing
young Chinese elements. And, what was more serious, it was incapable of coping with Communist infiltrators among the Chinese
in Malaya. Conversely, as far as Tan Siew Sin and the M.C.A. were
concerned, Lee was simply a "mischief-maker" who, after the formation of Malaysia, became its "greatest disruptive force."

In Singapore, Lee himself had some remnant disruptive forces to
contend with. In 1961 two Communist leaders then still in their
twenties, Lim Chin Siong and Fong Swee Suan, who had been
imprisoned but then let out of jail, had founded a Communist front
organization called the Barisan Socialis (Socialist Front), with ties
to Peking through the Communist Party of Indonesia—the P.K.I.
Two years later, even though Lee had put Lim and Fong back in
jail, along with about a hundred other Communists and pro-
Communists, the Barisan had managed to win thirteen out of fifty-
one seats in the Singapore Assembly and 33 percent of the popular
vote, while the P.A.P. got 47 percent of the vote and captured
thirty-seven seats. (There was one successful independent candidate, and the remaining votes went to losing independent candidates or were declared invalid.) Since the Barisan was anti-
Malaysia and the P.A.P. was pro-Malaysia, the Alliance Party in
Kuala Lumpur presumably should have hailed Lee's victory. However, the Alliance leaders were unhappy about the fact that three
Malay candidates they had backed had lost to three Malay P.A.P.
candidates, so not long afterward they activated a Singapore
counterpart of their party that came to be called the Alliance
Singapura.

The stirrings of the Alliance Singapura were largely responsible for a decision by Lee and his associates to enter P.A.P. candidates in the first federal elections in Malaysia, in April, 1964. As part of the agreement establishing Malaysia, Singapore had already been assigned fifteen out of 159 seats in the new Malaysian House of Representatives. Of these fifteen, the P.A.P. held twelve. Lee, who sat in the House as Singapore's Prime Minister, had previously indicated that his party would not contest elections elsewhere in Malaysia for at least five years, but now, spurred by two or three of his associates—particularly Rajaratnam, his closest friend—he changed his mind and decided to try to enter ten additional candidates. Whether or not the decision was wise—and most independent observers felt that it was not—Lee made it without preparing a proper political organization in Malaya. The P.A.P. members in the Malaysian Parliament had, from the outset, supported the Tunku and the Alliance Party, and Lee argued, somewhat sententiously, that he had entered the Malaysian elections in order to help the Tunku and his party even further by opposing Malaysia's pro-Communist Socialist Front. He added, rather contemptuously, that the stodgy Malayan Chinese Association was too weak to do this. Furthermore, he maintained that the United Malay National Organization was ill-equipped to fight the fanatic Muslims of the Pan-Malayan Islamic Party in the rural areas of Malaya. Therefore, he explained, he would enter the elections in just ten districts, where he could advantageously counter the Communists or the religious fanatics.

The M.C.A. naturally suspected Lee's motives and accused him of trying to split the Alliance by seeking to capture the Chinese vote; other Alliance leaders accused Lee of wanting to go even further and of trying to build up support for himself among the Malays as well so that he could challenge the Alliance as the head of a new multiracial party. If that were so, Lee replied, he would have waited until he was ready to enter a full slate of candidates. Whether that was true or not, it seemed apparent that Lee was already thinking of the P.A.P. as a Malaysia-wide force, and that he felt he could not afford to sit back and wait while the Alliance Singapura moved in on him in Singapore at the same time that its parent Alliance Party solidified its position in the rest of Malaysia.

The upshot was a sound defeat for Lee's slate. Only one of his ten candidates—Devan Nair, the vocal and able leader of the

Singapore trade-union movement, won in the Malaysian elections, and five did so badly that they lost their election deposits. The Alliance won eighty-nine seats and held a clear majority in the House of Representatives; the Socialist Front did no better than had been expected, winning only a handful of seats; but the Malayan Chinese Association, contrary to what Lee had hoped, more than held its own. Lee insisted that the P.A.P. had succeeded in its basic purpose of defeating some Communist and religious fanatic candidates, but this claim left the Tunku and his Alliance supporters cold. The most significant result of the elections was the aggravation of the animosities between Kuala Lumpur and Singapore. Instead of advancing himself as a national figure, Lee had primarily succeeded in spurring the conservative elements among the Malays into taking action against him. Until the 1964 elections these "ultras" had been held in check by the moderates, under the leadership of the Tunku. In the growing emotional campaign against the P.A.P. and against Lee in particular, they thereafter occupied the center of the stage.

After the election, also, racial tensions mounted in Singapore. In the late spring of 1964, while some slum areas were being cleared under the city's road-repair and housing program, about three thousand families, a number of them Malays, were evicted from their homes. The Malays claimed that they were being discriminated against, but the P.A.P. said that only 10 percent of the families evicted were Malay and that, anyway, all of them had received moving allowances and were getting new homes. Whatever the facts of the matter, the episode moved Syed Ja'afar bin Hassan Albar, the Secretary-General of the United Malay National Organization in Kuala Lumpur, to organize a new U.M.N.O. branch in Singapore and start a campaign to obtain for Malays there the same sort of privileges they were accorded in Malaya. Albar, a native of Indonesia who had become an ardent Malayan nationalist, was one of the most outspoken of the ultras, who constantly expressed the theme of "one race, one language, one religion." "Wherever I am, I am a Malayan," he proclaimed, and "If the Malays were split, the Malays would perish from the earth." Albar wanted Lee removed as Prime Minister and advocated a policy of keeping Singapore firmly in its place or even "crushing" it.

That summer, after the P.A.P. invited representatives of more than a hundred Malay organizations in Singapore to meet with Lee and some of his Cabinet to air their grievances, Albar countered by calling a meeting of his own. Albar's meeting took place first, in mid-July, and at it special new concessions were demanded for Singapore's Malays—including low rents and student allowances —and a partisan Malay Action Committee was formed. A few days later, Lee, at his meeting, rejected these demands and tried patiently to explain what Singapore was trying to do to help all races, whereupon the new Malay Action Committee denounced him bitterly and violently. Tension by this time was high, and on July 21, during a Malay religious parade, a Malay spectator got into a fight with a Chinese policeman, and a race riot started. It was several days before order was restored, and on September 3 new violence broke out when a Chinese trishaw rider was found murdered in a slum area; it was later pretty well established that he had been killed by Indonesian-hired gangsters, in an attempt to stir up more communal strife. During the two riots, thirty-five people were killed and hundreds injured, and property damage was extensive.

Around this time, Lee Kuan Yew had proposed to the Tunku the idea of establishing an Alliance-P.A.P. coalition government for Malaysia. The British apparently had suggested the same thing, but feeling was running too high, and the Tunku, who had begun to lose control over the Malayan extremists, was in no position to consider the idea seriously. Instead, he and Lee negotiated what they hoped might be a two-year moratorium on political debate, but this agreement was quickly violated by both sides. By early 1965, following the collapse of another tentative deal between Lee and the Tunku, whereby Singapore was to be given full responsibility for its own internal security in return for withdrawing completely from Malaysian politics, Lee and the ultras in Kuala Lumpur had virtually declared war on one another. Lee now constantly attacked both the ultras and the members of the Malayan Chinese Association, calling the latter "compradors" (Chinese managers for foreign interests) who had made their fortunes in business and had assumed the role of "haves" and started oppressing the "have-nots" of all races. He also began making the P.A.P. the spearhead of opposition to all those who conceded the Malays their various forms of special status, in business and education as well as in the Civil Service. He coined the slogan "Malaysian Malaysia," which he and his supporters declared to be the only possible alternative to a "Malayan Malaysia." Having originally conceded that the Malays deserved special rights, Lee now insisted that some of these rights should be eliminated in the interest of building a really multiracial nation.

The concept of a "Malaysian Malaysia" was formally adopted in May, 1965, by a Malaysian Solidarity Convention summoned by Lee and attended by representatives of the P.A.P. and of four other opposition parties in Sarawak and Malaya, and from these elements a new United Opposition was formed, as an outright national rival to the Alliance Party. The convention seemed to be inviting a showdown, and it came quickly, when, at the end of May, the Malaysian chief of state (a figurehead with the title Yan di-Pertuan Agong), in opening Parliament in Kuala Lumpur, spoke of "threats from within the country." He named no names, but Lee, in responding to the speech, made an impassioned plea for his Malaysian Malaysia, and added, threateningly, "We are for a Malaysian Malaysia or nothing." The Alliance leaders replied by attacking Lee as "unscrupulous," "pro-Chinese, Communist oriented and positively anti-Malay," and accused him of fomenting communal strife. From Lee's all-or-nothing approach, it was apparent that he was now ready to consider separation, and the Malayan extremists were urging that Singapore be thrown out of the federation.

In the summer of 1965, while things were growing worse, the Tunku was in London, attending a Commonwealth Prime Ministers' Conference. He professed to be hurt and puzzled by all the trouble in Malaysia. "Why do we want to say all these things?" he asked, plaintively. "We are a happy country, a happy people. . . . I wanted to be an elder statesman, and help resolve issues worrying one party or another." He added that, when he got home, "If there is still something worrying Mr. Lee, I will be glad to look into it and see how best we can settle things." The Tunku's return was delayed when he came down with an attack of shingles, and while he was in the hospital he apparently reversed his earlier views and determined to force Singapore out of the federation. Only two of his closest political associates in Kuala Lumpur knew of his decision

when he returned on August 5. Two days later, the Tunku summoned Lee and told him that if Singapore did not quit the federation there would be bloodshed. Lee, who had hoped that the situation could still be saved and had been formulating his own idea for
a looser federation, was shocked. He discovered that the Tunku
was adamant, however, and reluctantly accepted what he called
the Tunku's "intuitive" judgment. The separation was announced
simultaneously by both men on August 9, and took everyone, including the British, by surprise. The Tunku admitted that he had
been forced to his decision because he had been unable to control
the Malayan extremists. He said that the "ultra pressure groups"
had demanded "totalitarian methods to force the 'rebellious' state
of Singapore into submission." Lee, at a highly emotional press conference in Singapore, declared, "For me, it is a moment of anguish
because all my life I have believed in merger." He broke down and
wept, and when he had recovered his composure he said, "Nobody
in Singapore at this present moment and for the next five years,
maybe ten years, can persuade Singapore to go back to Malaysia
after our experience. But somebody will do it one day, perhaps in
different form, under different circumstances."

After separation, some observers commented that if the Tunku
had not succumbed to "crisis fatigue" and had exercised his talent
for reconciliation, the split might have been averted. One long-
time student of the area's politics wrote: "The especially alarming
fact is that the split signifies a failure of reason to prevail over
irrationality, unless, to be sure, the Malaysian merger was irrational in the first place." In the light of hindsight, it probably was
irrational for several reasons. Above all, there was a fundamental
difference of outlook among the partners in the federation, including different anticolonial attitudes that time had not yet had a
chance to alter or ameliorate. In Singapore, Lee and the extremely
capable and sophisticated fellow intellectuals who ran the P.A.P.
had fought their way to the top by pushing the British hard and by
outwitting and outmaneuvering the Communists of the Barisan
Socialis and their left-wing labor union supporters. In Malaya the
paternalistic Tunku and his aides, having moved more gradually
toward independence, had experienced little difficulty in sup-
pressing what had remained of the Malayan Communist Party in
the years immediately after the Emergency (though they were

soon to face a new challenge). When independence was gained, and when Malaysia was afterward formed, these same "old-line" British-educated leaders, many of whom had gone to school in England with Lee and other Singapore Socialists, had adopted a strategy of "consensus," forging the Alliance Party out of various elements that ran the gamut from liberals to ultraconservatives. The spirit that moved them was always one of compromise, and their motto was "Go slow." This was bound to conflict with the sense of urgency that Lee and his fellow Singaporeans felt, and their dynamic approach was bound to constitute a threat to the ordinary conservatives in the Kuala Lumpur government, let alone the ultras. Lee, from the outset, was regarded as a headstrong adventurer who had to be kept in check. In a bitter television interview a month after separation, Lee referred to "political eunuchs" hired by the Malays, who "otherwise might be impregnated with democratic Socialist ideas." The government in Kuala Lumpur sent a quick note of protest to Singapore, accusing Lee of "a wanton intrusion and interference in the domestic affairs of Malaysia" and of "an unfriendly act" which could only give aid and comfort to their mutual enemies. Lee replied by citing numerous instances of Malayan efforts to sow racial dissension and furthermore pointed out, with more humor than Kuala Lumpur was able to appreciate, that "in Chinese history, eunuchs have always occupied prominent and sometimes powerful positions as the *eminences grises* of Chinese emperors."

The Pangs of Separation

In view of the querulous note on which the separation began, it was hardly surprising that the provisions of the separation agreement, which were supposed to establish a workable continuing relationship between the two countries, on economic as well as defense matters, were never formally put into effect. The establishment of "a joint council for purposes of external defense and mutual assistance" was abandoned after a few abortive meetings, and very little in this field was accomplished until the British withdrawal was announced. In the area of trade and finance, where the creation of "joint committees" was supposed to spur agreements on economic matters of mutual interest, an atmosphere of suspicion, if not hostility, prevented progress in almost all areas. Both countries were at fault, but Singapore probably tried harder to reach an accommodation, or at least to avoid a complete break, than Kuala Lumpur. When I spoke with Lee Kuan Yew a few months after the separation, he made the point that, since Singapore was a small island with no natural resources, "We owe Malaysia their defense, and they owe us our living," but he emphasized that "there is an inexorable nexus between security and commerce and industry and economic development," and said that, if security and stability could not be assured, "we will trade with the Devil to survive." He acknowledged that "while we have a mutual capacity to destroy each other, Malaysia can do more things to us, militarily and economically, than we can do to it, but if the Malaysians try to capture us"—he smiled as he said this—"what then? In the end, it's a matter of reabsorption, and they just can't swallow us."

For Singapore, the greatest loss as a result of separation was a prospective common Malaysian market, which would have afforded her infant industries eleven million customers instead of two million. In preparation for such a market, quotas and restrictions on various goods and products had been drawn up before separation to apply to other nations; the moment separation took place, such quotas theoretically were applicable by both countries against each other. Sensing herself at a disadvantage, Singapore assigned quotas to Malaysian goods first, and Malaysia promptly retaliated. Economic war was slowed for a time by consultations, but because Malaysia remained unwilling to lower tariffs against Singapore goods Singapore increased her own protective tariffs on the products of her infant industries. As a result of Kuala Lumpur's tough policy, a number of Singapore factories, including a big Ford assembly plant that used to ship 70 percent of its monthly output of three thousand cars to Malaysia, had to cut back production and lay off workers. Kuala Lumpur next threatened to create its own rubber-processing and port facilities at Port Swettenham and Penang and to cut off most, if not all, of its trade with Singapore. Though this did not happen, the trade flow between the two nations continued to diminish.

Relations reached a new low late in August, 1966, when the two nations decided to issue separate currencies starting in June, 1967. Nair, the former trade-union leader who had been the only P.A.P. man to sit in the Malaysian Parliament, denounced the currency break as "shattering idiocy." When the move took effect, Singapore's currency was 100 percent backed by sterling and dollars, permitting foreign trade to be conducted without exchange controls, whereas under the Malaysian system the central bank could theoretically print extra banknotes to make loans to the government. Although the Malaysian arrangement was less conducive to long-term stability, the two governments ultimately agreed to accept at par, and in full, each other's currencies.

Not long after Singapore and Kuala Lumpur issued their separate currencies, full immigration controls came into effect, whereby persons moving back and forth between the two countries had to carry passports and noncitizen residents of both had to have visas. Early in 1968 Singapore's decision to repatriate some fifty thousand Malaysians working on the island was rescinded when the Malaysians retaliated by threatening to send an even larger number of Singaporeans in the federation back to the port. Although thereafter the two countries showed some signs of being more realistic in their dealings—personal relations between their leaders had taken a turn for the better, and they had started playing golf with each other again—their willingness to work together to create some sort of joint defense agreement in the wake of the British withdrawal did not altogether hide their mutual suspicions and fears, notably on economic matters. If, ultimately, through ASEAN or some other instrumentality, a start might be made toward the creation of a regional common market or some lesser forms of tariff and other commercial agreements, Singapore and Malaysia in the meantime were in open competition with each other to obtain foreign investments and to sell their respective products abroad. The Tunku, with his customary grace and spirit of optimism, declared, on his sixty-fifth birthday, that he favored a new approach. "Let us forget what happened in the past," he said, "and plan for close cooperation [because] we are so closely linked in all matters, in defense and economy." But the fact remained that, so long as the two nations stayed apart, their problems were bound to be vastly different.

Where Malaysia had a large economic base of its own, in rubber, tin, and palm oil, and a broad-scale rural development plan, Singapore's ability to survive and flourish depended more narrowly on its capacity to satisfy the needs of a large and young population by maintaining its traditional role as an entrepôt and trading center while at the same time building up its industrial base. Even before Malaysia was created, Singapore had concentrated on creating the necessary conditions for industrial growth —building power plants, improving port facilities, laying out arterial roads, and so on. Special stress had been placed on the Jurong Industrial Estate, an area twelve miles from downtown Singapore that was set aside for a whole new industrial complex built on sixteen thousand acres of what used to be low-lying swampland surrounded by hills. The earth from the hills was used to make a new dock area, and by 1969 nearly two hundred factories dotted the area, ranging from a Singaporean-and-Japanese-financed steel mill and fabrication plant and a big American refinery to smaller plants manufacturing some three hundred different products. The fixed capital investment at Jurong had risen from 20.4 million Singapore dollars to S$436 million in seven years of growth. Low-cost apartment houses, schools, and shops were also built there. Throughout the republic there was a total of nearly 250 so-called "pioneer companies" with an eventual total annual production worth nearly S$1 billion. These new firms, about a quarter of which were Japanese, which were given tax and other incentives, gave employment to about twenty thousand persons, a figure that would double when all the firms were in full production. In its second development plan, covering the 1966-70 period, Singapore concentrated even more on building up its industrial base, allotting almost S$1 billion out of a total of S$1.5 billion for this purpose. An Economic Development Board was set up to give investors all possible help in establishing either foreign-owned or joint-ventured firms, and persistent efforts were made to find markets abroad.

In an almost blatantly frank attempt to woo capitalists to Singapore, Prime Minister Lee, in mid-1968, forced through a new Employment Bill and amendments to the Industrial Relations Ordinance which, for a Socialist state, was tantamount to a small counterrevolutionary move as far as the workers were concerned. In order to make such things as working hours, conditions of service, and fringe benefits predictable over a period of years, and sufficiently attractive for investors, trade unions were barred from negotiating such matters as promotion, transfer, employment, dismissal, retrenchment, and reinstatement, all of which had accounted for more than half of the trade disputes in the colony in recent years. In order to spread the work and help alleviate the effects of unemployment, overtime was limited to forty-eight hours a month, and the compulsory retirement age was set at fifty-five. Lee's actions, which the militant unions opposed but could do little about, were an obvious effort on his part to create in Singapore the conditions and atmosphere of *laissez-faire* that had enabled Hong Kong, Asia's other city-state, to prosper. Survival was the theme Lee harped on, pointing out, as he had said before, that no one owed Singapore a living and that such measures as his new bill were the only way to draw business to the port. "Our best chances lie in a very tightly organized society," Lee had earlier maintained. "We must achieve an ability to mobilize the maximum we are capable of. Societies like ours have no fat to spare. They are either healthy or they die."

Nevertheless, some observers continued to feel that Singapore was demonstrating an odd mixture of tough self-reliance and colonial-minded dependence on others. Lee Kim San, who was Finance Minister before he took over the Defense Ministry, had asserted, for example, that Singapore had the "right" to count on the full cooperation of countries such as the United States and Great Britain, "which have a vested interest in ensuring that Singapore remains viable and stable so that, in turn, their own security interests are not jeopardized." Britain, it was hoped, would help out in the interests of protecting its vast commercial interests in Singapore and Malaysia, totaling about £700 million. After prolonged and often touchy negotiations, Singapore had obtained an agreement in 1967 from the United States whereby an annual export quota of thirty million square yards of textiles would be accepted in America, and a similar agreement to buy a lesser amount was signed with the British. Official diplomatic or trade relations were established with some eighty nations after separation, and everything possible was done to attract investors from all over the world. A 1967 agreement with the Russians to exchange S$30 million worth of goods during that calendar year was followed by similar deals with the Poles, Bulgarians, Czechs, and Yugoslavs, and in 1968 the Russians set up their first joint venture with Singapore, a shipping agency. Imports from China rose 50 percent in 1967 over 1966, and the Chinese became Singapore's third biggest supplier of goods, after Japan and Malaysia. The Chinese also set up ten department stores in Singapore, which were doing an annual business of S$300 million in 1968. Late that year the Singapore government set up a trading corporation for the specific purpose of developing further trade with countries of the Socialist bloc.

Successful Welfare State

Even before Malaysia had been created, Singapore had demonstrated a solicitude for its population's welfare that made the port one of Southeast Asia's most forward-looking communities. Despite separation, and the costs of supporting a new defense effort of its own, Singapore continued to spend heavily to carry on various social services—in 1968, before the heavy new defense outlays, such services comprised 43 percent of the total budget. In a five-year housing program ending in 1965, some 55,000 units were built, and slums were replaced by rows of skyscrapers, some of them twenty stories high. Another 60,000 units were to be completed by 1970. Public-housing flats of three rooms rented for between S$66 and S$95. As part of its social service program, the government also launched a widespread family-planning scheme to keep the rate of population increase below 2 percent, and by 1967 the birth rate had declined 25 percent in ten years. Government hospitals also announced that abortions would be performed on request for a nominal fee of S$5. The effort to keep the population down was primarily a preventive economic measure in view of the mounting problem of unemployment, but it was also designed to avoid overcrowding that would heighten the dangers of communal strife. Despite his considerable efforts to stress the multiracial approach, Lee and his fellow ministers remained fully aware of the constant, lurking danger of violence such as had occurred sporadically in Singapore over the past several years, and which would play into the Communists' hands.

During one of my trips to Singapore, I made some extended tours around the city with a friend who had lived in the port for several years and had been studying the complicated political and racial situation. We rode through a number of the areas where there had been racial friction between Malays and Chinese, including the Geyland district, where serious riots took place in 1960. Malay families, who had originally moved into the district when the government was building the airfield there, were living in rickety nipa shacks or in gaudily painted wooden houses—the Malays love bright colors. A big Malay market operated in the center of the district. On the fringe, however, and dipping into it, were scores of Chinese shops and some Chinese homes. Part of the area was still swampy, and in ponds where pigs raised by the Chinese were feeding on water hyacinths, ducks and geese raised by the Malays were also swimming. We passed through other districts where small Malay settlements were like islands in a Chinese sea, and it was easy to understand how trouble had occurred in the past and how readily a spark—an argument on a hot night in a shop or on a street corner—could ignite communal strife.

It was the government's hope that by slowly elevating the Malays' standard of living, it would eventually get them out of the slums, and it had begun a long-term program of urban renewal to clear up these areas and to fill in more of the tidal swampland and some of the low areas along the sea, thereby creating whole new sections for resettlement. Some of this work involved diverting river channels, rebuilding sewer systems, building new flood walls, connecting bridges and roads, and replacing blocks of tumbledown shacks and shops with new residential and commercial sections, as well as schools and mosques. These plans, as projected, would take years to complete, and the process of rebuilding men's minds so that the different races could live in harmony would undoubtedly take even longer, but this was part of Singapore's drive for survival. As Lee Kuan said in one of his postseparation speeches, "We believed, and we still believe, that our salvation lies in an integrated society. I say that integration is possible, not to make us one gray mass against our will, against our feelings, against our inclinations, but to integrate us with common values, common attitudes, a common outlook, certainly a common language, and eventually a common culture. . . . There is no reason why, with patience, tolerance, perseverance, we should not, in this hub, in this confluence of different civilizations, create a situation which will act as a yeast, a ferment for what is possible, given goodwill, forbearance, and good faith."

One of the consequences of Singapore's separation from Malaysia was the emergence of Lee, a Western-educated Socialist chief of a multiracial state with a progressive capitalist economy, as a potential regional and world statesman. Merger and Malaysia had for years been almost an obsession with him, and Lee's weeping when separation took place was essentially as much an intellectual as an emotional admission of frustration and failure. After his period of reflection, and his extensive travels through Socialist, Communist, and capitalist nations, he acquired a new and more mellow and larger outlook; he became less intense than when he still thought he might emerge as the leader of Malaysia. The illusion no longer existed, and the imperatives had been removed. For the first time since he had become Prime Minister, Lee was able to relax and to regard himself as the head of a small but potentially workable state, and, at the same time, as a practicing Socialist theorist whose ideas, if they were never workable in the restricted, communal atmosphere of Malaysia, could turn out to have a wider and more attentive audience in the regional context of Southeast Asian cooperation or in the larger context of Western-Asian relations. It was partly for this reason that, in the fall of 1968, he traveled again to America for what he described as "several months of sabbatical," basing himself at M.I.T. and Harvard. Although in his absence there were no serious crises, there were some left-wing student outbreaks and little progress had been made on new defense talks with Malaysia. Lee seemed more mellow when he returned, and while he still spoke self-confidently of Singapore's future, he was more subtle and cautious in his approach. "I take comfort from the fact that even in the Dark Ages there were places like Venice which shone out and lit the way back into the Renaissance," he said. "Perhaps that is the role we may be asked to play."

One of Lee's, and Singapore's, inhibiting problems remained the lack of an important political opposition. After separation, even more than before, Singapore was, to all intents and purposes, a one-party state. In fact, with the resignation late in 1966 of the nine

Barisan Socialis members of Parliament—two were in jail, two were underground and probably out of the country, and the other five had been boycotting Parliament for more than a year—there was no longer any legal opposition as such. This did not mean that a *sub rosa* Communist movement did not exist in Singapore; it operated within a dozen or so left-wing unions, which were still a significant minority among the 154,000 registered union members, and as a subversive political element throughout the city, even though the People's Action Party effectively destroyed most of the earlier left-wing movement by arresting and detaining its leaders for varying periods—many recanted and were released, but several of the more important ones, including Lim Chin Siong, the co-founder of the Barisan Party, were still in jail in 1968. Lee, Rajaratnam, and other government leaders acknowledged that the continuing influence of the Communists was "a real challenge" and said they would not consider it rebuffed until the strength of the Communists was "whittled down to 5 or 10 percent of the population." Essentially, however, as a result of tactical mistakes that played into P.A.P. hands, the Barisan, by 1968, had bankrupted itself as a Communist Party front; first it had opposed Malaysia as an "imperialist plot," then it had denounced independence as "phony" and another surrender to the imperialists. Instead of fighting the P.A.P. in an open constitutional fashion, the party had continued to take its orders from Peking, where the Malayan National Liberation League had its headquarters, and it had vacillated between pretending to be a legal opposition and representing itself as the Singapore spearhead of armed revolt, Peking style. Further, the party was rent by internal factionalism and had no respected leadership.

Nevertheless, by its very blunders the Barisan group to a certain extent succeeded in embarrassing Lee and his associates in the P.A.P., who became increasingly worried about their growing bourgeois image. In a television interview, Lee once said, "If I had a good lively opposition, a sane one, not an insane one that talks in terms of unreality, of course the joining of issues would be better," and he admitted that "if we are to succeed, we must eventually create a situation in which there is a viable, intelligent non-Communist alternative." There were Singaporeans who felt that he did not really mean what he said and that he was afraid of any real opposition. Through close licensing control of newspapers and a careful watch over public meetings, there was actually scant chance of any meaningful opposition growing up, Communist or non-Communist. The P.A.P. was consequently on the horns of a dilemma. It could not afford to give the Communists any leeway, and at the same time the appearance of a moderate party, while it would be healthy politically, would serve as a serious threat to the P.A.P. if it appealed, in more direct terms than the P.A.P. had proved able to do, to the fundamental chauvinism in the Chinese population. Similarly, a strong Malay Party would raise the danger of fresh communal strife.

In February, 1968, eight months ahead of schedule, the President of Singapore, acting at the request of the P.A.P., dissolved Parliament and called for a new election. The vote was sought in advance of the end of the party's second five-year term in power in order to obtain a new mandate to deal with the new problems arising from the British withdrawal. "We cannot have our mind half on elections and half on negotiations," Foreign Minister Rajaratnam, who was head of the P.A.P. Political Bureau, said. "Southeast Asia will become an increasingly turbulent area with mounting economic distress and political instability. We therefore require new approaches and new methods of tackling these problems." The Barisan Socialis boycotted the election, describing it as a "farce" and "a cover for the fascist dictatorship of the Lee Kuan Yew puppets." Five other small parties also abstained. Of the fifty-eight seats in Parliament, the P.A.P. won fifty-one on the basis of uncontested nominations, and then swept all the remaining seven in the balloting, held in April, when a handful of independents were defeated. The minority parties claimed that the P.A.P. had stuffed the ballot boxes and that there had not been time for them to prepare for the election, while Lee and Rajaratnam in turn said that the opposition had "cheated" the people by abstaining and that they hoped for a true contest next time—presumably in 1973. In the meantime, Lee said, he would increase the number of ministers and "over the next few years we will have a second team of leadership which will become the first team by the middle of the nineteen-seventies."

If the vote was, in fact, scarcely a successful exercise in democratic procedure, it did provide Lee and the P.A.P. with the desired mandate to move ahead in framing the tough policies that were deemed necessary to cope with the social and economic problems Singapore faced and to carry out negotiations with Malaysia on the subject of defense and other matters of mutual concern.

Malaysia's Ups and Downs

With his customary calm, Tunku Rahman continued to feel that the matter of joint security could be worked out satisfactorily. But the Malayans, having celebrated the tenth anniversary of their freedom in 1967, a decade that had been dominated by the Tunku and had been generally marked by the success of his moderate policies and his benign approach, admittedly had some serious problems of their own to contend with. Despite success in introducing Malay as the national language, though the use of English as a second language was still permitted, there were still some strong racial and communal undercurrents. Riots that broke out in Penang, in November, 1967, underlined this. Although ostensibly the weakening of the currency in the wake of the devaluation of the pound inspired the outbreaks, this was probably more of a pretext than a direct cause. Both the extreme left-wing section of the Labor Party and the extreme right-wing elements of the Pan-Malayan Islamic Party had for some time been brewing trouble, and there was evidence that they were encouraged by other *sub rosa* groups, including a secret extremist Malay religious organization known as the "Army of the Holy War," by remnants of Chinese secret societies, and, of course, by the Communists.

Shortly after the failure of the 1965 coup in Indonesia, there had been signs that instead of concentrating on a multiracial front designed to obtain more Malay support, the Communist underground had apparently received orders to return to the line of exploiting Chinese-Malayan communal grievances. There was certainly sufficient opportunity to do this. Chinese chauvinism remained a potent factor among elements of the Chinese population, and, while the Alliance Party had managed to introduce a multiracial educational program and had handled the language problem fairly well, there remained a sense of discontent and of smoldering revolt among the younger Chinese, who had little regard for the Chinese "establishment" exemplified by the Malayan Chinese Association. During 1967 and 1968, subversion of Chinese secondary-school students increased, and, while the government struck back to suppress these activities, the evidence showed that the Communists were having considerable success. Underground organizations in many schools had direct ties to professional Communist groups. Straight party-line secret pamphlets called on the left-wing leaders to persuade their fellow students "to leave the classrooms and participate in the revolutionary mass struggle so as to overthrow reactionary regimes and strive for complete liberation."

By the end of 1968, however, there was fresh evidence that the Malayan Communist Party, which continued to look to Peking for guidance, had received instructions to alter the communal line and to obtain as much support as possible from the Malays as well as the Chinese. The new line was to stress that, despite many differences, Islamic and Communist ideals and objectives were the same in most respects, and that they could be blended in a common program of "reform." The M.C.P. consequently sought to obtain a foothold not only in the Labor Party but also in the Partai Ra'ayat (People's Party), which was completely Malayan. Early in November, 1968, in nationwide raids, the government responded to the new challenge by arresting 150 alleged Communist agents, most of them in Johore, just north of Singapore, and in Selangor and Penang states. The arrests included many members of both parties. Simultaneously, the government, in a White Paper, said: "The Communist Party of Malaya has made it manifestly clear that it considers the present time ripe for preparations to be made to pave the way for the armed struggle." Along the Thai border, Malaysian security forces had uncovered more than one hundred Communist terrorist camps during 1968. This was regarded as proof of the resurgence of Chin Peng's old guerrillas of the earlier Emergency period. During the Muslim fasting period of Ramadan, at the end of the year, police discovered that Communist agents were taking advantage of the holiday time to distribute pamphlets in West Malaysia in a further effort to persuade Moslems that Communism was not anti-Islam. Most of this material was being smuggled in from Thailand, it was believed, and early in 1969 the government in Kuala Lumpur decided to evacuate some two thousand residents along the border and to resettle them in northern Kedah. The firm reaction, while seemingly justified by the evidence, forced the government to assume a tough line in advance of 1969 national elections and weakened the Alliance Party's democratic claims. The opposition, claiming a witch hunt, was quick to respond, and the Labor Party and the Partai Ra'ayat threatened to boycott the vote. Adding to the opposition was a new moderate left-wing party calling itself the Malaysian People's Movement (Gerekan Ra'ayat Malaysia), which appealed to intellectuals and trade unionists. Its chairman, Dr. Tan Chee Koon, echoed the sentiments of the left-wing parties by declaring that the Alliance was following "a set path of reviving the Communist bogey whenever an election is in the offing."

The forces of discontent were aggravated by a growing economic crisis, and by continued rumblings in Sarawak, where five hundred Communist guerrillas were still active and where, among other things, they were capitalizing on native complaints that Malays were still being given the best jobs and receiving the principal benefits of development funds. A decline of 17 percent in the unit price of Malayan rubber in 1967, of the price of tin by 7.5 percent, and of the price of palm oil by 5.5 percent threatened Malaysia's prosperity and also raised the likelihood of a slowdown in the national development plans that had been a major achievement of the decade of freedom. A 10 percent unemployment rate in the cities, where most of the Chinese population was concentrated, and of about half that in the rural areas, where underemployment was a graver problem, created an additional dilemma for the government, which was suddenly forced to count up its resources and decide where and when to allocate how much for what. Continued industrialization, which would help reduce urban unemployment, was held necessary, but this would take time, and, meanwhile, the situation in the countryside had to be alleviated; here the government was faced with a conflict between wanting to continue its policy of fragmentation of rubber estates into small holdings, while having to face up to the fact that falling rubber prices made it advisable to consolidate plantations into larger and more efficient enterprises.

The Alliance Party, confronted with the new national election, made no effort to gloss over the difficulties. Tan Siew Sin, the hard-headed Finance Minister, declared, in a budget speech, that "We do not have to fear the long-term outlook, though the immediate future may be somewhat less cheerful." In the face of British withdrawal, this meant that defense expenditures would have to be held down to 20 percent of the total national outlay, while money for education and other welfare and development projects would have to be restricted. District rural development schemes, a widespread and generally successful enlargement on the national development plan that had become a model for Southeast Asia, would surely continue as part of the government's concentration on "economic democracy," but some of the more dramatic examples of progress, as detailed and charted in unique "operations rooms" set up in the separate states and in Kuala Lumpur, would undoubtedly be less in evidence than previously. Essentially, despite an admirable rate of progress during the first decade of independence, Malaysia was still largely dependent on world economic conditions, and especially on rubber and tin prices, and though these improved somewhat in 1968, its internal troubles could easily be exacerbated by new declines.

In short, though Singapore's per capita earnings of US$510 a year and Malaysia's of $310 ranked only behind Japan's as the highest in Asia, the problems confronting each nation in 1968— including economic setbacks, currency troubles, unemployment, and the need to reorient defense plans, offered scant ground for complacency. The "silent revolution" each nation was embarked on would undoubtedly continue, with modified success, but foreign support and investment, which inevitably would play a key role in determining the rate of internal growth, were indeterminate factors. The prospects of hostilities ending in Vietnam, and of possible reductions in American aid to, and interest in, Southeast Asia, did not make the outlook any rosier. For Malaysia, there was the problem of bridging geographic and cultural and social differences in Sarawak and Sabah, and of dealing with conditions of political unrest and immaturity in those areas. For Singapore, the difficulties remained primarily those of a small island-republic with few resources and largely dependent on the economic decisions of others surviving during an interim period when it had to create a valid industrial base of its own. Regional cooperation and some forms of international aid promised to alleviate but not to solve the predicaments each nation faced. The end of the Malaysian-Indonesian confrontation had brought benefits to each ex-partner, but new political troubles threatened to upset the delicate internal balance in both Malaysia and Singapore. The Penang riots and the Sarawak situation, and the threats of the Barisan Socialis in Singapore to maintain a nonparliamentary opposition, were indications that the Communists had no intention of lying low and doing nothing. It was significant that, while the Peking government showed signs of continuing to fish in Southeast Asia's troubled waters, both Malaysia and Singapore were drawing closer to the Soviet Union, particularly on economic matters, and this perhaps represented a calculated risk on the part of each government to hope for a joint American-Russian effort to guarantee the neutrality of Southeast Asia after the end or the containment of the Vietnam war.

Whatever lay ahead for Malaysia and Singapore, nothing could gainsay the remarkable record of progress each nation had achieved in the difficult decade between 1958 and 1968. Much of this achievement was due to the vastly different personalities of Tunku Rahman and Lee Kuan Yew, each of whom, in his own way, had proved to be the right leader for his country at the right time. Despite their contradictory temperaments and approaches, each had come to have an increasing appreciation of the other's virtues and foibles, and if this had not altogether added up to mutual respect, it had gradually led to a more realistic attitude on the part of each man that was also reflected in the attitude of their aides. The irony of the British withdrawal lay partly in the fact that the departure of the old mother country had made both siblings realize that, after all, they had come from the same nest, and that they had better learn to fly together. If this awareness did not presage a new union, which conceivably might never take place, it at least made clear the necessity of a joint approach. And if this produced the expected results, on even a limited basis, the prospects of wider regional cooperation would also be enhanced, and Southeast Asia as a whole, despite the varying patterns of progress, and its separate histories of revolution and reaction, would move toward greater self-sufficiency and consolidation.

4

The Philippines:

SURVIVAL IN THE SUN

The New and the Old

Ever since the end of the Second World War, when the Republic of the Philippines came into being, it has alternately swung from periods of profligacy and corruption, during which little or nothing was done to cope with its many deep-seated economic and social problems, to moods of great zeal for reform, when the nation seemed suddenly to rediscover its capacities for growth and to realize the potential of its human and material resources. Yet despite the Filipinos' abundant zest, their spirit of contemporaneity and awareness of how fast the world was changing, the basic way of life of the republic's 35 million inhabitants—at least that of the great majority—has probably changed less during the postwar years than that of any other people in Southeast Asia. In fact, the first reaction of a visitor returning to the Philippines after an absence of a few years was that everything had stayed the same—the exaggerated and often shoddy imitation of American forms and ways of life, including advertising and journalism; the economic dislocation, producing poverty among the many in contrast to the wealth and profligacy among a few; the seemingly endemic crime and violence, which gave rise to private shame but no public remorse or national sense of guilt; and, finally, the perpetual frantic game of politics, which came to a quadrennial climax every four years in a Presidential election.

There were deep historical reasons for this peculiar state of affairs, for the odd mixture of panic and passivity that seemed to create nothing so much as a static condition among the Filipinos, who, in 1968, were the second most populous nation, after Indonesia, in Southeast Asia. After a number of dramatic and romantic though unsuccessful revolts in the nineteenth century and the beginning of the twentieth against their Spanish and then their new American colonial masters, the Filipinos were benevolently ruled by the United States until they were handed their independence in 1946 without having to struggle for it (and, as many, including some Filipinos, felt, without being ready for it). Since then they have been scarcely affected by the revolutionary tides that have swept Asia—the one rebellion they faced and extinguished in the early fifties, that of the Communist-led Hukbalahaps, was essentially internal in its inspiration, though it adopted some external Marxist ideological trappings.

With its many Hispanic and American influences, the Philippines inevitably found itself caught between East and West, but the tendency was to relish rather than resolve this psychological historic and geographic condition. Efforts to draw the republic closer to its Asian neighbors, such as President Ferdinand E. Marcos' goodwill tours to Indonesia, Thailand, and Malaysia early in 1968, and his espousal of regional solidarity, were quickly set back by the feckless prosecution of the Philippines' old but weak irredentist claim to Sabah, in northern Borneo, which had become part of Malaysia. The diligence and emotionalism with which for some years they had pursued this claim, and which at the end of 1968 resulted in a break in diplomatic relations between the two countries, demonstrated the Filipinos' continuing need for a meaningful national cause, which many observers all along felt might better be found at home, where poverty remained such a serious problem. It was not that the Filipinos were unconscious of this situation, for an almost flagrantly free press and rampant freedom of speech drew constant attention to it and served as outlets for demands for revolutionary change. Now and then some progress was made, as in 1967-68 a dramatic breakthrough in rice production took place, stimulated by the scientific discovery in the Philippines of new, high-yielding rice, and for the first time in its history the country began to export rather than import this staple. But, by and large, there was always far more talk than action, more criticism than achievement, and this inevitably has resulted in more drift than solid change.

It was easy and fashionable to ascribe the failure of a stronger response to domestic challenges to the twin bogeys of politics and privilege, and there was much to substantiate this, but there were also other social and psychological factors that were just as important and that underscored some of the larger contemporary problems of national and regional development. In his ten-year study published in 1968, *Asian Drama, an Inquiry into the Poverty of Nations,* Gunnar Myrdal, the Swedish social historian, noted a tendency among the Southeast Asian nations to "accept planning as an idea even before they are able to translate much planning into reality." Myrdal added:

Successful economic planning, with all its implications of conditioning and directing economic life—and, indeed, the prior ability to reach operational agreements—requires stable and effective, internally united government, conditions of law and order, social discipline, and, more generally, national consolidation. Even spontaneous, or nearly spontaneous, economic development, given the other necessary conditions, is hardly possible without a considerable measure of political stability.

Myrdal made the further point that "the feeling of nationhood" which systematic planning should engender is often vitiated by a lack of cohesion, with the result that "national consolidation" is actually retarded and the "cumulative processes" of planning can become as "vicious" as they are "virtuous." When the threshold of implementation is not properly passed, planning for development simply fails "to overcome and compensate for inertia and for forces working against it."

These seemed valid judgments that applied particularly to the Philippines. An American friend of mine who has lived in the islands for nearly thirty years, and who himself has been involved in the planning process, agreed with Myrdal when he conceded that there has been "motivation for progress, but no real awareness of concepts." As he put it, "The specifics are touched, tasted, felt and smelled, but it's all terribly slow, and the farmer, for example, even as he tests out the new methods of planting rice, remains stymied by the dead weight of tradition, of feudal social patterns. The old protective and paternal family and patron ties will only really begin to break up as independent and individual opportunity becomes more apparent, and that takes time, more time than we Westerners, who tend to forget our own slow development, are often willing to admit or grant."

Barring a more violent upheaval in the Philippines, which in 1969 seemed possible but not probable, the changes that either planning or a freer development of entrepreneurial opportunity could bring about were likely to continue to take place slowly. There were a number of reasons for this, including those that Myrdal had made about the absence of social discipline and political stability. These lacks, in turn, reflected established social patterns and embraced precolonial Filipino mores as well as the colonial impact of Spaniards and Americans over four centuries. Such patterns, particularly the Spanish-imposed ones, tended to be peculiarly fixed and hard to alter. Employers in the Philippines, for example, have through the decades been regarded as patrons, in the old Spanish style. I recall the rather pathetic sight, some years ago, of a group of insurance company strikers stopping their sidewalk picketing to greet the company president as he alighted from his car and to wish him a happy birthday. There was something totally anachronistic in the scene that brought to mind the whole heritage of Spanish colonialism that still undermines the social and economic fabric of the Philippines, particularly in the rural areas, where four-fifths of the population live.

The key to reform obviously continues to lie in the country's 28,000 barrios, or villages, where, in sharp contrast to the frenzy and opportunism of Manila, there remains a deep sense of isolation and an atmosphere of apathy broken only by the occasional fiestas that are like explosive forms of release and invariably consume whatever meager savings the people have. The average barrio is composed of about two hundred families, and three-fourths of the working men are farmers, a high proportion of whom have regularly produced only enough to feed their own households. Life in most barrios has remained extremely primitive; the majority of families have no toilet facilities, still superstitiously consult her-

balios, or medicine men, about everything from aches and pains to means of getting jobs or finding marital mates, and two-thirds of the people over ten years of age are still all but illiterate. The historical impact of poverty runs deep in the culture of these lonely, fragmented communities. The lack of energy and imagination on the part of the inhabitants must be attributed to their initiative and ambition having been purposefully destroyed by the Spanish overlords during four centuries of harsh rule, and, despite some individual examples of enlightened leadership under the Americans, little change in the basic outlook or the condition of the typical farmer took place in the ensuing half-century of United States dominion over the islands. On top of a deliberate policy of isolating the Philippines commercially by restricting its trade and intercourse with other Asian nations, the Spaniards created a massive, lumbering civil bureaucracy that, through sheer red tape alone, made it virtually impossible for the Filipinos to do any business in their own right and that cleverly facilitated the total domination of the Spanish religious and feudal landowners. The Spanish authorities acquired and administered the biggest and best tracts of land and turned the Filipinos into poor tenants or small private farmers trying to subsist on marginal acres in the wilderness.

The sharecropping system of cultivation that replaced the pre-colonial forms of communal land ownership became the single biggest factor in fomenting agrarian unrest in the Philippines. Under the plantation economy instituted by the Spaniards, the most fertile plantations in the nation, sometimes several thousands of acres in size, were held by the friar corporations, and hundreds of thousands of other acres were owned by the civil class of *caciques,* the absentee landlords, who by 1969, despite the break-up of a few estates under the long-delayed land-reform program, still owned most of the land in the rich plains of central Luzon. Whether he was a tenant or a struggling farmer on his own, the Filipino under Spanish rule had to pay tribute in various ways to his foreign masters. Under the *polo* system, he had to do military duty aboard a Spanish ship or on land, where he cut timber or made ammunition. Under the system of *encomienda,* the peasant had to pay an annual financial sum to the crown collectors, who were frequently crooks simply lining their own pockets. According to the system of *vandala,* each community was assigned a production quota, and everything that was grown had to be sold to the government, which more often than not took the produce on credit and never came through with any actual cash.

These old feudal forms of tribute have of course disappeared, but their effect has lingered and they have helped provoke the paralysis of incentive and the sterility that have seeped so deep into the countryside and that revolutionary writers since José Rizal, the Philippines' foremost national hero, have so vividly depicted. Not until Spanish rule was eliminated did the agrarian discontent come to the surface, but the protests seldom had any lasting effect. The biggest exception was the Hukbalahap rebellion of 1948-54 which Ramón Magsaysay, first as Defense Secretary and then as President, so brilliantly defeated by a combination of counterguerrilla military action and an amnesty program that ameliorated the land hunger of the rebels by giving them areas to farm in the southernmost island of Mindanao. But because so little was done about land reform in Luzon, the Huks were offering a new threat by 1967, and, more significantly, there were other radical movements burgeoning, both in the countryside and in Manila.

In addition to the economic strictures imposed by the Spaniards, there have been other social and behavioristic factors that have retarded development and have, in effect, "frozen" the Filipinos. For example, sociologists who have conducted numerous studies in recent years have generally agreed that the Filipinos, perhaps more than any other Southeast Asians, traditionally see themselves throughout their lives as belonging to specific groups, to which they remain intensely loyal. This group loyalty begins with the family and, as a man grows older, takes in the neighborhood, the town, the province, and a larger geographic area that has its own customs and dialect. The loyalty tends to diminish, however, as one sociologist, Richard Stone, has pointed out, in inverse proportion to the size of the group, though social mobility remains minimal. The Filipinos are, of course, inevitably victims of a literal insularity, in a country comprising more than seven thousand islands, including a dozen major ones, sprawled over more than twelve hundred miles of ocean, and in a society that uses nine different languages—Tagalog, the Luzon dialect, is the commonest, and English, taught in most schools, is the official one. In religion the Filipinos are predominantly Catholic, though there are more than a million Muslims and more than a million adherents of a local Christian sect known as Aglipayan. What seems to count most, though, in an ethnological sense, is territory—or "turf," in criminal terms—which undoubtedly helps explain both the stubborn Sabah claim and the prevalence of youthful armed gangs in the Philippines, especially in Manila and other cities and in Mindanao and the Sulu Archipelago in the far south.

This adherence to loyalty groups and the ardent defense of both territory and property have other sociological manifestations. Stone conducted a fascinating study of metropolitan traffic, and of what he calls "the driving game." Traffic jams, and wild driving, it should be said, have been notorious in Manila since the end of the Second World War and have grown worse each year. In analyzing the attitude of one veteran taxi driver named Lito, Stone concluded that, while Lito considered himself a member of the common people, the *tao,* and harbored a natural envy and resentment of the *malakas,* the affluent and powerful people, he also had a sense of humor and of the ridiculous and had come to view life as a series of contests, large and small, in which "winning" was, in effect, both part of the daily game and a self-protective necessity. Lito's "turf" was the street, and his natural opponents were other drivers—*barumbados* (reckless drivers), *swapang* (greedy drivers), and *buwaya* (crocodiles, or road hogs)—as well as pedestrians, all of whom, in Lito's world, were *tangá,* or stupid. A driver like Lito, after brushing a couple of pedestrians who were jaywalking, simply explained it away by saying, "When I'm driving here in the city, I drive like that. Because if you don't, they will *puck* you [push you around]. They look at me, those pedestrians, and they say, 'Oh, that is only an old man, I will *puck* him.' But me, I am driving in Manila now for thirty-two years. I will *puck* them first. I know how to play the game. If you don't *puck* them, they will *puck* you."

This urge to competitive self-preservation, which the American influence in this century has assuredly stimulated, considered in context with the older forms and inheritances of group loyalty, class structure, and the social and religious strictures of the Catholic Church, further helps explain why the Filipinos, despite their penchant for talking about modernization and change, have remained fundamentally static and passive. Under these circumstances, it seems all the more astonishing that the Philippines were able to make their breakthrough in rice production. The credit must be divided among the International Rice Research Institute, founded in 1961 in Los Baños, south of Manila, by the Ford and Rockefeller foundations; the United States Agency for International Development, headed in Manila in the mid-sixties by Wesley C. Haraldson; and President Marcos and his aides, particularly Rafael Salas, the able and reform-minded Executive Secretary at the Presidency, who devoted most of his time to the rice project and who, with Marcos' approval, performed what in the Philippines amounts to an administrative miracle by coordinating the activities of about a score of government agencies.

Despite the large rural population only a third of the nation's income has traditionally been derived from agriculture. Rice production per hectare (about two and a half acres) averaged less than thirty cavans (a cavan is equal to ninety-seven pounds of palay, or unhulled rice, which yields a little over sixty pounds of clean rice). With its fast-rising population, the Philippines was importing more than 300,000 tons of rice a year between 1963 and 1966. In 1968 it exported 60,000 tons, mostly to Indonesia, and the expectations were that within two or three years it would be exporting 200,000 tons, which should bring in about $30 million. The breakthrough began in 1966 when the first test plantings of a new rice seed, IR8, developed at the research institute, were made in Laguna Province, south of Manila. IR8's history dates back to 1962, when a scientist at the institute took pollen from a form of short indica rice grown in Taiwan and placed it on the pistils of emasculated flowers of a taller tropical native variety, known as Peta. Additional transplantings were made until a form of IR8 was developed which, while still susceptible to some forms of fungus and other diseases, and tending to produce too chalky a grain, was judged worthy of being tested in the field. The results were astonishing. The Laguna plantings brought a yield of 190 cavans per hectare, six times the normal Philippine average. Other tests were then continued, and new forms of IR8, as well as one known as IR5, were found, which produced a finer form of rice that was more blight-resistant and better-tasting, though some shortcomings remained. These new seeds were distributed in 1968, not only in the Philippines and Indonesia but elsewhere in Southeast Asia, including Vietnam.

Under Salas' direction, the Rice and Corn Administration and the various other agencies dealing with irrigation, banking and credit, and so on were brought together into a national Rice Action Group. Since IR8 cost four times as much as ordinary rice to cultivate because of the agricultural supplies and extra labor required, many farmers were scared to try it. But when the program was initially introduced in 1966 in twelve key provinces—ten on Luzon, and one each in the central Visayan Islands and in Mindanao—the receptivity of the peasants was encouraged by trained government "motivators" heading traveling teams of experts, and by A.I.D. distribution of 22,000 "rice kits," containing some seed, fertilizer, disease- and rate-control materials, and clear instructions. The average farmer planting the new seeds found his production tripled, which, despite his higher costs, made bearable by the government's new credit program operated through rural banks, brought him an income of a thousand pesos per hectare (four pesos equal one American dollar), which was three or four times what he had earned previously. Most farmers started off slowly by planting only part of their two or three hectares with the new so-called "miracle rice," but the program soon caught on and Salas expected to extend it to all the Philippines' rice-growing provinces —fifty-five out of a total of sixty-five—by 1970. The government's price-support scheme, which provided a guarantee of sixteen pesos per cavan of palay, specifically affected only about 15 percent of the total production, but it functioned as a protective device against price-cutting middlemen and speculators, although in 1968 they were not yet eliminated.

President Marcos' extensive road-building program, including feeder as well as major roads, was another vital factor. The success with new rice also led farmers to experiment with new higher-yielding corn seeds and with other vegetables, as well as with poultry and swine production, and the over-all result was a higher national agricultural income and the promise that the Philippines would become the leading surplus-food producer in the area. There were still some problems, among them a shortage of technicians and agricultural-school graduates, a shortage of modern farm equipment, insufficient warehouse space and marketing facilities, and the continued prevalence of plant disease and of rats, which together continued to destroy vast amounts of crops. There was also some doubt as to how long the government could sustain its price supports—it was up against the dilemma of raising the farmers' income and at the same time meeting the popular demand for cheaper rice. Some of the farmers using the new seeds had quickly been besieged by relatives and friends who made themselves dependents to the point where the experimental grower's added income was rapidly consumed and he was ready to give everything up and return to the old, simpler system. Nevertheless, the program could not be considered anything but a great success, and it was primarily due to what Salas called "the separation of the politicians from the administrators."

How Far with Marcos?

The solution of the larger program of land reform would not be so easy, although Marcos, on his way to becoming the first President of the Philippines to be re-elected to a second term, had his own compelling sense of history and of his role in it, and pledged to move ahead in this vital field, too. The problem was far more complicated than that of rice production, impinging as it did on the whole social-political spectrum of Philippine life and particularly on the traditional power of the wealthy landlord oligarchy, the dominant force in the country, whose influence reached deep into Congress and into Malacañang, the Presidential Palace. The background of land reform was as follows: Magsaysay, when he was President, was fully aware of the historical significance of the peasant problem and tried to cope with it in various ways that went beyond the solving of the Huk problem. In 1955, during his tenure, legislation was passed designed to break up the big landed estates and redistribute land to individual peasants. There was considerable debate, even among those favoring reform, about the efficacy of the bill. Many, if not most, experts agreed that, while something ought to be done to break up the biggest holdings and do away with absentee landlordism, the large size of the average Filipino family made too much redistribution unfeasible; the fragmentation that would result, it was feared, with each son of each father eventually inheriting an unproductive acre or two, might well do more harm than good in the long run.

A more hopeful solution, many believed, lay in the legal clarification of obscure and chaotic land titles and in the proper implementation of another bill already on the books, the Agricultural Tenancy Law, which provided the tenant farmer with the legal means to obtain a more equitable share of the harvest, security of tenure, and the option to become a lessee tenant. Specifically, this law gave the tenant the right to demand 70 percent instead of the customary 50 percent of what he grew, protected him—through the right to appeal to an Agrarian Court—from being arbitrarily thrown off his land, and allowed him the right to demand a lease-hold under a fixed rental that also permitted him to manage his own farm. What kept the law from working was the usual combination of red tape and inefficiency, plus the usual amount of politics and corruption. The legislation, furthermore, was extremely complicated and the average timid farmer knew very little about it, while the few dozen experts who were supposed to explain it were invariably hamstrung by local mayors who were in cahoots with the landlords and depended on them for political support. The tenants, for their part, had no organization of their own, which they drastically needed if they were to summon up sufficient strength and courage to fight for their statutory rights.

Magsaysay, who was a great inspirational leader but not a good administrator, was killed in an airplane crash in March, 1957, and was succeeded by Carlos P. García. Virtually nothing was accomplished during the García administration, and, after four lonely years as an opposition-party Vice President—Philippine law permits a splitting of the two top jobs along party lines—Diosdado Macapagal roundly defeated García's bid for re-election. Macapagal, a much more calculating and politically motivated man than Magsaysay, had carefully built up his grass-roots support as Vice President and he projected himself as the "poor man's" candidate. In academic background and administrative ability, he surpassed Magsaysay, whom he very much admired and whose spirit and dynamic drive he sought to emulate, but he altogether lacked Magsaysay's charismatic appeal, and his tendency to project himself as the best qualified of the six Presidents of the Philippines rubbed a lot of people the wrong way. By, in effect, placing himself above the crowd while pretending to be of it, and by admittedly adopting a number of legal short cuts to get his reform programs started—maneuvers for which the Supreme Court on several occasions peremptorily slapped him down—he spurred the opposition to charge him with dictatorial tendencies and a desire to establish some sort of system of "Guided Democracy" along Sukarnoist lines. Nevertheless, Macapagal did try to do something about land reform. As soon as he came into office, he introduced what he called his "Five Year Integrated Socio-Economic Program," to cost $6.5 billion through 1967; about a third of it was to come from foreign aid sources, and during this period both public and private investment was supposed to pump $12.7 billion into the economy. Macapagal stressed the fact that unless agricultural productivity, and therefore the income and purchasing power of the farmers, was increased, desirable new industries were not likely to develop and flourish.

One of the first emergency measures he pushed through Congress created a new Rice and Corn Administration, which by supervising the marketing and distribution of rice in particular managed to cut the retail price by two-thirds in one year, though by the end of his administration Macapagal was forced to import 600,000 tons of rice to keep the price down. The basic job of overhauling the marketing system in general, and getting rid of rapacious and unnecessary middlemen, while also revamping the corruption-ridden agricultural credit system, proved beyond the capacities of his regime. Along with many Filipino reformers, Macapagal believed that bettering the lot of the farmer had to go hand in hand with political reforms at the barrio level, designed to give the villages greater autonomy and control over their own affairs. Under a Barrio Charter Act, passed by Congress in 1959, the barrios for the first time elected their own councils, each headed by what was called a barrio lieutenant (subsequently a barrio captain), and these councils obtained limited rights to raise and collect some local taxes and to use 10 percent of all land taxes for their own purposes. Macapagal's other main accomplishment was to decontrol the peso as a stimulant to private enterprise, but, by and large, despite a plethora of plans, many of them extremely good on paper, there was little systematic implementation of them. Macapagal's failure as an administrator became more apparent as time went on; by mid-term he was so embroiled in politics and in his own efforts for re-election that virtually nothing was accomplished to refashion the clumsy government machinery, and increasingly the men around him became personal henchmen.

All in all, Macapagal was damned by his critics for being "all talk and no performance." It was commonly agreed, for instance, that beyond failing to come to grips with the critical rice situation —unfortunately for him, the scientific discoveries of new strains came too late to help his program—Macapagal let himself be frustrated and ultimately defeated by the land-reform issue. After having called a special session of Congress, he managed to push through a new reform measure, which, for the first time, abolished outright the system of agricultural-land tenancy dating back to Spanish times. Peasants could thenceforth become leaseholders with permanency of tenure, and with rents limited to 25 percent of an average normal harvest, after basic cost deductions. The government was supposed to take over, first, all idle and abandoned land, and then large estates, working by order of priority from the biggest ones down to those as small as seventy-five hectares; after expropriating such land and giving the landlords proper compensation, the government was to redistribute it in family-size farms to the peasants. There were various other sections of the act that were designed to furnish the peasants with loans at reduced interest rates and with other economic help and guidance, but the recalcitrant Congress that Macapagal faced, led by the dominant landlord elements in it, managed to emasculate the act in some important ways, notably by rejecting a measure to increase the land tax, by which the administration hoped to get enough funds to push the program. Ultimately, it was only set in motion in nine pilot-project areas, and relatively little land was redistributed.

Macapagal wavered between pride over the land-reform bill he pushed through and a feeling that he had been betrayed. When I saw him during this period, he said: "I used the strategy of surprise to get the bill through before the landlords realized what was happening. If I had implemented the land-reform program more fully, I think the outcome would have been even worse, because of the inherent frailty of the peasants. They do not yet understand the real implications of the program, and they are not yet mature enough to confront the counteractivities of the landlords. In other respects, because Congress turned down important economic or administrative reforms I sought, I was unable to satisfy the revolution of rising expectations. Our people are impatient for fulfillment of their hopes, and they will react strongly when they feel things are not moving fast enough. So, while I certainly brought about a substantial measure of improvement in their lives, and increased their income and raised their wages, they turned against me. I must accept this as the common fate of all reformers."

The 1965 election was one of the most bitter ever waged in the Philippines. As usual, the vital issues, though widely and heatedly debated, were over the heads of most voters and proved not as important as the candidates' personal qualities and characteristics. The result was that a majority of some 630,000 out of seven and a half million voters chose the more colorful Marcos, whose cause was immeasurably helped by his beautiful wife, Imelda, who campaigned both fiercely and tenderly for him, sometimes singing duets with her husband in various regional dialects for the highly musical Filipino audiences. Marcos himself described Imelda as his "secret weapon." Her help was especially valuable in countering the so-called "black propaganda" that the opposition Liberal Party disseminated against him. One of its main points concerned a typical family feud among the violence-addicted Ilokanos of northern Luzon, of whom Marcos was one. As a young man, he had been accused of murdering a man named Julio Nalundasan, who, on September 20, 1935, three days after he had defeated Marcos' father, Mariano, for a seat in the old Commonwealth National Assembly, was shot to death through an open window in his house. Young Marcos, who had just passed his eighteenth birthday, was accused of having been the trigger man in the plot because, among other things, he was an expert marksman and his college team used the same kind of .22-caliber rifle as the alleged murder weapon. Four years later, after having spent a considerable time in jail but still having managed to pass his bar examinations with what is still the highest record ever established in the islands, young Marcos argued his own case before the nation's Supreme Court and was unanimously acquitted after convincing the judges, in a brief of nearly a thousand pages and in an impassioned oral plea, that he had been the victim of a political frame-up.

The case, naturally, was a national sensation, and after it Marcos went on to become one of the Philippines' greatest war heroes. During the Japanese conquest of the islands, he successfully executed a daring delaying action in the retreat from Bataan, after which he survived the infamous Death March and a term in Fort Santiago prison, from which he escaped to become one of the war's boldest guerrilla leaders. He was wounded several times and was afterward awarded some of the highest Philippine and American decorations. After the war he practiced law, entering politics in 1949, when he was elected a Congressman; ten years later he became a Senator. He was a Liberal Party member in those days, and, in fact, gave way to Macapagal in the 1961 Liberal Party race for the Presidential nomination on Macapagal's reported pledge that, after four years, he would decline to run again and would support Marcos. When, toward the middle of his administration, it became apparent that Macapagal intended to run for re-election after all, Marcos was eased out as head of the Liberal Party, and he soon joined the opposition Nacionalista Party.

While there was nothing new about this kind of opportunistic party-switching, or "turncoating" as it is called in the Philippines —it goes on all the time, especially just before and after elections, and is the main reason for the lack of any permanent party structure and political stability—the background and circumstances of the Marcos-Macapagal dispute had been of such a special personal nature that they exacerbated the viciousness of the ensuing campaign and left a residue of recrimination. In the eyes of most Filipinos, even those who voted for him, Marcos remained an unknown quantity, and despite his acknowledged bravery and brilliance, there were aspects of his record that served to make him a suspect and mysterious figure as well as an alluring and dashing one. The charges that continued to be cited against him to impugn his integrity included a variety of complicated allegations—that he had been guilty of grabbing land from poor peasants by slick legal maneuvers; that he had knowingly used forged documents during a Senate investigation several years earlier into the illegal activities of foreign and Filipino businessmen; that he had used bad checks in business deals; that he had padded his Senate payroll; and that he had filed false personal war-damage claims. This was a pretty solid list of accusations, and, though Marcos countered some of them with aplomb and wisely ignored others, many people remained convinced that at least part of the alleged "black propaganda" had an element of truth to it.

Whatever the blemishes on his past, Marcos got off to a good start, especially with the rice program. I had the feeling, however, when I first spoke with him, shortly after his election, that despite his supreme self-confidence and his sense of authority, he was so overwhelmed with the manifold problems he faced that he had not even had time to think through possible solutions. He did say, even then, that he intended to push land reform harder, and that he hoped to do what Macapagal had not done—influence the wealthy Luzon landlords to surrender their properties for land in undeveloped parts of Mindanao or for shares in public companies, such as the government-controlled steel and cement corporations. And he talked about a "crash fertilizer approach" to increase the Luzon rice output severalfold in a few years. Four years later, when I saw him again, Marcos was more firm than ever about moving ahead with land reform. "This is an obsession with me," he said, adding that "I'm already in Dutch with the landlords for what we've done." Most observers, however, both Filipino and foreign, maintained that he had scarcely touched base with the program so far. "Marcos is a tough, sophisticated political animal with a good sense of timing," one of his more fair-minded critics said. "He does two or three things at a time, and then draws back and waits. During this administration he concentrated on food production and roads. If he is re-elected, the real test will come in those other two basic areas of reform—full implementation of the land-reform act and the establishment of peace and order in the country. The big question remains—will he be willing to buck the oligarchy all the way and prove himself the great President he says he wants to be, or will he back down and compromise?"

The Marcos land-reform program, which was being administered by Conrado Estrella, and which involved the activities of about a score of other agencies that were not yet as well coordinated as those dealing with the food-production scheme, embraced five areas of activity: the arrangement of leaseholds under which tenants would remain tenants but would run their own farms and pay a maximum of 25 percent of their crops to the landlords; the upgrading and improvement of landed estates, including the construction of roads and irrigation facilities, and of resettlement projects; the opening and development of new settlement areas in Mindanao and other southern islands; the acquisition by the government of private estates for ultimate redistribution;

and manpower training to furnish the technicians required. By mid-1968 some fifty towns, mostly in Pampanga and Nueva Ecija provinces in central Luzon, had been declared land-reform areas, and Marcos and Estrella promised that all of the central Luzon area would soon be brought under land reform. Some 85,000 farmers tilling more than 200,000 hectares had been affected so far, at least theoretically, and about ten thousand new leasehold contracts had been drawn up. While their implementation had lagged, in those cases where they had been carried out farmers had increased their production by about a third in their first year of "independence" from the landlords, and had doubled their output during the second year. However, there remained considerable reluctance on the part of the many peasants to be on their own, even as leaseholders; and without proper education, through farm extension courses, and without enough credit facilities, they frequently failed to benefit from their new opportunities and some even chose to return to the landlords' fold. The government had purchased six haciendas in central Luzon by 1959 and planned to buy another twenty or so, but the trouble was that the Land Bank and the Agricultural Credit Administration had insufficient funds to move ahead with these plans, despite the fact that only 10 percent in cash had to be paid out and the rest was in the form of government securities. Some of the landlords were willing to sell their properties and accept the securities for reinvestment, but most were still resistant.

All in all, there was considerable skepticism about the program's future, and doubt that Marcos would really face up to the landlords and the other oligarchic elements and force through the revolutionary changes that were necessary beyond the purchase of land, including administrative changes. As one knowledgeable American said, "Land reform has been talked about for years here, but there has to be more to it than political oratory. The problem is to get the peasants used to living in a landlordless world. If you can't make the farmer productive, leave him alone. Those whose income is already increasing as a result of the new rice- and corn-growing techniques couldn't care less about owning their own land. Prosperity can actually come to the Philippines without land redistribution. Marcos may know this and may not want to risk the political dangers of pushing ahead."

Law but No Order

The land-reform program and, in fact, all the planning that went on but remained unimplemented were closely tied to another fundamental problem, analogous to the United States one of "law and order." Ever since independence the republic's social and economic growth had been retarded by the violence that was endemic throughout the islands, but especially in the Greater Manila area, where the crime rate continued to soar almost steadily and where more than a thousand murders occurred in 1968, about half the recorded national total—untold others went unrecorded. While Manila was by no means a mirror of the country as a whole, it reflected the awful cleavages of wealth and poverty and demonstrated the social and emotional unrest that pervaded so much of the Philippines. On the surface, the city—which, next to Warsaw, had been the capital worst damaged in the Second World War —was largely rebuilt by 1968. The harbor had finally been cleared of sunken and shattered hulls, while Dewey Boulevard, renamed Roxas Boulevard, had had its waterfront face lifted and new buildings had replaced the bombed-out and shell-pocked old ones. Even Intramuros, the old walled city near the downtown area where the Japanese made a bitter last-ditch defense, had finally been cleared of its miserable hovels of squatters' huts. However, as one rode through the more populated parts of Manila to the rich outlying suburbs, it was easy to see why crime flourished. Driving, for example, to Forbes Park, the new, wealthiest part of Greater Manila, where hundred-thousand-dollar homes had become commonplace, one passed along potholed and often flooded streets through drab neighborhoods packed with ramshackle houses, around which half-naked youngsters played or came to beg or offer cigarettes for sale through car windows whenever one of the never-ending Manila traffic jams brought the long lines of vehicles to a halt. Perhaps nothing so much epitomized the contrast between poor and rich as the sight of a huge Cadillac or a Mercedes-Benz stranded in traffic in a bad neighborhood amid a flock of "jeepneys," the remodeled war-surplus jeeps that the Filipinos had fitted out with seats along the sides sheltered by canopies that bore such colorful names as "Manila Boy," "Starlight Lover," and "Jilted Joe."

Early in 1968 the seriousness of the crime situation led all of Manila's seven English-language newspapers to run a common editorial, calling on Marcos to take steps to curb the crime rate, which promised to be one of the main issues during the 1969 election, as it has been in the United States. Much of the crime that took place was difficult or impossible to track down, but the fact that there were some thirteen hundred separate law-enforcement agencies, the great majority of them ill-equipped, poorly trained and underpaid, and many of them corrupt, did little to help solve the problem. Political murders were among the most frequent forms of killing; there were sixty-two such crimes reported during the mid-term elections in 1967, when Marcos secured a Nacionalista majority in both houses of Congress; the opposition Liberals charged him with having mounted a campaign of threats and terror. Much of the killing that occurred was done by alleged murder syndicates—the papers in the summer of 1968 were full of reports of the existence of eleven such mobs, including one said to be composed of six hundred armed men. Loose, unregistered guns remained one of the major problems; officials said there were 55,000 such weapons in the country, but the actual number was believed to be nearly ten times that. As Teodoro Valencia, the veteran columnist of the Manila *Times,* wrote, "The gun should cease to be a status symbol. This can only happen if public officials were to start hiding their guns and stop hiring them."

Aside from murder and other crimes of violence, including armed robberies, all of which made Manila the most unsafe place in Asia, not excepting Saigon, there was a vast amount of corruption in business dealings tied in with those in the highest levels of the government. The graft involved ever huger sums—including, for example, kickbacks of as much as 50 percent on millions of dollars of road-building and other construction projects, on the building of new and, many maintained, unnecessary sugar mills, and on the sale of former American-owned properties to Filipino syndicates. All of this could be ascribed to the competition for power that was intense in the Philippines, as well as for survival on many different levels. There is said to be no such thing as a satisfied Filipino victor in *any* sort of contest. When a politician made a fortune as a result of being elected to high office, he seldom stopped to count his blessings or his bounty and simply kept on trying to make more money. Similarly, a loser, whether he was a businessman or an ousted officeholder, or a simple barrio citizen who kept dropping half his paltry income by betting on cockfights or playing the numbers game—the two most popular barrio pastimes—would never give up. He would go on losing until someone, a better-off member of the family or a friend, bailed him out, whereupon he would start all over again, or, if he was really cornered, resort to violence.

Only once since independence, during Magsaysay's administration, could there be said to have been a significant improvement in the moral climate, and this was due, above all, to Magsaysay's own incorruptibility and to his proving that wrongdoing could be curbed, by means of tactics that he used across the board, against important and powerful officials and wealthy private individuals as well as lesser lights. President Macapagal attacked a few sources of corruption—most notably, he broke the extensive business empire of Harry Stonehill, an American with many Filipino connections, and forced Stonehill and his associates out of the country—but here again Macapagal's lack of administrative ability kept him from accomplishing any real reform. Marcos, when he came into office, promised, as every President before him had done, to concentrate on the moral issue, and he did crack down hard on smuggling (though piracy was increasing). By facilitating the further independence of barrio administration, he also reduced ordinary crime in some parts of the country. But no more than his predecessors, with the exception of Magsaysay, did he attack corruption from the top down.

The Communists, of course, have always insisted that corruption is a by-product of capitalism, but, in the moral atmosphere of the Philippines in 1968, it seemed no accident that the erstwhile Huks, the remnants of the Communist-inspired rebels of the fifties, had become primarily "mafioso" types whose business was business rather than revolution, and whose simulated Robin Hood activities in the central Luzon countryside were more akin to those of syndicate protective associations in America than to the conduct of other left-wing agrarian reformers in Asia. The Huks—the full name is *Hukbon ng Mapagpalay ng Bayan*, which in Tagalog means

People's Liberation Army—were primarily active in four Luzon provinces in the late sixties. Their armed strength was variously estimated at only two to three hundred men, many of whom carried excellent M-16 guns stolen from nearby Clark Field, the vast 157,000-acre American air base, which served, among other things, as a transit point for weapons shipments to Vietnam. At the height of their earlier power, in 1950, the Huks had had a hard core of some fifteen thousand, most of them armed, and about thirty thousand supporters among the Luzon peasants. When they were subdued, in 1952, by Magsaysay, who broke the back of the movement by capturing its Politburo in October, 1950, their organization fell apart, but they managed to keep some small armed bands going. By 1964 their estimated support among the peasantry was still twelve thousand; this was said to have increased four years later to a point close to the 1950 figure, and recruiting of sympathizers was continuing. These peasants, for the most part, were simply people who were harboring or helping the armed elements and the fifteen hundred or so additional members of the "legal" cadre, the political organizers, feeding and protecting them from the Army and the constabulary units that sporadically tried to track them down; the farmers voluntarily gave, or were forced to give, donations of rice, as did many of the landlords in the key provinces, who followed the path of least resistance by establishing an accommodation with the Huks, even allowing the roving bands to hide out on their haciendas.

In a series of skirmishes in the spring and summer of 1968, two of the Huks' ten top commanders, Gregorio García, alias Yoyong, and Alberto Mercado, alias Tronco, as well as half a dozen lesser leaders of bands that numbered anywhere from six to thirty men, were killed by the Army or the constabulary. But the other main commanders were still at large, directed by the two heads of the movement, Pedro Taruc, alias Pedring, and Faustino del Mundo, alias Sumulong, who had prices on their heads of 150,000 and 100,000 pesos respectively. Pedring and Sumulong, and another commander, Bernabé Buscano, alias Dante, were all veterans of the 1950 movement, as was Sumulong's chief alleged rival, Alibasbas, who was killed early in 1968 after being betrayed to the constabulary by Sumulong.

The stronghold of the Huks had long been Angeles City, adjacent to Clark Field, where they completely controlled the administration and dominated the rackets involved in the operation of night clubs, prostitution, taxis, and even the collection of garbage. Since Angeles was not off limits to the American servicemen at Clark, which had a total regular population of 62,000, including dependents and a steady flow of transients, the American community there was directly supporting the Huks' Angeles economy to the tune of an estimated $30 million a year. Some transient airmen were billeted in Angeles hotels because there was no space for them at Clark. It was estimated that Sumulong's take from the Angeles operation alone was at least $15,000 a week. The Huks had even moved into Clark itself, taxing the maids at American billets twenty-five cents a week, for instance, and one of the reasons that $250 million worth of matériel, ranging from iceboxes to electronic equipment and cars, was being stolen from the base each year was the Huks' ascendancy over the private guards and some of the constabulary elements patrolling the base, as well as their ability to cut at will through the barbed wire surrounding the huge installation.

The Huks had sought brazenly but unsuccessfully to take over the entire security of the base, offering the Americans a $450,000-a-year "protection" contract. The offer was turned down, whereupon the man who made it, Ben Serrano, who was associated with Sumulong, set up a new night club in Angeles called the Oasis, where American servicemen and their wives were soon losing thousands of dollars a week gambling. When some American women, whose husbands were in Vietnam, were unable to pay up, they were forgiven their debts if they agreed to sleep with the operators of the club. In May, 1968, Serrano was shot and killed in Angeles following reports of rift between him and Sumulong, but according to the best available evidence he was not actually murdered on the orders of Sumulong, who may have planned to kill him shortly, but by the so-called "Monkees," a select group of government-hired killers who got to him first when he refused to turn openly against Sumulong. Such mystery killings were commonplace in what was still called "Huklandia," the area where the Huks roamed more or less at will, and in Angeles alone in 1967 more than one hundred persons simply disappeared and were presumed to have been killed. Among those murdered during 1968 was the acting governor of Tarlac Province, presumably a victim of the Huks, though they issued a public denial, claiming he was eliminated by his government opponents, and conducted their own "investigation." Generally, in their assumed Robin Hood role, the Huks killed officials or informers only in ostensible defense of the peasants, whom they claimed to be protecting—from cattle rustlers, for example—but they were also known to have murdered soldiers or members of the constabulary who had fought against them back in the fifties, thus obtaining revenge in American gangland style.

The New Left Wing

Although they still talked about land reform and the destruction of all imperialist and landlord elements, the contemporary Huks, compared to their forerunners, appeared to lack an ideology. To all intents and purposes, they were plain racketeers, and Sumulong and his top aides, in particular, were being accused by some members of the movement of having become "capitalists" themselves. Whatever truth there was to rumors of a split in the ranks, what was taking place was a far cry from the events of the late forties and early fifties, when the Communists gave the movement its direction through the ten-member Politburo headed by José Lava and, later, by his brother Jesús. From time to time, since the late fifties, a score of so-called political transmissions had been clandestinely distributed, and these mixed ideological and tactical directives, it was believed, may have come from members of the old-guard leadership in Manila, such as the Lava brothers, or from other left-wing intellectuals who had played an active role in the nationalist movement in the past and were still felt to be acting in an advisory role. The latest of the "transmissions" came out in June, 1968, when evidence of some effort to reinstill an ideology among the Huks was obtained in a raid conducted on what was apparently a training camp for Huk soldiers in an isolated area north of Clark Field; documents were seized indicating attempts were under way to re-establish the Stalin University of the fifties and to give members of the movement lessons in doctrine as well as in methods of guerrilla warfare. Interestingly, these documents were written in the flowery dialect of Pampanga Province, in contrast to the documents of the fifties, which were in Tagalog and were much more easily translatable.

During 1967 and 1968, too, both Peking and Moscow, in Communist Party publications, for the first time since the earlier rebellion took note of the Communist Party of the Philippines, which had been dormant for many years. These outside references reflected signs of a split among the Filipino left-wing intellectuals, which was borne out in the bitter factional fighting taking place among the students and labor leaders. On May Day, 1967, a statement purportedly issued by the C.P.P. and subsequently printed in a New Zealand Communist Party paper and picked up in Peking, called for "nation-wide party re-building, development of rural bases," and declared that the "outlawed situation of the party dictates clearly that there is no path to national and social liberation except armed struggle." The statement, further, assailed the Moscow "revisionist" position. In December the "Information Bulletin" of the *World Marxist Review,* a Moscow publication, reprinted a statement supposedly issued by the pro-Soviet C.P.P. which fully aligned itself with the Moscow point of view on all international matters and took issue with the summons of the pro-Peking group for "armed struggle," emphasizing that while this was an ultimate "necessity," such an order "ignores the present state of objective conditions and subjective forces in the Philippines," which calls instead for combining "dialectically parliamentary struggle and armed struggle, legal and illegal forms of action." Some observers felt that both Moscow and Peking were simply putting liens on the movement in the Philippines for future purposes, while others felt that the renewed international Communist recognition signaled a forthcoming fresh attempt to start another, more effective insurrection, this time with more outside guidance, and possibly more material help.

Despite careful intelligence surveillance, there was no evidence that any new "Politburo," Moscow- or Peking-oriented, had as yet been established in the Philippines, though there might still be a small secretariat of three or four members that was secretly giving interim advice to the small underground movement. Certainly, the whole left-wing complex of groups and organizations in the islands was thoroughly fragmented in 1968, and what had been taking place in recent years amounted to the building of a new cart, composed of various front organizations, without a horse to pull it. "In a way, this is just how the Filipinos do things," one long-time American observer commented, "and in this sense we're lucky that no one has come along to pull the whole thing together. But all of these organizations are building up, and we can't afford to sit back and assume that nothing is going to happen."

The emergence of new left-wing groups had a strong bearing on the direction in which the Philippines was likely to go in the next few years. The question in turn involved not only the solution of such domestic problems as land reform and peace and order, and the various plans to do something about poverty and unemployment, but also the reorientation of the republic's relationship with the United States; this would include the rewriting of trade agreements that were shortly due to expire, the conditions for the continued use of American Army, Navy, and Air Force bases, the prerogatives of Americans who resided and did business in the islands, the status of American-owned properties, the assistance that had been rendered by the Filipinos to the Americans in Vietnam, and, in general, the whole American impact, psychological as well as material, which had undoubtedly inhibited any stronger effort the Filipinos might have made to orient themselves more toward Asia.

The most important left-wing nationalist organization, more important than the Huks in the opinion of most competent observers, was a peasants' group formed in 1964 called *Malayang Samahan ng Magsasaka*, or Masaka for short. The hard-core membership of Masaka was said to be about four thousand, but the group claimed more than twenty thousand. Like the Huks, Masaka was active in central Luzon, particularly in the province of Nueva Ecija, and it was also extending its influence to the provinces south of Manila. It had a stronger ideological bent than the Huks, based mainly on agrarian reform—it insisted, for example, on the breakup of all large estates and the distribution of hacienda land to the peasants—and it also took a strong nationalist and antiforeign stand on other matters. The head of Masaka in 1968 was Felixberto Olalia, a sixty-five-year-old former Huk who served a jail sentence after the last rebellion, and, according to the government, was a former member of the Communist Party. Olalia personally professed a strong anti-American line and believed the Philippines should be allowed to go its own way, "without any interference." While he did not advocate violence for the present, Olalia saw "trouble ahead," he told me, if the government failed to implement its land reform and other social programs, and he didn't seem to have much faith that it would. At Olalia's invitation, Governor Estrella, of the Land Authority, had attended Masaka meetings, jocularly addressing the peasants in the audience as "fellow Communists." Although there were a number of old-time Huks in Masaka, and while the organization cooperated on the surface with the Huks, there was some evidence that the two groups were competitive and that Masaka considered itself the rightful heir to the revolutionary cause of the peasants. During 1968 three Masaka men who were operating in the heart of Huk territory were mysteriously killed in sudden gun assaults, apparently by the Huks.

Masaka and Olalia were closely associated with the Socialist Party of the Philippines, which in 1966 replaced the left-wing Labor Party. The head of the S.P.P. was Ignacio Lacsina, a forty-year-old, urbane, articulate, and well-educated man. While Lacsina also said he favored a "parliamentary solution" to the crisis in the Philippines, and hoped to project his party politically over the next few years, he, like Olalia, foresaw armed rebellion within a decade if the problems of land redistribution, unemployment, and higher wages, among others, were not dealt with boldly by the government. To deal with the land question, the S.P.P. was creating its own peasant cadres, which presumably would cooperate with Masaka's. A Socialist state alone could solve the nation's economic mess, Lacsina maintained, though he acknowledged the need for some joint ventures between the state and Filipino capitalists once the tight hold of the "present oligarchy" was broken. Like all nationalist leaders in the Philippines today, Lacsina was strongly against the maintenance of American bases and of any continuation of the "special relations," created by the Laurel-Langley trade pact, due to expire in 1974. Negotiations between Washington and Manila had already begun—the Filipinos were seeking continued bilateral preference for some of their goods sold to America, but were unwilling to grant much in return.

All the nationalists, loosely banded together in the Movement for the Advancement of Nationalism, were propagandizing for

trade with the Communist nations, and a number of trade delegations, led by the Czechs, were in the process of discussing the
possibility of trade relations with the Philippines. Groups of Eastern European tourists had also started to visit the Philippines—in
mid-1968 seventeen Russians visited Manila for several days. Those
who most feared the growing influence of the left-wing movements
pointed out that the political situation was so chaotic, and so
uncontrollable, that the permanent presence of Communist trade
delegations or the regular appearance of tourists might lead to
serious infiltration by foreign Communist agents; such agents
might be able, far better than the Filipinos themselves, to pull together the various native factional groups that had been spending
most of their time fighting each other. This was especially true of
the left-wing students in the universities—of which there were no
fewer than thirty-three in the Manila area alone, though most of
them were mere "diploma mills" which each year were "graduating"
thousands of young men and women who, unable to find jobs, were
simply joining the ranks of the discontented.

The center of student activity was the University of the Philippines. The two top student leaders, José Sison and Francisco
Nemenzo, Jr., were young firebrand teachers who had maintained
their student status by occasionally taking a graduate course and
affiliating themselves with student organizations. Both men had
extended their areas of activity as New Left spokesmen beyond
the campus, to labor unions, other nationalist organizations, and
journalism. Sison, following a trip he made to China in 1967, with
some forty Filipino students, journalists, and politicians, became
the chief pro-Peking spokesman, while Nemenzo was regarded as
more pro-Moscow. Their battle for control of the student movement was a bitter and divisive one involving not only the Kata-
baang Makabayang, the main New Left youth organization, which
laid claim to five thousand members and from which Nemenzo
withdrew in 1967 and formed his own rival group, but also the
Bertrand Russell Peace Foundation, which also split in two. Sison
for a time was running everything, from the Movement for the
Advancement of Nationalism to the *Progressive Review*, a left-wing
periodical that appeared several times a year, but his star in 1968
seemed to have set, and Nemenzo, the more professional of the
two in tactics, loomed as the more important leader. Significantly,

Lacsina was moving into the student picture, too, and was instrumental in a violent attack on the "Americanization" of the University of the Philippines, alleging that American money had been carefully applied to stress courses that would help to keep the Philippines in a "neocolonial" state.

Aside from factionalism, the passivity of the students was ascribable to their basic middle-class mentality, which had led them to forget their ultranationalist aims the moment they either found jobs or attached themselves to a political party or group that could help project them up the ladder of influence. Marcos had succeeded in luring a number of the nationalist leaders, led by Blas Ople, the Secretary of Labor, into his administration. There were signs, however, that the New Left was getting ready, late in 1968, to play a more active role in influencing national and international issues. Oddly enough, such matters as student influence over the curriculum of the universities, and tight faculty control of campus activities, which have stirred students in the United States, France, and elsewhere, had not moved the Filipino students very much, but this, too, could change. "If they were smart," one foreign observer noted, "they'd not only concentrate on what concerns them most, right on the campus, but also on such social matters as unemployment, favoritism for government jobs, poor garbage collection, and bad administration generally. These are the bread-and-butter issues—not the future of Clark Field and parity."

The criticism seemed a valid one, but the New Left figured to get more mileage out of the larger issues of anti-imperialism. The paucity of ideology on the left had forced its leaders to flog the same old horses. In the fall of 1968 a number of anti-Vietnam rallies were held, and several demonstrations took place in front of the American Embassy to protest the shooting of a Filipino civilian by an American Marine guard at Sangley Point, a naval base—the civilian had been suspected by the guard of trying to steal a bicycle. The whole question of the American bases in the Philippines, the duration of leases and matters of jurisdiction, had been one of the issues over which there had been a growing nationalist and anti-American sentiment. In 1965 the United States made clear its willingness to reduce the length of its leases on Clark Field, and on Subic Bay, the major naval base, from ninety-nine to twenty-five years, and the Americans granted the Filipinos jurisdiction over American military men accused of criminal offenses. The United States also agreed to relinquish some 25,000 acres of the 175,000 acres of the vast Clark Field base. Despite these concessions, there remained a considerable nationalist element in favor of the bases being relinquished completely, or at least placed under the jurisdiction of an area-wide defense system. Marcos was in favor of the bases being retained, with possible further modifications being made on the lease terms.

The general issue of continued "colonial domination" which the nationalists kept bringing up centered on the trade agreements between the United States and the Philippines. These involved intricate questions that were in the process of renegotiation anyway. The total American investment in the Philippines was only about a half-billion dollars, so there was scarcely much substance to the "colonial domination" issue, and most observers felt that both this and the matter of the bases could easily be resolved. But the bedrock of xenophobia, and the ambivalence about America and Americans in particular, were more difficult to deal with. "Filipino nationalism of the responsible kind need not be incompatible with friendship for other nations, especially the United States," Marcos said blandly. The trouble was, so much of what was written and said on the left was irresponsible. The lack of bona fide student and intellectual leaders was perhaps the chief reason why there was not more dynamic social action, and this had resulted in the Communists and their witting and unwitting allies filling the void. These elements, in fact, had for several years obtained an influence in the universities and in the press that far transcended their actual numbers. Among the plethora of columnists on the English-language and dialect papers, there were a dozen or so who regularly espoused ultra-left-wing and anti-American causes. One of the leading magazines, the *Graphic*, was a virtual mouthpiece of the left, and its publisher, J. Antonio Araneta, was openly accused early in 1968 by a prominent Senator of having helped shepherd around a Chinese Communist general who visited the country incognito several months before, and who reportedly was trying to set up a spy net at Clark Field until his identity was discovered and he was quickly and quietly deported. In addition to the *Graphic* and the *Progressive Review*, there were

three other monthly or bimonthly publications that ardently espoused the left-wing line, while the *Philippines Free Press*, a long-
established and highly regarded weekly with a reputation for complete honesty and fairness of reporting, had become increasingly
anti-American and shrill in its policy.

As was so often the case, there was precious little countervailing
journalistic activity on the non-Communist left or among middle-
ground liberals. Only one magazine, *Solidarity*, published and
edited by F. Sionil José six times a year, stood in opposition to the
New Left. José, a man of many parts, was a novelist, bookshop
owner and art dealer, among other things. His editorials often
went to the heart of the matter. "The tragedy of the nationalist
movement," José wrote, in one issue of *Solidarity:*

is not that it has no leaders or followers, but that it has alienated itself
from the people. And the main reason for this cleavage is in the leaders
themselves, those who have been corrupted by ambition and desire for
acceptance into the restricted enclaves of the elite. Compounding this
tragedy is the absence of a class consciousness in the nationalist
movement. . . . Twenty years of independence have borne out the fact
that the politicians of both our parties have no ideology that can
energize us into lifting this country from the dungheap.

José, along with many other non-Communist Filipinos, believed, in
1968, that "a revolution is in the near horizon and not even Marcos'
call to greatness can stop it. . . . The elements of this revolution are
all around us, in the continued dissidence in Central Luzon, in the
paralysis of the Army, particularly the Philippine Constabulary,
and in the anarchy which pervades all sectors."

Another man who spoke of the "vacuum of ideology" was
former Senator Raúl Manglapus, who in the summer of 1968 was
preparing to launch a new Christian Social Movement based on
Latin-American and Italian models. Manglapus, one of the earliest
ardent advocates of land reform and decentralized government—
he ran a poor third for President in the 1965 election but, with
justification, blamed part of his poor showing on the fact that only
the two leading parties were legally entitled to poll watchers—had
come to feel that the best hope for the Philippines lay in "a democratic coalition of the left, composed of the working class, progressive intellectual and social-minded middle- and upper-class people

who believe in the same ideas for peaceful social revolution."
Whether Manglapus' search for a form of "Christian humanism"
and "social justice," with evangelical overtones, could obtain a
hearing among the masses remained to be seen, but the movement,
which was expected to have the backing of some students and
perhaps of some elements in the Socialist Party, as well as of the
Jesuits and other liberal-minded Catholics, was an interesting new
phenomenon, and would bear watching.

The Tempest over Sabah

President Marcos himself had increasingly taken note of the
seriousness of the Philippines' social and economic situation, in a
series of television speeches he made in 1968 and in other public
addresses. "We are sitting on top of a volcano," he said on one
occasion. "If we don't get rid of our social inequities, show some
responsibility toward the unfortunate, and utilize our resources, we
will explode, with or without Communism." While the country had
made some economic progress, especially in rice production, many
of the other gains were due to artificial circumstances, and financially the situation was not sound. While the total national
growth rate in 1967 was 5.5 percent, the rising population curve
and continued inflation diminished the effect of the over-all growth.
A liberal credit policy in 1966, subsequently cut back, encouraged
new business but created a surfeit of imports over exports and a
trade deficit of nearly $250 million, the highest in twenty years.
Foreign reserves increased by $100 million, to $221 million, in
1967, but this was mostly due to added loan receipts from foreign
banks and from the International Monetary Fund and to reduced
repayments schedules to American banks on earlier loans; private
capital, in fact, continued to flow out of the country. The hope of
obtaining more loans from Japan was set back by restrictions
placed on Japanese retail businessmen by the Mayor of Manila,
Antonio Villegas, who had his own political ambitions, and the
Philippines could not depend indefinitely on other windfalls from
abroad, such as war damages and dollar benefits accruing from the
Vietnam war.

One of the big failures was the promotion of tourism. Manila had two fine new hotels in 1968, the Hilton, overlooking refurbished Luneta Park, and the Sheraton, and others were being built, but virtually nothing was being done to lure visitors, and the tourist facilities that existed were invariably badly run (when I visited Corregidor, the battle-scarred island in Manila Bay, for example, the only way to get about was in a dilapidated Army truck run at the whim of a casual sergeant). The ultimate solution to the financial problems faced by the republic was obviously more exports and more taxes, but the economy was not yet geared to encouraging the former, and Congress had given Marcos a hard time on the latter. It passed only six of thirty-five tax bills he submitted in the regular session in 1968, and a special session during the summer did not accomplish enough to avoid an estimated budget deficit of two hundred million pesos or more. A consequent tightening of the belt thus seemed likely, but this would hurt the poor more than the rich and make it harder for Marcos to achieve his broad goals.

One way or another, whether Marcos became the first President of the Philippines ever to win a second term and won the chance to make good on his call to greatness, or whether the New Left or some sort of middle-ground coalition would move into a dominant political position, the Filipinos seemed to be on the verge of some dramatic change they had both so long sought and denied themselves. There were those, such as the youthful and articulate Senator Benigno Aquino, Jr., of the Liberal Party, who accused Marcos of wanting to create a "garrison state," even citing the Army's "civic action" programs, which had helped build roads and other installations, as a sign of the growing militarism in the country. Aquino, who may himself be President someday, had all along been Marcos' strongest critic, and had attacked him on a whole swath of issues, from padding the budget to messing up the Sabah issue by permitting a secret training program for "special forces volunteers" to get out of hand. The trainees, Muslims from Mindanao and Sulu, were brought to the island of Corregidor as an ostensible counterinsurgency force to deal with infiltrators supposedly coming from Malaysia or to serve as a potential invasion force against Sabah—it never became clear which was true. At any rate, a scandal developed in mid-1968 when at least three of the trainees were shot and killed, on the orders, apparently, of the man who sold the idea of the training program to Marcos—they had rebelled against the treatment they were receiving, and against not being paid. The Corregidor incident served to heighten the dispute over Sabah, and to aggravate the issue of Muslim separatism in the south, where the citizens of Mindanao and the Sulu Archipelago had long felt neglected by Manila. The Sabah question, which some suspected Marcos was using as a campaign issue for 1969, though he had shown little interest before in pressing the claim, quickly roused the emotions of virtually all Filipinos, few of whom were aware of its legal intricacies.

In 1764 the Sultan of Sulu ceded most of what is now North Borneo to the British East India Company, and although the company did not develop the area, the cession was never rescinded. Then, in 1851, Spain routed the Sultan's forces, and claimed sovereignty over all the "Territory of Sulu and its Dependencies." Britain, arguing that the earlier agreement between the East India Company and the Sultan of Sulu was still operative, refused to accept the Spanish claim to Borneo, and, as things worked out, the Spaniards never really moved in. Ultimately, in 1885, they renounced their claim. Meanwhile, various foreign individuals and firms had been obtaining concessions of one sort or another in North Borneo—sometimes dealing with the Sultan of Brunei, sometimes with the Sultan of Sulu. In 1865, an American named Claude Lee Moses, who was United States Consul in Brunei, and a confidence man of some skill, persuaded the Sultan of Brunei to give him a ten-year contract in a large, vaguely defined chunk of North Borneo for the paltry sum of about three thousand dollars a year. Among other concessionaires were a pair of American freebooters named Torrey and Harris, who in the eighteen-sixties founded something called the American Trading Company and projected the building of a capital to be called Elenna. However, Elenna never was built, and, in fact, the American Trading Company never got going. The next large-scale concession went to Gustavus Baron de Overbeck, the Austrian Consul General in Hong Kong, who took over and renewed Torrey & Co.'s arrangement with the Sultan of Brunei and, playing it safe, made an overlapping deal with the Sultan of Sulu. Presently, Overbeck bowed out, and shortly afterward his partners handed the concession over to the British North Borneo Company, which received a charter from the British crown. This company managed to establish some law and order in North Borneo and to initiate some improvements in education and communication, but it didn't manage to thrive commercially. In 1888 it successfully appealed to the British government to make the territory a protectorate. During the Second World War, when the Japanese moved in, the company, in effect, died, and on July 15, 1946, it quietly transferred its authority to the British Colonial Office, which declared North Borneo a crown colony.

The Philippine Republic insisted that the British North Borneo Company had no right to hand over the area to the British, and that the British in turn had no right to hand it over to Malaysia. The Filipino argument began with the point that the sultanate of Sulu came under United States rule after the Spanish-American War, and then under Filipino rule in 1946. Thus, in the minds of the Filipinos, who still recognize the spiritual and ceremonial status of the sultans, everything that belonged to the sultans before subsequently came under their jurisdiction. The nub of the case in 1968 concerned the language of Baron Overbeck's 1878 agreement with the Sultan of Sulu. The document used the Malayan word *"padjak."* The Filipinos insisted this meant a lease, and the British argued that it meant a deed in perpetuity.

The Filipinos, having lost out in their argument with the British, both legally and politically—after insisting that they had a better chance than Malaya of keeping North Borneo from entering the Communist orbit—did not let the matter drop after the formation of Malaysia, in 1963, and the issue became more intense through the years. Several meetings between Malaysian and Filipino representatives failed to resolve it, as the Malaysians, not wishing to jeopardize their own weak hold in Borneo any more than they had to, refused to let the matter go to the International Court of Justice. In September, 1968, President Marcos signed a controversial measure passed by Congress that declared Sabah, as well as a piece of Indonesian Kalimantan, to be within the territory of the Philippines. Beyond the matter of pride, the claim of the Filipinos was obviously being pushed for economic reasons too, since Sabah is rich in timber and other resources. Although it was apparent that neither Malaysia nor the Philippines wished to get involved in a shooting war over Sabah, there were belligerent gestures on both sides and the Filipinos were making every effort to force the

Malaysians to take the issue to the World Court or some other impartial forum. (In view of their own problems with the Muslims in Mindanao, many observers thought they were playing a dangerous game.) The Malaysians responded by "suspending" diplomatic relations with the Philippines and abrogating a year-old anti-smuggling pact between the two countries. Demonstrations were held in Kuala Lumpur and Manila by angry partisans, and the situation threatened to get out of hand until, late in October, the Malaysians agreed to hold some more talks. Tempers, however, continued to flare and for a time a full break in relations seemed imminent. There was a possibility that the United Nations might try to resolve the complicated problem. Some face-saving move for the Philippines seemed to have become almost essential in view of the emotionalism that the issue had stirred up; the fact that Marcos had got involved in it, by signing the territorial bill, did not make things any easier, particularly since it thereby promised to become an election issue. The most unfortunate part of the whole matter was its detrimental effect on the progress made over the past few years by regional associations in Southeast Asia, particularly the Association of Southeast Asian Nations (ASEAN), to which both Malaysia and the Philippines, as well as Indonesia, belonged.

Whatever resolution there might be to the "crisis"—whether it remained a tempest in a teapot or developed into something more threatening—it contributed to the overwhelming search for "color" and "excitement" the average Filipino thrives on. Without some scandal, without at least one major issue like Sabah or the killings on Corregidor, and a host of minor ones, the Filipinos feel starved. They have become accustomed to living in their own constant limelight, and they love it. There are no secrets in the Philippines. Every last detail of who could be blamed for something like the Corregidor mess, for brownouts due to water shortages, for the poor telephone system, for major violations of the law as well as for such lesser infractions as allowing parties of strip-teasers to visit the Manila jails and entertain selected prisoners, and every last smidgen of gossip about what politician is planning to switch parties, and why a current beauty queen wants to get married instead of taking part in some obscure international contest, continues to be splashed across the front pages and television screens *ad nauseam*. This endless display of national and personal problems has turned the democratic process into a form of diversion, while decision-making has become gamesmanship. More than anything else, all this has delayed the emergence of the Philippines from adolescence into nationhood. What the republic needs, and what Marcos by 1969, at any rate, had not yet given it, was a thorough social shake-up, a set of widespread reforms that would really jolt the country's old and outworn foundations. Shortly before the earthquake that struck Manila late in July, 1968, causing the deaths of some two hundred people, most of them caught in a five-story apartment building that collapsed, a Filipino social scientist cogently said, "Whenever I see our volcanoes erupting, as they have recently, I have the strange feeling that these natural disturbances we are prone to are symbolic stirrings of our shackled society trying to free itself from its age-old bonds."

5

Thailand:

DAM OR DOMINO?

Again at the Crossroads

Thailand, situated north of the stirring Malay world, north of bustling Singapore, and south of Vietnam, found itself, in 1969, at one of those difficult turning points frequently confronted in the past by that independent kingdom. Through compromise or opportunism, and by sheer luck, Thailand had always before managed to stay out of trouble and preserve its status, but the circumstances now were more complicated and the outlook more serious in its implications for the nation's well-being and security. In fact, of all the countries of Southeast Asia except Vietnam, Thailand appeared to have the most uncertain future. The reasons were several. Ever since 1964 Communist terrorists in the northeast and the south, and then in the far north and northwest of the country, had been conducting a widely dispersed but partially synchronized campaign of terror and aggression. This campaign was directed against both local government authority and the national government in Bangkok. Although this activity was part of the larger pattern of Communist insurgency in Southeast Asia, and was similarly directed by Peking and Hanoi, it seemed aimed, as long as the war in Vietnam lasted, at establishing a covert rural foundation for a subsequent major effort in the only nation in the area that, although it had never been a Western colony, had openly aligned itself with the West—particularly, since 1965, with the Americans in Vietnam. Thailand had furnished its strongest support by allowing the Americans to build six major air bases, from which the United States Air Force conducted most of its missions over North Vietnam and the Communist infiltration trails through Laos. These bases would revert to Thailand, and theoretically could become permanent Thai installations, to be reactivated in any further emergency, but there was some doubt, by 1969, as to how many of them the Thais would want to use. Thailand had also sent some troops to Vietnam, promising ultimately to contribute up to twelve or fifteen thousand men, but as the fighting there slackened and the peace moves progressed, there was some doubt, too, as to how many of these troops would be used.

The Americans, in return for the Thais' support, had helped strengthen the Thai military forces and contributed money and technical advice to Thailand's counterinsurgency program, which, after a slow start, showed some signs, by 1968, of holding the Communist threat in check. To be sure, since there were only about two thousand insurgents in the country, and perhaps some fifteen thousand sympathizers, it could not be said that any substantial challenge had yet been made by the Communists. Both militarily and diplomatically, however, the Thais were painfully aware that their future internal safety and international stability depended on the outcome of the Vietnamese war, over which, despite their commitment to the Americans, they had little or no leverage. This lack of control over their own destiny, with its consequent impact on the situation within Thailand, was making the Thais edgy. If the Americans ultimately pulled out of Vietnam, which seemed inevitable, and if they further reduced their military and political role throughout Southeast Asia, Thailand, with a population of 33 million, could find itself in a highly vulnerable position, isolated from possibly pro-Communist or neutralist governments in the former Indochina area and exposed to stepped-up Communist subversion if not aggression, which could come from all directions. Whatever decision the Thais made—to string along as a junior partner of the United States in the continuing battle against Communist expansion, or to formulate another historic compromise which might ensure some kind of neutrality while they gained time and tried to improve their relations with their ideologically alien neighbors—they accordingly seemed less likely than before to escape unscathed from the outside forces impinging upon them.

Thailand's historic capacity to "bend with the wind" had served it well. In the early nineteenth century, when the Chinese were the dominant influence in the area, the Thais had maintained close relations with the Chinese. From the mid-nineteenth century until the beginning of the Second World War, the orientation was British. The Thais then adjusted to the Japanese conquest of Southeast Asia, but with the help of patriotic elements both in Thailand and abroad maintained their links with the United States. Field Marshal Phibun Songgram, the Army strong man who led the 1932 coup against the arbitrary rule of the Siamese kings (Thailand was known as Siam until 1939), declared war against the United States in 1942, but the Thai Ambassador in Washington, Prince Seni Pramoj, refused to deliver the declaration. After the war, while insisting that Thailand restore to its neighbors the territories the Japanese had awarded Phibun, the Americans supported Thailand's entry into the United Nations and the two countries drew increasingly closer, especially after the victory of the Communists in China in 1949. Between 1932 and 1968 there were some fifteen different governments and seven military coups in Thailand, but the strongest political element remained the Army, and, though seven different constitutions were proclaimed during this period, none of them created more than a democratic façade. The King remained a figurehead, though a revered one, and the military ran the show. In elections in 1957, Phibun lost out to one of his rivals, Marshal Sarit Thanarat, who a year later dissolved the newly elected National Assembly and reimposed dictatorial rule. Though Sarit, who had installed himself as Premier, instituted national development plans and encouraged private enterprise, with the help primarily of the assimilated Chinese, he did little to help improve the lives of the common people. He amassed a personal fortune, the details of which only came to light in a series of scandals involving his mistresses after his death in 1963, when the Deputy Premier, Marshal Thanom Kittikachorn, took over. Thanom eliminated most of his military rivals, who had been involved in Sarit's scandals, and established a strong and effective government, with the help of General Praphas Charusathien, who among other things controlled the Bangkok area.

Thanom also set in motion the process of preparing a new constitution, and after nearly a decade of delays Thailand finally, in mid-1968, promulgated its eighth constitution since its emergence from feudalism and absolute monarchy in the nineteen-thirties. Democratic elections for a House of Representatives were set for February, 1969. If the nation now seemed determined to work out its own future in a careful fashion, the earlier failures of parliamentary democracy were still remembered, as were its leaders' frequent decisions to follow the path of least resistance, including the deal with the Japanese in the Second World War to avoid occupation. Whether these leaders would now stay on the path of democracy, no matter what happened in Vietnam, and would also continue to play a key role in furthering programs of regional economic development and military cooperation, remained one of Southeast Asia's moot questions.

The Thais, as many Americans had begun to realize, after several years of close relations with them, were perhaps the most contradictory and confounding people in Asia. They were, at once, delightful and exasperating, determined and vacillating, modern and backward. Since they had their own definite ideas about how, when, and why they wanted to do things, this sometimes made them, as allies, difficult to deal with—which is precisely what, on occasion, they thought of the Americans, whom they looked upon as charming and annoying, positive and changeable, efficient and obtuse. Under the circumstances, the relationship between the two countries was bound to be uneasy, and there were many subtleties that made the association more tenuous than it appeared on the surface or in the communiqués. In some respects, the alliance seemed like a marriage of convenience. On the one hand, this made it more practical and less subject to pretense and to crises of conscience than the frequently tortuous relationship between the Americans and the Vietnamese. On the other hand, simply because it was more of an arrangement than an involvement, the differences that arose were not unlike those that might occur between two successful business partners whose sensitivities were easily aroused whenever mutual obligations and responsibilities became subject to conflicting interpretations.

On the matter of the air bases, for example, neither the Thais nor the Americans would admit for more than a year that they existed, although the whole world knew that, one by one, they were being built and becoming operational. It was not until January, 1967, that the then American Ambassador, Graham A. Martin, admitted that bases were being used "in carrying out defensive measures." Martin, a highly able man who was considered by his State Department peers to be something of a maverick in the Foreign Service because he believed in making decisions on the spot with a minimum of interference from Washington, "revealed" another long-known fact, that there were at the time some 35,000 American troops in Thailand, eight thousand of them "engaged in construction and maintenance of strategic roadways, communications networks, port facilities, military supply depots, and other installations." Practically all the rest were Air Force personnel working on the bases or supporting elements for a large-scale American logistics operation involving heavy stockpiling of military supplies. During the long months of "secrecy" about the air bases, when correspondents were writing about the air attacks against North Vietnam and the Ho Chi Minh trail though they were not allowed to visit any of the bases, Ambassador Martin had kept silent in deference to the wishes of the Thais, whose intense aversion to publicity in such matters was in inverse ratio to the Americans' fondness for it. Part of the Thais' feeling was predicated on their lingering doubts over American intentions of sticking it out in Vietnam, and on their not wanting, publicly at least, to put all their eggs in one basket, which they had never liked doing. As events developed, by the spring of 1968, when there were 45,000 American troops in the country and a new ambassador, Leonard Unger, and as the Thais found themselves bound to the indecisive American effort in Southeast Asia, it was not surprising that they were the first to express their fear that the projected peace negotiations in Vietnam would herald an American withdrawal from the whole area.

There was a certain precedent for American assistance to Thailand, which, among other things, covered the stockpiling operations. When asked about this, for example, the Americans and Thais always pointed out that it was in accordance with the Southeast Asia Collective Defense Treaty of 1954, which established the

Southeast Asia Treaty Organization (SEATO). In March, 1962, two months before five thousand American combat troops had been temporarily sent to Thailand as a precaution against an expected major Communist drive in Laos (they were withdrawn early that summer), the SEATO agreement was simplified by a joint statement of Secretary of State Dean Rusk and Foreign Minister Thanat Khoman, of Thailand, in which Rusk reaffirmed that in aiding Thailand, "its ally and historic friend," the United States believed that its obligation "does not depend upon the prior agreement of all other parties to the treaty, since this treaty obligation is individual as well as collective." The chief purpose of the Rusk-Thanat statement, in its emphasis on the bilateral as well as the collective nature of the treaty, was to anticipate the objections of the two recalcitrant SEATO partners—France and Pakistan; the other signatories, in addition to the United States and Thailand, were Australia, New Zealand, the Philippines, and Great Britain, and they generally approved of the American position on Thailand. Indeed, Britain, Australia, and New Zealand had small contingents of troops in Thailand themselves, making for what Ambassador Martin liked to refer to as "a multilateral effort."

The reluctance of the Thais to speak frankly about their emerging alliance with the United States was essentially a reflection of their long experience in maintaining their independence not only through their unique combination of luck and skill but also because of their singular capacity for adroit imprecision. An earlier American Ambassador to Thailand, Kenneth Young, once observed that Thai foreign policy "is always fending off alien and external influences, keeping its distance, separating out the dangerous from the useful, remaining uninvolved as long as possible, and always leaving room for maneuver and a margin for options with at least two in hand at one time, never to be faced with an irrevocable alternative or an involuntary retreat." Mixed elements of tough practicality and guarded skepticism accordingly have traditionally guided Thai foreign policy. Self-reliance has been another historical key. Through the past seven hundred years the Thais have regularly applied two other principles in maintaining their independence—a multiplicity and diversity of contacts with both Asian and Western nations, and a policy of seeking counterweights in their foreign associations so as never to be overdependent on any one nation or set of factors. Several American representatives in Thailand from time to time have commented, out of a sense of bewilderment and dismay, over the Thais' ability to pursue tactics of maneuver and delay until they got what they wanted. Consequently, many an "agreement in principle" one day turned out to be no agreement at all the next. In pursuing a policy of balance, of frequently playing one nation or group subtly off against another, the Thais have also always been strongly guided by the precepts of their national religion, Buddhism. These precepts have permitted them to see the world as a moral whole, in which elements of power, virtue, and value are neatly counterbalanced; the human world is regarded as but one of many worlds in what has been described as "a timeless, spaceless universe of eternity and endlessness." Prince Wan Waithayakorn, who had been a Foreign Minister and in 1968 was a Deputy Prime Minister, used to point out that Buddhism permits the Thais to have close relations with many countries at once because "the Buddhist Law of Karma, according to which a person doing good will get good and a person doing evil will get evil, is applicable to all mankind without any distinction whatever." The sort of objectivity that such thinking allowed was one of the qualities of the Thais that puzzled the Americans most. One Thai military chief answered a question about the use that Americans were making of bases in his country by saying, "I'm just a hotelkeeper who rents out rooms. I don't care what my guests do in the rooms or who they invite up there."

Whether because of the Buddhist spirit of live and let live or merely because of the financial temptations provided by the presence of so many American servicemen—in addition to the thousands stationed in Thailand, five thousand a month from Vietnam shuttled in and out of Bangkok, more for recreation than rest—the city by 1967 had become the liveliest, the loudest, and probably the most licentious city in Southeast Asia. New restaurants, bars, night clubs, and "massage parlors" were opening every week—some avenues and streets became literally lined with them—and most did a thriving business. Many of the clubs featured stripteases, which were supposed to be illegal, but despite sporadic official clean-up campaigns the strippers on New Petchburi Road, which was nicknamed The Strip, kept playing to large audiences, and daily advertisements as well as the columns in the Sunday supplements were comically blunt in their come-ons and comments. "The strip show at the Progress Bar is as raunchy as any you'll find in town," the entertainment section of the Bangkok *World* typically wrote. The beautiful Buddhist temples and the Floating Market on the canals remained standard tourist attractions, but the tone and tempo of the town inevitably changed greatly during the Vietnam war years. By day, the once languid, sun-soaked streets became heavy and odorous with traffic, and at night the city heaved with the sound of jazz and was ablaze with neon lights. Much, if not most, of the conspicuous and inconspicuous consumption presumably would vanish when the American servicemen left, but in the meantime it spread beyond Bangkok to the towns in the north where the bases were located—Udorn, Nakhon Phanom, Ubon, Korat, and Takhli—and south to the new $100 million B-52 base at U Tapao, alongside which a tremendous new naval base, at Sattahip, was built by the Americans and turned over to the Thais in the spring of 1968.

Although it was obvious that it was the Thais who were providing the *sanouk*—the pleasure—and reaping the profits, and that the authorities could have closed the "massage parlors" and the dance halls if they had wanted to, the Americans were increasingly blamed for ruining the morals of Thai girls and for their blatant exhibitionism. In December, 1967, one of Bangkok's best-known columnists blasted the Americans as "beasts" and "sexual perverts." He further accused the Americans of exploiting Thailand economically and of seeking "to destroy Thai independence." There was more to this sputtering hostility than met the eye. The Thais resented the license granted visiting American correspondents, in contrast to that accorded Thai journalists, to criticize Thai attitudes and Thailand's lack of national discipline and political organization, and they were particularly disturbed over some unfair slurs against the bravery and patriotism of King Phumiphon Adulyadej and the royal family, who have always been revered in Thailand and are the principal source of national unity. Ambassador Unger did his best to mollify the Thais, but the misunderstandings continued, though they did not noticeably impede the war effort.

Fortunately, the Bangkok boom was economically sound enough in other respects to withstand the inflationary effects of the American military "invasion." The Thai economy enjoyed one of the highest rates of expansion in the Far East, if not in the world, during the sixties, the gross national product having risen from 59.9 billion bahts in 1961 to 86.5 billion in 1966—twenty bahts are worth one American dollar. During 1967 the growth rate dropped from 9 to 6 percent, due principally to a drought, but this was only a temporary setback and, for the new Six-Year Plan beginning in 1967, the Thais projected a yearly rate of growth of 8.5 percent. A trade deficit was more than made up for by invisibles—tourism, private investment, and foreign aid—and gold and foreign exchange reserves were up to almost one billion dollars by the end of 1967. Though the budget deficit was about 25 percent, equal to the increase in budget expenditures, the consumer price index that year rose less than 5 percent.

Thailand was still essentially an agricultural nation—the per capita income was only $125 a year—but it was rapidly developing new industries, which by 1968 accounted for more than 30 percent of the total national product. As in Singapore, generous tax incentives were being offered for foreign-capital investment, and import duties on raw material were also being relaxed, with the result that new factories—for the production of tires, pharmaceuticals, light steel goods, electronics, and plastics, and for the assembly of automobiles—were springing up all around sprawling Bangkok and in Phra Padeng, its industrial surburb on the twisting Chao Phraya River. Thailand's primary export products, rice and tin, continued to provide the bulk of the country's income from foreign exchange, and the Thais maintained a revolving export credit fund that, for example, enabled South Vietnam to obtain much-needed rice from Thailand in 1966 and 1967. During the coming Six-Year Plan, for which 56 million bahts would be spent, nearly twice as much as during the first plan, the Thais planned to concentrate on correcting the many regional inequalities that had for so long made for such contrasts within the country between wealth and poverty. The poverty remained worst in the northeast, where the soil was poor and there were few natural resources—the per capita income in this region was only forty or fifty dollars a year—which was the reason the Communist guerrillas had attacked there first.

Prelude to Insurgency

The level of the insurgency in Thailand was often compared to that in South Vietnam in 1958 and 1959, when the Vietcong began to step up assassination and terror activities, striking primarily at officials such as hamlet and village chiefs. The Communist terrorists in Thailand similarly assassinated village headmen, policemen, and government teachers—the most influential people in the rural communities—but what the guerrillas seemed to lack, in sharp contrast to the Vietcong, was a solid organization built tightly into the village structure. This did not mean that the insurrection in the northeast and the north, and in the middle and lower parts of the southern peninsula that dangles like the stem of a flower down to the Malaysian border, might not in time acquire this kind of organization, but there were reasons to doubt that it could easily be done. Certainly, in contrast to the activities in Vietnam, the Thai insurrection, with the exception of the movement in the far south, revealed a lack of experienced cadres. Above all, it lacked a man of the caliber of Ho Chi Minh, whose special genius had always been organizational, and who, in 1945-46, while outwitting and then eliminating all other nationalist groups, welded the Vietminh into the dominant force in his country while his closest associate, General Vo Nguyen Giap, was creating what became perhaps the most effective guerrilla army in history.

Before the Second World War there was a Moscow-oriented Marxist Study Group in Bangkok, and even earlier, in the late twenties, Ho Chi Minh, disguised as a Buddhist monk, took refuge for a year or two in the province of Udorn, from which he not only directed the Communist apparatus in Indochina but also ran the Third International in the Far East. But Ho never concentrated on the Thai Communists as such. During the war the Free Thai Movement, an underground paramilitary organization that fought the Japanese in the northeast, included among its leaders a forceful figure named Tiang Serikhan. Tiang advocated independence for northeast Thailand and its integration with Laos—the population of the northeast is largely an admixture of Lao and Thai stock, and the people are, in fact, known as Lao-Thais. After Tiang's death, in

1952, many of his followers were absorbed into the so-called Solidarity Movement, which openly professed Communism and whose several thousand adherents in the northeast had links with the Communist-led Pathet Lao in Laos. This group also maintained some contact with the Communist Party of Thailand, which had been organized in 1935 in Bangkok and had become legal in 1946, but had later been outlawed and, after being entirely taken over by Peking, had gone underground in 1952. In 1960, a newly established Thai Exile Association, based in Laos, had among its members a number of leftist leaders still in northeast Thailand, including Krong Chantawong, the leader of the Solidarity Movement. A year later Krong and a hundred other left-wing politicians in the northeast were arrested by Field Marshal Sarit, and Krong was executed. Krong's widow was subsequently arrested, but their daughter, Krungstem Chantawong, was still at liberty in 1968 and was said to be leading a Communist terrorist band in the Phu Phan Mountains of the northeast-central region.

The execution of Krong and the break-up of his group slowed down subversive activity in the northeast, but in the middle of 1964 it began a steady increase as a growing number of infiltrators, including some Pathet Lao and North Vietnamese and probably a scattered number of Chinese Communists, crossed the Mekong River into Thailand from Laos. Primarily, though, these insurgents were Thais who had been recruited in the northeast and in other parts of the country and who were sent to a Communist indoctrination school at Hoa Binh, north of Hanoi, or to one in Yünnan Province in southwest China, where they were given six-to-nine-month courses in various phases of guerrilla warfare. Late in 1967 two graduates of the North Vietnamese school who had returned to Thailand and had been captured in the northeast were interviewed at a press conference in Bangkok. There had been 120 students in their guerrilla class, they said, and since the school at Hoa Binh had then been in existence for at least five years, Thai and American officials estimated that some seven or eight hundred terrorists had been already trained by then in North Vietnam alone, and perhaps another three or four hundred in China, though not all had necessarily remained loyal to the Communists. The two prisoners and others who were arrested after them indicated that Communist promises to pay the recruits well and to train them for a profession had not been carried out, and that a number of the returning trainees had also been disillusioned by the hard life of a guerrilla. In addition to the Thai recruits, several thousand young Chinese or Sino-Thais from Thailand were believed to have gone to China for training in the mid-sixties, but the Chinese Communists may have kept most of them in China to work on farms or in factories, possibly with the view of sending them back to Thailand at a later date.

The open Sinofication of the Communist Party of Thailand can be said to date from October 1, 1964, when Radio Peking broadcast a message of congratulations from the C.P.T. to Communist China on its fifteenth anniversary. The message made clear that the C.P.T. sided with the Chinese against the Russians in their ideological struggle and called on "all forces that are against the U.S. imperialists and their lackeys to unite immediately and form a patriotic democratic united front." The following month, a Communist publication called *Ekaraj* (*Independence*) repeated the united-front theme in announcing the formation of the Thailand Independence Movement, whose aim was described as the overthrow of the dictatorial Thai government and the severing of all relations with the United States. Early in January, 1965, in a remark that has been widely quoted since, Foreign Minister Chen Yi of China told the French Ambassador in Peking that there would be "a guerrilla war in Thailand within a year." Two weeks later, the Voice of the People of Thailand, a clandestine radio station that had started up in Laos in 1962 and had moved to North Vietnam and then to China, announced the creation of the Thailand Patriotic Front, "a political organization willing to cooperate with all compatriots of all sexes, ages, professions, political affiliations, and religions who love peace and democracy." The Front's program included the cancellation of all "military, economic, and technical aid agreements" between Thailand and the United States. During 1965, as the establishment of various other front groups, recruiting farmers, workers, young people, monks, and teachers, was announced, the Thai Patriotic Front took on the shape and coloration of the National Liberation Front of South Vietnam, and at the end of 1965 the Thailand Independence Movement and some of the other shadow front groups merged with it. Peking was clearly trying to create the illusion that there was a mass base of support for these various fronts, but there was never much indication that they were anything but names.

Two Thais have been mentioned from time to time in Peking broadcasts as leaders of the front organizations. One of them, a former Army officer named Phayom Chulanont, who vanished after a government round-up of left-wing elements in 1963, was frequently described as the "permanent representative" of the T.P.F., while the other man, Mon Kon Nanakon, a former sawmill owner who was arrested for conspiracy against the Thai government in 1953 and disappeared after his release two years later, was called the "liaison delegate" of the Thailand Independence Movement. Both men have turned up as "official Thai representatives" at international Communist meetings in such places as Cuba and Ghana. A third man, former Premier Pridi Phanomyong, whose People's Party had been a dominant influence in Thailand in the thirties and forties but who was overthrown by a coup in 1946 and forced to flee the country, was also sometimes mentioned by Peking, but Pridi was living quietly in Canton and was not believed to be openly associated with any of the Thai front groups.

At the beginning of 1966 the Thailand Patriotic Front declared that "we have no alternative but to take up arms to repulse the enemy," adding that "the only way we will be able to destroy the enemy forces and to score a final victory is to enlarge the armed struggle into a people's war." By mid-August Peking was making no effort to hide its ultimate aims in Thailand, though, as with the North Vietnamese, the Chinese were exhorting the Thais to take action while making no promises about aiding the revolution themselves. Quoting the precept of Mao Tse-tung and Lin Piao that "a single spark can start a prairie fire," the Peking press agency said: "The armed strength of the Thai people was very small at first. But in a little more than a year, this tiny spark of revolution has indeed spread like a prairie fire. The more U.S. imperialists and Thai reactionaries try to extinguish the fire, the higher it burns. This is the law governing the development of all people's revolutionary struggles."

Terrorism was unquestionably on the increase. In 1962 only three assassinations of government officials or government supporters were reported in Thailand. There were four in 1963, and twelve in 1964. In 1965 thirty-three such people were killed, and by this time the guerrillas were no longer trying to avert open clashes with the Thai police but were willing to meet patrols and shoot it out and even conduct ambushes and attacks against police installations; the result was a total death toll, including ordinary villagers defending their properties, of about ten a month. In the first half of 1966, sixty-five civilian officials, mostly *pubaiyans*, or village headmen, and teachers and alleged police informers, were killed in the northeast, in addition to forty-five police and security officers, while the terrorists themselves suffered eighty-five dead. The worst month was June, when there were twenty-seven reported killings on the government side, including seven *pubaiyans*. The figures dropped off during the fall harvest season, but then picked up again, and the year-end total of officials alone killed was 150. In 1967 it soared to over two hundred. The total number of incidents had risen from twenty in 1965 to three hundred in 1967.

In most areas where they operated, the terrorists used the device of the armed propaganda meeting. A group of thirty or so guerrillas—occasionally there were as many as a hundred—would throw a cordon around a remote village. A few armed cadremen would then pound the village headman's drum to summon the populace. Once the audience had gathered, the Communist agents would harangue it for an hour or two, sometimes using the question-and-answer technique. The themes were always the same: "the corrupt Thanom-Praphas clique"—referring to Prime Minister Thanom and Minister of the Interior Praphas—was declared to be interested only in making the rich richer while ignoring the poor people of the northeast; it was extracting money from the people by unjust taxation and using what it collected to oppress the people even more; the government was turning Thailand into an American colony and a base for the further suppression of all the people of Southeast Asia (mention was frequently made of the American air bases); Communism alone would bring improvements to the people, including better jobs and better farm equipment. These themes, though by no means ineffective, lacked a specific revolutionary appeal. In Vietnam the Vietcong had always been able to cite examples of corruption by specific officials; in Thailand both the *pubaiyan* and the *kamnan*—who head groups of villages— were elected and, even though they carried out assigned government duties, they invariably retained the respect of the villagers, as did the government-appointed teachers. The best target the Thai Communists had was the Provincial Police, who had the deserved reputation, as a group, of being lazy, corrupt, and cruel.

Perhaps most to their disadvantage, the Communist terrorists in Thailand did not have the issue of land reform to play upon as the Vietcong had; where the Vietcong made a great point of distributing land belonging to wealthy French or Vietnamese landowners, most farmers in Thailand already owned their plots, poor and small though they were. Finally, the Communists in Thailand had to contend with the two strong, unifying national themes—Buddhism and the King. King Phumiphon, who was born in 1928 in Cambridge, Massachusetts, where his father was enrolled in the Harvard School of Public Health, is in direct line of the popular Chakri dynasty that has sat on the throne in Thailand for more than a century. He and his wife, the beautiful Queen Sirikit, have from the outset of their reign been highly popular with the Thai people, chiefly because they have proved themselves to be a disarmingly natural couple and have taken an active and continuing interest in the people's welfare. Pictures of the King hang everywhere in the country, even in the farthest northeast villages, and the national respect and reverence for him are genuine. This has also been the case with the Princess Mother Saengkwan Mahidon, who in her capacity as head of the Thai Red Cross has spent much of her time flying around and visiting the troops and villages in outlying areas, often hopping in and out of helicopters in dungarees.

Despite the handicaps the terrorists faced and the losses they suffered—some 250 dead and 400 captured, and 2,000 defectors in 1967—they continued to make headway and to gain adherents, even though, beginning in 1966, they had been placed more on the defensive because of the increased mobility of the government forces, especially the Provincial Police, whose principal elements were ferried about by helicopter. As a rule, the terrorists continued to move about in groups of thirty or forty from forest or mountain bases, where they maintained training camps and stored what food they could get. Rice and other grains were traditionally scarce throughout the northeast, and the guerrillas had to depend mostly on getting food from the local villagers, either by solicitation or, sometimes, at gunpoint. They seemed able to sustain themselves in this fashion, but there was no indication, by the end of 1968, that they were managing to build up the kind of support in the northeast villages that could keep them going indefinitely, as the Vietcong had done. They did not, however, seem to suffer a lack of arms—most of their weapons were Second World War American ones obtained from Laos, where control over guns and ammunition has been lax and they can be bought through smugglers or from the Pathet Lao. Some new Chinese AK-47 rifles were also coming in. The Thai government claimed that unidentified helicopters sighted over some of the guerrilla areas were carrying food and weapons to the terrorists, but the Americans in the area believed these were simply smugglers' craft carrying opium or gold.

The Thais were particularly worried about the participation in the insurgency movement of North Vietnamese who had been living in the northeast of Thailand for a number of years. During the Indochina War some eighty thousand North Vietnamese, many of them enthusiastic supporters of Ho Chi Minh, sought refuge in northeast Thailand. The North Vietnamese Red Cross repatriated about 35,000 of these refugees, in 1959 and 1962, and several thousand more were sent back in 1964. Hanoi refused to take back any more after that, however, claiming they couldn't because of American air raids. About half of the original number of refugees, therefore, remained in five northeast provinces, and births had probably raised the total figure to sixty thousand by 1968. The North Vietnamese had always lived in their own villages under tight control of their own organizations, such as the Overseas Vietnamese Mutual Aid Association of Thailand, which provided a handy front for carrying out propaganda and indoctrination as well as for gathering intelligence. Pictures of Ho were openly displayed in these Vietnamese homes, and youngsters were taught to speak Vietnamese in clandestine schools, in violation of Thai law. For the most part, the Vietnamese in Thailand fulfilled a useful function, working as electricians, machinists, carpenters, truck farmers, and small merchants; they kept to themselves and generally obeyed Thai regulations, including proscriptions against moving around. But even by 1966 there was evidence that some of them had begun to serve as advisers in the ranks of the terrorists, and that they were shielding the infiltration of new North Vietnamese elements from Laos. Some North Vietnamese documents were captured during raids on terrorist camps. There was no evidence that large numbers of North Vietnamese had joined the terrorists, but the possibility of their becoming a dangerous fifth column in a general insurrectionary offensive was recognized by the Thai government. Early in 1967 the first of more than a hundred Communist Vietnamese were arrested and sent to detention areas, and additional arrests were made during that year, continuing in 1968; the government let it be understood that, if necessary, the whole North Vietnamese population would be moved to some rather uncomfortable offshore islands, but in order not to upset Hanoi the Thais hoped to avoid such a drastic step.

The Counterinsurgency Program

By the middle of 1967 the Communists had not only stepped up their actions in the northeast but had begun to move into the area close to Burma and not far from China. Even before this happened, a number of experts had suggested that the activity in the northeast was a possible diversionary move for a larger assault down through another corridor from China that runs alongside Burma and then strikes into the heart of the central plain toward Bangkok. This has served as a traditional invasion path, and the ultimate strategic objective of such an offensive would be to cut the whole northern half of Thailand off from the south and tie it into a Communist Laos and Vietnam. The Communist attacks in the north began in the province of Nan and then spread gradually westward into Chieng Rai and south into Phetchabun Province. The north and northwest provinces were the home of some 250,000 tribal peoples, of whom about a quarter or a third were Meos and an equal number Yaos; most of these tribal elements have remained apart from the Thais, who in turn have paid little attention to them. The Communists, in concentrating on the hill people and promising them their autonomy, were therefore on fertile ground, politically, and they quickly took advantage of their adjacent bases in Laos, where they controlled both Phong Saly Province and parts of Sayabouri, from which infiltration into Thailand was easy, even though the Thais sought to seal the border.

The Thai government claimed, early in 1968, that there were no more than five hundred Communist agents among the Meos and other tribesmen, but it was obviously worried, and its initial reaction was not calculated to win the support of the Meos. Tribal villages suspected of harboring Communist terrorists were bombed with napalm after some eight thousand villagers and those in other places nearby were evacuated to the lowlands. The Meos were also ordered to stop growing opium, their favorite crop. The Communists capitalized on these harsh measures and propagandized the ignorant tribesmen further about the wicked ways of the government. Meo-language broadcasts were said to be emanating from Peking, and both the Meos and the Mossos, in the north, were wooed with gifts, including amulets and charms to ward off troubles, as well as with brand-new AK-47 rifles and machine guns. After a number of ambushes of government patrols, Bangkok finally responded by beginning a counterinsurgency effort in the northwest, too, with the main emphasis on health and education. The situation, in mid-1968, was regarded as serious, though if the government proved able to ameliorate the predicament of the tribal people, it was in a position to place the Communists on the defensive. On the other hand, by moving farther south, the terrorists threatened to cut communications between the north and the northeast, and there was a further danger of a more serious outbreak to the far west, along the Burmese border, where there were some twenty thousand members of the Lahu tribe, considered to be among the best fighters in Southeast Asia. According to some reports, the Communists had been secretly training the Lahus for years in terrorist tactics and were ready, by the summer of 1968, to move them in force into the northern and northwestern provinces, where they could constitute a new major threat.

As had happened in Vietnam, the counterinsurgency program in Thailand underwent several reorganizations and shifts of emphasis during the 1966-68 period, and there was considerable difference of opinion as to the merits of the various changes. When Ambassador Martin was in Thailand, what he felt was a "quantum jump forward" was made when the Americans helped persuade General Praphas, who was Commander in Chief of the ninety-thousand-man Royal Thai Army as well as Deputy Prime Minister and Minister of Interior, to create a central Communist Suppression Operations Command. General Praphas himself headed it formally, but the real operating chief was Lieutenant General Saiyud Kerdphol, a forty-five-year-old staff officer with a brilliant record partly based on his graduate work at American and Australian military staff colleges. Saiyud adopted an unusual approach to counterinsurgency by telling the local officials that their job was not only to suppress the terrorists but to get out among the villages and "listen to the people, and win their confidence by helping to protect them."

Under his direction, with the help of Air Chief Marshal Dawee Chullasapya, the Deputy Defense Minister and Chief of Staff of the Supreme Command, Saiyud established seven civilian-police-military units in the key northeast provinces—they were afterward extended to some of the northern and southern provinces as well. These C.P.M.'s were composed of Provincial Police, of whom there were some 32,000, of Border Patrol Police, an elite group numbering 6,300, and of Army troops, and they averaged in size between one thousand and fifteen hundred men, totaling, in all, about ten thousand. One of the things they helped do was reduce tensions among the police elements and the regular Army. The head of each C.P.M. was the provincial governor, who was assigned special deputies for security, for administration, and for what was called Accelerated Rural Development. One of the most important factors in the general improvement of the situation that took place in 1967 was the high caliber of leadership supplied by the good crop of northeast governors, who were civil servants and who were specially selected, on the basis of their past records, to take over the troubled provinces. Beyond their C.P.M. function, the police, as the principal counterinsurgency elements, operated independently. The Provincial Police conducted patrols of twenty or thirty men each in conjunction with Volunteer Defense Corps units organized in the villages, while the Border Patrol Police had two sets of thirty-man platoons, one group static and the other mobile, and these platoons concentrated on the key border areas where the majority of infiltrators from Laos entered Thailand. It was impossible to watch the whole border, particularly the long stretch of the Mekong River that divides Laos and Thailand, but with the help of helicopters the police could at least respond more quickly than before to reports of terrorist movements. To increase the rate of response, new police stations were established in 250 northeast *tambols*—

tambols were groups of anywhere from five to twenty villages. Radios were distributed at the *tambol* level, so that when an attack occurred a *tambol* head, the *kamnan,* could radio his *nai amphur,* or district chief, who could in turn summon help from the governor and the C.P.M. at the provincial capital.

Quick local response was still the most vital aspect of counterinsurgency, and to aid the police and the Volunteer Defense Corps in the villages the Thais also tried the Vietnamese formula of People's Action Teams; groups of ten men from key villages were selected and sent to Bangkok for training, after which they returned to their villages and served as the main local defense elements, freeing the police and the volunteers for wider patrolling duties. Another Vietnamese scheme that was adopted was the formation of Census Grievance and Aspiration Teams; specially trained groups of interrogators were sent into the villages to make complete blueprints of the population, house by house, to determine the loyalties of the people, to find out which families had relatives with the terrorists, and to analyze the complaints as well as the wants and aspirations of the people. It was hoped that these census squads, when there were enough of them, would reduce some of the resentment that still existed in many parts of the northeast as a result of tough police measures. In far too many cases the provincial police still came into a village where there had been reports of terrorists and arrested virtually every young man over sixteen years of age. Because they lacked interrogation experts themselves, the police took most or all of this male population to district headquarters or to the nearest Joint Security Center, which were cooperative intelligence units composed of several police agencies and the military in a number of northeast provincial capitals.

These security centers amassed a file of ten thousand suspected terrorists or sympathizers in the area, but many of the names were aliases and were thus duplicates for the same person. Not much was known about individual Communist leaders in the northeast, though the names of some regional commanders were on file. The terrorists maintained radio contact with each other, and on occasion North Vietnamese voices were intercepted by the police, further indicating the presence of North Vietnamese cadres. That there was coordination among the rebel groups was also indicated by their manner of movement; when they came out of the hills, they generally traveled along the borders of provinces and districts, an old Vietnamese trick to create confusion among the government patrols, which usually operated within specified geographical limits.

Although the over-all counterinsurgency program seemed to be making headway, the Army resented the increasing civilian role in it, and in October, 1967, it received permission from General Praphas to take over full control. This all but eliminated the Communist Suppression Operations Command and placed Saiyud in a virtually inactive advisory role, while martial law was imposed in *all* the sensitive provinces. The Americans disapproved of the change, but there was little they could do but go along with it. One of the first things the Army ordered was the creation of a new Village Security Force system in the northeast. Members of the force, who would receive eleven weeks' training, would gradually replace the mixed groups of local auxiliary troops and police in the remote areas and would, it was hoped, provide the kind of constant protection that was necessary if the northeast villagers were to be able to live in peace without raids by roving terrorists. Whatever success the new program might have, however, the Americans continued to emphasize to the Thais that no counterinsurgency scheme could succeed on the basis of military response alone, and that the key to defeating the Communists lay in reconstruction and development.

Thai officials were sensitive to the charge that they had neglected the northeast in the past, and they cited the fact that the region had always been poor and not worth developing, but as they became more convinced that they had to deal with the terrorists on a broad basis, they began stepping up the various programs to improve living conditions for the ten million people—almost a third of the total Thai population—in the area. The bureaucratic wheels, while they still ground slowly, moved somewhat faster than they once had. Requests for assistance were funneled by the Army through the respective ministries directly to the district level, where the appointed chiefs, the *nai amphurs*, who were also improving in quality, worked with the local ministerial representatives in dispensing it. Despite the improvement, there was still too much of a time lag in dispatching essential equipment and material, and, more significantly, there remained a dearth of men in the field who knew how to use machines when they got them. As had been the case in Vietnam, the rate of educational reform and vocational training lagged behind the availability of aid; there were too few good elementary and secondary teachers, for example, and few experts to train young men to run tractors, bulldozers, and road scrapers. To fill in until more teachers could be sent out, and more local people trained as technicians, the Border Patrol Police established nearly two hundred schools in the more remote villages, where they taught the first four grades and gave some technical and medical training to older youths.

Under the auspices of the National Security Council, the Thai Army, by mid-1968, had established twenty-two Mobile Defense Units in the field. These units, initially composed of 120 men, including teachers, medics, mechanics, and agriculturists, would settle in villages for forty-five days and institute a crash program of road-building, crop improvement, and so on, encouraging the people to develop their own community projects. After the forty-five-day period, an M.D.U. would be gradually reduced to about twenty people, and this smaller group would remain in a village indefinitely. When the village was judged sufficiently secure to be left on its own, the M.D.U. turned it over to the Ministry of Interior and moved on.

Early in 1967 I visited a twenty-man M.D.U. that had been in the village of Ban Pone Toom, in the district of Na Kae in Nakhon Phanom Province, for three years. This district, lying in the shadow of the Phu Phan Mountains, was one of the most insecure in the northeast, and the M.D.U. was sent there shortly after a hundred of Ban Pone Toom's young men had gone into the hills to join the terrorists. The M.D.U. appeared to me to have had considerable success in the village. It had got the people to build connecting roads to nearby villages, to erect a dam for the storage of water during the rainy season, to plant tobacco, cabbages, onions, and watermelons to supplement the rice crop, and to grow jute for gunny sacks—improvements that, according to the colonel in charge of the team, had raised the villagers' per capita income from six hundred bahts a year to two thousand. In addition, the team had helped the people clean the place up by building fences to keep livestock out from under the houses. Medical aid and health education had notably decreased the incidence of infectious diseases, mostly intestinal disorders and liver fluke sickness, from eating raw fish. (The worst cases had been evacuated by helicopter.) New wells had been dug, and latrines built. The local school had been improved, and a new library had been built and filled with books. Finally, a twenty-man local security force, consisting of fourteen village volunteers and six Provincial Police, had been formed for regular patrol duty.

Despite this apparent progress, I heard some criticism afterward from Americans in the area that the M.D.U. team had not really gained the villagers' confidence. I was told that the failure was due to a lack of understanding and consideration on the part of many of the M.D.U. workers, which was said to typify a general inability on the part of many government officials in the region to realize that no matter how much equipment and technical aid a village might get, the people would not develop any deep loyalty to a government they felt treated them with contempt rather than with respect. Material results were too frequently a reflection of an M.D.U.'s or a district chief's eagerness to meet government goals, without enough attention being paid to what the villagers themselves wanted. Many northeast villages that were considered to be 90 or 100 percent pro-Communist, these critics said, were really on the fence, and could be won over with the proper approach. But all too often something like an ill-considered mass arrest could nullify all the aid efforts.

The M.D.U.'s were essentially spearhead units, operating mainly in the most remote and critical areas. Basic reconstruction work, however, was under the direction of the Accelerated Rural Development program, a long-range plan supported entirely by the American aid mission in Thailand for bringing permanent improvements to the northeast. The program concentrated at the outset on building roads, an important factor in helping farmers get their produce to markets, but it also sponsored such things as agricultural and fisheries improvements, and health and educational projects. Mobile Information Teams, supported since 1962 by the United States Information Service, were also brought into the new program and widened the scope of their activity, which included the showing of government propaganda films in the outlying areas and periodic appraisals by Thai specialists of local conditions and attitudes.

Another American-supported program was the training of so-called village organizers and, through them, village leaders. A selected village organizer was given six months' training by the community development department of the Ministry of Interior and was then sent into the field to survey a group of four or five villages. After he got to know the local people and familiarized himself with social and economic conditions, the organizer picked thirty leaders or potential leaders, who were then given a five-day course on the rudiments of self-government. Upon returning to their communities, the leaders—with the help of the organizer, who took up residence in one of the villages and moved about constantly among the others—called meetings and tried to get the villagers working on local improvements, such as well-digging and the construction of water towers, irrigation and dam projects, or roads. When outside help was required—for instituting a new system of planting crops, for example—the village leaders, with the encouragement of their organizer, put in requests for tools or equipment or seeds.

One American official in Bangkok remarked expansively to me one day, "There are a lot of tough, able, bushy-tailed Thais around —we have a lot more talent here than we ever had in Vietnam." Most Americans in the field agreed that there were indeed some talented Thais, and that they had a tremendous advantage over their counterparts in Vietnam in being able to operate under political conditions that were more conducive to getting things done; there were no bitter regional quarrels in Thailand, for example, as there were in Vietnam, and the nation as a whole had a stability that never existed in Vietnam. In the vital middle and lower Thai official echelons, however, the quality of government officials still left much to be desired. The individuals who seemed most aware of the enormity of the tasks ahead, and of the problems that would arise if the Communists choose to raise the ante in Thailand, were the governors. Their success depended on their spirit of independence, which had freer rein before the Army took over the counter-insurgency program, but the best of them were still performing the most important roles in the region.

In Udorn, Governor Winyu Angkanalaks, in his late thirties and the youngest governor in Thailand, was concentrating on agricultural productivity—a matter of considerable urgency throughout Thailand, since the soil is generally poor and the birth rate high.

Governor Winyu had devised what he called the three K's program
—for *kai*, or chicken; *kaotang*, or sorghum; and *ko*, or cattle.
Chicken-breeding and egg production could easily be improved,
and there was a ready market for eggs in the region, particularly
with large numbers of American troops there. The yield of sorghum
per *rai*—two and a half *rai* equal an acre—was far greater than
that of rice; also sorghum required less water and could be double-
cropped each year, which was rarely the case with rice in this
barren land. As Governor Winyu saw it, a farmer could earn eight
hundred bahts per year by planting sorghum, as compared to only
230 bahts if he planted rice. As for cattle, though it would take
some time to improve breeding methods and to obtain good bulls
and oxen, the financial rewards would be worth it, and there was a
ready market for good beef in Thailand and elsewhere in Southeast Asia. While he was encouraged by the amount of progress
being made, Governor Winyu told me that the terrorists in 1967
seemed better trained and better organized than they had been
previously. "Their ambush tactics are better," he said. "We need to
improve our communications system in order to react faster, and
our radio net is only now starting to work effectively."

In Sakon Nakhon, reportedly the province with the most terrorists, Governor Bodaeng Chantasen told me they were concentrated
in four different locations. He felt that with the improvement of
government tactics, especially the use of American-supplied helicopters, the situation could be handled, but he was worried about
the increase of activity on the part of the North Vietnamese in the
province, and by the reported influx of cadres from outside. He,
too, said that a vital factor in dealing with the terrorists was the
road-construction program, and he was encouraged by the
progress being made, especially in the southern part of the province, where three road projects were under way to connect a hundred kilometers, including one stretch that would cut right across
the Phu Phan Mountains. The Thai road-builders in Sakon Nakhon
were being assisted by the 809th United States Army Engineer
Battalion, which the Communists referred to in their propaganda
as "the dirty imperialist road-builders."

The last province in the northeast I visited was Nakhon Phanom,
which borders the Mekong for more than a hundred miles, facing a
part of Laos that is heavily infested with bands of Pathet Lao.

Governor Saswasdi Meephiem said that in the six bad areas of his province there were a number of villages that were almost completely pro-Communist, but that elsewhere the government was making headway with programs for clearing land and supplementing the rice crop by introducing silkworm cultivation, as well as cattle-raising. He predicted that it would take three years for the reconstruction program to take effect, but said that he thought the terrorists could be contained in the meantime unless the large North Vietnamese population—there are some ten thousand North Vietnamese in Nakhon Phanom—become directly involved. He added that an increasing number of Communist sympathizers had begun to come out of the woods and surrender, professing to be willing to return with government troops to urge their friends to come out. These returnees spoke of being disillusioned by the failure of the terrorists to make good on their promises to pay them eight hundred bahts a month and give them free farm equipment, including tractors.

Throughout my 1967 trip around the northeast, I was impressed by the number of new schools and health stations that had been built since I had last been in the area in 1964. Mobility here, too, was important, especially in dealing with matters of health, and the Americans were providing a unique helicopter service to help the Thais. Air Commandos were flying five-man teams consisting of two medics, one corpsman, a dental technician, and a doctor all over the northeast and to some northern and central parts of the country as well, from the Cambodian border to the borders of Burma. A team remained in a remote area two to three weeks and then, after a few days' rest, took off again for another spot. In an average week, each team was treating between two and three hundred patients, mostly for parasites, anemia, and skin diseases, and also performed minor medical and dental surgery. Some of their patients inevitably included terrorists who took advantage of a team's presence to come out of their retreats for expert care. In addition to this medical work, American civic-action workers among the flying commandos were repairing and building wells and latrines and conducting a veterinary service to control rabies. There had been some difficulty in convincing the Buddhist monks that rabid dogs should be destroyed, but after some dickering the monks said it would be all right to feed the dogs poison meat if good meat were also offered them, so that they would have a choice. The veterinarians used their own judgment as to how much good meat and bad meat to serve, and the rabid-dog population had diminished accordingly.

Although many of the programs being carried out in the northeast, and the ones just beginning in the north and northwest, appeared to be accomplishing something, the sense of overoptimism I encountered among both Americans and Thais in Bangkok struck me as oddly and perhaps ominously reminiscent of the situation several years earlier in Vietnam, where rosy hopes that the end was in sight were being expressed in Saigon, in sharp contrast to the opinions formed by American advisers and correspondents—not to mention many Vietnamese—in the provinces. Admittedly the situation in Thailand was not yet nearly as serious and might never become so, but for all the effort that was being made to contend with it, what was lacking, as in Vietnam, were consistency and cohesion and an abiding sense of purpose. Some of the problems were still purely bureaucratic, but others, such as providing enough security through far-ranging patrolling and local self-defense training to stimulate villages in the more remote areas where the terrorists were strongest, were more basic to the success or failure of the whole counterinsurgency scheme; it was too soon yet to tell, late in 1968, whether the new Village Security Forces and a stepped-up program of American support for the Thai police would be able to achieve this. The prospective end, or slowing, of the war in Vietnam raised the danger of a fresh letdown, though this was obviously the moment when special vigilance was required. As this point approached, a report issued in mid-1967 by the American aid mission in Thailand seemed more than ever germane:

Changes in the desired direction are occurring, but they are so limited in extent and impact that they cannot accomplish the basic objective of securing the allegiance . . . of the ten million northeasterners which is absolutely essential for security and rural development. . . . The villager wants a dialogue between himself and his officials on an egalitarian basis that aims at eliminating corruption, modification of regulations and adjudication of differences. We should more carefully consider what the villager himself wants, not what officials who rarely get out to the village think he wants.

The Threat in the South

If this was true of the Communist insurgency in the northeast and northwest, it was perhaps even more true of the situation in the south, where there was a potentially even more dangerous guerrilla thrust. Just below the center of the eight-hundred-mile-long southern peninsula, only about twenty miles wide at its narrowest point, a group of several hundred hard-core Communists and several thousand sympathizers were operating much as their comrades in the northeast were, except that the southern terrorists were stressing persuasion and propaganda more than terror and assassination. By thus slowly and deliberately building up support in the area, they were believed to be laying a solid groundwork for a future offensive. These central-southern guerrillas were known to be in touch with the Communist groups in the northeast, contact being maintained by couriers who traveled north and south along the Burmese border. Chinese cadres under direct Peking orders were said to be the leaders of this mid-peninsular group, which also maintained some liaison with the small but tightly organized Communist Party of Thailand, in Bangkok. In late September, 1967, the government rounded up thirty-three Communist leaders in Bangkok, including a man said to be the chief organizer of the guerrilla movement and another one described as its principal quartermaster; the successful raid undoubtedly put a crimp in the Communists' plans but did not stop them from continuing their nationwide terrorism.

Separate from this central peninsular organization was a group of seven or eight hundred terrorists in the five provinces further south, two of which bordered Malaysia. These included the experienced remnants of the ten thousand guerrillas of the earlier Emergency in Malaysia said to be still directed by Chin Peng, who next to Ho Chi Minh was perhaps the most experienced Communist leader in Southeast Asia. Chin, who was fifty years old in 1968 and who had won a British medal for his anti-Japanese underground work in the Second World War, had fled into the jungles of northern Malaya and Thailand when the British finally defeated his force in 1959; there were reports from time to time that he had gone to China or to some other part of Southeast Asia, but the Thai and Malaysian police who were conducting joint patrols in the jungle border region felt that he was still in the area, moving back and forth across the border. Chin's small but highly trained and efficient organization was more sophisticated than the terrorist bands in the northeast and, unlike the central southern Communists, did not maintain much contact with them, at least not regularly. Instead, this deep-south group was taking its orders straight from Peking, though it also had close connections with the Malayan National Liberation League and the Malayan National Front, both anti-Malaysian bodies that had representatives in Malaysia and headquarters in Peking, as well as with the Malayan Communist Party, which had slowly taken Thais of Chinese extraction into its ranks as well as some Thai Muslims in the effort to broaden its racial base.

In the three southernmost provinces—Pattani, Yala, and Narathiwat—the population is between two-thirds and three-quarters Muslim, and long-standing opposition to Thai (Siamese) rule culminated after the Second World War, in an insurrection in Narathiwat, in 1948, that coincided with Chin Peng's Communist insurrection in Malaya. The Thais put down the Narathiwat revolt, which they said was due to the activity of Muslim separatists who sought to incorporate the southern provinces with the northern Malayan sultanates. Continuing sentiment for separatism among the Muslims in the area was being capitalized on by the Communist guerrillas, as well as by ultranationalist Malayans on both sides of the border, and by roving bandit gangs. The Thai Muslims have retained their own language and their own religious practices. Moreover, a large number of Chinese merchants and small landholders in the region have maintained their own customs and language. As a consequence, the peninsula was thoroughly fragmented, which served Communist purposes well.

The terrorists were strongest in the Betong district of Yala, a rubber-growing area that was predominantly Chinese. They moved about in bands of fifteen or thirty and sometimes fifty men, and both their organization and discipline were better than that of the northeast Communists. In most villages they had permanent male and female agents, and once a month or so a number of uniformed terrorists visited each village to conduct propaganda meetings and collect food and taxes. Small individual rubber planters were taxed moderate monthly amounts of twenty or thirty bahts, while the larger rubber-estate owners paid as much as ten thousand bahts monthly and were assessed on the basis of the number of workers they employed. The Communists also distributed money and medical aid to the poor. Generally, though well armed with American weapons, the terrorists were not seeking out fights with Thai or joint Thai-Malaysian patrols, but occasionally a patrol was ambushed. Late in 1967 the Thai Provincial and Border Police were just beginning to be strong enough to go out searching for the guerrillas, but there was some friction between them and the Malaysians, who privately accused the Thais of not trying very hard. It was true that the Thais were sometimes reluctant, since they were a minority in the south and did not relish being marked for assassination.

The seriousness of the situation in the far south was brought home to both the Thais and the Malaysians on June 17, 1968, when Chin Peng's guerrillas carried out their most successful raid in twenty years. Striking from the dense jungle only a hundred yards or so from a Thai check-point in Betong district, they killed sixteen Malaysian border policemen and wounded seventeen others. So far as was known, the Communists suffered no casualties in their quick withdrawal. The attack led to an immediate series of high-level conferences between the Thais and the Malaysians, with the latter doing their utmost to persuade the Thais that the time had come to take the southern guerrillas as a real threat and to step up the joint border patrols. The Thais still did not want to move in armored tanks and helicopters, but they did agree to increasing the surveillance of the guerrilla areas on both sides of the border, and to engage, when necessary, in "hot pursuit" across it. Control of supplies on the Malaysian side was established, but, unlike the Malaysians who also moved out residents on their side of the border to places farther south, the Thais registered their residents in the border area and then began moving in the first of some fifteen thousand more families (sixty thousand persons) from other parts of the country, specially chosen for their apparent loyalty and their patriotic and pioneering spirit. It was hoped that they would act as the eyes and ears of the government patrols in tracking down the terrorists. A price of $83,000 was placed on

Chin Peng's head, and lesser amounts were offered for other known guerrilla chiefs, including two Thai Muslim lieutenants of Chin.

The guerrillas were as elusive as Chin's gangs had been during the earlier Emergency. During three years of operations, the Thais, on their side of the border, had discovered some 150 guerrilla camps in the jungle, many of them elaborately surrounded by trenches and booby traps and including barracks, dining halls, training rooms, and recreation halls, but not once had the patrolling troops been able to reach a camp before it was abandoned. Frequently it took them a week of cutting their way through the jungle, only to find that the guerrillas had fled a day or two, or even hours, before; on other occasions, while moving through rubber plantations, the patrols would hear the local rubber tappers apparently warning the guerrillas.

The confused political and racial situation in this southern region was made more complicated by the activity of several hundred bandits, with whom the Communists cooperated when it suited their purposes—in the killing of Thai village chiefs, for example —and attacked when they sought to pose as "defenders" of the poor. The bandits derived most of their income from smuggling, which was traditional in the area and was a source of official corruption; government controls over the price of rice were difficult to enforce, and the smugglers, with the connivance of local officials, were able to sneak large amounts across the border to Malaysia, where they could get higher prices. Economic conditions in the southern provinces, while generally better than in the northeast, were growing worse because of the decreasing world price of rubber. More and more peasants were subsisting by raising what crops and catching what fish they needed for themselves, but not much more. The government's development program in the south had a lower priority than the one in the northeast and was complicated by language difficulties and by the fact that the Thais had done little or nothing to bring the Thai Muslims into the official hierarchy beyond the comparatively low level of assistant district officer. Though by 1968 the government had started building schools and had established a university and a development center at Yala, and had moved in some Mobile Development Teams and a summer student program modeled on the Peace Corps, Thai officials in the south seemed to lack the zeal of some of those in the northeast, and they were still subject to overcentralization and bureaucratic infighting in Bangkok. One high official, worried about the growing strength of the Communists and the danger of a southern Communist drive to match a northeast offensive, said, "We're taking care of the head of the body, up there, but not the legs, down here." In general, there seemed too much inclination among the Thais to protect their own position in the south rather than improve the economic and social conditions of the Muslims and make them believe in the beneficence of Thai rule, rather than in the blandishments of the Communists and the Muslim separatists. The Thais themselves often seemed uncertain of how to deal with the vacuum in the region. They helped repair mosques, for example, and at the same time erected huge new images of Buddha.

Assimilation and Politics

Behind the whole question of insurgency in Thailand lay a factor of uncertainty about the Chinese population and its sympathies. Four million people in the country were described as "Chinese," but at least a million were regarded as Sino-Thais as a result of intermarriage, and another million or so had been born in Thailand. Of the remainder who were Chinese-born, perhaps a quarter of a million were believed to be pro-Peking, and the rest, though chauvinistically pro-Chinese, were essentially apolitical. Many of the Chinese regularly sent remittances to their relatives in China, but the great majority seemed to have fully adjusted themselves to the Thai way of life. A sizable number, especially those with their own businesses, had adopted Thai names. Ever since they had come to Thailand three centuries ago, the local Chinese, undoubtedly because of the country's long tradition of independence, had made a point of establishing close relations with leading Thais in the government, in the military, and in banking and business. This was usually done in the form of an outright deal, with the Chinese "partner" in the relationship, often described as a Thai's "Chinese tail," supplying the capital while his Thai associate provided local contacts and influence. The system extended to all areas of enterprise in Thailand, and during the Vietnam war boom produced ample dividends from the construction of hotels, office buildings, and pleasure palaces.

All in all, the Chinese in Thailand had done well, and had been more successfully assimilated than anywhere else in Southeast Asia. There remained the question of how far their loyalty to Thailand would extend if events took a turn for the worse, if the insurgents in the northeast and south increased their position and influence, if China pushed its policy in support of "wars of liberation," and if, above all, Vietnam became reunified under a pro-Communist or leftward-leaning "neutralist" government. General Praphas, when asked about the Chinese in Thailand, said he foresaw "no problems, if we can manage as we do today," and he pointed out that "some of us around here may be 5 percent, 20 percent, or even 50 percent Chinese, even though we consider ourselves Thais." But Praphas also emphasized that, no matter where the Chinese emigrated, they always looked upon themselves as Chinese. This was something, of course, that was worrying all Southeast Asian nations with large numbers of Overseas Chinese, including not only Indonesia but also Burma, where, alarmed at the prospect of a Chinese power thrust, General Ne Win had moved firmly to eliminate all Chinese businessmen, which had scarcely alleviated his already considerable economic woes but had given him more political peace of mind. The Thais did not consider such a move practical, nor desirable, under the mixed racial circumstances in the country and the benefits they derived from doing business with the Chinese, but they, too, had their moments of worry. If the Communists did win the battle of negotiations in Vietnam, and the Americans did back away from Southeast Asia, the chances were that, despite its almost pathological fear of Peking, Thailand would turn neutral and look toward China— especially if that country displayed a more restrained foreign policy—as much as toward the West. This would be perfectly in keeping with its historical traditions and diplomacy.

Much admittedly depended on the degree of political progress the Thais were able to make. There had been considerable debate over several years about whether the country should move quickly to adopt a new Constitution and hold parliamentary elections or

wait until the insurgency was better contained. Those against rush-
ing the democratic procedure, not unexpectedly, had gravitated
around General Praphas, whose power base lay in his continued
firm control of the Army and the police. But by 1967 Praphas
seemed reluctantly ready to accept the constitutional procedure.
Despite his obvious power, the Thai government was actually a
neatly balanced wheel, with the quiet but persevering and honest
Prime Minister Thanom as one center spoke and the King as the
other; notwithstanding Praphas' great strength, these two invariably controlled the wheel's movement, seeing to it that the power
and push supplied by Praphas and his friends were braked by
their own restraining influence and by that of a number of civilian
democratic-minded leaders, notably Foreign Minister Thanat and
former Premier Pote Sarasin, who was Minister of National Development.

The new Constitution was finally promulgated in June, 1968,
after the long months of argument and procrastination. The 183-
article document scarcely provided for full representative government and there seemed little doubt that the present ruling group
would remain in power. Among other things, the new upper house,
the Senate, would continue to be appointed by the King, in consultation with the current political leaders in control of the military
elements and therefore of the country; the lower body, the House,
while elected on the basis of one member in each province for each
150,000 people, would enjoy far less power and prerogatives, and
since the Senate was to have a total membership equal to three-
fourths of the House, control of both for the ruling government
group could be assured by only one-quarter control of the House.
As for the Cabinet, or Council of Ministers, it would have more
powers than the legislative branch; appointed by the King, the
Council could not include any members of the legislature, and
there was no need for it to submit its programs for any vote of
legislative endorsement or confidence. There was nothing to indicate, either, that the Prime Minister had to be a member of the
party that obtained the most votes in the House elections. Civil
rights were guaranteed fairly well, but nothing in the Constitution
precluded the continuation of martial law, which has existed in
Thailand since 1958 without a break, and, in fact, continued after
the Constitution went into effect.

When the old Senate passed the election law late in 1968, it demonstrated a last-minute bit of independence it had not previously shown by rejecting the recommendation of the Cabinet that all candidates for the forthcoming House election had to belong to political parties. Prime Minister Thanom, honestly seeking to promote the new constitutional experiment, took the Senate move in stride, but Praphas, who was out of the country at the time, was said to be furious, as were other members of the military. Despite the lack of recent political party experience in the country —like labor unions, parties and political activity had been banned for years—one of the healthier signs of development was the quick emergence of eight dormant or new party groups. The ninth and the largest and most powerful was the government party, which was pondering a new name, and which was headed by Praphas; Pote Sarasin was Vice Chairman and Air Marshal Dawee was Secretary General. Of the other old parties, the most important were the Democratic Party and the People's Party, which together would probably form the strongest opposition. The Democratic Party was headed by Prince Pramoj, who had led the anti-Japanese resistance from Washington during the Second World War and then had briefly served as Prime Minister. Pramoj claimed that the new Constitution "almost achieves immortality for the [incumbent] Thai government," and thereby immediately placed himself in the vanguard of the new opposition. In the Bangkok municipal elections, held in the fall of 1968, his party won twenty-two of twenty-four seats, but the government chose not to put up any candidates —mostly because its own party was still in the process of being reorganized. Pramoj recommended that the Thais determine to stand up against Communist aggression—in concert with the Americans, if the Americans could be persuaded to help out no matter what happened in Vietnam, but, if necessary, alone.

The People's Party hoped to draw most of its strength from the northeast. Although several other new smaller parties that sprang up did not have much following, another encouraging sign was the burgeoning youth activity. The day after the new Constitution was promulgated, the students startled the government by demonstrating against the continuation of martial law, and the government responded sophisticatedly by meeting most of the students' demands—lifting the ban on public speaking and rescinding an increase in bus fares. Subsequent demonstrations on issues of student participation in the administration of the major universities were less successful, but the students had made an impression that stirred many of their elders. As the time for the February, 1969, elections approached, there was divided feeling about their significance, but at least a growing interest. Pramoj, and others of the opposition older guard, said they could win a majority if the vote was clean, but predicted that, through bribery and other means, the government would see to it that it obtained a majority in the House; in describing the Constitution further as "a set of false teeth—not very real, but with some bite," Pramoj scarcely won many friends for his cause among those who were either close to the government or who depended on officials for their own survival, and that included a great many people. It was the hope of foreign observers that a new liberal non-Communist element would eventually emerge in Thailand, one that could offset threats both from the right and the left and that would act as a balance, but this would surely take time in view of the long period of political and intellectual stagnation. In the meantime, though banned, the Communists would undoubtedly try to operate behind the scenes or underground as a political force, chiefly among the poor peasants.

How effectively the leaders of the government would respond to a new political climate and to political methods and practices that were different from their own was at best problematical. It was widely believed that Prime Minister Thanom would stay on as the formal head of a new government, at least for a time, although an alternative was Pote Sarasin, whose administrative and political experience qualified him as perhaps the leading civilian politician. The fact that he was Chinese might have more advantages than disadvantages in a changeover period. As for Praphas, pending the elections he was biding his time about his future official position. Though he had not been well for years—he suffered from severe eye trouble—he was not likely to surrender his great prestige and power willingly, any more than he would easily give up the financial prerogatives of his position, which helped him distribute largess to his friends in the Army as compensation for their low salaries and their high degree of loyalty. At a press conference, he once jokingly compared himself to Hanuman, the lithe magical monkey in the epic *Ramayana*, whose ability to assume different forms and perform miracles for his sovereign, Narai, enabled him to be highly important but to keep in the background and at the same time enjoy life as something of a free-wheeling sybarite. Praphas raised a few eyebrows when, in expressing some reluctance to be the leader of the new government party, he added, loftily, that "being engaged in politics means standing in filth and becoming stained with the filth." The longer he and his cohorts remained in office, he added, with more apparent reference to himself than to anyone else, "the more things are said against us, in coffee shops and other places," and he didn't relish having his children and grandchildren be tarnished by a bad family name. A few more eyebrows went up when he qualified this, however, by saying, "As a soldier, I will not be able to remain quiet if the nation is in trouble. I am willing to lay down my life for the country. I am not afraid of hard work." Praphas' new frankness, and his enjoyment of his bantering sessions with the press as he let himself become more of a public and less of a shadowy figure, seemed to indicate that, whatever the political developments in Thailand in the next few years, and barring problems of health, the General, one way or another, would still be around.

6

Cambodia:

THE EYE OF THE STORM

❧

Cambodia Is Sihanouk

In recent years the visitor making the half-hour plane trip from Saigon to the Cambodian capital of Phnom Penh has invariably experienced the sensation of having momentarily escaped the turbulence of the Southeast Asian hurricane for its calm eye. The differences between the two cities became manifest the moment the plane set down at Phnom Penh's Pochentong airport, where it was likely to be the only one on the field, in contrast to the scores of fighters, bombers, transports, and helicopters on the ground or overhead at Tan Son Nhut, in Saigon. The ride into town was swift and smooth, along clean, broad avenues and streets relatively free of traffic and of the cloying smell of exhaust fumes. The stucco houses and villas of residential Phnom Penh, painted serene pastel colors, stood far apart amid lush, well-tended lawns and imparted an air of comfortable and unhurried living. The food and wines in the French restaurants were still good, and the Vietnamese-run dance halls and cafés, although their operators had begun to acquire some of Saigon's money-grabbing habits, retained much of the old French atmosphere of *joie de vivre.*

Such manifestations of contentment, however, could not conceal that the storm was close by, and to watch Prince Norodom Sihanouk, the Chief of State, perform his extraordinary feat of navigating above it was an often breath-taking experience. Sihanouk, the former King who stepped down from the throne in 1955, at the age of thirty-three, to take over the controls of his flimsy state, continued, for the most part, to meet with astonishing *élan* and vitality the challenge of staying politically aloft. He not only forecast the political weather, in all its variability, but frequently played the exciting role of daredevil barnstormer and test pilot, and, while the crowd gasped and sometimes criticized his swift and sudden maneuvers, he repeatedly proved his ability to entertain but more importantly to survive as the leader of a people and a country he has both personified and dominated.

Sihanouk always liked to refer to his Khmer people as his "children," and they, for their part, cherished and revered him, but in a wider sense the relationship went far beyond that of parent and offspring, to that of a Superman-style hero and his audience. In a more historical and sophisticated sense, he looked upon himself as an Asian knight-errant engaged in a sacred mission to save his nation from the Infidels and the barbarians, which included, in varying degree, both the Communists and the Americans and their allies. Although the situations and the circumstances kept changing, there was a certain consistency to the story line—the predicament of the beleaguered hero-prince surrounded by enemies seeking to devour or destroy him; his compulsion to preserve Cambodia's sovereignty at whatever cost, including his own life; his repeated narrow escapes and re-emergence, girded in fresh moral armor, to do battle yet again with the wicked forces of the world who would not leave him alone. For all his protestations, it is doubtful that Sihanouk ever wanted to be left alone—neglect would probably have caused him to languish sadly—but as he moved from crisis to crisis, some imposed upon him and others created by himself, his assurance and bravado increasingly failed to hide the uneasy desperation beneath the suave exterior. With the passing of the years, anger and frustration on more than one occasion prompted him to succumb to near-hysterical outbursts, followed by periods of dejection and depression. There was never much doubt that Sihanouk, as a self-driven and dedicated man, was sincerely striving to remain neutral and independent while the countries surrounding him in Southeast Asia were at war, but the more I observed him during several visits to Cambodia between 1965 and 1968, the more he seemed to me a tragic and lonely figure out of the past, and at the same time something of a medieval flagellant. In his rear-guard campaign to hold on to what was left of the ancient and remarkable Khmer empire and heritage, he sometimes drew so much attention to his own vulnerability as to increase rather than diminish it. One could readily sympathize with his predicament of feeling himself surrounded by the Vietnamese on one side and the Thais on the other.

At its height, between the ninth and thirteenth centuries, the great Khmer empire had conquered much of Southeast Asia, including what is now Vietnam and Thailand, and had ten million subjects when England had only about five million. Thereafter, beginning in the fourteenth century, the Thais and the Vietnamese, yellow mainland people—the Khmers are darker-skinned and are related to the Polynesians and the Indonesians—moved in, and would have destroyed the kingdom altogether had it not been for the arrival, in 1863, of the French, who thus, in a sense, became the saviors as well as the colonial rulers of Cambodia. Sihanouk often accorded public credit for his country's survival to the French, who, largely as a result of his efforts, granted Cambodia its independence in 1953, and he consistently referred to President Charles de Gaulle—who, like him, later urged the neutrality of all the former Indochinese states—as one of the great men of history. Cambodia, he liked to say, was the most "unabashedly Gaullist" and genuinely Francophile nation in the world outside of France.

For all his maneuvering, one somehow suspected that sooner or later, as Sihanouk himself often predicted, his people were likely to be swallowed up by some form of Communism. And although he repeatedly proved to be what he claimed to be—an anti-Communist monarch with Socialist leanings—he also repeatedly said he would prefer to have his country succumb to Communism rather than to American-style capitalism. Much of this was undoubtedly defensive, but as the war in Vietnam dragged on and grew fiercer, the danger of its spreading into Cambodia and engulfing Sihanouk increased. By 1968 the danger had become manifest through a series of scattered Communist rebellions in a number of provinces. If Sihanouk had an understandable obsession about the sanctity of his frontiers and lived in constant fear of a larger invasion, there seemed little he could do about it. South Vietnam and Thailand, both at war with the Communists, pecked away at his borders, purposely or accidentally; in the case of Vietnam, Sihanouk unquestionably had invited such incursions by allowing the Vietcong and the North Vietnamese to use his territory for sanctuary and supply, or by stressing his inability to deny them the use of it. The United States, though sympathetic to Sihanouk's predicament, was also at war in Vietnam, and while he constantly accused the Americans of violating his frontiers on the ground and in the air, Washington's orders to military commanders in the field were to exercise restraint in pursuing Communist troops across the Cambodian border. Not all the American commanders necessarily agreed with these orders, but they had to accept them and try to abide by them.

When I interviewed Sihanouk in Phnom Penh in the summer of 1966, he declared emphatically that only when the United States recognized his "existing borders" and put an end to "military action against our country" could an American-Cambodian reconciliation become possible. Diplomatic relations between the two countries had formally been broken off by Sihanouk in May, 1965, following two years of deterioration that had begun with Sihanouk's renouncing American military, economic, and cultural aid because, as he claimed, it was not unconditional and violated his neutrality. There had been a number of moves made by both Sihanouk and the Americans to establish the terms and conditions for a dialogue that might lead to better relations again, but something had always happened to upset things, mostly border violations by the South Vietnamese, who used American equipment and were sometimes accompanied by American advisers into Cambodia, or accidental attacks by American fighter bombers on Cambodian villages. Despite apologies from Washington, which emphasized the unavoidability of such mishaps in time of war, especially under the circumstances of the borders being differently or unclearly defined on the available maps, Sihanouk had remained unmollified. During my conversation with him, he pointed out that the Soviet Union had officially recognized Cambodian independence, neutrality, and territorial integrity, and he asked why the United States could not do likewise. The answer was apparent, but Secretary of State Dean

Rusk had, in fact, told a press conference early in 1966, "We support fully both the neutrality and the territorial integrity of Cambodia."

The United States, moreover, had offered to underwrite an increase in the personnel and equipment of the International Control Commission in Cambodia. The 1954 Geneva agreements, ending the war between France and the Vietminh and dividing Vietnam at the Seventeenth Parallel—supposedly on a temporary basis until free elections could be held there—had also guaranteed the independence of Cambodia and Laos and had set up an International Control Commission, to be staffed by representatives of Poland, India, and Canada, that was supposed to supervise the peacekeeping efforts in the entire area. Primarily, the strengthening of the I.C.C., as endorsed by both the State Department and Cambodia, would have involved the use of helicopters to patrol Cambodia's six-hundred-mile border with Vietnam. Sihanouk had first proposed such an increase in December, 1965, and had since repeated the proposal several times, but the Russians, as co-sponsors of the 1954 Geneva accords, had refused to go along with the idea. The Cambodians, protesting that they were constantly being called upon to prove their innocence in the matter of helping the Communists, argued that the Geneva agreements provided sufficient legal grounds for proceeding with the expansion of the patrols. The trouble was that the Poles and the Indians—particularly the former—were loath to take any action that the Russians had not approved, and the Russians had not seemed eager to interfere with any activities of the North Vietnamese and the Vietcong along the border, even though, as in Laos, they were in favor in principle of keeping the war in Vietnam from expanding. Even if some agreement about an expanded I.C.C. had been reached, and perhaps twenty special helicopter-borne teams had been put in the field, their efforts, it was thought, would be pretty much hamstrung by continuing juridical and procedural arguments among the three Commission members, as for so long had been the case both in Laos and Cambodia, as well as in Vietnam.

Blowing Hot and Cold

Perhaps more than any other ruler in Southeast Asia, Sihanouk has all along felt, rightly or wrongly, that the fortunes of his country, as of other nations in the area, would in the final analysis be determined not so much by itself as by the policies and roles adopted by those two great powers, the United States and China. Over the years, China had kept looming above him like a great Cheshire cat, alternately grinning, vanishing, and reappearing. The United States, farther away, had been more like a big Saint Bernard dog, with the proverbial bell and cask of brandy tied around its neck for rescue operations, but Sihanouk, like some of his fellow Asians, often wondered about the dependability of the beast—when and where it would show up, and if it did how long it would stay. Moreover, his doubts about, and some of his railings against, the United States were based on a conviction that the Americans had not only supported his two traditional enemies, Vietnam and Thailand—"eaters of Khmer earth," as he called them—but had encouraged them in their plots against him. His accusations to this effect centered particularly on what he alleged was American as well as Thai and Vietnamese support of the Khmer Serei, an opposition organization that was formed just after the Second World War by an exiled former Cambodian Prime Minister named Son Ngoc Thanh. The Khmer Serei, which used to operate along the Vietnamese border, had its headquarters somewhere in Thailand. Though it once claimed a strength of ten thousand men, Western military observers and even Sihanouk himself privately estimated its number of armed men at no more than six or seven hundred. Nevertheless, Sihanouk made its existence a pretext for keeping almost two-thirds of his Army, or about twenty thousand men, along the Thai border. He accused the Thais of using the Khmer Serei as a screen for launching attacks of their own against Cambodia; it was true that they had held three of its provinces during the Second World War, and he claimed they still coveted these areas. The Thais continued to probe into Cambodian territory, and in May, 1966, they attacked Preah Vihear, the venerated temple returned to Cambodia by a decision of the International World

Court in 1962. The Cambodians retaliated sharply and effectively.

The United States quietly sought to restrain the Thais from engaging in such provocative actions, and the United Nations sent a representative to the border area in an effort to reduce the number of incidents, which kept continuing, but Sihanouk remained deeply disturbed about the possibilities of a large-scale Thai attack that would catch him in a pincer movement in the event of a simultaneous invasion by the Vietnamese from the east. Deploring what he described as "de-Asianized Asians," he berated the United States for aiding such "imperialist renegades" all over Asia, particularly in Thailand and South Vietnam. In an editorial in the monthly magazine *Kambuja*, Sihanouk wrote, early in 1966:

> The warmongers wage war in Vietnam in the name of "anti-Communists." While they contribute more than the best agents of Mao Tsetung and Ho Chi Minh to favor, to hasten the Communization of South Vietnam, the interventionists have the nerve—or the ignorance—to consider themselves as a "solid wall" against the Communization of our continent and they are angry with us because we do not display our gratitude. . . . The reason for our attitude is simple. First of all, we hold them responsible for the arrival at our doors, too soon for our liking, of Communism. The United States attracts Communism as sugar attracts ants.

At another point in the same editorial, Sihanouk spoke out in defense of the South Vietnamese people, and declared that

> the Americans and their mercenaries of various nationalities occupy their country as formerly Hitler's Germany and its henchmen occupied the Balkan states. They have imposed a reign of terror and in order to get at one doubtful Vietcong they kill ten or a hundred times more noncombatant Vietnamese, whose only desire is to live peacefully in their country.

These were harsh, exaggerated statements. Unfortunately, many Americans, including officials in Washington, took a great deal that Sihanouk said far too seriously. Sihanouk, for his part, was inordinately hypersensitive about what the Americans, and especially the American press, said about him; as a journalist himself, and one who wrote constant editorials and supervised the contents both of *Kambuja* and the weekly *Réalités Cambodgiennes*, he found it hard to believe that what appeared in American magazines and newspapers did not reflect official or semiofficial opinion. He also deeply resented what he considered personal attacks on him, for he considered himself the embodiment of the Khmer spirit. He once explained in an article: "For a well-born Asian and above all a Khmer, gratuitous slurs and unfairness are the worst of things. We can bear anything, suffer without saying a word the cruelest physical suffering, but slights, scorn, injustice, no matter where they come from, are intolerable to us." On another occasion, he wrote: "For me to die in battle would be nothing; but to be insulted and slandered before all my fellow Cambodians is absolutely intolerable. Through me, the entire Khmer people feels lessened in its honor and its dignity. . . . To insult me, to hurt me or to humiliate me, is to do the same to the Cambodian nation."

Sihanouk's attitude had its origin in the period after the defeat of France in 1954 and her departure from Indochina. At that time Sihanouk felt firmly that Cambodia's security and sovereignty depended on the friendship and support of the United States, whose anticolonialism the Prince admired and whose support at the Geneva Conference—although he afterward did not like to admit it—had alone helped him stand firm against the partition of Cambodia, which the Vietnamese Communists sought. When the Southeast Asia Treaty Organization was created in September of that year, Sihanouk welcomed its so-called "umbrella of protection" over Cambodia, Laos, and South Vietnam. The following year Cambodia accepted American economic aid. Sihanouk's fear of encroachment by the Communist Vietminh kept him close to the United States, though Prime Minister Nehru of India warned him that he was being too "pro-Western." The turning point for Sihanouk came at the Asian-African Conference in Bandung, Indonesia, in April, 1955, where he fell under the influence of Chou Enlai of Communist China, who dominated the meetings. Both Chou and Pham Van Dong, the Foreign Minister of North Vietnam, assured the Prince that they would respect the integrity of Cambodia if he followed a neutral course. After Bandung Sihanouk decided that Cambodia's internal unity, which had been weakened because of his pro-Western feelings, depended on his maintaining a posture of neutrality in his relations with both the Communist and Western worlds.

At this point, many observers still feel, the United States made a mistake in pressuring Sihanouk too strongly to join SEATO and to respond with positive expressions of friendship to offers of economic and military aid. Whether or not there were ever any formal "strings" attached to American aid, Sihanouk felt that he was being blackmailed, and it was primarily for this reason that, in February, 1956, he made his first pilgrimage to Peking. The Chinese proved splendid hosts, and Sihanouk was impressed by what he saw in China. He was even more impressed by Chinese promises of economic assistance, which gave him a lever to use against the Americans. During the following year the Prince cemented his relations not only with China but also with the Soviet Union, Poland, and Czechoslovakia. Late in 1956 Chou En-lai returned Sihanouk's visit, and not long thereafter Cambodia's new policy of neutrality was formally written into its Constitution and it was announced that Cambodia was no longer interested in the "protection" offered her by the SEATO pact. Thus, in the short space of two years, Sihanouk had switched from a policy of neutrality that favored the West to one that disposed him to lean more heavily to the East, and particularly toward the Communist countries of Asia and those nations, such as India and Indonesia, which professed a policy of nonalignment.

Sihanouk's leftward-turning neutrality and his growing conviction that the United States would always favor South Vietnam and Thailand more than Cambodia were further encouraged in June, 1958, when three thousand South Vietnamese troops invaded Stung Treng Province and took up fortified positions at a point several kilometers inside the Cambodian border. The United States refused to condemn the invasion as "aggression," maintaining its impartiality and even reminding Sihanouk that the arms aid he had received from us was meant for use only against the Communists. The following month Sihanouk gave de jure recognition to China, and in August, after he had again visited Peking, the two countries established full diplomatic relations. In September Sihanouk journeyed to the United Nations and was also received by President Eisenhower and by Secretary of State John Foster Dulles, the architect of SEATO. The Prince tried, without much success, to explain that his policy of counterbalance was necessary if Cambodia was to survive pressures from both the right and left. Sihanouk's suspicion of American motives deepened in 1959 when he accused the Central Intelligence Agency of being behind new Khmer Serei and South Vietnamese plots to overthrow him, and he used the C.I.A. constantly thereafter as a whipping boy for everything about American policy he disliked in Southeast Asia. In September, 1960, he suggested that both Laos and Cambodia be neutralized and their neutralization guaranteed by the Western and Communist powers and also by North Vietnam, South Vietnam, and Thailand. The Communists and the French supported this idea, but the United States refused to go along with it, feeling that it would favor the Communists, and Washington also rejected a plan submitted by Sihanouk in 1961 for the neutralization of Laos alone. When Laos finally was neutralized by a new international agreement supported in Washington in 1962, it was too late, just as Sihanouk had feared, and the guarantees that were given did not work. From this point on, relations between Sihanouk and the United States moved inexorably to the final rupture in 1965, and during this period Cambodia moved steadily closer to its former colonial parent, France, which increased its economic as well as its military and cultural stake in the country.

As Sihanouk became more convinced that the Communists would win out in Vietnam and Laos, he continued to move closer to China, too, and at the same time he tried unavailingly to obtain guarantees of his borders from North Vietnam and from the National Liberation Front. His aim was still to foster an independent neutral bloc composed of all the former Indochina states, which was logical enough, although impractical under the circumstances since none of the combatants, either in Laos or Vietnam, was willing to negotiate. Sihanouk kept trying, and in March, 1965, he summoned a Conference of the People of Indochina in Phnom Penh, at which he planned to propose that, in keeping with the Geneva principles of 1954, there should be a simultaneous withdrawal of all combatant forces in Vietnam and that the I.C.C. be given sufficient powers to guarantee a condition of total neutrality pending a satisfactory political solution. The North Vietnamese and their Communist associates insisted on prior American withdrawal, and they threatened to walk out of the conference if Sihanouk delivered his speech. The Prince did not deliver it, though he afterward distributed copies, and the conference turned into a Communist-dominated anti-American propaganda forum. Sihanouk was confronted with a worse dilemma than ever. While he still excoriated American imperialism, he also felt, as he told a Cambodian audience that same month, that "if the United States leaves South Vietnam, we will be face to face with Communism and, worse, with the Vietnamese Communists, which are for us the worst kind of Communists."

Equally distrustful of the Vietnamese Communists and of United States policy, Sihanouk now turned more hopefully than ever to China. He felt that China alone could protect him from all his enemies, including the Cambodian Communist movement, which he had so far managed to keep in check but which remained a threat because of North Vietnamese, rather than Chinese, support. He went as far as to say that "if our region is one day to be overrun by Communism, let us very much hope that it will be China, and no other Socialist power, that takes over the reins in our country, for we know that she understands us and will preserve our territorial integrity under any circumstances." Sihanouk soon became fulsome in his praise of China. In addition to his other talents, he is a prolific song writer, and he entitled one of his compositions, which regularly appear in *Kambuja*, "Nostalgia for China." A literal translation of some of the lyrics goes:

> Oh, beloved China!
> Steadfast is my heart.
> Deeply it yearns for Thee!
> Oh, Affectionate Friends!
> You have set Khmer fears at rest
> By your decision to give us
> Firm and brotherly support.
> Great Power, great among your peers!
> You might have draped yourself,
> As others do, in egoism and pride.
> But "great" and "small" are both alike to Thee.
> Noble defenders of humanity,
> Whose banners bear the proud device,
> "Equality," "Independence," "Liberty"
> For all the Peoples in the World!
> Oh, People's Republic of China!
> The Khmers ever your friends will be!

Despite such lush encomiums, it is doubtful that any Cambodian, including Sihanouk himself, ever really believed his repeated assertion that "China is our best friend." One veteran diplomat in

Phnom Penh observed, "It would be a total misreading of Sihanouk to think that he is convinced China will win out. Chinese
hospitality mesmerized him at first, but he never really felt at home
in Peking. His Sinophilism remains a sign of his exasperation with
the United States, which is what caused him to turn to Peking in
the first place. American actions, not Chinese pressure, will determine the future; and since Sihanouk is not a man to be anyone's
puppet or satellite, any pressure on him will inevitably produce a
negative reaction." Sihanouk certainly realized that the Chinese
were bound to be in Asia a lot longer than the Americans, but he
unquestionably resented Peking's pressure the more the possibility
arose of his starting a new dialogue with the Americans. Furthermore, the Prince was not happy over the continuing refusal of the
Chinese to support another Geneva conference on Vietnam, and he
had been even less happy about Peking's earlier negative reaction
to a British suggestion for another Geneva meeting on the question
of Cambodian neutrality.

Sihanouk has always operated on the theory that no policy is
ever irreversible, including his; while his in many ways was far
more consistent than that of most countries in that he never devi-
ated from his primary aim of seeking protection for Cambodia,
his tactics, his principal weapon, inevitably shifted from time
to time, and, starting in mid-1966, there were signs that he was
veering back toward the West, or at least tentatively away from
China. There was interesting evidence of this in July, when a series
of seven editorials appeared in the left-wing newspaper *La Dépêche,* which was under the direction of Chau Seng, who was then
Sihanouk's leftist *chef de cabinet* but who was in Paris at the time.
The editorials were written by Tep Chhieu Kheng, who had been
known in the past as pro-Chinese, and it is reasonable to suppose
that they would not have been allowed to appear if they had not
had Sihanouk's blessing. Among the titles were "The Grand Illusion," "An Exploded Myth," and "The Wrong Horse," and the
point that all seven of the editorials made was that the real "paper
tiger" in Asia might not be the United States, after all, but China,
which had recently reacted to the bombing of the Hanoi and
Haiphong fuel dumps with more wordy promises of support and
aid but did nothing to substantiate earlier threats to intervene in
behalf of the North Vietnamese. The prospect, Tep Chhieu Kheng

said at the time, was gloomy, since it meant that the Americans were more determined to pursue the war in Vietnam than either the Chinese or the Russians, whose own destructive ideological battle could have disastrous consequences for Asia; the Vietnamese would be left to tear each other to pieces, and nonaligned countries like Cambodia faced the prospect of foundering helplessly in a possibly American-dominated sea. The tone of the editorials was one of marked disrespect for the hollow promises and general inadequacy of the "Socialist camp" and, at the same time, of grudging respect for the imperialist Americans, who at least were sticking to their guns and were also supporting Cambodia's proposal for an enlarged International Control Commission.

The editorials had a considerable impact among the foreign diplomats in Phnom Penh, who debated whether or not they represented a significant turning point for Sihanouk and Cambodia. When not long afterward I went to the palace in Phnom Penh and spoke with the Prince, who looked very much the royal personage —he likes to be called *Samdetch* (Prince) or Monseigneur—I asked him about his own views. He carefully pointed out that his National Sangkum Movement, though basically a single party, still had a left, a right, and a center wing, and that he stood in the center. As for the left wing, he said with a smile, presumably referring to its members' current disappointment with Red China, "They have been deceived in love."

Early in 1967 Sihanouk was given reason for serious qualms about the intentions of the Chinese, who for the first time showed signs of wanting to interfere directly in the country's internal political affairs. Essentially, this represented a spillover of their chaotic Cultural Revolution, and it coincided, more or less, with Peking's "recall for consultation" of its Ambassador to Cambodia, Chen Shu-liang, with whom Sihanouk had always got along well. As soon as Chen had left the capital, local Cambodian and Chinese Communists, whose combined strength was probably no more than two thousand, began a typical Red Guard campaign in Cambodia's Chinese schools and in the press, distributing Mao Tse-tung propaganda and Mao buttons. (The Cambodian Communists, known as the People's Party, were allowed to operate openly at the time, although, under Sihanouk's peculiar ground rules, they could not, as a party, run candidates for election.) Whether or not, as some people suggested, the Chinese effort was designed to compensate for current defeats and mistakes of Chinese foreign policy in Indonesia and Burma was immaterial to Sihanouk; he simply and suddenly realized that there was an imminent and dangerous threat to Cambodia. Simultaneously, his own theretofore unchallenged rule was facing an internal threat from conservative elements led by the then Prime Minister, General Lon Nol, and the Prince's reaction was adroit: he used the Chinese threat, and a threat provided by a separate leftist rebellion in the northwestern province of Battambang, as a two-edged weapon to eliminate his internal opponents both on the right and on the left.

The Cambodian Left

The prelude to Sihanouk's moves had been the election of September, 1966. In what was officially described as a "step forward" to stimulate democracy, Sihanouk for the first time did not personally select all the candidates for the National Assembly but allowed any member of the one-party, all-inclusive, National Sangkum Movement who wanted to run to do so. The result was that more than four hundred candidates, ranging from extreme left-wingers to extreme right-wingers, entered the race for eighty-two seats. Sihanouk's private hope was that the three leading left-wingers, Hu Nim, Khieu Samphan, and Hou Youn, and one conservative incumbent he did not like, Duc Rasy, would fail to be re-elected, but, despite behind-the-scenes maneuvering by government security agents, all four kept their seats. In his opening address to the new Assembly, which was considerably further to the right than its predecessors, Sihanouk asked that the members try not to give vent to "personal animosities," and to refrain from "Byzantine quarrels and extranational deviations." The new Assembly was permitted, also for the first time, to choose the Prime Minister and Cabinet— actions Sihanouk had always taken himself in the past. General Lon Nol, who had most recently been the Minister of National Defense, was selected to be Prime Minister by a narrow margin. According to persons in a position to know, Sihanouk actually engineered the choice of Lon Nol, in order to remove him from his key military post, where he was regarded by the Prince as a more immediate threat as the leader of the nation's essentially conservative military forces.

After considerable bickering, which Sihanouk, emerging from the hospital where he was being treated for chronic insomnia and nervousness, unavailingly sought to ameliorate, the Assembly ignored his recommendations to "regroup" and form a broad-based government. When the left-wingers refused to cooperate, a predominantly right-wing government was selected. Sihanouk thereupon created a loyal opposition—or "countergovernment," as he called it—composed of left-wing members of the Assembly, and including the three men he had originally hoped to see defeated in the election, along with some leftist outsiders. He gave them the right to publish a daily bulletin, and said that he hoped the group would spur the established government, through its criticisms and suggestions, to be "aware, attentive and correct."

Acrimonious relations between the countergovernment leaders and the regular Cabinet members quickly plunged the whole Assembly into turmoil. If Sihanouk's initial motive in sponsoring Lon Nol had been to remove him as a threat to his own dominance and at the same time to please the conservative elements, things obviously were not turning out as the Prince had hoped. In November, 1966, there were rumors of a right-wing coup. As the left-wing elements became more fractious and fought back, Sihanouk first decided to get rid of the countergovernment, then reversed himself and invited Lon Nol's Cabinet members to resign if they wished. When most of them did quit, the Prince again reversed himself and, refusing to accept the resignations, re-established the Lon Nol regime and diminished the effectiveness of the shadow Cabinet by dismissing Hu Nim, Khieu Samphan, and Hou Youn. Sihanouk's mother, Queen Kossamak, who is perhaps the only person in Cambodia who has any real influence over him, was reported to be displeased by his erratic handling of the whole situation, and she was instrumental in persuading him, early in 1967, to take a two months' trip to France, where he often goes for an elaborate health regimen. During his absence there were reports that the Lon Nol government was seeking a rapprochement with the United States —a maneuver that Sihanouk may have condoned or pretended to condone for the time being, even though he distrusted Lon Nol more than the left, which he thought he could better control.

By the time Sihanouk returned, on March 9, an internal revolt had broken out in Battambang, a southwest farming region with a turbulent history. Until 1907 Battambang was part of Thailand, and during the Second World War the Thais, under the dispensation of the Japanese, controlled it again. Consequently, Battambang had retained a large restless Thai minority. Also, members of the Khmer Serei, part of the right-wing opposition, were active in the border areas of the province, where they had some protection from the Thai Army. Traditionally, there have always been bandits in the region, too, and they were cooperating with the Khmer Serei. Since early 1967 incidents involving attacks by Khmer Serei or bandit elements had increased, and these were quickly exploited by the local left wing—primarily by what Sihanouk calls the Khmer Vietminh. As early as 1947, during the French war in Indochina, some Vietminh elements that included pure Vietnamese as well as Vietnamese of Khmer extraction set up Communist cells in some remote parts of Cambodia, Battambang among them. After the Geneva agreements of 1954 the Vietminh forces had withdrawn from these areas, but they left behind some political cadres and a network of underground cells. These groups were able to take advantage of the unfortunate economic and social conditions in the province. Battambang, unlike most other parts of Cambodia where the peasants own their own land, has always had a wealthy land-owning class and what amounts to an agrarian proletariat, which had gradually become further alienated from the government as a result of official distribution of land to families resettled from other provinces and to war refugees from the delta in South Vietnam, who were of Cambodian extraction. The resentment of the local peasants was further encouraged by the activities of Chinese rice merchants and middlemen who, reacting to efforts to put them out of business, had convinced many villagers that they were being swindled by the government cooperatives, in spite of an increase in the price the farmers were getting for their rice.

Just before Sihanouk returned from France, Lon Nol took action against the unrest in Battambang by dispatching a battalion of tough paratroopers to the province, whereupon the Cambodian Communists in Phnom Penh, probably with the approval of the Chinese Embassy there, began to demonstrate against the "assassins of the Khmer people." In Battambang three small provincial guard posts were attacked and three government patrols ambushed by Khmer Vietminh rebels, whose total strength was estimated at between one and two thousand. A camp of Royal Khmer Socialist Youth in the town of Stung Kranhung was burned down, and demonstrations and distribution of Communist propaganda also began in a number of other provinces. Lon Nol dispatched more troops to Battambang—at one time seven battalions were operating in the province—and some of them took harsh measures against villagers accused of harboring the rebels, or sympathizing with them. However, Sihanouk, in a message to the nation, accused the "Khmer Reds," as he also called the Khmer Vietminh, of having "forced these people to go to the forest in order to attack the national forces." He further charged that the Cambodian Communists were taking orders from "their great chief in Phnom Penh," adding that he did not know "whether this great chief is a foreigner or a Khmer." In any event, he said the Cambodian Communists now wanted "to create a civil war," despite the fact that "the government of Lon Nol, Nhiek Tioulong [the new Defense Chief], and even Sihanouk have given a great deal of aid to the Vietminh and the Vietcong." He went on plaintively, "The Americans are aware of the fact that we have aided [the Vietnamese Communists] in the political and diplomatic fields. We have also given them aid in many other fields, which I cannot explain in detail. . . . But why have they allowed their Khmer Vietminh children to kill my partisans who are only nationalists? . . . The Khmer Vietminh has repaid me by saying that Sihanouk has sold the nation to the Americans, because Sihanouk is rotten and a lackey of imperialism. Such an accusation is very unjust. . . . The Khmer Serei, the [South] Vietnamese, Thai, and South Koreans have joined forces in attacking us because we do not want to be a lackey of the free world and only want our independence and neutrality."

Toward the end of April, 1967, following the arrest of about 150 Khmer Vietminh in Battambang, Sihanouk publicly named Hu Nim, Khieu Samphan, and Hou Youn as the three top ringleaders of the Communist conspiracy. Since they were still members of the Assembly, he granted them parliamentary immunity for the time being, but ordered them to answer questions before a military tribunal, at which Prime Minister Lon Nol would "confront" them. He also named two other men as lesser conspirators—So Nem, the Minister of Health, and Chau Seng, who had been Minister of Education as well as director of the Cabinet until the crisis of the previous November, when he had been relieved and made a member of the High Council, a group around Sihanouk the Prince has used, whenever it suited his purposes, as a kind of supercabinet. The fortunes of Chau Seng, a Vietnamese with strong pro-Chinese Communist leanings, had risen and fallen depending on the Prince's whims and changing needs, but he had continued throughout to prosper financially, and had reportedly become one of the richest men in the country. By this time it had become known that the Chinese Communists living in Cambodia were taking an active part in the dissemination of propaganda, especially in the secondary schools, where they also had fostered a number of antigovernment demonstrations. In addition, they were known to be propagandizing among the Buddhist monks of the country.

After naming the Khmer Communist leaders, Sihanouk made a special point of appealing to the tribunal that would hear their evidence, and to the people as a whole, not to make martyrs of the three men by putting them to death. Khieu Samphan and Hou Youn chose not to take any chances: shortly after they were denounced, they disappeared from their homes, and Hu Nim later also fled. They were variously reported afterward to have been murdered by the security police, to have fled to remote parts of Battambang, or to have fled into Vietcong areas of South Vietnam or to China.

At the end of April, with the local Communist threat at least momentarily in check, Sihanouk accepted Lon Nol's resignation as Prime Minister and took over himself as the head of a new Special Government, which he declared to be not accountable to the Assembly. The move was undoubtedly facilitated by an auto accident Lon Nol had suffered in March, which had temporarily disabled him, but most observers in Cambodia believe that Sihanouk used the Battambang disturbance as an excuse to get rid of Lon Nol, having continued to regard him as a serious threat to his own power. No matter who had been Prime Minister, Sihanouk had always run Cambodia pretty much as a one-man show anyway, but Lon Nol, more than any other single individual in recent years, was, and remained, in a position to oppose him; it was conceivable that, with the cooperation of a group of young Army colonels, he might even lead a pro-American military coup against the Prince. The Army, which had deteriorated sharply in both training and equipment since American assistance ended in 1963, remained strong in its pro-American sympathies, and Sihanouk undoubtedly was aware of this.

Sihanouk was slower in facing up to the challenge of the local Chinese Communists than in dealing with the Khmer Communists, although he very likely was aware all along that the latter were receiving aid and encouragement from the Chinese Embassy in Phnom Penh. When he reassumed direct control of the government at the start of May, 1967, he devoted himself initially to improving the economic situation in Battambang and elsewhere, hoping that he would thereby diminish the Communist threat. Although Sihanouk technically became Prime Minister, while retaining his title "Chief of State," Son Sann, a financial expert who is a political moderate, was in day-to-day charge, with the title of Chief Minister. The rest of the new ministers were mostly political moderates regarded mainly as technicians, but among them was the perennial Chau Seng as Minister of Economics, and So Nem was retained as Minister of Health. As a consequence, the new government was more acceptable to the left than Lon Nol's. On May 9, following a four-day trip through Battambang, during which he promised amnesty for those arrested and pledged a program of all-around aid for the province, Sihanouk declared in a broadcast that "though China is a very great friend of our nation, only the Chinese in Peking respect us while the Chinese in Cambodia grow ever bolder and more arrogant toward us. They have quit the Chinese schools to join ours, where they bring in Mao Tse-tung's books and carry out all types of subversive activities. They are Sino-Cambodians."

Although there are only about three or four hundred thousand Chinese in Cambodia, they have traditionally played the most active commercial role, along with an equal number of Vietnamese. The Chinese were mainly responsible for facilitating the smuggling of an estimated 100,000 tons of rice a year to the Vietcong and the North Vietnamese, who were willing to pay twice as much for it as the Cambodians. The smugglers, who sometimes worked with profiteering elements in the Army, took a considerable rake-off, however, so unless the farmer dealt directly with the Vietcong, which he could do only if he lived near the border, he didn't come out with much of an added profit. Usually, the Chinese trucked the rice to points near the border, where the Vietcong agents, picking it up from secret dumps in the jungle, paid off in paper pledges redeemable through Chinese Communist channels in Phnom Penh. During May several Chinese who were caught engaging in these rice deals were given twenty-four hours to leave the country, but in taking such reprisals Sihanouk found himself in a difficult position, because the actions obviously were detrimental to the Vietcong, whom by his own admission he was aiding.

In his next challenge to the Khmer Communists, Sihanouk suggested that they form a government—on condition that a national referendum be held to determine whether they should stay in power. Not unexpectedly, the Communists did not accept this gambit. He then repeated his charges of increasing propaganda activities in schools and extended it to cover the Khmer-Sino Friendship Association, an organization he had formerly sponsored. But, apparently hoping that the more moderate elements would prevail in the Cultural Revolution in China, and hoping to avoid a serious confrontation, he still said publicly that there was no proof that China was responsible for subversive acts within Cambodia. He persisted in this charitable attitude even after a group of fifteen Chinese technicians who had arrived at a military base near Phnom Penh to unpack some Chinese aircraft parts began handing out *The Thoughts of Mao Tse-tung* and making propaganda speeches; when they were told to stop, they went off in a huff to the Chinese Embassy, but they returned in a few days to finish their job in a more subdued mood. Early in August, when Sihanouk's Special Government had been under more constant left-wing attack because it had refused to account for the disappearance of the three left-wing Cambodian leftist politicians, the Prince, bluffing once more, resigned and again asked the left to form a new government. The offer was again rejected. Sihanouk then said he would carry on, commenting, "What impudence, what hyprocrisy from these leftist pigs!"

A week later, when Prince Norodom Phurissara, a cousin of Sihanouk's who was serving as Foreign Minister, made a visit to Peking, Premier Chou En-lai declared that "the Chinese government respects the neutrality, independence, and territorial integrity of Cambodia within its present frontier" and spoke of "strengthening our present relations" on the basis of the five principles enunciated at the 1955 Bandung Conference, including noninterference in each other's affairs. This apparently conciliatory mood did not last long. On September 1 Sihanouk announced the dissolution of approximately a score of Khmer Friendship Associations originally founded to promote friendly relations with foreign countries. He was prompted mainly by the subversive activities of the Khmer-Sino Friendship Association, and he explained that if this association were allowed to continue it would destroy rather than improve relations between Cambodia and China. All the old committees were replaced by government-controlled bodies that were kept under close surveillance and were ineffectual. Disregarding the announcement, the Chinese, on September 4, sent their old friendship association in Phnom Penh a telegram of congratulation on its third anniversary. The wire expressed fulsome praise for the joint struggle against "American imperialism" and "revisionism" and appeared to be a calculated attack on Sihanouk and his government.

Sihanouk reacted violently, calling the telegram "an extraordinary interference in the internal affairs of a sovereign state." He became even angrier a few days later when the Chinese telegram was published by *La Dépêche,* still directed by Chau Seng, who was still Minister of the Economy. The Prince thereupon demanded that Chau Seng, and So Nem, who had been head of the old Khmer-Sino Friendship Association and was still Minister of Health, both resign their ministerial posts. Then, declaring that "the truth must be disclosed," Sihanouk called for a national referendum in January or February, 1968, so that the Cambodian people could choose between "Sihanouk and the Sangkum on the one hand and those who wish Cambodia to be dominated by China on the other." Twenty Phnom Penh newspapers—Chinese, Vietnamese, French, and Cambodian—were suspended and were replaced by four controlled papers, one in each language. The Prince capped his performance by telling a cheering crowd in front of the royal palace that he would recall his diplomatic staff from Peking, leaving a "caretaker" there to signify that he did not intend to break off all relations with China. But within forty-eight hours, after another conciliatory message from Chou En-lai, he changed his mind and said he would let the staff stay on.

The Prince afterward summed up his new approach to China by saying, "I have prepared to stop the Chinese ideological invasion rather than wait for gangrene to start in my country. My counter-offensive came too quickly for the Chinese—before the enemy was in position. I am only a David, but I am not afraid to confront all the Goliaths on earth." In defining the "evolutionary trend" of "the gradual deterioration of our relations with China," Sihanouk spoke of the "first phase" of Cambodia's relations with China, from 1955 to 1965, when they were "distinguished by complete respect on China's part," and the "second phase" that began in 1966, "with the start of the Cultural Revolution." Since then, he declared, "China inundates Cambodia with propaganda, and indulges in widespread subversive activities in the mistaken belief that the 'fruit is ripe' and can be eaten. Unfortunately for China, the Cambodian fruit is far from ripe for Communism, even in Asian form. Naturally, I have never harbored any illusions in regard to the real nature of Communism. I have meditated upon the works of Marx, Lenin, and Mao, and I have always realized that Asian Communism could not continue to coexist forever with a monarchist Cambodia, with its nationalist regime committed to a form of socialism modified in conformity with Buddhist doctrine. But I do confess to an error of judgment: it was my belief that China would leave Cambodia alone until the Americans had withdrawn."

In taking note of several messages he had received from Chou En-lai and other Peking officials, which kept stressing the Bandung principles again and again and pledged to respect Cambodia's integrity, Sihanouk carefully and calculatedly emphasized the Chinese "retreat" in the attempt to make Cambodia a "satellite," and spoke of being "friends with China again—*until the next time . . . China starts trying to subvert us.*" It seemed doubtful that he would any longer depend on China as he once had, or that he would again refer to China as "our best and closest friend." He added to a group of correspondents, "I have said that sooner or later Asia will be Chinese and I still maintain that, but that is no reason why I should bow to China. The Chinese, I know, will not spare me. On the contrary, the more you lick China's boots, the more they scorn you." During this difficult phase of his crisis with China, however, Sihanouk went to some pains to reiterate that he was not gravitating to the West. "I am no weathercock rotating to face the prevailing wind, nor am I a cynical opportunist," he declared. Sooner or later, he insisted, the Americans would be forced to get out of Vietnam, "where there is no prospect of a military, and still less of a political, victory," but "our behavior toward China is not related in any way to American intentions."

The Border Issue

Sihanouk was obviously stretching the point somewhat with such a statement, for the Vietnam war, and the American role in it, had by this time become something of an obsession with him. "Americans understand Asians very badly—and the opposite is also very often true," he had told me, earlier. "I, as an Indochinese, am convinced that extending the air escalation against North Vietnam will in no wise result in the Vietnamese deciding to accept negotiations—least of all surrender. Certainly they have suffered, and will continue to suffer, very heavy damages and loss because of the Americans' overwhelming superiority of equipment. But they will grit their teeth and they will not ask for pity—moreover, the Cambodians would do the same under similar circumstances." From almost the start of the American build-up in South Vietnam, Sihanouk had maintained that the United States would have to come to terms, eventually, with the National Liberation Front, "making them their only interlocutor," as he put it to me. For the Americans to leave South Vietnam, he said, "would be to the honor of your country and would strengthen its moral prestige, much damaged throughout the world because of this aggression against a much weaker people."

While he was telling the Americans that they ought to quit the war, Sihanouk also was advising the Communists to negotiate in Vietnam, suggesting that this was the best way they could win. How little he actually relished this alternative, however, was indicated by what he had told an earlier Sangkum meeting, that "if the Vietnamese are reunited and become strong, they will remain Vietnamese and they will come to seize more territories from us." Caught as he was, therefore, between distasteful possibilities, the

Prince stepped up his effort to obtain guarantees of his borders from both the National Liberation Front and the North Vietnamese. "If we ask them to recognize our frontiers, it would be better for us to sign an agreement with them," he maintained. "If they respect their own signatures, it will be a very important thing for our future. . . . If we sign an agreement with them, we must also recognize them and exchange diplomats. . . . Without this agreement I feel very cold." He told the Sangkum that he was planning to give the North Vietnamese in Phnom Penh ambassadorial status and also give the National Liberation Front representative "the status of a diplomat without an embassy," even though the Front had not yet established a government, and he added that he wanted to do this before the Communists won the war "because [then] they will already be too strong and it will not be necessary for them to oblige and please us." Such recognition, he later stated, afforded him "a minimum of risk instead of a maximum of risk." Sihanouk's game of diplomatic definitions included a good many other nations, Communist and non-Communist, whose governments he treated according to his own basic philosophy of "reciprocity." Friends of Cambodia, especially those who respected its territorial integrity and offered unconditional assistance, were rewarded, while enemies were downgraded. The results often made for strange companions at Phnom Penh dinner tables, but the Prince relished his role as the creator of a sort of Cambodian Social Register for diplomats.

The situation on and around Cambodia's borders remained murky, and Sihanouk went to great pains to prove that reports of the Vietnamese Communists' isolating large parts of his frontiers were false. In 1967 I was one of several correspondents invited by the Prince to inspect the country's borders, something that Western military attachés were also interested in doing as regularly as they could, which was not often. The best evidence we all gathered was that the Vietcong and the North Vietnamese were probably sneaking over into Cambodia from time to time in military groups, possibly up to regimental size, but that it was unlikely they ever stayed more than a few days, at least not in the northeastern area bordering on South Vietnam—first, because food was scarce there; second, because the various tribes that inhabit the region were generally hostile to any Vietnamese; and, third, because there were ten thousand Cambodian soldiers along the Vietnamese border, bolstered by about twice as many provincial guards and armed civilians, and they all had orders from Sihanouk to fire on any invaders. Some of the incidents that took place did involve exchange of ground fire, though most of the attacks Sihanouk talked about were bombings from the air. The attachés and other impartial observers, however, readily admitted that the wild border provinces in the north, mostly mountainous jungle, were so difficult to patrol, or even to keep watch on from the air, that no one could say for sure that the Communists could not or did not regularly move back and forth. Sihanouk himself, at one point, admitted that four-fifths of the Vietnamese border area facing Cambodia was occupied, "either permanently or occasionally, by National Liberation Front troops."

The Western attachés, notably the Australians, British, and French, made a few arduous treks through the remote northern provinces, where there were few roads, to search for signs that the Vietnamese Communists had extensively used Cambodian territory for rest and resupply. Among other things, they looked for hacked-down trees and bushes, indicating that trails had been recently used; evidence of camps and of depletion of local food supplies; and, perhaps most significant, nervousness among the native tribal people. While they found no trace of these things on the trips they made (they were particularly impressed by the fact that the roads built by the French in colonial days had dwindled into overgrown timber trails or scarcely usable foot trails, or had simply disappeared into the jungle before they reached the border), the attachés were the first to admit that they had only scratched the surface in exploring suspect places, especially in the two northeast provinces of Stung Treng and Ratanakiri, and in Mondulkiri, just to the south. They agreed that it was perfectly possible for the Communists to hide out, with their own food, in the jungles indefinitely. No foreigners, for example, nor any Cambodian representatives either, ever carefully explored the area where Laos, Cambodia, and Vietnam join, and where a branch of the Ho Chi Minh trail was believed to cut across Cambodia from Laos and into Vietnam. As for the so-called Sihanouk trail, the attachés tended not to believe the allegations by some Americans and South Vietnamese that this was an elaborate network reaching all the way up from the southern port of Sihanoukville, on the Gulf of Siam, and moving northward through water routes or roads into the Sekong, a tributary of the Mekong. Although Saigon insisted that sizable Chinese and/or Russian arms shipments were moving into South Vietnam from Sihanoukville and other small ports on the gulf, neither the attachés nor the International Control Commission could find any hard evidence to prove this. (During 1968 the American command in Vietnam charged repeatedly that both military and nonmilitary matériel was coming in from Cambodia, and the evidence of captured new weapons in the delta was convincing. It seemed likely that at least some of those weapons and ammunition had been brought by sea to Cambodian ports and then smuggled overland to Vietnam. This was a faster and more practical route than via the Sekong.)

The Sekong was navigable part of the year, but there were no signs of any special traffic on it or of anything more than rough trails running alongside it from northern Cambodia into Laos. Some traffic in rice and medicines probably did move into Laos through the north, and joined the Ho Chi Minh trail there, but the flow, the observers thought, was not sizable. What took place on the Laos side of the border they were not prepared to say. The attachés did not deny that considerable smuggling took place from all parts of Cambodia along interior routes, trails, and waterways into South Vietnam; such smuggling has always gone on, and there was little doubt that the smugglers were reaping special profits out of the war. In 1966 and 1967 I saw considerable evidence of open contraband trading taking place in the southern province of Svay Rieng, where in the village of Bavet, right on the border and two hundred yards away from a military and police headquarters, there was a bustling open-air market, in and out of which scores of Vietnamese and Cambodian peasants were moving across the border to sell or exchange all manners of food as well as cigarettes and beer. It was certainly possible for the Vietcong in the delta areas to cross the border here almost at will to obtain food, especially at night.

The most important evidence of Vietnamese Communist activity across the Cambodian border came to light in November, 1967, just after the visit to Cambodia of Mrs. John F. Kennedy and four friends of hers, including Lord Harlech of Britain. Mainly because of her trip, Sihanouk had temporarily lifted one of his periodic bans on foreign correspondents and had allowed more than a hundred television and press representatives, most of them Americans, to come to Cambodia. The Prince delights in displaying his country to prominent guests, whom he selects with a care that is always based partly on shrewd political calculations and partly on his mood of the moment. His innate sense of showmanship and his graciousness as a host make his sporadic unveilings of the country seem like Happenings, during which any number of seemingly magic and mysterious things may occur, all of them blending, in retrospect, into something with the quality of a fable, with obscure overtones that Sihanouk will in time define and explain in the manner of an Oriental astrologer, as in one way or another he explains everything that happens in Cambodia. Despite his disclaimers, as expressed in his controlled press, Sihanouk was fully aware that the invitation to Mrs. Kennedy to make a trip to Cambodia that she had previously postponed would be interpreted as a gesture of reconciliation to the United States and "a change in policy" toward China. Sihanouk, for his own tactical reasons, was willing to let the Chinese think so, too, and he outdid himself in trying to please Mrs. Kennedy (who, most of the correspondents thought, did not always respond, perhaps because of natural shyness or aloofness, as warmly or spontaneously as she might have to the Prince's gracious gestures).

After Mrs. Kennedy left, Sihanouk had various other events prepared for his Happening, including an unveiling of his latest film, starring himself and his beautiful Cambodian-Italian wife Monique, and the annual Water Festival, which heralds the autumn harvest. The correspondents were supposed to join Sihanouk's customary captive audience of some 6.2 million Cambodians and to be equally docile onlookers. However, Sihanouk had earlier made the mistake of inviting the reporters to go anywhere they wished in search of evidence that the Vietcong or the North Vietnamese were using Cambodia as a sanctuary, as a source of supply, or as a headquarters.

This time, in contrast to the previous occasions where such invitations had always resulted in officially guided tours, three correspondents were not so easily manageable. They were George Mc-Arthur and Horst Faas, of the Associated Press, and Ray Herndon, of United Press International; they were all veterans of the Vietnam war and had obtained information from intelligence sources in Saigon about the exact positions of a number of Vietcong or North Vietnamese installations and secret trails in Cambodia. In Phnom Penh they rented a car and drove to one of these sites, in Kompong Cham Province. There they found, just as they had expected, an inconspicuous trail leading into a forest. Summoning as witnesses a reluctant group of local Cambodian soldiers and government officials, they followed the trail, which soon ran into a well-constructed corduroy road of the sort that was regularly being built by the Vietcong across the border in South Vietnam and is capable of carrying heavy trucks. A few hundred yards down the road, in a camouflaged clearing only four miles from the border, they found a score of small, newly constructed huts, with wooden beams and thatched roofs and bamboo tables and chairs inside; nearby there were drainage ditches and latrines, a parking area capable of accommodating twenty trucks, and a series of loading platforms. Other evidence, including a quartermaster record sheet in Vietnamese and a North Vietnamese medical kit, firmly indicated that the camp, from which many oxcart tracks led toward the border, had been used by the Communists as some sort of headquarters, capable of secreting a battalion. The fact that it seemed to have been recently built, and was only a dozen miles away from Loc Ninh, in Vietnam, made it likely that the camp had been used as a staging area for the big battle that had taken place around Loc Ninh earlier in November.

The discovery of the camp spoiled Prince Sihanouk's Happening. News of it came in the middle of the Water Festival, which always takes place at the time of the November full moon, when the Mekong, at full flood stage and backed up into the Great Lake of Cambodia, reverses its current and starts flowing south again, while the silt-covered land slowly dries and the rice harvest ripens. This happy occasion is celebrated by three days of pirogue-racing, during which these long, brightly painted native boats, each manned by forty paddlers, pass in front of the royal barge, the paddlers chanting to the imprecations of clowns who proclaim the seasonal rejuvenation with earthy verses. At night there are fireworks, and on the last evening a series of floating barges, lit with flares or electric displays, extol the grandeur of Sihanouk and set forth the accomplishments of the kingdom. On the third night of the show, I was sitting only a few feet from the Prince, who was perched alone on a platform overlooking the gay events; he was glum and silent—more so, I was afterward told, than at any public occasion in years, and it was obvious that the news about the discovery of the camp, which had reached him that afternoon, had thoroughly upset him.

In the days that followed, the Cambodian government reacted slowly. First it denounced previous stories from Saigon about the existence of such camps, and took seventeen correspondents on a guided tour of Ratanakiri Province, in the northeast, where, to no one's surprise, nothing indicating any Communist activity was found. The Cambodian officials who had accompanied the three other correspondents to the camp meanwhile tried by turns to pass it off as a place used by the Cambodian forestry service, a refugee center, and a "secret" Cambodian Army installation. As it became apparent, however, that no one would believe these explanations, Sihanouk and the government simply started categorically denying that any such camp existed. A government statement denounced the camp story as representing "completely unfounded accusations which aim without doubt to explain the setbacks of the United States Army in South Vietnam, and to prepare international opinion for the extension of United States aggression in Cambodia." The statement admitted that small infiltrations of the border occur but said it was "impossible for Vietnamese armed units of any size to cross into Cambodian territory, because in spite of their limited effectiveness the Royal Cambodian Armed Forces would not allow it." The correspondents were accused of having taken advantage of the freedom of movement they were given during Mrs. Kennedy's visit, and Sihanouk's chagrin and displeasure were reflected in a new ban on all American newsmen.

The Prince's stubborn reaction to the discovery of the camp—Western diplomats had hoped that he would respond more calmly—did little to strengthen his position of neutrality. Almost masochistically, he seemed to have invited some kind of reprisal against himself. Apparently, by closing his eyes to the Communist sanctuaries within Cambodia, he had thought he could maintain at least a pretense of ignorance. His denials, in the face of the evidence, more than anything else showed he was convinced that the inevitable American withdrawal from Vietnam would leave him totally vulnerable to the Vietnamese, whom he continued to fear more than any other people. The only way to survive later, he had concluded, was to mollify the Vietnamese Communists now, which was why he had moved to give the North Vietnamese and the National Liberation Front diplomatic recognition. If it was true that the Prince had decided irrevocably to consolidate his relations with Hanoi and the Front, setting them up as the best bulwark against Chinese Communist expansion in Southeast Asia, then his elaborate game of semantic diplomacy involving recognition of his borders was little more than a meaningless charade, which a good many diplomats thought it was anyway. Sihanouk, however, had gone so far with it that he could scarcely turn back.

Actually, ever since the Geneva Conference of 1954 he had been seeking to have his frontiers more carefully defined and guaranteed. He had made little headway until de Gaulle, during his state visit to Cambodia in 1966, had rather offhandedly made a comment about respecting Cambodian integrity "within the limits of its existing borders." Sihanouk had since then made demands for similar declarations on virtually the whole international community, much in the manner of an Oriental potentate ordering kowtows and tribute from those who wanted to deal with him. The response had been slow during the first part of 1967, but by mid-year it had begun to pick up. Singapore came through with a French-type declaration, and so did the East Germans (theirs was later dismissed by Sihanouk because their Consul General in Phnom Penh had issued it on his own without consulting his government). Early in June the Russians, seeking to take advantage of the uneasy relations between China and Sihanouk, had complied with his request, followed in rapid succession by the North Vietnamese, the National Liberation Front, the North Koreans, and then the Chinese. When Hanoi and the Front included the word "recognition" as well as "respect" in their declarations, Sihanouk tried to persuade the French to rephrase their statement, but Paris politely pointed out that, since France had drawn the borders in the first place, it scarcely needed to give formal recognition to its own handiwork. All this added to the semantic byplay, and when the West Germans, with a flourish, added the phrase "recognition without reserve" to their declaration, Sihanouk raised the verbal ante.

The first people to balk at this were the Australians, who, despite the presence of their troops in South Vietnam, had remained close friends of Cambodia, giving Sihanouk the kind of unconditional economic aid he sought, and, through the efforts of their able Ambassador, Noel St. Clair Deschamps, remaining the only non-Asian nation besides France to retain Sihanouk's complete respect—a feat that was all the more remarkable since they were also representing the Americans in Phnom Penh. But now Canberra refused to alter the language of its original declaration on the border issue. Two other major nations, Great Britain and Japan, had delayed in issuing any statements at all, and it was not until early 1968 that Sihanouk obtained declarations that satisfied him from all three nations, as well as from a score of others that were diplomatically represented in Phnom Penh. He had won the battle of words, although it was doubtful whether the border statements in any way denoted legal responsibility on the part of the declaring countries. What, for instance, could or would West Germany or, say, Cuba conceivably do if Cambodia were invaded?

Shuttlecock Diplomacy

It may be, as Sihanouk maintained, that Mrs. Kennedy's visit was not meant to initiate any "opening to the West," but most observers in Phnom Penh felt that the Prince at least had put up some trial balloons. He had let it be clearly understood that he held the Johnson administration responsible for prolonging the war in Vietnam—if President Kennedy had lived, he said at one point, "no tragedy would have been able to occur between our two countries." Thus the visit gave him a wished-for opportunity to make it clear that, even though he continued to oppose American policies he was not anti-American—something he had obviously wanted to say at that particular time because of his disillusionment with the Chinese. But since he was convinced that the Americans would sooner or later leave Asia, and that the Chinese were obviously going to stay there, he was playing for time with Peking, too, in the hope that Chou En-lai and the moderates would win out in the Great Proletarian Cultural Revolution, just as he hoped that some new Kennedy-like leader would become President in the United

States and end the war. Having shifted away from China and made his big gamble with Hanoi and the Vietcong, with the aim of holding off those he most feared by helping them, he thereupon made another calculated year-end move toward the United States.

Only a few days after he had warned that if any American or South Vietnamese troops entered Cambodia he would call for volunteers from Russia, China, and other Communist nations, he told the Washington *Post*, in reply to some cabled questions, that he would not object if American forces entered Cambodia in pursuit of Vietnamese Communists illegally present in the uninhabited parts of the country—meaning the northeast. At the same time, he invited President Johnson to send an envoy to discuss ways of ending the border tensions and strengthening the role of the International Control Commission. In the first week of 1968 Chester Bowles, who was on his second tour of duty as the United States Ambassador in India, arrived in Phnom Penh as the President's selected representative. After several days of talks an agreement was reached to firm up the I.C.C., with the United States pledging to give it two helicopters, and Sihanouk agreed to give it two more—so that it could better investigate complaints and inspect border areas. Bowles told Sihanouk that the Americans had no desire to spread the war by indulging in "hot pursuit" of Vietnamese Communist elements into Cambodia, but a day later the State Department "clarified" this by emphasizing that American troops still reserved the right of self-defense, which just about left things where they had been before. It soon became apparent that neither the Polish members of the Commission in Cambodia nor the Russians, who had been co-chairmen of the Geneva Conference, were eager to see the Commission expand its role, and the all-important question of whether it could act by the majority vote of two of its three members or unanimously in investigating complaints remained undecided.

As for the future of the war itself, Sihanouk said after his talks with Bowles, "We are not on the same wavelength." The matter of American "recognition" of Cambodia's borders, which alone, Sihanouk said, could lead to a resumption of full relations, was left in abeyance—neither he nor the Americans seemed to think this would be settled until the war was over. If there was little that came out of the meeting—the border violations continued and the

I.C.C. did little or nothing about them—there had at least been a rapprochement between the two countries and a useful discussion that pointed up the problems of policing troop movements, which would have to be dealt with again in any negotiations to end the war in Vietnam. The role of the I.C.C. remained essentially ill-defined and obscure, and in Cambodia even more than in Laos most observers doubted that the Commission would ever be able to perform a worthwhile function in the making and keeping of the peace, unless its prerogatives were made much clearer and it could move around much more freely.

Any assessment of Sihanouk must always be tentative. He is a compulsive poker player, of the sort that never drops out of a game, and he plays politics the same way, with a mixture of bluff and guile as he tries to catch his opponents off guard and make them believe he holds more cards than he actually has. His impulsiveness and incaution frequently get him into trouble, but if he tends to magnify his predicament and protests too much, he still sees Asia, and the threat of Communism, perhaps more clearly than any other Asian leader, with the possible exception of Prime Minister Lee of Singapore, who is more hardheaded and shrewd because he has had an even greater internal Communist problem to handle. Both men are supreme egoists, but Lee is less Orientally complex. Sihanouk is fond of denying that he is "changeable"—"I don't go from left to right, I am always in the middle," he says—but the middle can be a void, which is actually what he fears most, and that is why he has constantly kept moving, and playing one side off against another. As long as he could do this and still keep Cambodia unified internally, the policy paid off, but it had become apparent, by the beginning of 1968, that he was facing a serious domestic situation, both politically and economically, and that his enemies on the right and on the left were forcing the challenge.

Late in February, 1968, rebel bands became active again in five separate areas of the west and southwest of Cambodia, including Battambang. As the guerrilla activity continued throughout the spring, Sihanouk became more and more jittery. He called out the Army reserves and ordered search-and-destroy sweeps in Battambang—where eighty-nine terrorists were killed and thirty-two others captured—and in the provinces of Kampot, Kompong

Thom, and Koh Kong, all in different parts of the country. Sihanouk authorized *Réalités Cambodgiennes* to comment: "No one forgets that the subversion and armed agitation [in the provinces], 'teleguided' from abroad, is directed from Phnom Penh by a handful of intellectuals, some of whom still occupy important positions in the heart of the administration." The Prince cited several examples of Communist infiltration, including a Vietnamese junk intercepted off the Cambodian coast full of Chinese weapons for the Cambodian Communists, some Chinese documents captured in Battambang, and other Peking propaganda found in Phnom Penh in the home of the former president of the Cambodian Students Union, who was sentenced to death by a military tribunal. While he still shied away from accusing the Vietnamese or Chinese Communists outright of launching attacks against Cambodia, he had less hesitation in charging the Pathet Lao, the Communist guerrillas in Laos, with inciting rebellions in Ratanakiri and Stung Treng provinces, which have a common frontier with Laos. "The Thai Patriotic Front [the Peking-supported Communists in northeast Thailand] and the Pathet Lao have always refused to recognize our frontiers," he said, "and therefore even if North Vietnam and China keep their promises, nothing will bar the road to the Siamese Communists and the Laotion Communists." He cited further evidence that some of the tribal elements operating in the Lao-Cambodian border areas had been armed with new weapons to take part in the rebellions.

During the summer the guerrilla activity slackened, but Sihanouk's complaints continued. In an unusually frank letter to the French newspaper, *Le Monde,* he wrote,

It is perfectly clear that Asian Communism does not permit us any longer to stay neutral and withdraw from the conflict between the Chinese-Vietnamese and the Americans. Not being able to make us—we who have no intention of dying for Hanoi or Peking any more than for Washington—into allies offering unconditional support, Asian Communism strives to overthrow our regime from within. The tournament has only just started.

In another interview the beleaguered Prince declared, "It is all-out war, a fight to the death between them and us." Late in September, for the first time, Sihanouk conceded what he had been trying to deny for years—that the North Vietnamese and the Vietcong were indeed using Cambodian territory as a sanctuary. "Many of them have come to live on our territory," he admitted. "I do not dare solve this problem, so I bring it to the attention of the people and all high personages so you may ponder it." The Prince's Secretary of State for National Security, Sosthene Fernandez, issued a report substantiating the activities of the Vietnamese Communists, in which he said that "the Vietnamese are becoming increasingly hostile to the local people and the authorities." Early in October some thirty Cambodian Communists were arrested by Sihanouk's police in Phnom Penh as he continued to crack down on local "traitors" he could at least control.

Although the Chinese continued to mollify Sihanouk publicly and to send him some fresh aid, including three Mig-17 fighters, some training planes, and spare parts, it seemed apparent that the break between the two countries had become virtually complete as Peking continued its aid to the various subversive groups that were operating all around Cambodia as well as inside the country. Increasingly, the struggle in Vietnam by both sides to strengthen their positions pending negotiations placed new strains on Sihanouk's neutrality. "China is not at all happy to see Hanoi negotiating," he said, at one point. "China's interest is that the war continues, that a defeated America retreats from Asia, and that Vietnam is so devastated that it will depend heavily on China for its reconstruction. Then China will become the only great power of Asia. Whether China wants it or not, Asia will naturally fall under its control." Unless the war in Vietnam were brought to an end soon, he intimated, his own balance-of-power position would become completely untenable, and he would face destruction. France alone, he continued to stress, had refrained from interfering in Cambodia's affairs, but he was obviously also worried about how much France would go on supporting him after de Gaulle passed from the scene. As for the United States, to which he was increasingly willing to draw closer, he was equally worried about its confused political situation and how this would affect his future relations with Washington. Like other Asian leaders, he wondered what effect the election of Richard Nixon as President would have on United States policy in Asia. When he was asked if he would like to see the Americans withdraw completely from Southeast

Asia, he replied, "The United States is an imperialist force, but the United States presence helps Cambodia indirectly. You are welcome in Southeast Asia so long as you are not inside Cambodia. We would be happy if you continue to occupy Thailand and the Philippines—that will maintain the balance of power. If the United States withdraws completely, the small nations of Southeast Asia will be Maoized."

Domestically, Sihanouk also was having more and more problems. He astutely saw the activities of the Communists as an effort to discredit him with the Sangkum and to force him to surrender power to the Army, in which case the Communist movement would be given a justification it had previously lacked. He faced the challenge realistically. "When resistance will no longer be possible," he said, "Sihanouk will withdraw and the Army, which is anti-Communist, will take power." It was more than a matter, however, of General Lon Nol and the colonels around him, backed by some leading conservative figures of the royal court and government, taking over. Sihanouk had stepped aside before and then, by popular demand, once a new crisis arose, had resumed his role of personal leadership. In fact, in September, 1968, this happened again when the Cambodian Royal Council and National Assembly, following an emergency session, voted him full powers as Head of State as a result of Cambodia's being "threatened from without by aggression and from within by the actions of traitors."

Even so, it seemed to many observers that Sihanouk was becoming more and more isolated. He had fewer friends and confidants and, in a sense, was acting more and more like an Oriental potentate. His strongest critics accused him of operating a medieval state masquerading as a democracy. Actually, of course, Cambodia had never pretended to be a democracy, and when Sihanouk spoke of Buddhist Socialism and of the Sangkum Movement as "the embodiment of the people's will," he was fully aware that for many years he had been the lone interpreter of that will. He was probably also aware, although he said little about it, of certain changes that had begun to take place in Cambodia, and of the existence of a large body of youth that was restless, impatient, and dissatisfied, and of which the young Communists were only a fraction. Almost from the outset, Sihanouk had stressed education and built scores of elementary and secondary schools as well as new universities, but what he hadn't been able to do was find jobs for those who graduated, and by 1968 he was confronted with the grave problem of what to do with thousands of unemployed young men and women, a good many of whom, if they could not find work at salaries that were too low anyway to meet the rising cost of living, were bound sooner or later either to turn to the right or the left and involve themselves in an active political opposition. Some of these young men had already joined the rebels in Battambang and elsewhere. Others were forming quiet alliances with the conservative elements, including those in the Army as well as in politics, who firmly believed that Sihanouk, in economic as well as political ways, was leading the country to destruction. By this time it had become practically impossible for foreigners in Cambodia to talk to anyone except Sihanouk and his pet officials. The students were far too scared to meet with Americans, or with any Western strangers, and their fears were justified, for their activities were being constantly scrutinized by the security police.

Sihanouk's greatest internal problems have been economic and financial, and economics and finance, unfortunately, were never his strong points. Four-fifths of Cambodia's small population lived within walking distance of the Mekong or its tributaries, and there was always enough to eat and, in good years, a surplus of rice for export. But the rice crop in recent years had not been consistent, and some of what was available was smuggled to the Vietcong. Rubber production, which remained under the control of the French, had continued to increase, but world rubber prices had continued to go down. Even if the rice crop improved, Cambodia's economic base needed to be widened to include not only more diversification but more agricultural and industrial development. Sihanouk's program to develop the frontier provinces were commendable, and nearly half a million people, mostly ex-Army men and their families, had been resettled in these areas, where they got land, a house, some cattle, and some money to get started. The Army itself spent considerable time helping the "pioneer communities," many of which had been literally carved out of the wilderness, by building roads, dams, and factories. But the new political disturbances in these provinces had created new problems.

In the early and mid-sixties Sihanouk managed, with help from abroad, mostly from China and other Communist nations and

France, to build up a small industrial complex, dealing in cement, textiles, canning, timber production, and so on. But many of the infant plants suffered from a lack of efficient management and also lacked enough raw materials. Modest foreign exchange reserves had to be held intact for internal emergencies and for buying limited amounts of raw materials for factories already in existence, but there was not enough cash to support the Army, keep the government running, and also build up the national industry to the point where it could both afford employment to young persons and produce profits. Increasingly, and somewhat paradoxically, Cambodia was in danger of going broke.

Through the late sixties the total budget deficit had kept mounting, and Sihanouk found himself, in effect, in a financial vise. The nationalization program that had been begun after the cut-off of American aid, when banking and all export-import business had been nationalized and a national campaign of austerity introduced, had signally failed in its aim of eliminating corruption, graft, and smuggling, and had dried up the private commercial sphere to the point where scores of Chinese and Vietnamese businessmen had simply shut down their shops. The attempt to "Cambodianize" private trade having proved unsuccessful, a new course was adopted. Areas of private, mixed, and public enterprise were redefined and the private sector was again encouraged; plans were announced to create a free port of Sihanoukville, which would enable raw materials to be brought in and stockpiled at low cost while facilitating the flow of exports. The country still needed major development, however, such as would be afforded by the long-discussed plans for the Mekong that would create large dams for power and irrigation. The Australians and Japanese were, in fact, engaged in planning just such projects for Cambodia, but the war had delayed progress. In his political isolation, Sihanouk was reluctant to join other new regional groupings that might help him, such as the Asian Development Bank. "We cannot join these 're-grouping' schemes that are more political than economic and cultural," he stubbornly maintained.

The future of Cambodia obviously depended, in 1969, on the outcome of the long war in Vietnam, and on what kind of peace could be made. If the Vietnamese Communists could be contained, devoting themselves to their own problems of recovery and development in North Vietnam and to an ultimate peaceful effort to reunify South and North Vietnam, Sihanouk's chances of survival, let alone progress, would be infinitely enhanced. The Chinese were another matter. After their recent setbacks abroad and convulsions at home, it was difficult to gauge their long-term program in Southeast Asia, but their short-term strategy and tactics seemed based on simply keeping the pot of local rebellions boiling throughout the area, including in Cambodia. Much would depend, as Sihanouk himself realized, on the outcome of the bitter conflict between the revolutionary expansionist forces, still dedicated to wars of liberation, and the more moderate elements that believed in refashioning and completing the Chinese revolution and living in relative peace with their neighbors and, perhaps, with the Soviet Union and the United States as well.

Another important factor in Sihanouk's calculations, of course, was the highly useful role he envisaged the United States could play, after the Vietnam war, economically and socially, if it agreed to give its aid completely without strings and allowed the nations of Southeast Asia to go their own way, politically. In Cambodia's case, there was little danger, if Sihanouk continued to have anything to say about it, that such a way would be Communist. There was no disputing his thorough understanding of Communism, and his assertions that his peaceful Buddhist population would not live happily under Communist rule were well founded. The danger was that, through his own actions, his penchant for getting himself overly involved in international verbal gymnastics, he would fail to come to grips with the basic internal economic and social problems that required more than merely genuine affection and concern for his "children" if Cambodia was to grow and prosper. His own and his country's survival, at the start of 1969, seemed to depend as much on his own restraint as on what he judged to be the lack of restraint in others.

7

Laos:

THE UGLY DUCKLING

The Seesaw War

Laos has always seemed like lotus land—a place the hippies were bound to discover, as they did in the spring of 1968, because they could live cheaply, on noodle soup and pot, in a carefree, permissive atmosphere that included easy access to girls and gurus. The atmosphere was genuine but misleading. Though virtually self-sufficient and potentially prosperous, with a lucrative traffic in gold and opium, Laos was easygoing on the surface, but it had for years been umbilically linked to the war in Vietnam, and during the early months of 1968 it experienced its most trying moments since that war began, with North Vietnamese troops mounting major offensives in the northern and southern parts of the country. These attacks were widely believed to have been coordinated with the Tet offensive of January-February in South Vietnam and to have been part of Hanoi's strategy to prepare for negotiations. There was no reason to suppose that in Laos the Communists would not plan to "negotiate and fight at the same time," however, just as they were prepared to do in Vietnam, and the feeling in Vientiane was that they would do a lot more fighting than talking.

The immediate reaction to President Johnson's announcement

late in March of a partial halt in the bombing of North Vietnam, and to Hanoi's reply expressing a willingness to hold discussions, was therefore a mixed one, compounded of as much skepticism and fear as hope. This response, like that of other nations throughout Southeast Asia, was based on the suspicion that the United States was preparing to pull up stakes, even though the President had made it clear that we would stick fast to our principles and programs of support and development. Notwithstanding, the Lao were afraid that the North Vietnamese would feel they had a free hand to do what they wanted, and that at the same time the Americans, who had carefully and covertly been giving various forms of military as well as open economic assistance to Laos over a period of years, would immediately plan to reduce military aid in the greater interests of achieving peace in Vietnam. At a Polish reception a few days after the President's announcement, this apprehension of the Lao was enhanced by the joyful manner in which the North Vietnamese representatives entered the room, hands aloft and all smiles, like triumphant boxers. As they took the Russian Ambassador in tow and moved among the guests, their satisfaction, which seemed real, apparently reflected their conviction that the United States had, indeed, finally shown signs of backing down in Vietnam and that American popular opposition to and distaste for the war had forced the change in policy, as Hanoi had all along been predicting.

Whatever form the negotiations ultimately took, it seemed likely that the Lao would have to be included eventually, if on a separate level, and that the final settlement of the long conflict in Vietnam would in all probability determine the future of their country, too. It was equally apparent that the Communists were determined to carve out a special position for themselves in Laos, one that would be based on their own interpretation of the Geneva agreements of 1954 and 1962, the latter dealing solely with Laos, and that they would try to consolidate politically the gains they had achieved militarily. By early 1969 there was evidence that they were preparing their negotiatory strategy to deal with what they cogently described as "the realities of the present situation" in Laos. What they meant by this was clear: the 1962 Geneva formula of a tripartite government, including right-wing, neutralist, and Communist representatives, which had proved unworkable as far as they were concerned, was now a dead issue, but other parts of that agreement, and of the earlier one in 1954, that dealt with such matters as the mechanics of policing the country through some form of international inspection and control, could be continued and interpreted as they saw fit. In effect, this meant that they would operate on the principle that possession is nine-tenths of the law: they would keep the territory they held, and would apply their own political yardsticks to manipulating the "new" political situation in ways that would ensure their predominance in whatever type of refurbished government evolved, whether a form of neutralism or something else. Among other things, this meant that, no matter what new political formula was devised, they would seek to obtain more than four out of the sixteen Cabinet seats that were accorded them in the 1962 agreement.

The "realities" were not altogether bleak, as far as the non-Communists were concerned. While their fears and their particular suspicions about North Vietnamese intentions were justified, there was also a rosier way of looking ahead toward the prospect of peace. Ironically, although Laos had been artificially created in 1950 out of the former French Indochina empire and had been shakily sustained ever since under the Geneva agreements and other corollary ones that had consistently been flouted or ignored, Laos might yet emerge, it was felt, as a more viable entity than either North or South Vietnam. For one thing, it remained small enough in population—there were less than three million people in Laos in 1969, as compared to nineteen million in North Vietnam and seventeen million in South Vietnam—to preclude its being a threat to any of its neighbors. For another, Laos had been a foil or a pawn of the major powers for so long that it had become a sort of international responsibility, preying on the consciences of larger nations, and it might end up being a combination ward and buffer state to the mutual advantage of the United States and the Soviet Union, both of which had all along been eager to contain the expansionist aims of China. And, finally, because they *had* shown themselves to be pliable and amenable to compromise, and because their nationalistic spirit was not highly developed, the Lao might eventually be able to work out a formula for neutral survival that other nations in the turbulent climate of Southeast Asia might yet come to envy.

Should this someday happen, the Lao would undoubtedly

ascribe their good fortune to the *phi*, the multifarious animistic spirits whose worship is possibly more of a national religion than Buddhism, with which it has been assimilated. The *phi* exist everywhere—in the earth, the heavens, water, and fire, and in the organs of man, in the household, and in the jungles and forests. The Lao regard the *phi* as immortal and as possessing the powers of reincarnation as well. They can be influences for evil as well as good, and they are constantly being propitiated or exorcised, depending on their natures and qualities. Just about everything that happens in Laos, or to a Lao, is ascribed to these unpredictable and invisible moral spirits. This helps account for the Laotian sense of fatalism, which is sometimes misread for laziness—to be sure, there are times when the first seems to engender the second. It is no wonder that the hippies were attracted to Laotian lore, and that they took to the *phis* as enthusiastically as to pot. About a hundred of them were in Vientiane in the spring of 1968, forgathering nightly in such pads as Psychedelic House and The Third Eye, where they smoked marijuana and drank beer and shrieked cacophonic songs of social and sexual significance that must have sent shivers up the spines of even the most responsive *phi*.

The atmosphere of license and gaiety in Vientiane, which was reflected in the easy informality and ebullient exchange of conversation at diplomatic gatherings as well as in the night clubs and other more intimate parlors, was scarcely matched elsewhere in the country. This was particularly true in the north, where the Communists were making their strongest assaults against government forces during the 1968 dry season in an apparent effort to grab as much territory as they could before any negotiations began. Ordinarily, following these dry-season offensives, which were spearheaded by the North Vietnamese Army in behalf of the less efficient native Pathet Lao Communists, the N.V.A. troops had afterward withdrawn and the government forces had struck back during the wet season, starting in June. This seesaw conflict had left the government in control of only about two-fifths of the country's land area but of 80 percent of the population, while the Communists held or dominated the rest. During 1968, however, the North Vietnamese demonstrated an intention to remain and consolidate the dry-season positions in their own behalf as well as in support of the Pathet Lao.

The offensive began early in January, when the N.V.A. reacted strongly and swiftly to a government attempt to strengthen its hold in the Nam Bac Valley, north of the royal capital of Luang Prabang. Initially, the government had twelve battalions at Nam Bac, and the N.V.A. had only one division, the 317th, the victors at Dienbienphu fourteen years ago, plus some smaller elements; but the government troops lacked cohesion and aggressiveness, and, finding themselves caught in the valley with the N.V.A. artillery on the heights in a situation undoubtedly reminiscent of Dienbienphu, they withdrew. They failed to close ranks properly, however, and under heavy pressure lost a lot of equipment and disintegrated, with the result that fifteen hundred men remained unaccounted for, although the majority had probably simply gone off to their homes and would eventually straggle back to their units.

The N.V.A. capture of Nam Bac, in mid-January, was only a beginning. Thereafter, the Communists pushed down through Houa Phan (formerly Sam Neua) Province, bordering on North Vietnam, and into Xien Khouang Province, just to the south, and captured a score or more government landing strips that were primarily used to supply Meo tribesmen and other tribal people in the northeast. The tenuous hold the government had maintained on parts of this area was lost, and nearly ten thousand refugees fled south while twenty-five thousand tribesmen came under Communist control. During this drive the N.V.A. also captured an important secret communications installation at Pathi, near the North Vietnamese border, which the Americans had been using in connection with the bombing attacks on North Vietnam.

From Luang Prabang I flew east in a small single-engine plane called a Helio to Sam Tuong, where the main refugee center in Xien Khouang is run by the Americans. The Communists had been taking pot shots at small aircraft recently, bringing down a number of helicopters and putting holes in some Helios, and as we flew between the mountain peaks of this rugged country the Air America pilot, Gene Britzius, commented, "I can use up a whole year's supply of adrenalin out here in half a day." The atmosphere at Sam Tuong was tense, with the N.V.A. only a day's march away. Caribou transports were shuttling in and out with refugees being ferried from airstrips to the north. Mostly Meo, but including some Lao and some Thai Dam, or Black Thais, they were clustered in their various native dress alongside the runway, and among them were a dozen Buddhist monks who wore machetes under their saffron robes.

Dr. Charles Weldon, a Public Health Service doctor who gave up his practice in a small Louisiana farm community in 1962 to come out to Laos with his wife, who was also in the service, took me through the Sam Tuong hospital, which last year handled 12,400 casualties and which was now packed with victims of the current offensive, mostly young men with bullet wounds in their faces and chests, or shattered limbs. "We picked them up wherever we could and carried them to the nearest secure area, and then flew them down here," Dr. Weldon said. "The whole region up north is falling to the Communists. This year they're fighting harder than they ever did before, and they've brought in the first team. The situation is now hopelessly mixed up with the Vietnam war, and these poor people are taking a beating because of that. Once we assumed an obligation to help them, we should not have abused them because of Vietnam. We should have defended and helped them in their own right."

Dr. Weldon, a soft-spoken and gentle man, was less severe in his criticism and less bitter than his boss at Sam Tuong, Edgar (Pop) Buell, a fifty-five-year-old Indiana farmer who had been in Laos for eight years, mostly working among the Meos. I had first met Buell in 1963, when he was already becoming a legend as a result of his passionate dedication to the Meo cause, and, if anything, he had become more impassioned since then. There are about 250,000 Meos in the country; a ruddy-complexioned, Tibetan-Burmese people who migrated south from China originally and who hate and fear the Chinese, they have been regarded as among the best fighters in Southeast Asia, and their leader, General Vang Pao, was rated by the Americans and others as one of the two best commanders in Laos. The Meos, who grow rice on the mountain slopes and like to live at altitudes above 3,500 feet, practice a slash-and-burn system of cultivation, remaining in one place five or six years and then moving to another hill after burning off their first holding so that it will not erode and so the trees will grow back normally in about twelve years. They also grow opium, which they sell in the cities, and their fervent devotion to their land is partly due to their determination to hold on to this profitable crop. Buell, who had hardly slept in days because of the refugee crisis, was in a highly emotional state, which, considering what was happening to his beloved Meos, was understandable.

"This may be the forgotten war in Laos, but some of us will never forget it," he said. "General Vang Pao [Buell kept referring to him as "V.P."] told me six years ago, 'O.K., we're willing to do our part because we feel it's for the free world and it's our duty, and all we ask of you is that you support us.' But that's the last damn thing we've done! Their only real weapons are what they've captured from the enemy. Otherwise all they've got is old World War Two stuff, carbines and some mortars, which was good four years ago but not against the new AK-47 rifles the North Vietnamese now have. V.P. has lost at least a thousand men since January 1, killed alone, and I don't know how many more wounded. He's lost all but one of his commanders. Was it their war at Pathi? We asked them to go in and defend our lousy installation because of the Vietnam war. Why didn't we defend it? We destroyed their homeland in order to keep that installation secure, and it was lost anyway. What's more important, I've just lost twenty-five thousand people to the Communists, and they're all my friends. A short time ago we rounded up three hundred fresh recruits. Thirty percent were fourteen years old or less, and ten of them were only ten years old. Another 30 percent were fifteen or sixteen. The remaining 40 percent were thirty-five or over. Where were the ones between? I'll tell you—they're all dead. Here were these little kids in their camouflage uniforms that were much too big for them. But they looked real neat, and when the King of Laos talked to them, they were proud and cocky as could be. They were eager. Their fathers and brothers played Indian before them, and now they wanted to play Indian. But V.P. and I knew better. They were too young and they weren't trained, and in a few weeks 90 percent of them will be killed. For what?"

It was easy to sympathize with Pop Buell and Doc Weldon. Here were two middle-aged men who had devoted the better part of their remaining professional years to working themselves almost to death—Buell had already one heart attack and he was due to retire in a few months—for something they deeply believed in, for a people they genuinely loved as well as admired, who had a capacity to learn as well as simply accept assistance, and who had a staunch belief in their own national identity and destiny as well as the will to oppose any invader, especially the Communists. Both men told several stories of Meo heroism and martyrdom in the face of Communist aggression in northern Laos. In 1965, for example, when the North Vietnamese and the Pathet Lao moved to consolidate themselves in the area east of the Plaine des Jarres in the north-central part of the country—this followed the breakdown of the tripartite system of government and the withdrawal of the Communists from the so-called government of union—some nine thousand Meo tribesmen were forced to flee from their homes, much as they were doing now. After several days, they stopped in a bowl-like valley similar to Sam Tuong, a small enclave surrounded by hills. The North Vietnamese pursued and attacked them with mortars and machine guns in an attempt to stop their flight. The Communists were ruthless, killing a total of twelve hundred, including women and children, many of whom were literally battered to death with clubs and the butts of guns. As Doc Weldon told the story, "At the last moment, facing capture by the North Vietnamese, the Meos killed scores of their own children and old people to avoid having them seized by the Communists. That's what these people are like."

In another case, cited by Buell, some North Vietnamese troops came into a village, grabbed all the rice they could get from the old men and women—the young men were off fighting—and, the following morning, before they left, collected the seven old men in the village and shot them all through the legs. "It was a very simple lesson," Buell said. "The Communists were letting them know: 'Stick with us or you die.' It's not like Vietnam in Laos. There is no shadow government here—oh, sure, the North Vietnamese use the Pathet Lao as a front, and in some places they put a cadre or two in a village to stay a while and organize things, but there is nothing like the fancy infrastructure they've built up in South Vietnam. Here it's either one side or the other. This is a war of invasion and extermination."

General Vang Pao had the reputation of being a hard man to see, and at the moment he was busy fighting off a North Vietnamese battalion about fifteen kilometers away, but Buell managed to persuade him to drive over in his jeep to Sam Tuong to talk to us—the fact that he would have a chance to visit with some of the newly arrived Meo refugees from the north was undoubtedly the main reason he agreed to come. A handsome man in his late thirties, who had five wives and twenty children, Vang Pao was commander of Region Two, one of five military areas in the country. Trained by the French in Hanoi, he spoke both French and English, as well as a variety of Meo dialects and Lao. He lost no time telling us that the situation was more serious than it had ever been before.

"We're losing ten or twenty men killed a day," he said. "The North Vietnamese have us outgunned, with heavy mortars and artillery as well as AK-47's. We've respected the Geneva accord on armaments, though they haven't, but we didn't expect a conventional war of this kind. We need modern weapons and more than the few T-28 bombers we've got. We must mobilize all the hillmen in this part of the country. The Communists are building up a political as well as a military offensive. They're determined to throw us out of Sam Neua and the other northern provinces, and after that the cities, including Luang Prabang and Vientiane, won't be safe either. It's finished up here unless we get help quickly. Please hurry up, because we're nearly all dead." Vang Pao said all this impassionedly yet calmly, which made it all the more impressive. He added that there were 46,000 North Vietnamese troops in the northern part of Laos, and that "the Pathet Lao is nothing but a camouflage." Furthermore, he said, there were four Chinese Communist battalions fighting alongside the N.V.A. They had been identified by documents and insignia, he claimed, and his men had come across five bodies of Chinese soldiers only twenty kilometers from Sam Tuong.

The presence of Chinese fighting elements in Laos had frequently been rumored but never proved, and both American and Lao officials in Vientiane, when I spoke with them after my visit with Vang Pao, tended to doubt the General's intelligence sources, though they admitted the reports could be right. "We've simply never seen any documentary evidence," one embassy officer said. He added that some Chinese troops were known to be in the country, but they had not been actively engaged in combat. Between two and three hundred were located in the Pathet Lao–held area of the Plaine des Jarres, where they were serving as a sort of military advisory group to the local Communists and as a security force. The Chinese also maintained a cultural and economic mis-

sion there. Another three hundred were in Phong Saly Province, in
the northwest part of the country, just below China. This undersize
battalion was bringing in supplies from China and helping train
the pro-Communist neutralist forces led by Colonel Deuane Sou-
vannarath, which totaled about two thousand, and which were
mostly in and around the Plaine des Jarres, too, southeast of Phong
Saly. Unknown additional Chinese troops were moving in and out
of Laos farther west to guard the supply route from Yünnan, in
China. Phong Saly had for years been the domain of Khammouan
Boupha, an independent war lord under the domination of the
Chinese Communists, and he depended on them to supply his
fifteen hundred troops, some of whom were Chinese-speaking
members of the Ho, or Haw, tribe, and they, too, moved back and
forth between China and Laos. There were three known roads
along which the Chinese could readily move combat forces into
Laos if they ever chose to do so, but so far they seemed to have
confined themselves to logistics support for the North Vietnamese
and the Pathet Lao.

"We would like to be able to prove that the Chinese are fighting
here," another ranking embassy officer said. "Vang Pao may be
personally convinced they are, but he's an emotional guy, like all
the Meos, and he's in a real bind right now. Our guess is that the
Chinese, who have got their own problems, would want to be very
careful in Laos because of the Russians, let alone the Americans.
You've got to remember that when the Chinese attacked India, the
Russians moved in Mig aircraft to help protect the Indian forces.
Essentially, the Russians want to keep the fragile structure in Laos
intact, and they have all along tried to keep the Vietnam war from
expanding. Any expansion would simply mean an added drain on
them to help Hanoi even more than they have been doing."

Laos has always been one of the best listening posts in Southeast
Asia, and the possibility that the Russians in Vientiane may have
influenced Hanoi to begin serious negotiations was suggested to
me during my 1968 trip by several diplomats. Moscow's desire for
peace was generally accepted—an end to the war would both encourage better relations with the United States and enable the
Russians to improve their position in Southeast Asia, in competition with the rather discredited Chinese. On the other hand, if the
Chinese stopped aiding the North Vietnamese—Peking had already

expressed its disapproval of the pending Paris negotiations—the Russians might be called upon by Hanoi to help rebuild and develop North Vietnam, with or without the cooperation of the United States, and they would probably have to keep the Hanoi government suitably rearmed as well. The same would hold true, though to a lesser extent, for Laos. "Peace could turn out to be even more expensive for the Russians than war," one Western diplomat commented. For the moment, in Laos, they were treading softly and being very polite, while they were monitoring everything the Americans were doing. What was interesting was that in Laos, as elsewhere in Southeast Asia, they were sending top-flight people out to represent them, and they were showing every indication of wanting to stay in the area.

The Struggle in the South

How difficult the prospects for negotiating peace and then maintaining it in both Laos and Vietnam were was made apparent during a second trip I took in 1968 to the southern section of Laos designated as military Region Four. This region contained much of the Ho Chi Minh trail complex that twisted down from North Vietnam and through Laos before it cut back eastward along various jungle routes into South Vietnam. From Tchepone, on the Vietnamese border just below the Seventeenth Parallel, the trail widened into a new road that moved southwestward toward Saravane and Attopeu in Laos, from which it narrowed again into smaller dirt roads and trails. South of Attopeu, it more or less joined the so-called "Sihanouk trail," which here was the Sekong, as that river emerged from Cambodia into Laos, and small dirt paths alongside it. Barges and sampans brought mostly rice and medical supplies from Cambodia, and when and where the river ceased to be navigable the cargoes were hauled by truck and then on foot east into South Vietnam, joining up with the flow of material and men coming down from North Vietnam.

During the 1968 dry-season offensive, the North Vietnamese, of whom there were about ten thousand in southern Laos, had sought with some success to widen the area of security flanking the Ho

Chi Minh trail in the area between Saravane and Attopeu and around the Boloven Plateau in the middle. In threatening these two cities, and the town of Lao Ngam on the western side of the plateau, they had also shown their intention of permanently achieving control, in behalf of the Pathet Lao, over Laotian territory in the south. Presumably, when negotiations really began, they would claim this newly won ground, just as they intended to do in the north, where their 1968 campaign had been even more specifically aimed at grabbing territory. The task of ultimately determining who controlled what area, or of trying to halt the arms and other traffic, and of policing this whole region of Laos and adjacent portions of South Vietnam, let alone the rest of that country, was a monumental one that seemed bound to occupy the attention of the negotiators for months, if not years. Here in southern Laos, as well as up north, it seemed illusory to think that the Communists would readily give up all the ground they had gained or regained, or to believe that they would altogether stop their build-up and resupply, or their political activities, once the peace talks began, whether or not there was any more fighting.

Traffic on the Ho trail, according to what I was told, had run 40 percent heavier in 1968 than in 1967, and the American air attacks on the trail, mounted from Thai air bases, consequently had been more intense. As many as eight hundred trucks a month out of a total on the trail of six or seven thousand were being destroyed, the bulk of them north of Tchepone, below the Mu Gia Pass, through which the vehicles moved south, some of them branching off to the east through the A Shau Valley, in support of the Communist offensives in the 1st Corps area of South Vietnam, and the rest moving farther south toward Attopeu and then eastward into the Vietnamese highlands. The air attacks, of course, were still not officially admitted to be taking place, in deference to Prime Minister Souvanna Phouma's policy of neutrality, although he had now condoned the returning of fire by the American "reconnaissance" planes, which is what the bombers from Thailand were called. In addition to the air attacks, and even less often mentioned, were the trail-watching activities on the ground of the Americans, the South Vietnamese, and the Lao, which were conducted from both sides of the border. Since the United States was seeking to live up to the spirit of the Geneva accords of 1954 and 1962, it officially maintained only a large staff of military attachés and clerical assistants in Laos, and there were no acknowledged military "advisers," or any American troops, in the country. It was no longer much of a secret, however, that the trail-watching represented a vital under-cover operation that required considerable military and civilian cooperation and logistics support, and that as a joint intelligence effort it had been one of the most successful of the war.

In Pakse, a town of some 32,000 on the banks of the Mekong not far from both Thailand and Cambodia, I spoke with some Americans and Lao at the Region Four headquarters of General Phasouk Somly, who, like Vang Pao, was a highly regarded commander. They all agreed that the North Vietnamese, far better armed with 120-millimeter and 140-millimeter rockets, heavy mortars and AK-47 guns than the Lao Army, could take Saravane, Attopeu, and Lao Ngam if they wanted to attack any or all of them in regimental strength, but the consensus was that the Communists would probably not go that far, despite their having laid siege during the previous three months to these as well as to other towns in Region Four and to some places bordering Thailand. At one time they had attacked Thakhek, on the Mekong in Region Three to the north. The seizure of a provincial capital, however, would have constituted an open violation of the Geneva accords, and the North Vietnamese were thought eager to avoid this, especially at this juncture, though their very presence in Laos was already in contravention of the Geneva agreements.

By subjecting the government troops to heavy threats and harassment, including two big mortar and rocket barrages at Attopeu, the Communists may have been hoping that the government would be forced to evacuate one or more of the capitals, which would have enabled them to maintain the fiction that they were not actually "captured." General Phasouk's forces had defended them well, however, and had done some of the best fighting by the Royal Lao Army since the war had begun. Late in February, the outer defenses of Attopeu, Saravane, and Lao Ngam had all been surrounded and attacked at once. Although some North Vietnamese elements had briefly entered Lao Ngam, all three places had ultimately held and the Communists had lost about five hundred men killed. All in all, over the past two months, the North Vietnamese and their Pathet Lao underlings had suffered between one thousand and fifteen hundred dead in the south, many of them having been killed by T-28 bombing strikes, which were serving as the best equalizer the Lao government forces had to make up for their poorer ground weapons. During the same period the government had had five hundred men killed in action. Since early March there had been skirmishes and continued shellings by the Communists, and some ambushes of roads in Region Four, which had slowed down communications, but no further all-out attacks, and it began to look as if the Communists would settle, for the moment at least, in this prenegotiatory posture.

During the 1968 attacks in the south the International Control Commission in Laos had conducted its first investigation in about three years when the Indian and Canadian members visited Saravane for several hours in late February at Prime Minister Souvanna Phouma's request. The third member of the Commission, the Pole, had refused to go along. The two inspectors had found the city two-thirds deserted but the government garrisons well dug in. Because of the Indian's reluctance to go too far—he had only recently arrived in Laos, and was far more willing to support an active Commission role than his predecessor had been, but he wanted to move slowly—the report of the two commissioners had been based on only fragmentary information, but the Canadian had found ample evidence that Saravane was under siege. The trip appeared to be a good augury of what lay ahead for the Commission, even though it also focused attention on what the problems of such a policing group were. The role of the I.C.C., in any event, which theoretically included inspection of places already under attack and of the whole trail complex in the Laos-Vietnam border area as well as the more debatable function of preventive activities, was thoroughly basic to any negotiations. But differences over interpretation of the I.C.C.'s obligations and functions had all along rendered the Commission, in Vietnam and Cambodia as well as Laos, virtually helpless, and this had served to emphasize, as clearly as anything else, the terribly complicated problems involved in the tortuous making of any future peace in Southeast Asia.

The Commission in Laos, despite having more leeway than its Vietnamese and Cambodian counterparts, had still been hamstrung in various ways. The Neo Lao Hak Sat, the local Communist front organization, claimed that the Commission had no right to function because the Communists had quit the coalition government created under the 1962 Geneva agreement—which incorporated two earlier agreements, one at Zurich in 1961, which determined the broad basis of Laotian neutrality, and another one prior to Geneva in 1962, known as the Plaine des Jarres agreement, which determined the composition of the tripartite government, in which Communists, neutralists, and rightists would be equally represented. There was a fundamental discrepancy involved here, since the Plaine des Jarres agreement had stipulated that government decisions had to be unanimous, while the Geneva terms for the operation of the I.C.C. permitted it to conduct investigations by a majority vote of two out of the three members. The Communists argued, with some legal justification, that this investigatory function was secondary to the fact that the government of the neutralist Premier Souvanna Phouma had no right to order any kind of investigation without the participation of the Communists. This was the main reason the Polish member of the I.C.C. had regularly refused to take part in the rare investigations that had been conducted.

The Poles had also abstained on the theory that the Commission didn't really exist any more, since it was supposed to have been formally continued by a unanimous vote of the Geneva participants every three years. This was done once, in 1965, but thereafter Communist China and North Vietnam had voted against its continuance and both had since refused to pay any dues. The Commission had continued to exist anyway. The Poles, as well as the Russians, who with the British were co-chairmen of the Geneva accords, wanted to keep the I.C.C. alive in principle but under wraps, and they had argued that its role should only be one of offering "good offices." The Canadians, with the support of the United States, said that such a good-offices function implied the right if not the duty to investigate violations, and that this was a proper execution of protocol, as set forth in the original Geneva agreement.

This whole confusion of function and purpose underlined the feeling of doubt that the I.C.C. could operate successfully anywhere in the former Indochina area unless the procedure was completely re-evaluated and new rules and regulations governing its performance were set up. Under the circumstances of the war in Vietnam, such re-evaluation and reordering might prove impossible. There were those, however, including the Canadian participant members, who felt that the Commission could and should be continued, in view of the experience it had gained and the fact that a framework for cooperation still existed. Once some sort of unitary government had been re-established in Vientiane, they said, I.C.C. teams should be placed in the field to police a cease-fire and supervise the garrisoning of the various military groupings. Each of these groupings would move only at the discretion of the Vientiane government. Next, about fifty fixed and mobile teams would be needed to supervise activity on all routes, passes, and trails, and these teams would have complete freedom to maneuver. Once these two things were done, a new national gendarmery, including some special Border Police, should replace the Army in the countryside as a peace-keeping instrument, to deal with banditry, insurrection, and other disturbances. This broad outline of a method for policing a peace agreement perhaps sounded overoptimistic, particularly since the Communists showed every indication of insisting on retaining their veto power and defining the ground rules as they interpreted them; but unless something of the sort was created, and made at least partially effective, in Vietnam as well as in Laos, the chances of maintaining peace, or of avoiding a gradual Communist takeover in both countries, had to be assessed as slim.

The entire difficult question of whether coalition and neutrality could work, even under the best of conditions, was of course crucial to the peace effort. No amount of policing, even if it was effective, would be able to ensure a satisfactory peace and pave the way for a hopeful amount of social and economic progress if the political formulas that had to take precedence could not be found, and, once found, accepted and implemented. In the fall of 1968 there seemed far more willingness on the part of the government in Laos to accept and reimplement a coalition solution than there was in Vietnam, where the government of President Nguyen Van Thieu, and the National Assembly, had taken strong stands against any kind of coalition with the Communists, though other Vietnamese believed just as firmly that some sort of process of accommodation with the National Liberation Front there was inevitable and that the sooner it was attempted, within a separate southern framework, the better. In Laos, Prime Minister Souvanna Phouma was still holding the door open for the Communists to re-enter the central government in Vientiane, but their most recent statements evinced no further desire to do so under any circum-stances, and the only "compromise" they envisoned at the close of 1968 was one predicated on their retention of the territory they then held, which was roughly the same, with a bit more added, than they had had in 1962. Control and influence were two different things, however, and whether they could be rationalized and ultimately resolved in the context of a new national-unity government based on a sharing of ministerial posts and popular elections would have to be seen. It was apparent, though, that there might be a greater willingness among all political elements in Laos to move in this direction than there was in Vietnam.

This was not to say that there were no skeptics and dissenters about. Among them, for example, was Prince Boun Oum, the col-orful patriarch and dominant figure in the south. Boun Oum, who had helped negotiate the Geneva agreement though he never be-lieved in its efficacy, even after he became part of the resultant tripartite government, bluntly told me, "I don't believe in Lao neutrality. Geneva was all done for geopolitical reasons. It had no sense of reality. It was an artificial myth created by the big powers. I told Harriman [W. Averell Harriman, a principal negotiator then and President Johnson's chief negotiator at Paris in 1968] that I saw no point to sitting down and talking to Prince Souphanouvong [the erstwhile Communist representative in the Vientiane govern-ment and Souvanna Phouma's half-brother]. Why make us sit down with a bunch of pirates? Harriman was locked in his own contradictions, as you Americans always are. Why try to force us into fictitious neutrality deals? We've been neutral from time im-memorial actually, in that we don't want to pick a quarrel with anyone. We trusted the French. We didn't ask for independence. They betrayed us, and forced us to become independent, in the fifties, just as they have since betrayed you Americans—I don't know what's happened to France. I'm touched by what the United States is doing here now. Your intentions are pure. If anyone has a heart, it's the American people. But we're maladroit. Without a white protector we'll just become a battlefield between the North Vietnamese and the Thais, and then the Chinese will walk in and pick up the pieces. It's essential to re-establish equilibrium in this part of the world, and it calls for a united white effort, mostly American and Russian but including some French administrators. We must live with a protector or disappear."

Souvanna and the Americans

Boun Oum's views, whatever degree of postcolonial nostalgia they revealed, nevertheless represented a certain tough-minded realism and, at the same time, a legitimate degree of disillusion with earlier theories and concepts about the Indochina area. Certainly these ideas were not fully or carefully formulated at the time of Geneva, in 1954, or again in 1962; as a consequence, and because of the natural unfolding of political events, in North and South Vietnam especially, the Geneva agreements had proved unworkable or abortive. A more carefully calculated American commitment, followed by a continuous and not sporadic and crisis-oriented use of leverage, would have achieved much more than it did. In a certain sense, this is what the Americans were now belatedly trying to do in Laos, which was one of the reasons to have some hope for the country's future. This restrained American approach, if it was not in tune with that of Boun Oum or some of the generals, including Vang Pao and Phasouk, who wanted more and better guns and planes with which to fight or hold off the North Vietnamese later as well as now, was very much in keeping with the policy of Souvanna Phouma, and it was Souvanna who almost singlehandedly had guided national policy.

When I spoke with him during my 1968 visit, he was as firm as he had been three years earlier, when I had last seen him, about maintaining his position of neutrality and of operating within the context of the 1962 agreement, if only the Communists would, in effect, repent and rejoin the family in Vientiane, which he privately agreed was increasingly unlikely. He readily admitted that the situation, militarily, was more serious than it had been before, and that the "lack of tranquillity," as he quaintly put it, was due to "the violations by the North Vietnamese of our territory, and the ideological war of subversion that emanates from North Vietnam."

A political solution in Vietnam was inevitable, he said, and peace there would bring peace in Laos. Once the "foreign troops" of Hanoi left Laos, there would be no reason why the Pathet Lao and the Neo Lao Hak Sat front should not be represented in the Army and in the Vientiane government, and for this reason he was still keeping the four ministerial seats they once held reserved for them. He foresaw a neutral bloc of nations composed of both Vietnams, Laos, Cambodia, and Burma, all of them Buddhist nations—he excluded Thailand because of that country's association with the Southeast Asia Treaty Organization (SEATO). He did not seem especially worried about any possible intervention on the part of the Chinese, and he echoed what the Americans had said about their being no proof that any Chinese battalions were fighting on Laotian soil. "But don't stir the anthill," he said. "It might get the ants started." As for more American military aid, there was no need for it. "If we want more, we'll ask," he said, "but the help we have now is enough." A few days after my talk with him, Souvanna Phouma seemed less confident. At the Polish reception, following the news of President Johnson's speech and of Hanoi's response, he appeared in need of fresh assurances from the Americans that the help he was getting would at least be sustained, let alone increased.

There was less likelihood that the successful American economic aid program, which amounted to $57.6 million for fiscal 1967 and was expected to run about the same for fiscal 1968, would be curtailed than there was of a cutback in our unpublicized military or semimilitary assistance, much of which was being distributed and supervised by the Central Intelligence Agency. In this sense, Souvanna's fresh fears, and the previously expressed fears and complaints of some of his generals, seemed well founded. In its eagerness to prove its good intentions to Hanoi, the United States had already cut down on some of the air support it had been rendering General Vang Pao in the north, although there were some other forms of aid to him that had recently been increased. There was no indication, as yet, that the daily average of 250 bombing attacks on the Ho Chi Minh trail had been diminished since President Johnson's speech—this would not occur until Hanoi gave some assurance that the rate of infiltration would be reduced. As far as the Lao were concerned, support within Laos was more important than interdiction of traffic on the trail, which mostly, though not entirely, affected Vietnam. Washington had indicated previously that it would not send the Lao more than the forty T-28 propeller-driven bombers they already had—the Communist position was that *all* bombing within Laos should stop, as well as the Ho trail bombing. Actually, not more than thirty trained pilots were available on any given day, and only about the same number of planes were operational.

As for the ground forces, the Lao officers kept saying that they would like to see their whole army of some 55,000 men, plus about 10,000 progovernment neutralists, supplied with M-16 rifles in place of the older M-1's and M-2's these forces now mostly had, but, as the Americans saw it, the M-16 was too complex a weapon for the average Lao soldier to handle, and, while the older weapons were not the equal in firepower of the Communists' AK-47's, they had proved suitable so far in defensive action, particularly with the help of air support. Four battalions of the government's forces, primarily those engaged in guerrilla activity in the north and south, had, in fact, received M-16's for special patrol and reconnaissance action, and more were being slowly distributed. Although the caliber and fighting ability of the Army had slowly improved, the consensus among American military observers was that the government troops already had what they could use with respect to technical ability and training, and that they still needed considerable work on such basic things as fire planning, coordination with artillery, communications, and intelligence. Giving them too many sophisticated weapons would be futile, these experts said, especially in the face of demographic realities; if the North Vietnamese, who were far superior in fighting ability and weaponry, wanted to make further inroads into Laos, there was very little the Lao by themselves could do about it anyway. This became apparent toward the end of 1968 and the beginning of 1969, when the new dry-season offensive coincided with an increase of North Vietnamese troops in Laos, following their withdrawal from South Vietnam. The Communists again threatened Attopeu and Saravane and other towns around the Boloven Plateau, as well as the key area northeast of Vientiane. The government troops managed to hold their own, but the threat remained serious as negotiations on Vietnam got under way in Paris. As the American bombing of the Ho Chi Minh trail increased with the suspension of the bombing of North Vietnam, Souvanna said he hoped it would soon stop and that a Laotian peace settlement would follow one on Vietnam.

Approximately two-thirds of American economic assistance in Laos was under the heading of project aid. Special stress was being placed on agricultural improvements, including irrigation schemes ranging from the building of large and small dams to the use of pumps, the distribution of modern fertilizer, the facilitation of credit to encourage self-help projects, and experiments with the new high-yield rice seeds developed at the International Rice Institute in the Philippines. These seeds, as in other Asian countries, promised to revolutionize Laos' rice economy. The nation produced about 500,000 tons of rice annually, and had regularly imported between 70,000 and 100,000 additional tons. The use of the new seeds, it was hoped, would bring about a surplus for export of some 50,000 tons by 1969, which would jump to 200,000 tons within a few more years; but the increased military activity and the North Vietnamese seizure of more territory, including rice lands, threatened to hold this program back. There had been a large rise in vegetable production over the last few years, and Laos was even sending some vegetables to Thailand instead of buying them from there, as had traditionally been the case. The care and cultivation of forest lands and lumber production were also increasing. The construction and improvement of roads, both large ones and feeder roads for bringing crops in from outlying areas, either to the main highways or to the Mekong River, was rapidly progressing. The other fields in which American aid had been important were education and health. Hundreds of elementary and secondary schools had been built all over the country, and teacher-training programs had been instituted. Some 250 rural dispensaries had been built and staffed.

The central idea behind the development aid program, and the commodity-import program that included bringing in such things as petroleum products and necessary vehicles and other equipment, was to move Laos from a subsistence to a market economy as soon as possible, which meant no faster or slower than the capacity of its people to learn new methods and techniques would permit. As Ambassador William Sullivan, one of the ablest American diplomats in Southeast Asia, explained it, "We want to try to help the Lao escape from living by the seasons, but we have to deal carefully with the rising-expectations equation." Sullivan and Joseph Mendenhall, the experienced chief of the American aid program, pointed out that while the Lao, like any other people, wanted to be able to buy such things as motor scooters and transistor radios, they had to become fully aware of their responsibilities in dealing with the machinery of credit relationships set up with the government or with cooperatives if they were to avoid falling back into patterns of corruption imposed by moneylenders or grasping landlords. "We can be catalysts," Sullivan says, "but we also have to make sure the Lao understand what's taking place, and we have to find a way for them to carry the ball themselves."

Financially, Laos in 1968 was in considerably better shape than most other Southeast Asian nations. In fact, the kip, the national currency, had become one of the soundest in the world, thanks to the Foreign Exchange Operations Fund which supported it. This was a five-nation stabilization mechanism backed by the United States, Great Britain, Japan, France, and Australia, which was created on the recommendation of the International Monetary Fund late in 1963. The Americans in the 1967 fiscal year had contributed $13.8 million to the fund, about 70 percent of the total provided. The fund supplemented the stabilization process of the commodity-import program, which made dollars available at the artificial rate of 240 kip to the dollar for authorized commodities; this program had been cut back somewhat since 1966 because too many Lao importers and dealers had been making big profits out of imports by falsifying invoices, pricing goods at the 500-to-1 rate, and re-exporting them to Thailand. As in many underdeveloped countries, Laos also obtained financial benefits from a counterpart fund, through which aid dollars kept by a bank or an import firm were paid for in kip, which then became available for government use. The proceeds were used, with the approval of the United States, mostly for humanitarian projects, including supplemental support for some 250,000 refugees whose primary needs were supplied by the United States through air drops that totaled sixteen hundred tons of commodities a month. Of the national budget of $32 million, the Lao were raising $15 million themselves, over and above the foreign aid they were receiving, and almost half of this came from an 8.5 percent tax imposed on the transit of gold, which was flowing through Laos at the rate of five or six tons a months, mostly to Vietnam.

The able Minister of Finance, Sisouk na Champassak, had become Souvanna Phouma's protégé and heir apparent, and the mere fact that his chances of one day becoming Prime Minister were considered good if he stayed in politics was an indication that, after years of political uncertainty, Laotian politics had settled down, although, as one American observer remarked, "projecting them into the future is a little like trying to package smog." It was a fact, however, that there had been no major turbulence since early in 1965, when General Phoumi Nosavan, the right-wing leader who had once been the favorite of the United States Central Intelligence Agency, had made a final, abortive attempt to grab power and had then left the country for what appeared to be permanent exile in Thailand. In October, 1966, there had been another brief coup attempt by a popular Air Force leader, General Thao Ma, but this had been more of an erratic outburst directed against General Oun Rathikoune, the Army Chief of Staff, and his deputy, General Kouprasith Abhay, than a real political power play.

The political power structure in Laos in 1969, as had always been the case, was based on regional and family loyalties and alliances, except that they now balanced each other in such a way as apparently to preclude any rash action. Furthermore, Souvanna Phouma, who at sixty-six had solidified his own position in the prime ministership as the years had passed, had managed to benefit from the rivalries that still existed among the generals and sectional groups by keeping them all in line while playing them off against each other, thus diminishing the dangers of the military trying again to make him a captive. The only man who could cause trouble, it was generally agreed, was Kouprasith, whose private and profitable power base reached into the civilian branches of the government as well as through the key Vientiane garrison, but the other general officers, notably Vang Pao and Phasouk, would move against him, it was said, if he tried to grab control. Souvanna had, furthermore, managed to diminish the power of some of the old-guard political and officer elements by bringing some younger men into his Cabinet and other administrative areas, and this, too, promised to make for a more peaceful and orderly turnover when the transition to Sisouk or to someone else was made. Though a southerner himself, from Champassak Province, which was Boun Oum's domain, Sisouk was not altogether admired by the right-wing southern leaders, or by some of the generals, who looked upon him as something of an outsider and a technocrat. This old-guard element was also either skeptical or contemptuous of Souvanna's continuing belief in Laotian neutrality. Nevertheless, they seemed to realize that Sisouk had a good standing abroad and, next to Souvanna, was probably the man best capable of running the country. However, as peace negotiations in Vietnam came to a head, Souvanna, who had spoken earlier of retiring, as he had from time to time before, declared that "in the present circumstances, I believe I can be more useful to my country by staying at my post." As for Sisouk, who was under fresh pressure from the old guard, he indicated that *he* might quit, which would not necessarily lessen his chances of succeeding Souvanna in the future.

In the central part of the nation, including Vientiane Province, political power still rested fairly solidly in the hands of the large and wealthy Sananikone family, with which General Kouprasith was allied. The Sananikone clan, run by the venerable Phouie Sananikone, former Prime Minister and head of the National Assembly, was a force for stability rather than dissension, though there were rivalries and jealousies among its many members. In the north, aside from Vang Pao, who did not seem to have any political ambitions beyond the protection of his beloved Meos, the only other important political force was the King, Savang Vatthana, in Luang Prabang, the royal capital. Souvanna Phouma, who held his princely title as a result of his family's having inherited vice-regal duties under the crown, had his political base in Luang Prabang, too, as did General Rathikoune, the Army chief. The old-line family and military groups held political power by dint of wealth and tradition. What was still lacking was any real political party development, either at the center or in the regions and grass roots, where the competition from the Communists was keenest. The fifty-nine members of the National Assembly—nine of them held ministerial posts and retained their seats but didn't vote— were almost all connected, one way or another, with the important regional families, or were beholden to the key generals. In mid-1966, a rebellious group of conservative younger Assembly members had led a campaign against government corruption and had then succeeded in forcing through a rejection of the government budget. Furious, Souvanna got the King to dissolve the Assembly, and a new body was chosen in an election held in January, 1967, which, as they had before, the Communists boycotted. The new body was "more responsive" to Souvanna's wishes, which meant that it would not try to upset the applecart by demanding, among other things, that Souvanna discard the 1962 formula for a union government and pass around the four Cabinet posts and other jobs he was still holding open for the return of the Communists. The Assembly customarily operated through its standing committee, which met regularly in Vientiane in order to pass decrees sought by Souvanna and the Cabinet, and the body as a whole, unlike its more rambunctious predecessor, once again played little more than a ceremonial role. One of its northern members, Sopsaisana, had made an attempt to start some sort of political action by getting thirty-eight assemblymen to join what he called the Parliamentary Group for the Implementation of the Geneva Accords, and he hoped this might germinate a new "national movement" that in time could become a party; but by 1969 the group had done nothing but issue some manifestoes.

The King remained a strong force for unity in the country, and in 1968 he was traveling around increasingly, though his name and face were still unknown to many back-country peasants and hillside tribesmen. It was significant that, at the end of the year, the Communists were playing up the King as the "Supreme Power" in Laos, which underlined their apparent abandonment of the old tripartite principle of government. When the time came for political peace talks, they were saying, the King should preside over them and help provide a new mechanism. There were various ways in which the Communists were demonstrating their respect for the King. After their 1968 offensive, though they did not withdraw troops anywhere else, they did pull out some battalions from the Nam Bac area near Luang Prabang. This seemed an obvious gesture of deference to the King and perhaps a subtle form of pressure on him to pay less heed to Souvanna Phouma. The North Vietnamese in Vientiane also increasingly snubbed Souvanna and Sisouk and paid direct homage to the King—their ambassador visited with him on one occasion in the fall of 1968, and sent a representative to attend the wedding of one of his sons, as did the Lao Communists. The Russians, too, were going out of their way to please the King. For the time being, so long as the Royal Army did not flex its muscles, the regional-family balance of power under Souvanna's firm hand and under the benevolent gaze of the King seemed likely to be maintained, but it was perfectly possible, in the long run, that the Communists' appeals to the King, given their strength, would influence him to play the peacemaking role they desired, and that this might lead to a downgrading of Souvanna and hasten a new Laotian compromise. "Right now it's like a series of lumps stuck together," one ranking diplomat observed. "If Laos can only have a breathing space, once we can figure out what the North Vietnamese will really settle for, these people could make it, with a little agriculture, a little public health, and a few roads."

It might not be as easy as that, but a number of veteran observers of the Laotian political scene felt that the best hope for the future lay in the villages, among the local headmen, who were slowly becoming aware of the possibilities of progress. "You don't need a social revolutionary figure here," one of these observers said. "You need political leadership that knows how to come to grips with the realities of daily life, men who can explain to the people why it's important to pump water up from the rivers for irrigation instead of depending on the seasons for rain and mud. It will be some grubby little guy in the village who will move the country from the seventeenth to the twentieth century."

The possibility remained, of course, that the grubby little guy would turn out to be a Communist taking orders from the Pathet Lao, or, more specifically, from the Phak Khon Ngan, the clandestine nucleus of the Communist Party in Laos directly tied to the Laodang (Workers) Party of North Vietnam. The Phak Khon Ngan was operating on the surface through the Neo Lao Hak Sat, the most important of various political or social fronts, and it maintained a system of cadres which, while not comparable to those in South Vietnam, could easily burgeon into a full-fledged political apparatus. The Communists were devoting increasing attention to rural problems and were also concentrating on indoctrinating Laotian youths, including those who had been studying in France— some of these were being trained in North Vietnam and then sent back to Laos. They had stepped up their propaganda and regularly broadcast reports of their military victories, in English as well as Lao.

The leadership of the Communist movement in Laos had remained much the same for a number of years. The secretary general of the Phak Khon Ngan was Kaysone Phomvihan, a half Lao, half Vietnamese who, in 1945, after studying medicine at the University of Hanoi and engaging in Vietminh youth activities, had been sent back to his native Savannakhet, in southern-central Laos, by Ho Chi Minh. Initially, he worked for Prince Souphanouvong, but he had soon eclipsed Souphanouvong politically and was still, in 1969, the principal Laotian link with the Laodang in Hanoi. Aside from the Prince, three other old-time leaders remained in the party hierarchy—Phoumi Vongvichit, who specialized in culture and the dissemination of information; Nouhak Phoumavan, who prided himself on his peasant background, and Singkapo Chounlamany, a member of a leading southern family who had abandoned his wife and children in 1945 to become a guerrilla. A fifth man, Sithone Kommadan, a member of the Lao Ven tribe, was still the Pathet Lao chief in the south, where he had inherited the domain of his father, an old-time revolutionary who was killed by the French. Early in 1968 a new name, Sisana, had been heard. A poet and historian, he was being extolled by the Russians and Eastern Europeans and was apparently becoming a powerful figure; for the moment he was in charge of propaganda and was the chief denouncer of the Americans. Souphanouvong was still the most often quoted—late in 1967, in an Eastern European radio talk, he had admitted publicly for the first time that he was a Marxist and a Communist—and it was anticipated that he would again become the dominant public figure on the left if a new coalition was formed, though the strings would undoubtedly be pulled for him by Kaysone and by the Laodang in North Vietnam. There was fresh talk of the possibilities of a reconciliation between Souphanouvong and his half-brother Souvanna, who was said to be willing to meet Souphanouvong at the latter's headquarters to discuss an end to the war and a joint declaration in favor of the United States' stopping the bombing in Laos. This might prove the best way to get direct Laos peace talks started between Hanoi and Vientiane.

A large-scale shift in Communist political strategy and tactics began in the spring of 1968, following a series of meetings of the Laodang Central Committee in Hanoi. There were indications that the Phak Khon Ngan might come out from underground, and that, despite Souphanouvong's Marxist admissions, he and the Neo Lao Hak Sat would be presented as "neutral" elements for the purpose of negotiations. By June, following meetings among the Lao Communists, in line with Hanoi's orders, the tripartite governmental formula was no longer officially expressed as an ultimate solution—this was when the new phrase about "the realities of the present situation" began to be heard. Further evidence of the shift came when Souphanouvong and Vongvichit dropped the titles they had held in the tripartite union government—they had continued to use them even after their boycott of it. Everything pointed to the Communists' desire to sit down to a brand-new table, under the eye of the King. And as far as the International Control Commission, or something like it, was concerned, the Communists indicated they would still abide by the Geneva principles, but would go on interpreting them in their own way, which meant through the full use of their own veto power over and above the veto of the Polish representatives. This new policy, as it emanated from Hanoi, was gradually passed on down the line in Laos, through the Lao Communist Party to the Neo Lao Hak Sat front and on down through the village cadre level. A Joint Union Conference of the Neo Lao Hak Sat and the Patriotic Neutralists of Colonel Deuane and other left-wing neutralist officers and politicians was held, and the new policy was outlined and explained. Interestingly, too, in this apparent approach to negotiations, which had previously never been broached as the fighting had waxed and waned, was the translation into English of Lao Communist propaganda, and its dissemination in the United States as well as in Europe. The stress in much of this propaganda was on reaching a Lao solution—an internal one that would be separate from the solution in Vietnam. This did not mean, of course, that the situation, as the Communists saw it, was not dependent on the outcome in Vietnam; what it did mean was that, once the substantive Vietnam discussions began, and even if Laos was brought into them as part of the re-establishment of a Geneva mechanism, detailed Lao political talks should be conducted apart from those on

Vietnam, and that, furthermore, the United States should have no part in them.

Within these broad possibilities, the survival of Laos, against all earlier odds, seemed possible. The ugly duckling, who had been given short shrift over the past two decades, might make it, after all. What Laos above all needed, as veteran diplomats had repeatedly emphasized, was time to consolidate the leap into the twentieth century that the defeat of the French, the Geneva experiment, and the war in Vietnam had forced upon this gentle, landlocked country. Neutrality might be a myth, as Souvanna Phouma's critics maintained, but as part of the Indochina peninsula that might well have to live within an orbit dominated by Communist North Vietnam, Laos' best hope was to remain neutral and to maintain its rate of growth long enough so that it could stand on its own feet as a nation, which it was just beginning to do for the first time since its test-tube birth. If, in early 1969, it was on the edge of delayed puberty, its nurturing into adolescence and nationhood would require the care and kindness, as well as the protection, of others, above all that of the major powers, eventually including China. Perhaps the greatest danger was that it might yet become a prize over which China and North Vietnam would fight, but, so far at least, the Chinese were behaving prudently. The protective role of the Soviet Union and the United States would probably remain the most important restraining factor.

8

Vietnam:

REAPING THE WHIRLWIND

The Vietnamese and the Americans

Not since the seventeenth century, when the Germans were ravaged by the Thirty Years' War, has a people been so steadily afflicted by strife as the Vietnamese since 1941. And no city in Asia has been subject to as many pressures and conflicts during this period as Saigon. Two wars, from 1946 to 1954 against the French colonialists and from 1959 to 1969 against native Communists, as well as countless internal riots, rebellions, and coups, have left an indelible mark on what was once the most gracious and charming capital in Southeast Asia. During many visits over two decades, I saw the mood of Saigon shift over and over again, but not since November, 1963, when a military *coup d'état* overthrew the autarchic regime of Ngo Dinh Diem, did I feel such an impending sense of change as I noted in the early days of 1969. After the anti-Diem coup there had been a feeling of exhilaration and hope, but the atmosphere by 1969 had become heavy with uncertainty and apprehension over the possible course of events both in Vietnam and at the peace conference in Paris. The apprehension on the part of the South Vietnamese seemed duly justified. The year-old Second Republic of President Nguyen Van Thieu, while ostensibly a democracy with an elected bicameral legislature, was in many respects still an authoritarian regime. It lacked, as had all the governments since the birth of Diem's First Republic in 1954, an effective organization and true nationalist zeal. However one criticized the Communists, for whatever degrees of terrorism and other violations of human freedom, the Vietcong and the North Vietnamese could rightfully claim to be well organized and totally dedicated to the goal of attaining their form of national independence for Vietnam. Almost from the outset of their thirty-year struggle against the French, the Japanese, and the Americans, they had shown a remarkable sense of discipline, an enduring fervor, and a capacity to suffer unremitting hardships. Without these qualities no amount of Chinese Communist or Russian military and moral assistance would have enabled them to continue struggling so perseveringly and at such a cost, especially since 1965, against the massive weight of American manpower and firepower.

Once the peace talks had begun, though fighting continued, often fiercely, the phrase one heard most in Vietnam was "gaining time." The South Vietnamese were afraid that, having been rushed into negotiations by the Americans without proper preparation, they would not have enough time to collect and consolidate themselves before a settlement was reached in Paris—even a preliminary one involving some troop withdrawals and a cease-fire, let alone a more complicated political solution that would undoubtedly be based on some sort of compromise with the National Liberation Front. If the Vietnamese, for this and other reasons, had become ambivalent about the Americans, there was also considerable mixed feeling among the Americans about the Vietnamese and about the frustrating, brutal, and inconclusive war. Such opinions on the part of both partners were inevitable under the circumstances of the complicated United States role in Vietnam, dating back to American support of the postwar effort of the French to reclaim their Indochina empire. The legitimate Vietnamese nationalists, as much as the Communists, had resented that policy, which had included military as well as economic and financial aid. When the French were defeated at Dienbienphu and withdrew, the United States began its own commitment, at first a modest advisory and economic one but one that grew rapidly after 1961. By 1968 its cost had grown to $30 billion a year, spent mostly to support the 545,000 American troops in South Vietnam and the fighters and bombers that were attacking South Vietnamese targets, that blasted North Vietnam—from March, 1965, until October, 1968—and that continued thereafter to attack North Vietnamese infiltration routes in Laos from bases in Thailand.

In 1961, and for several years after that, most Americans still felt that our commitment in Vietnam was a justified effort to stop the spread of Communism in Southeast Asia by supporting a non-Communist government. Many, however, opposed the bombing of the North from the outset. And by 1968, if not sooner, many others had come to believe that the war had grown intolerable, particularly in the face of the problems America was facing at home, of the divisiveness the conflict was causing in our society. Even those most involved in the Vietnam situation felt that our purpose had been vitiated, if not invalidated, by our failure to comprehend the real nature of the war, and to match our military effort with a positive and flexible political policy. What seemed a series of lost opportunities to apply our political leverage and foster democracy slowly and reasonably, especially after the fall of Diem, had been compounded by our mistaken belief that, once the political situation got out of hand after 1963, we could create stability and strength out of mounting confusion and chaos and inject quick doses of democracy, like penicillin. In an earlier book, *The Lost Revolution* (1965), I discussed some of our errors of omission and commission and suggested how they might have been avoided if we had been firmer and had had a more realistic and resolute set of objectives in Vietnam, and if we had acted on them with a proper combination of tough practicality, imagination, consistency, and foresight. As time went on, and despite an improvement in the military situation, I became increasingly convinced that we had missed the boat. We could not recapture lost revolutionary ground because we had failed to grasp the nature of the Vietnamese revolution in all its multifarious and complicated aspects, and because, among other things, we had experimented with various tactics of counterinsurgency instead of first developing a larger strategy of counterrevolution. In short, we had drifted into the situation primarily to stop Communism but without enough of a policy or program capable of coping with the peculiar set of revolutionary imponderables in an Oriental setting. By 1969, while we could not simply write off Vietnam and withdraw precipitously, I came to feel, along with many others, that we had no alternative but to diminish our commitment as best we could, keeping in mind that the manner and method of our withdrawal were not only vital to Vietnam but even more vital to the rest of Southeast Asia.

The ambivalent feelings of Vietnamese and Americans toward each other, which had greatly increased by 1969, revolved primarily around the question of our withdrawal. It may well be true that as a result of our inconclusive and even contradictory policies in earlier years, reflecting the larger Western failure to understand Asian ways of thinking, we not only unduly confused the Vietnamese but suppressed a natural revolution in South Vietnam, or even a normal evolutionary process. One can go back further and put the proposition differently. If it was possible that by dealing with Ho Chi Minh and the North Vietnamese in 1945-46 we could have encouraged an independent form of national Communism— embracing all of Vietnam and ultimately creating a Tito-like buffer state against the Chinese Communists—then it may also have been possible that once that opportunity was lost we could have achieved more by doing less after 1954. Which is also to say that, having supported the benighted colonial effort of the French and then replacing them as a foreign though not a comparable colonial influence, we perhaps unwittingly hindered rather than helped foster a separate development in the South. Even though this might from the outset have been dominated or guided by the tough Communist regime in the North, the South, with its unique traditions, might at least have retained an identity of its own under a more resilient type of Communist rule. The argument can be countered by considerable evidence that the Communists would simply have moved in and taken over, as they had elsewhere, and that any South Vietnamese show of independence would ultimately have been treated the same way that the Russians dealt with Czechoslovakia in 1968-69. Nevertheless, there are staunch Vietnamese nationalists, including pro-American ones, who have always believed in the case for separate identity and who remain convinced that, under different conditions and circumstances of Western involvement after the Second World War, such a development could have been inspired and prosecuted from the start. Other Vietnamese in the South have always admittedly operated in a different context, one of dependence rather than independence. Their attitudes and actions have contributed to the basic fragmentation and to the failure of nationalism in South Vietnam, and have made easier the process of Communist subversion. One manifestation of this in the latter nineteen-sixties was the growing power and prestige of an "American privileged" class of Vietnamese, who had replaced the earlier "French privileged" class and whose peculiar ambivalence about the Americans derived from their fear and resentment over our eagerness to leave: once the Americans were gone, they would not only lose their profits but might also lose their heads.

The contemporary American ambivalence about the Vietnamese has had different sources. Some Americans, including ever-revolving embassy officials, became so convinced of the growing strength and stability of the Thieu government in 1968, and of the new regime's democratic pretensions, that they deemed it not only capable of standing up to the Communists in a negotiatory contest but felt that it could hold its own in an electoral contest, too. Even when they conceded that the government left something to be desired, that inefficiency and corruption were still widespread, and that no national consensus had been created, these protagonists maintained that the Vietnamese had to stand on their own feet. They could do that only, it was argued, by learning how to confront a peremptory challenge. Others, more aware of the historic southern fragmentation, counseled further patience and tender counsel. Still others, epitomized by the outgoing Secretary of Defense Clark Clifford, who was chiefly responsible for persuading President Johnson to call the bombing halt, believed firmly that the time had come to cut bait, and had no compunctions about criticizing the South Vietnamese for dragging their feet on negotiations. In contrast, many American military men in Vietnam saw victory within grasp and maintained it was a tragic mistake to start negotiating so soon. Some other officers, more wary and bitter, felt that the military establishment had been betrayed, that it had allowed itself to be caught in a limited war with limited objectives on the vast Asian continent, and that, once committed, it had suffered from the restraints placed upon it—from bombing the North more fully and from applying greater military strength on the ground in South Vietnam and perhaps in North Vietnam, too. Whatever the generals thought, the American people were disposed to end the war as soon as possible, but most of them seemed to want to do it in such a way that the Vietnamese would not be abandoned and that the American willingness to lend support to the rest of Southeast Asia would be sustained, if restricted.

While these mixed and contradictory opinions among the South Vietnamese and the Americans sometimes served to help the Communists, it could not be said that the North Vietnamese and the Vietcong were having an easy time of it. After so many years of waging war, the North was obviously feeling the strains, emotionally and economically as well as physically, while the southern Communists and their supporters were suffering a growing demoralization and depletion of their ranks. Late in 1967 an important change in policy set the stage for the historic Tet offensive of January-February, 1968. This change had its origin in events starting in 1965 when the tide of the conflict began to change to our advantage militarily, even though the political advantage remained with the Communists or hung in the balance.

The Turning of the Screw

In March, 1965, when the United States had just begun its steady bombing of North Vietnam and had landed the first 3,500 Marines in the South, the war still looked favorable for the Communists. By the end of that year, when there were 150,000 American troops in South Vietnam, the Communists retained control over about half the population and somewhat more of the nation's territory, but they had probably already lost their chance to win the war militarily. They had hoped, during the summer of 1965, to have climaxed major victories in the central highlands and on the coastal plains by effectively cutting South Vietnam in two across its narrow belt. (It is interesting to note, however, that long afterward Le Duan, Secretary General of the Laodang [Communist Workers] Party, admitted that "the situation had developed more rapidly than we had anticipated," adding that "at that time we had not yet acquired adequate conditions . . . to make the puppet Army disintegrate in a basic and irretrievable manner.") By keeping open their lines of communication and supply eastward from Laos, southward across the Seventeenth Parallel, which divides North and South Vietnam, and westward from the China Sea, the Communists had expected to maintain military control of the situation while continuing to build up their political offensive in the countryside and in the cities. The quickly imposed superiority of American firepower and mobility—the latter primarily through the remarkable use of helicopters—had upset the Communist timetable and strategy and had proved the decisive factors in averting the "irretrievable" collapse of the South Vietnamese. This was notably demonstrated in 1965 in the big central highlands battles of Plei Me and the Ia Drang valley, on the coast in Binh Dinh and Phu Yen provinces, and on the Chu Lai peninsula in the northern part of the country. During the next three years, this advantage of mobility and ever greater firepower, including B-52 bombers from Guam and heavy naval guns firing inland from the sea, was proved repeatedly. The Vietcong and the North Vietnamese infiltrating into the South—and increasing from 1,000 a month to as many as 25,000—were constantly kept off balance and began to suffer large losses. Forced on the run by the Americans, who in due course attacked their long-held secret jungle bases where they had their principal headquarters, underground hospitals, and ammunition and food caches, the Communists lost the initiative and had to resort to hit-and-run tactics while trying to stay out of sight between assaults. Eventually, whole North Vietnamese divisions were forced to take sanctuary across the borders in Laos and Cambodia, where they could not be pursued and were safe from the bombers, and where they could rest and be resupplied.

The American mobile tactics, most significantly, deprived the Communists of the time they had always needed to "prepare the battlefield" for a major attack. This meticulous planning had included political and economic as well as military preparation—the injection of agitation and propaganda teams into the villages, the use of terror where necessary to obtain food and intelligence or avoid the rendering of them to the enemy, and detailed studies of terrain, among other things. The inability any longer to prepare for a battle in this fashion was perhaps best demonstrated in the spring and summer of 1966, during what the American Marines named the battles of Hastings and Prairie in Quang Tri Province, the northernmost in the country. Like the highlands fights the year before, the Quang Tri engagements, which lasted much longer, were an important turning point in the war. For the first time, the North Vietnamese sought to invade the South in strength directly across the six-mile-deep Demilitarized Zone, or D.M.Z., and to capture both Quang Tri and Thua Thien, the province below it, of which the ancient city of Hué is the capital. The North Vietnamese Army, or N.V.A., had depended on their Vietcong supporters in the two provinces to give them intelligence and, even more importantly, to store rice and other food in various secret places. But during the spring of 1966, in a series of so-called rice-protection campaigns known as Golden Fleece operations, the Marines and elements of the Army of the Republic of Vietnam, or A.R.V.N., had successfully kept the Vietcong from carrying out these vital preparatory tasks. During the same period, beginning in March, General William C. Westmoreland, the commander of the American forces in Vietnam, and his intelligence staff had slowly accumulated evidence of the forthcoming D.M.Z. attack from several sources. These included reports from local agents and ordinary peasants of North Vietnamese units moving separately and gradually through the D.M.Z. into Quang Tri and Thua Thien; in mid-May a deserter from North Vietnamese Division 324B, the major invasion force, reported that his unit, which had just crossed the Ben Hai River in the middle of the zone and moved into South Vietnam, was supposed to explore routes and suitable base areas for the main elements of the division. When the battle was joined, in July, the Americans had enough information to blunt the Communists' attack from the start, and the North Vietnamese could never gain the upper hand; the Marines were able to jump their battalions around by helicopter, putting out fires wherever they flared up and finally forcing the Communists to move back across the D.M.Z. into North Vietnam. In the ensuing two years, they repeatedly tried to cross the D.M.Z. again and mount a major offensive in Quang Tri. While for several months they pinned down a large Marine force at Khe Sanh, a mountain base in the western part of the province, and caused considerable casualties by artillery shelling of this and other Marine bases, the Communists were never able to make much headway, and in their abortive efforts they suffered much heavier losses than the Americans.

As the United States sent more troops to Vietnam—by the end

of 1966 there were 350,000 in the country, and the peak of 545,000 was reached in mid-1968—they increasingly took over the burden of fighting the so-called main-force Communist elements, while the South Vietnamese were assigned the tasks of pursuing the regional and local guerrillas and providing security for the government's pacification programs. By then, enjoying somewhere between a three- and four-to-one edge in combined manpower, including some fifty thousand Koreans and smaller contingents of Australians, New Zealanders, and Thais, as well as about 700,000 armed South Vietnamese, the Allies were able to prove that the traditionally accepted ten-to-one ratio for successfully engaging a hidden jungle-based enemy could be reduced through the overwhelming use of techniques of modern warfare. Successful engagement, however, was one thing, and eliminating the enemy and breaking up his political apparatus was another. The "search-and-destroy" operations of the Americans undoubtedly turned the tide of the war, but the corollary formula of "clear and hold" was less successful. Invariably, an area—even a ridge line or a single hill—was fought for and captured, frequently at the cost of heavy casualties, only to be reoccupied by the Communists once the United States forces had been withdrawn and ferried by air to another battle, perhaps two hundred miles away. This resulted in the Communists' regaining much of their control over key parts of the country. The inability of the Allies to remain and pacify these areas, as in Binh Dinh Province, for example, traditionally a cradle of Vietnamese revolt, made the people doubt the government's purpose and led them to continue helping the Communists, willingly or unwillingly. Thus, in spite of isolated examples of successful follow-up security measures and social and economic development, among them some exemplary American and South Vietnamese combined operations, the Allies were seldom able to capitalize on their military victories, and the war consequently drifted into a state of irresolution. Whether another 400,000 or 500,000 American troops would have made any difference is problematical. Probably they would have altered the balance further, especially as the Vietcong experienced more difficulties in recruiting replacements for losses, but it is doubtful that the difference would have proved decisive, particularly in view of the ability of the North Vietnamese to continue infiltrating large elements into the country despite the American bombings.

Political Half-Measures

Whatever victories they won in the fluid war, the Allies' failure to achieve more than they did politically was the vital factor in producing a stalemate. The two elements, military and political, could not be separated. While there were many things the Americans might have done to stimulate action in both fields, the political failure was primarily a South Vietnamese one. It involved above all the insufficient and improper use of manpower, a lack of organization and, in the final analysis, of will. Among the specific shortcomings was the inability to come to grips with military reorganization, which itself was a political problem. Back in 1954 the United States Army set about creating a conventional force in Vietnam, ill-equipped to fight the Communists' type of unconventional warfare; fifteen years later there was still nothing resembling a guerrilla force of any size and strength among the South Vietnamese, and in this sense the whole American effort could be compared to a series of blood transfusions without any attempt to operate and seek the source of the disease. The Army was always a political force in its own right, and the general officers who ran it were loath to brook any interference from the Americans that might affect their own power structures. As a result, A.R.V.N. continued to suffer from lack of leadership, especially at the important junior-officer level, while political and family influence, to say nothing of corruption, remained rife throughout the Vietnamese military system. When the Americans, between 1962 and 1965, made some efforts to advise on and reorganize the system, the Vietnamese, for the most part, paid no attention or merely gave lip service to American suggestions. After the Americans assumed the brunt of the major fighting, the advisory role slackened, though when General Creighton Abrams became General Westmoreland's deputy in 1967, and later took over the command from him, efforts were resumed to improve the caliber of A.R.V.N., to make the Regional (provincial) Forces more efficient by giving them M-16 rifles, to improve the quality of the Popular Forces assigned to pacification and local defense duties, and to increase the number of National Police and weld them into a common offensive and defensive scheme.

What was still talked about but never attempted was a complete revision of the whole military structure that would conceivably have enabled the South Vietnamese to fight the Communists more effectively, in the Communists' own style. Such a revamping would have called for the abolition of the four basic Army corps into which the country was divided, and which for years were separate fiefdoms of the generals who commanded them, and for the breakdown of the Army's eleven divisions into mobile battle groups operating at brigade size in regions more or less corresponding to the Communists' military zones. Battalions and companies would function at the provincial and district level, with village self-defense elements protecting their own communities with the help of the Regional and Popular Forces. When he took office in January, 1968, President Thieu pledged himself to reorganize both the military and the civilian administrations, as several of his predecessors had also promised, but he did little or nothing to make good on his pledge, chiefly because it would have threatened his own power base. Early in 1969 American officers noted an over-all improvement in the aggressiveness and fighting capabilities of the Vietnamese armed forces, but even then only one division and some elite elements were rated as excellent, two of the eleven divisions were still considered downright poor, and the rest were improving at varying rates. Many thoughtful young lieutenants and captains, as well as some field officers, were fully aware of the need to overhaul the entire structure, but like their young counterparts in the administrative field, including scores of bright students with foreign university postgraduate degrees in special fields of study, they were ignored or lost in the bureaucratic shuffle. When they spoke their minds, they were invariably regarded as upstarts or troublemakers and demoted to lesser jobs.

If the failure to reorganize the creaky military and government machinery represented an inability to deal with traditionalism and with the stubborn resistance to change that was so characteristic of the survival-minded Vietnamese ruling circles, the failure to prosecute more successfully the many programs designed to create a "social revolution" in South Vietnam was another commentary on the over-all ineffectiveness of the various Saigon regimes. The reconstruction and development of war-torn hamlets and villages was basic to the struggle to "win the hearts and minds of the people," as the cliché went. Here was an area of activity in which the resources of the government, backed by those of the Americans, were far superior to those of the Communists, except with regard to two vital elements—political motivation and leadership. Part of the South Vietnamese difficulty was administrative; at one point, early in 1966, when the Americans sought to rationalize the program of rural development, or Revolutionary Development as it was eventually misnamed, there were no fewer than thirty-nine different Vietnamese groups or agencies engaged in the attempt to bring reforms and benefits to the villages and to provide them with some degree of security. Basically, however, the lack of progress through the years, dating back to the Strategic Hamlet Program of Diem and his mystique-ridden brother, Ngo Dinh Nhu, was due to the lack of good political conception and effective organization. The failure was at least twofold: it was due to insufficient covert activity to match the secret tactics of the Communists and to complement the overt programs of assistance the government had at its disposal, and it was predicated on a vertical rather than a horizontal approach. That is, instead of beginning at the hamlet and village level, where some degree of quiet preparation should have been carried out first among the peasants in order to remove their deeply imbued suspicions of the government, the series of overlapping programs were always superimposed from the top down—from Saigon through the traditional channels of corps and division commanders, to the provinces and districts, and to the villages and hamlets.

Initially, a small group of American counterinsurgency experts had tried to avoid this, working with a number of Vietminh officers who were versed in Communist methods of indoctrination and propaganda. As far back as the spring of 1964, a program had been started to train six-man covert groups known as Advanced Political Action Teams, consisting mostly of ex-Vietcong agents, to enter Communist-controlled hamlets and, dressed in black pajamas like the Vietcong, to engage in armed counterinsurgency; once they had killed or dispersed the handful of Communists in a hamlet, the team members would stay on the scene and help the people harvest their rice and repair whatever damage had been done. Later, this scheme was enlarged and young men were selected from hamlets and villages to undergo training at Vung Tau, on the China Sea near Saigon, after which they were sent back to their native

places to conduct political and development programs as members
of what were then called Political Action Teams, or People's Action
Teams. These were the genesis of the fifty-nine-man Revolutionary
Development (R.D.) Teams that began to operate in 1966-67, and
by 1969 there were some fifty thousand individual R.D. workers
assigned for the most part to priority areas—around Saigon, on the
central coast in Binh Dinh, around Danang, and to parts of the
delta. Perhaps two-thirds of these teams returned, after their thirteen weeks' course at Vung Tau, to work in or near their home
areas. This was practical enough, but it did not prevent the R.D.
cadres from acquiring a government stigma, and too often they
were mistrusted, even by their own villagers, particularly in contested places where Communist reprisals for cooperating with the
government were common. This is not to say that these teams
failed to accomplish many worthwhile projects and to instill a
fervor that had been sorely lacking, but, like so much else the
Americans became involved in, the scheme became overstructured.

In 1967 a system was devised by Robert Komer, the American
pacification director, to rate about two-thirds of the nation's 12,500
hamlets where the government had established some influence on a
scale of "A" to "E," by computers, according to eighteen indicators,
half having to do with the villages' state of security and the other
half with development factors. By this time the American military
command had taken over the rural development program on the
American side, and while Komer, as General Westmoreland's deputy for pacification, had striven to maintain a sound civilian image,
the computerized scheme had resulted in a weakening of the earlier personal and local quality of the program. There were still some
covert aspects of it that were run by the American Central Intelligence Agency, such as the operation of ten-man assassination
teams called Provincial Reconnaissance Units, but most experienced counterinsurgency experts felt that the program had become
too mechanized to be politically effective. A new counterintelli-
gence operation known as Phoenix, which brought together all the
Vietnamese and American intelligence facilities from the district
level up, began to achieve some success in apprehending members
of the Vietcong infrastructure (V.C.I.), but it could not be said, at
the start of 1969, that either the Revolutionary Development or the
Phoenix program had yet made notable progress except in hamlets

where the government could provide some reasonable degree of security. Perhaps two-fifths of the nation's hamlets could be included in that category, but even in many of these the amount of consistent security varied greatly.

The Failure of Reform

If the inability to make more headway on pacification was half of the political failure in Vietnam, the other half was the even greater inability of all the post-Diem governments to create any sort of consensus among the diverse factions and groups, including the various religious elements—the Buddhists, the Catholics, the Hoa Hao and the Cao Dai sects. As negotiations approached, this incapacity to foster unity within the Saigon regime's own ranks became an increasingly serious problem, and it inevitably added to the growing confusion and debate about how to deal with the National Liberation Front. The Communists, on the other hand, knew what they wanted, and if the initiative was taken away from them militarily, they did not lose their ability to prepare the political battlefield. This preparation was simply a further reflection of the incontrovertible fact that, under that redoubtable superorganizer Ho Chi Minh, the Communists had captured the nationalist movement of the country back in 1945, killed or dispersed the anti- or non-Communist leaders who had originally joined them in the broad Vietminh Front, and ever since had guided the course of the Vietnamese revolution. It was also significant that the dozen or so members of the ruling Politburo in Hanoi, whether they belonged to the pro-Chinese or pro-Russian factions, had stuck together more tightly than any other Communist ruling body in the world. Despite some internal conflicts, they were always able to shift their military and political strategy as they saw fit—advancing, retreating, and modifying. On the other hand, countless successive governments in the South, under the French, under Emperor Bao Dai, under Diem, under the seemingly endless procession of military and shadow civilian bodies and leaders—juntas, councils, troikas, directories, Chiefs of State, Presidents, and Prime Ministers— sought unavailingly to contend with this precisely steered Communist machine. And countless political experiments, from hand-picked advisory councils and national assemblies under the French and Diem to hamlet and village councils and the new National Assembly, elected in 1967, failed to rally or to inspire the country or to counter effectively the better-organized, more single-minded Communist apparatus.

The 1967 elections in South Vietnam, and the vote for a Constituent Assembly that preceded them in September, 1966, must be considered against the backdrop of the coup that overthrew Diem and against the so-called Struggle Movement in the spring of 1966 that saw the defeat and political withdrawal from the scene of the militant Buddhists. The protracted power contest, marked by several coups and attempted coups and culminating in the ascendancy of Nguyen Cao Ky as Prime Minister and of Nguyen Van Thieu as Chief of State, served to debilitate further whatever will was left in the South to create some sort of solidarity among the bickering military, religious, and political groups. The fact that the contest was allowed to continue for so long without a firmer American effort to ameliorate it, and even to force a solution sooner, may be regarded as one of the foremost failures of American policy in Vietnam. By the time Thieu was elected President and Ky Vice President, energies had been dissipated, emotions had worn thin, and a new cynicism had set in. As for the Struggle Movement, which was both a symptom and a cause of the disunity, it developed as it did chiefly because of the infighting among the military, although there were deeper causes that reached to the very roots of the revolutionary crisis in Vietnam. In being allowed to come to a violent head and to be resolved as it was, it did nothing so much as to exacerbate regional as well as personal and religious differences and hand the Communists a perfect issue to use for their own advantage.

The Struggle Movement, initially begun as a campaign of demonstrations and boycotts by the Buddhists for the election of a civilian government, was then subverted by the Communists. However, from the outset it drew together a whole cross-section of critics of what was then the ruling military Directory, a group of ten generals often in conflict among themselves and with Ky, who was Premier. The ground swell of opposition to the Directory was concentrated in Danang and Hué, in central Vietnam, where the militant Buddhists headed by Thich (Venerable) Tri Quang had their strength, but it quickly spread to other cities, including Saigon. The role of the enigmatic Tri Quang was always much debated. He was one of the leaders of the Buddhist campaign against Diem, during part of which he took asylum in the American Embassy, but in subsequent years he became increasingly anti-American, feeling that Washington's policies of supporting one general or group of generals after another had delayed the democratic process in Vietnam, out of which he hoped the Buddhists would emerge as a new political force. Frequently accused of being close to the Communists (although some members of his family had been persecuted by the Vietminh), Tri Quang actually saw himself primarily as an *éminence grise;* if his political opinions seemed to parallel those of the Vietcong, he was apparently conscious of what he was doing, and he thought he would be able to outwit the Communists —an error of judgment many men in similar circumstances have made.

Early in 1966, as the Struggle Movement gained adherents among the students as well as the Buddhists in central Vietnam, and as the Vietcong began infiltrating it, Premier Ky, with the support of the Directory, moved against it—first abortively, in early April, and then successfully, in May. His response was partly motivated by a desire to eliminate one of the four independent-minded "war lord" corps commanders, General Nguyen Chanh Thi, who ran the I Corps area, including Hué and Danang. Thi was ousted, but before being banished from the country he emerged as something of a popular and Buddhist hero. The role of the Americans in the whole affair was a questionable one. Eager to encourage the development of civilian rule through elections, they nevertheless helped provoke the crisis by urging Ky privately to get rid of Thi—or at least they condoned Ky's action on practical power-play grounds—and then they urged him to crack down on the Buddhists who had got out of hand. In the second attack on the religious rebels, which ended with a bitter siege of a number of pagodas and with the 1st Division and some other units of A.R.V.N. siding with the dissidents in what almost became a full-fledged civil war, American transport planes ferried Ky's paratroopers north. Ironically, having been in the vanguard of the campaign for civilian elections, the militant Buddhists, after being defeated and having many of their followers jailed, called for a boycott of the Constituent Assembly vote in the fall of 1966. The boycott was only partially successful and the Buddhists participated more fully in the subsequent elections, but by 1969 they had not yet re-emerged as a meaningful political force.

The Constituent Assembly elections, in which 81 percent of the registered voters in the 55 percent of the country under government control participated, were widely regarded as a demonstration of the Vietnamese eagerness to take part in the democratic process. This was perhaps too sanguine a view. There was very little actual interest in the forthcoming new Constitution itself, and the candidates for the most part discussed matters that had a greater political appeal, such as food shortages and the rising cost of living, local security in battle areas, and the hopes for peace. Nevertheless, after an initial lethargy, the new Assembly of 117 delegates got down to work on writing a new Constitution under the watchful eye of the military Directory, which through friendly delegates controlled approximately half of the Assembly and maintained a considerable veto power over its deliberations and final product. The Constitution, as drafted and accepted after prolonged discussion, set up a strong executive with some checks and balances held by the legislature and the new judiciary. It was subsequently criticized by Vietnamese experts on a number of grounds, mainly these: that it left the Prime Minister, who was appointed by the President, in too weak and anomalous a position, even as an administrator; that the bicameral legislature was too divisive and ineffective a parliamentary instrument, and that in Vietnam's state of development a single chamber would have been better; and that a clause prohibiting "every activity designed to publicize or carry out Communism" would make it difficult if not impossible to foster any legal and workable accommodation with the National Liberation Front.

Thieu and Ky, despite their pledge to the Americans that they would not provoke a new crisis by running against each other for President, both became candidates. After a typically Vietnamese secret meeting of all the generals in June, 1967—a three-day session marked by tears, accusations, and recriminations, as well as by intrigue—Thieu emerged as the winner, heading the military ticket with Ky running with him for Vice President. The Americans, behind the scenes, encouraged this "solution," which scarcely proved to be a satisfactory one. The more popular, if more irascible and unpredictable, Ky never fully forgave the United States for dropping him in favor of the more stable, if also more crafty and suspicious, Thieu. In the September, 1967, elections the two uncomfortably linked generals won about a third of the total vote, and the surprising showing of the peace candidate, Truong Dinh Dzu, who finished second with about half as many votes as Thieu, drew world-wide attention. Dzu and eight other defeated Presidential candidates claimed that the balloting was rigged, disputing the judgment of a group of American and other foreign observers who briefly watched and overly praised the process. The consensus of more experienced Americans and of most Vietnamese was that, with some discrepancies, particularly in the final juggled choice of six ten-man slates for the Senate, the election was relatively fair but not particularly impressive; the fact that Dzu, even though somewhat of a charlatan, was later jailed for his peace activities did nothing to increase Vietnam's new democratic image.

The assumption, primarily an American one, that the vote would have any salutary effect on the war, or on the internal political situation, was regarded by most Vietnamese as unwarranted and unrealistic. Part of this reaction could be attributed to national cynicism, but much more was due to the conviction that the whole elective process had simply been an American-directed performance with a Vietnamese cast. American officials argued in its favor that at least it replaced a military junta with a legally elected government—one that could negotiate on a more nearly equal and a more honest footing with the Communists. The case against having held the elections so quickly was a more subtle and substantial one. Despite the logic of establishing some framework of legitimacy, most experienced observers maintained that more harm than good was likely to result from force-feeding democracy to the Vietnamese at such a chaotic moment in their national life. It was pointed out that a third of the country, held by the Vietcong, was unrepresented and that no adequate groundwork for real representative government had been prepared in the two-thirds where the voting did take place. This was said to be true both of the countryside, where security was still spotty and the Revolutionary Development program had only had a scattered impact, and of the cities, where the intellectuals, professional people, and the various religious elements—if they had had more time—might at least have created some sort of political framework and party system before the voting occurred.

Beyond the fact that the elections had not provoked much popular enthusiasm, what happened afterward appeared to justify much of the criticism of the whole procedure. Thieu and Ky immediately began a new contest for power which was quickly exacerbated by their respective entourages. This new infighting, which went on for many months, demonstrated that there was not one government, as had been hoped, but a whole series of governments and would-be governments. At the top was Thieu. Sitting alongside him, as Secretary General of the newly established office of the Presidency, was Nguyen Van Huong, a former leader of the old Dai Viet (nationalist) Party and a close friend of Thieu's who had power pretensions of his own and, as a sort of Assistant President, sought to express them by overseeing the work of the Cabinet. The first Prime Minister, a lawyer named Nguyen Van Loc, chosen as a sop to Ky, proved weak and ineffective. His successor, the popular Tran Van Huong, an elderly man who had held the prime ministership briefly in 1964-65 and who had finished fourth in the race for President, was widely respected for his integrity, and many felt he should have been prevailed upon, despite his reluctance, to take Loc's spot originally. By the time he agreed to become Prime Minister, his area of maneuver had been reduced as a result of the Thieu-Ky struggle, in which Thieu, with the increasing backing of the Americans, gradually emerged the victor. Ky, his office of the Vice Presidency having few constitutional prerogatives to begin with, had to depend on keeping his own men in enough jobs to maintain his influence. His options were slowly reduced, particularly after his friend, the chief of the National Police, General Nguyen Ngoc Loan, was dismissed, and other officers close to him were either dismissed, killed in action, or resigned. In addition to these individual power centers, the four corps commanders, though they were supposedly shorn of their political duties, remained strong military-political figures; there was a further vestigial influence held by the former National Leadership Council of generals, and by a smaller "inner" military committee headed by Thieu.

Below this executive area, the Senators and Representatives, who had their own internal conflicts, sought to express their respective prerogatives vis-à-vis Thieu or Ky. Thieu tended first to ignore them. When this simply aggravated the Assembly further, the President backed off and started to deal with it more carefully, like a man with a nagging wife. Increasingly, as Thieu gained strength and confidence, he shared his thoughts with fewer and fewer people, even among the members of his own entourage. Unlike Diem, who had had his brother Nhu to advise and ultimately to guide him, Thieu seemed to trust no one. He was his own Nhu. Even when he did solicit the opinions of others, including those of his brother Nguyen Van Kieu, he remained as suspicious as he was cautious. As he made more and more decisions by himself, he slowly gained a mystique of his own. "Thieu will never be a statesman, but he is becoming a politician," one of his less ardent Vietnamese admirers grudgingly admitted.

In the period after the elections, when I talked with old Vietnamese friends both in and out of the government, it was impossible not to sense that they were becoming more and more impatient with the Americans' continuing miscomprehension of Vietnamese attitudes and Vietnamese affairs. Much of this was due to the constant turnover of American personnel and some of it to a seemingly deliberate ingenuousness on the part of American officials. At the same time, the Vietnamese resented their growing dependence on the Americans, militarily and economically; they recognized that although the Americans were not colonialists, there had evolved in Vietnam a colonial ambiance that sometimes seemed worse than colonialism itself. In spite of the improved coordination between the American and Vietnamese armed forces, the Americans were increasingly fighting their own war and the Vietnamese theirs. If a true joint command was ever advisable (and it may once have been), it no longer seemed possible. Economically, the United States had managed to shore up the country artificially, saving it from a total economic breakdown by pumping in a variety of miscellaneous exports to soak up excess piastres; by building up the infrastructure of bases and harbors, which furnished well-paid employment to the Vietnamese; and by bringing in some much-needed "crisis commodities," especially rice. The Vietnamese had little to say about all this, and their main reaction had just been to hope that it would ultimately do more good than harm. At the same time, having been prodded by the United States into making an experiment with democracy, they at least wanted to carry it out in their own way—which meant they might listen to American advice if it was realistic or consistent. But, in the post-election period, American inconsistency became a particular grievance. For instance, in the matter of facilitating peace negotiations —which was part of the rationale for holding elections in the first place—the Vietnamese found it hard to understand why, having encouraged the new government to make its own approaches to Hanoi or to members of the National Liberation Front in its own time and way, the United States should almost immediately after the elections have begun a whole fresh set of private maneuvers designed to bring Hanoi to the bargaining table. "Either Washington wants us to make our accommodations or it doesn't," one of my Vietnamese friends commented. "If it does, then it should at least give us an opportunity to do so. The Americans should stop talking so much, both about peace and about our great democratic prospects."

Background to Tet

By the fall of 1967, coinciding with the confusing postelection period in South Vietnam, the North Vietnamese were already planning their astonishing 1968 Tet offensive—a violent assault on Saigon and Hué and a hundred other cities and towns. The offensive, which represented a real turning point in the war, although politically more than militarily, was a combination of desperation and daring. Not until the end of the war, if ever, will we know what the Communists really expected to achieve. Their ultimate goal was undoubtedly to provide a General Uprising in the cities that would bring about the climactic collapse of the Saigon government and the establishment of new revolutionary committees which would then negotiate for peace—*both* with the National Liberation Front and with the Americans. However, despite their preliminary agitation and propaganda and their impassioned last-minute exhortations and instructions, it seems unlikely that they believed the so-called General Attack would result in such an uprising. The

Tet offensive was probably viewed as only *the first step*—at least this is how the leading members of the Politburo in Hanoi and the top generals must have regarded it, though not all of them were by any means in agreement over strategy and tactics. Ironically, the offensive was a military failure, one that caused losses far greater than the sizable ones General Vo Nguyen Giap, who planned the so-called 1967-68 winter-spring campaign, had allowed for; but politically and psychologically, the attack brought dividends the Communists had not anticipated. It led directly to the partial halt in the bombing of North Vietnam at the end of March, 1968, and then to a complete halt and to the formal beginning of the period of "fighting and negotiating at the same time" at the end of October.

What were the circumstances that produced the Tet offensive, how was it planned and executed, and what were its specific failures and accomplishments?*

One must first try to comprehend the predicament the North Vietnamese found themselves in by the spring of 1967, or even earlier. The American dispatch of troops to Vietnam two years before had completely upset the Communists' three-stage plan for victory in accordance with the strategy they had used to defeat the French. This now-famous concept, elucidated mainly by Giap and by Truong Chinh, a top member of the Politburo, was based, first, on a so-called period of contention or defensive guerrilla warfare, during which the guerrillas gradually would increase their probes of enemy-held areas and take some offensive action. Next came the period of "equilibrium," during which, as Truong Chinh wrote, "our military and political aim is to wear out the enemy's forces, annihilate them piecemeal, sabotage, disturb, give the enemy no

* In reconstructing the situation that obtained before Tet, in analyzing what took place and appraising the results, militarily and politically as well as psychologically, I have depended primarily on a careful reading of scores of captured North Vietnamese and Vietcong documents; on intelligence reports of the offensive and its aftermath (and of the subsequent one in May, 1968) that were made available to me; on conversations with a number of Communist defectors and prisoners; and on interviews with many American and Vietnamese officials and private observers. I am also indebted to Douglas Pike, a United States Foreign Service Officer and author of *Viet Cong* and of numerous articles and papers on the National Liberation Front, and to P. J. Honey, lecturer at the School of Oriental and African Studies of the University of London, who is a specialist on North Vietnam.

peace to exploit the people easily." This stage was essentially one of growing mobile warfare and of preparation for the third stage, that of "the general counteroffensive," when the enemy would be placed on the defensive and, as Truong Chinh explained, the aim would be to have "the whole country rise up and go over to the offensive on all fronts, completely defeat the enemy, and achieve true independence and unification."

The American counteroffensive in 1965 and 1966 threw this tested timetable way off and forced the North Vietnamese and their Vietcong accomplices, directed by Hanoi through the Central Office for South Vietnam and the People's Revolutionary Party, reluctantly to make some drastic re-evaluations. This reappraisal began in mid-1966. Despite the dedicated desire of men like Giap, Ho Chi Minh, and Premier Pham Van Dong to bring the war to a successful conclusion and to unify Vietnam in their lifetime, it was apparent that events were moving slowly, that the Communists had not even succeeded in advancing into the second period of "equilibrium," and that some readjustment was necessary in the face of the tremendous American superiority in firepower and mobility. Such a reappraisal called for an admission that the war would remain more "protracted" than had been hoped. In the words of Ho Chi Minh himself at the time, it "may last another five, ten, twenty years or longer." Instead of forcing the issue into the counteroffensive stage, with the odds against them, the Communists thought of engaging indefinitely, if need be, in what Douglas Pike, the American expert on the Vietcong, has aptly described as "neo-revolutionary guerrilla war." This concept, essentially one of compromise and adaptation to the awesome challenges posed by American might, envisioned the achievement of ultimate victory at the second stage of the classic three stages. Although Giap was still insisting, as he always had, that victory would be won on the battlefield and not through negotiations, other members of the Politburo in Hanoi were already thinking in terms of fighting and negotiating at the same time. The neo-revolutionary guerrilla war concept was adaptable to the fight-talk strategy—in fact, it virtually assumed a prolonged period of such fighting and negotiating during which the Americans, Hanoi hoped, would become increasingly impatient to get out of Vietnam. While much of the difference may have been semantic, the new strategy seemed to be an admission that the third stage of the originally planned counteroffensive might never be reached, at least not in the classic sense in which it had been employed against the French.

The reasons for this change of attitude were apparent. Nothing so much served to underline the problems the Communists were facing as the attrition they were already experiencing in their paramilitary guerrilla ranks in the South—the basic regional and local forces which were supposed to be the revolutionary shock troops. Though they did all they could to rebuild these elements, they were already confronted, by early 1967, with the apparent need to send more and more North Vietnamese troops into South Vietnam, and to try to blend these fresh and inexperienced forces with the depleted guerrillas as well as with the main Vietcong force, which wasn't always easy. Thus they found themselves on the horns of a growing military dilemma: on the one hand, they were engaged with the Americans in a number of costly major battles, in the highlands and on the central plateau and south of the D.M.Z., and, at the same time, they were experiencing difficulty in reorienting their main force and guerrilla elements in a manner that would enable them to fight an effective second-stage mobile type of war.

There is another factor that at this point was deeply troubling the North Vietnamese—the Sino-Soviet dispute and its effect on the prosecution of the war. It was obvious, as captured documents and letters showed, that the conflict of the two Communist giants was deeply disturbing to the hardheaded men in Hanoi, both in theoretical and practical terms. The Chinese, as is generally known, favored the protracted-war theory and believed that the time was not yet ripe for negotiations. For this reason, Peking was against sending large North Vietnamese troop elements to the South, believing the guerrillas should handle the situation. They spoke of the war lasting at least "seven years" before they, and other Socialist nations, would be in a position to come to Hanoi's rescue, "using all types of weapons and heeding no frontiers," as General Nguyen Van Vinh, chairman of the National Reunification Commission of North Vietnam, which directed the war in the South, somewhat sarcastically said in describing Peking's views. General Vinh, though he admitted the possibility of "four more years" of fighting to achieve decisive victory, went more directly to the point when he said that Hanoi's policy was "to continue fighting until such time as we can fight and negotiate at the same time," adding that "while negotiating, we will continue to fight even more vigorously." He also said, prophetically, that "it is possible that the North will conduct negotiations while the South continues fighting, and that the South will also participate in negotiations while continuing to fight." Vinh left little doubt that he was far more appreciative of Moscow's position than Peking's, vis-à-vis Hanoi. He admitted quite openly that "We are worried" about the split in the Communist ranks and remarked that "We cannot just sit by and wait until the Socialist camp is united to achieve decisive victory." He may have gone further than the Russians liked when he declared that "the Soviet Union will support us under all conditions, whether we fight, or negotiate, or fight and negotiate," but he left little doubt of his lack of appreciation for China's views when he said, "China gives us wholehearted support, but she has weak points," including her "technical ability [which] is inferior to that of the Soviet Union."

The North Vietnamese were quite aware of their necessary dependence on China, not only for their basic guns and ammunition but for assembly plants and for manpower to help repair the bomb damage, as well as for extra food to bolster the shaken agricultural economy in North Vietnam. But in their mood of justified exasperation they did not relish Chinese interference in the field of strategy, nor did they relish the prospect of fighting for seven years, or longer, simply to wait for the time when the Chinese came to their rescue—something no Vietnamese would ever welcome anyway. At the same time, while grateful for the help the Russians were giving them, particularly sophisticated weapons such as antiaircraft guns and missiles, Hanoi did not relish Moscow urging negotiations *too* soon. Had it not been so serious, the situation would have had its comic overtones. In fact, in a speech he made in mid-1966, General Vinh found himself talking out of both sides of his mouth when he said, as P. J. Honey has quoted him, "The contents of the guidelines and strategy involving protracted fighting and the contents of achieving decisive success within a relatively short period of time are not mutually contradictory," and then added, moments later, "In a resistance war it is right to speak of protracted war and self-reliance, and the urge to fight and win quickly represents a rightist tendency."

The near-trauma the North Vietnamese thus found themselves in became more apparent. As they increasingly stressed their self-reliance ("Our attitude is very independent . . . we will follow neither Russia nor China . . . we ask for money and weapons only . . . we place our trust only in our own party," as Vinh insisted), Hanoi had to admit that the situation in South Vietnam was becoming "indecisive" and that the time had truly come for negotiating while also continuing to fight. Perhaps the key sentence in a speech General Vinh made while visiting the troops in the South was this: "In fighting while negotiating, the side which fights more strongly will compel the adversary to accept its conditions." Therein was an explanation for the startling reversal in strategy the Communists made early in 1967, when the Central Committee of the Laodang Party met in Hanoi and framed Resolution 13, which called for a "spontaneous uprising" in order to win "a decisive victory in the shortest time possible." In April, according to the testimony of top-level prisoners, at a secret meeting in the jungle northwest of Saigon, the important cadres of the South were informed of this monumental decision. They were also told that Pham Van Dong had traveled to Moscow and had obtained the Russians' pledge of continued military and economic aid, after they were informed of Hanoi's plans to fight and negotiate simultaneously. Le Duan had visited Peking at the same time and, not unexpectedly, had run into greater resistance; the Chinese were still insisting that the North Vietnamese continue fighting indefinitely, but Le Duan made it clear that the Laodang Central Committee, or more specifically its eleven-man Politburo, would stick to its decision. (It is worth noting here that, two years later, early in 1969, the Chinese had become far more amenable to the Hanoi viewpoint and seemed willing to accept the fight-talk strategy as the best way to get the Americans out of Vietnam eventually.)

As a southerner, and the principal creator of the Vietcong, who were the successors of the earlier Vietminh, Le Duan's political strategy had for years had its military complement in General Giap's three-stage program for victory in the South. Both men, as well as Truong Chinh, who followed the same line, had been criticized in the Politburo for the failures and defeats since the massive American intervention. The military commander in the South, General Nguyen Thi Chanh, also a Politburo member, had been responsible for implementing the old strategy until his death early in 1967 from what Hanoi said was a "heart attack" but what was apparently the result of a B-52 bomber attack on his jungle headquarters in Tay Ninh Province. His job was thereafter split up among two or three generals—the senior man was General Tran Do—while the political direction on the ground in the South was assigned to another veteran southern revolutionary, Pham Hung, a Politburo man who had for many years been a top security specialist. Giap, however, probably reassumed over-all direction of the southern military campaign and may have made a number of trips South himself. Certainly he was the author of the winter-spring campaign of 1967-68, which had three phases.

The first phase, in the October-December period, was an attempt to pin down large numbers of American troops below the D.M.Z. and at Loc Ninh and Dak To in the highlands near Cambodia. The battles that took place in these areas were in the classic mold, but they did not represent a counteroffensive strategy in the old sense. Giap's apparent aim was to force the Americans to send reinforcements into the mountains, thereby spreading themselves thin and permitting the Communists, among other things, to move back into the coastal regions. However, Giap suffered heavy losses, especially at Dak To, and he was unable to take advantage of the American troop shifts because he simply lacked enough men himself to reoccupy the key areas in Binh Dinh and Phu Yen provinces along the coast. He did achieve some psychological benefits by arousing further dissatisfaction in the United States over the seeming futility of the war—the idea of fighting bitterly for a hill, taking it, and then abandoning it when the fight was over. During this first phase Giap also stepped up his attacks against Allied air bases, communications and transportation facilities, and logistics centers like ammunition dumps and warehouses.

While this was going on, Le Duan and Giap were preparing for the second phase, the Tet offensive. In this phase, in contrast to the almost exclusive use of North Vietnamese troops in Phase 1, Giap used some seventy thousand troops of the southern Liberation Army. By attacking a great many places throughout the country with relatively few forces in each case, he hoped to seize as many district and provincial capitals as possible and hold them as long as he could, with the basic aim of proving that the South Vietnamese

troops were incapable of defending the people. When that happened, Giap hoped, there would be mass uprisings in Saigon and
other places; though it remained doubtful that he and his associates in Hanoi expected the full *Khoi Nghia*, or General Uprising,
they probably did believe that the attacks would arouse more popular support than they did, and that this would set the stage for the
third phase, scheduled for the spring of 1968, to last until June. By
then, Giap hoped, he would have shaken the American command
structure, whose troops he figured to hold off during Tet by using
the North Vietnamese as blocking forces around Saigon, Hué, and
the other major cities. He then foresaw a final "set piece" battle
that would cause the Americans to become fully disillusioned and
give up the war. At that point he also hoped to incite the final
collapse of the Saigon government, though it was conceded this
might take more time. As a subsequent Communist analysis put it,
representing Giap's viewpoint, "Unless a major victory is achieved,
nothing can be expected from the diplomatic struggle. . . . The
diplomatic struggle is intended to bolster the military and political
struggles only, and not to be a substitute for them." If the General
Offensive could not be carried off, the document concluded, the
only two alternatives would be renewed and protracted war or the
acceptance of a coalition government.

In understanding this shift in Communist strategy, there are two
other factors that must be taken into account as reasons for Le
Duan's and Giap's risking it: the situation in North Vietnam and
the relationship between Hanoi and the National Liberation Front.
Although North Vietnam had remained a "young country"—75
percent of the population in 1967 was said to be under thirty-
five—and although only about 11 percent of the total available
manpower was engaged in military duty, according to American
analysts, there was no doubt that the pressures of the long war,
and especially of the American bombing, had caused considerable
economic deterioration and dislocation. The effect of all this on the
population, estimated at about nineteen million, was "cumulative,"
as Honey has noted. Diversion of labor on a local basis for repair
work, he pointed out in a summary written in the fall of 1967, had
given way to more permanent reassignment of workers in agriculture and industry to the tasks of repairing the mounting bomb
damage. Furthermore, there was the job of building seven thou-

sand antiaircraft gun sites and hauling shells from the Chinese frontier or the ports to those sites. Aside from the fact that ordinary production output suffered accordingly, the people were experiencing increasing shortages of food and clothing, as well as medicines. In spite of censorship, they had begun writing to their relatives abroad and even in South Vietnam for assistance (I read several such letters in Saigon in the second half of 1967). It was difficult to tell how long the stoic North Vietnamese would continue to fight unquestioningly for the revolutionary goals they undoubtedly still believed in, but the fact that trouble might be brewing was evidenced by the speeches of a number of Politburo members, which already were warning about the lack of sufficient zeal among cadres, about the prevalence of profiteering, and about black market practices. It may thus have been true, as Honey said, that Foreign Minister Nguyen Duy Trinh deliberately lied in January, 1968, just before the Tet attack, when he declared that a stop in the bombing would lead to a discussion of "relevant questions" concerning peace; but there was no doubt that the North Vietnamese were hurting, and that they were particularly eager for the bombing to end. The General Offensive at Tet was therefore decided on, at least in part, as the first step to obtain a cessation of the bombing—and to that degree it worked.

As for the Hanoi-N.L.F. relationship, this, too, was undoubtedly a source of some worry to the Politburo. The key date in the history of the relationship was January 1, 1962. It was on that day that the People's Revolutionary Party was founded. The P.R.P. was described as the "Marxist-Leninist element of the National Liberation Front," and, privately, members of the Laodang in the South were told that the P.R.P. thenceforward would represent the party there. According to what Pike and other analysts have since concluded, Hanoi decided to set up the P.R.P. as a hard "inner pyramidal core," reinforcing the loose Front pyramid with its village base, because the North Vietnamese felt that a sense of "ideological isolation" was growing in the South and that this could lead to separatism. (The Russians, incidentally, had warned of this.) The P.R.P. moved slowly into a position of command, emphasizing a new proletarian line, which the predominantly peasant population may have found strange but which did serve to tighten discipline and provide a fresh source of faith and doctrine. The P.R.P.

gradually assumed direct control in all Front villages, with P.R.P. cadres handing down orders to subgroups and local bodies, and establishing all the policy guidelines and directives. In a paper in 1967 which projected the possibilities of accommodation in the South between the Front and the Saigon government, Pike wrote:

> The P.R.P. is a Janus-faced organization. In the South, it insists to the Vietnamese people it is not Communist but Marxist-Leninist, indicating philosophic but not political allegiance and implying some sort of national Communism. And it asserts internal control of the N.L.F. In the North, the D.R.V. (Democratic Republic of Vietnam) characterizes the P.R.P. as a vanguard of Marxist-Leninist organization, indicating it is in the mainstream of the worldwide Communist movement, both spiritually and materially connected to the North Vietnamese, the D.R.V. government and the Laodang Party. Regardless of its ideological image, there is no ambiguity in the N.L.F.-P.R.P. relationship. The N.L.F. is dominated by the P.R.P. as an organization, by P.R.P. goals, and by P.R.P. cadres.

As long as the twin objectives of these two elements—political power and unification of the two Vietnams—continued to run parallel, the N.L.F.-P.R.P. machine would remain in running order. But once a crossroads was reached—which could easily be over the question of a political settlement—a break within the N.L.F. seemed inevitable. As Pike said, "The size of the breakaway N.L.F. force will be determined only by the success which the P.R.P. cadres have, between now and the day of the future split, in 'regularizing' or Communizing the movement and weeding out the potential deviationists." It was significant that, while the North began to formulate more clearly the policy of fighting-and-negotiating simultaneously, the Front began to speak increasingly of "national salvation." In a 1967 program statement, the first one issued since the founding of the Front in 1960, this theme of national salvation was constantly reiterated: "Unite the entire people, fight the United States aggressors, save the country." While it speaks of reunification as an ultimate goal, the stated principal objective was to build "a broad, national, democratic, peaceful, neutral and prosperous South Vietnam." In detailing its aims, the program stressed such things as a broader and more tolerant land-reform policy, an amnesty program, veterans' benefits, and integration of minority elements. Although the word "coalition" did not appear, Front leaders acknowledged that the coalition idea was implicit in the platform, and captured documents repeated this theme, while making it perfectly clear that any coalition in which the Front participated would have to be completely dominated by the Front, using the techniques of the well-organized minority that gains and holds power over an amorphous, less deeply dedicated, and poorly in· doctrinated majority.

In an article that appeared in *Foreign Affairs* in October, 1967, I discussed the possibilities of local accommodation as a challenge to the South Vietnamese. I suggested that if a civilian government chosen in Saigon could win the respect of the Vietnamese people, such a process of accommodation in the hamlets and villages might lead, first, to selective dialogues and then to new local elections, followed by larger negotiations at the Hanoi-Saigon-Washington level. A contest and a race against time would develop, in which agents of the government and of the Communists would seek to obtain a presence and influence in the hamlets (in fact, such a contest did begin after Tet). Whether a separate solution for the South could evolve, permitting "a more free revolutionary expression of its own ethos," still seemed to me the paramount issue early in 1969, when negotiations were already seriously under way. However, this was certainly not the way Hanoi was looking at it in the period just prior to Tet, 1968, although the Front may by then have had other ideas, including potential accommodation. As I noted in *The New Yorker* at that time:

It would appear to be more prudent for the N.L.F. to protect and sustain its guerrilla organization in the villages, which is now being weakened by attrition, than for it to continue fighting and losing as many men as it is and thereby making itself increasingly dependent on northern replacements. It may be, of course, that Hanoi is fearful of losing control over the Front, which presumably could happen if it allowed the Front to revert to the old style of independent guerrilla warfare while negotiations dragged on.

It was apparent, certainly, that if it lost its guerrilla identity, and if its southern image was also weakened, accommodation of any sort in the South would be more difficult.

This is not to suggest, in the light of hindsight, that the Tet offensive was decided on by the Politburo in Hanoi in order to maintain its hold on the Front and on the political situation as a whole in the South. However, it is not too much to say that *one* of the reasons for the change in strategy may have been the fear in Hanoi that the general deteriorating situation in South Vietnam might lead to a breakaway movement, particularly since the Front was more willing than Hanoi to go on fighting a guerrilla-type war indefinitely; or, alternatively, the Front might make its own accommodations with other southern elements, including liberal breakaway groups and individuals from the government, and thus politically outflank the North Vietnamese, who were thoroughly dedicated to reunification in the shortest possible time.

Such, then, was the situation on the eve of Tet.

The Attack—Failure and Success

At 8:40 P.M. on January 29, 1968, Lieutenant General Frederick Weyand, Commander of the American II Field Force embracing the Vietnamese III Corps area around Saigon, sent the following message to all his unit commanders: "There are a number of positive intelligence indicators that the enemy will deliberately violate the truce by attacking friendly installations during the night of January 29 or during the early morning hours of 30 January. Addressees will take action to insure maximum alert postures throughout the Tet period. Be particularly alert for enemy deception involving use of friendly vehicles or uniforms." Several hours after General Weyand's message went out, Communist forces attacked a number of places in II Corps, the highlands area just to the north. At 9:45 on the morning of January 30, the government canceled the nationwide three-day truce for Tet, the Vietnamese New Year, that both sides had separately called, and just after noon a full alert was announced in the Capital Military District, though it was too late to recall most of the government soldiers who had been released for the holidays and had gone home— roughly half of all units. One exception was the police: a week earlier, when a large cache of AK-47's—the Chinese-type guns in widest use among the Vietcong—had been discovered in Saigon, General Loan, the police chief, had ordered his own alert, and more than half of his men were on duty during Tet. At 10:15 P.M. on January 30, a Vietcong agent with three AK-47's in a burlap bag was captured in Go Vap district of Gia Dinh Province, right outside of Saigon. He revealed that his unit planned to attack Tan Son Nhut airport on the outskirts of the city that night and said that some of the Vietcong forces would be dressed in A.R.V.N. uniforms.

While it had been apparent for some time that the Communists were planning a major attack around Tet, neither the Americans nor the government had believed the assault would occur on Tet itself, in violation of the year's principal holiday. Even when the evidence during the last day or two indicated that this was indeed likely, General Weyand and his staff believed the enemy was incapable of attacking Saigon, and they felt it would be the height of foolishness if he tried to do so. Over the previous several weeks, however, it had become clear that something big was brewing. Following the defeat during the fall of a number of Vietcong units in skirmishes in the so-called priority area—the provinces ringing Saigon—the main Communist forces had withdrawn northwest and west to the Cambodian border. South Vietnamese troops were then assigned responsibility for continuing tactical operations in the Capital District and the priority region, while the Americans took over in the outer provinces. After the border area battles in October and November, at Loc Ninh and elsewhere, the Communists sought to establish a new base area further east in Binh Long Province, and in Phuoc Long. In response, anticipating that this was a prelude to another attempt to infiltrate troops back toward Saigon, the Americans launched a number of special operations to keep the enemy off balance. They also set up a series of blocking forces along the expected infiltration routes. This plan was carried out between mid-December and mid-January, but when General Weyand's intelligence indicated that the Communists were shifting their forces again—south, southeast, and west of Saigon—he informed General Westmoreland and suggested a change in the pre-Tet posture. Three attacks on populated areas near Saigon enhanced Allied suspicions that the Communists would shortly try to assault additional district capitals and other population centers. Further suspicion was aroused by a build-up of depleted local Vietcong forces with North Vietnamese replacements and by intelligence indicating a heavy influx of new AK-47 guns and new Chinese and Russian rockets in the jungle belt around Saigon. Although it was not verified until after Tet, there was also some evidence that the Communists were reorganizing their command structure around the capital. In fact, they had created six subregional commands around Saigon, like the slices of a pie; each had its own supply sources and was operationally under the direct control of COSVN (Central Office for South Vietnam) headquarters. To meet this changed situation, General Westmoreland abandoned the earlier blocking-force plan and moved about half of his forty-nine Allied maneuver battalions in III Corps closer to Saigon. He also used heavy Rome plows to clear as much of the suspected rocket-belt area as possible and destroyed some old unproductive rubber plantations the Communists might seek out for sanctuary.

During the night of January 29-30, when attacks took place on the cities and towns of Danang, Hoi An, Kontum, Pleiku, Qui Nhon, Tuy Hoa, Ninh Hoa, Nha Trang, and Ban Me Thuot in II Corps and I Corps, there were some probes on outlying areas of Saigon. The main attacks in the capital—on the American Embassy, the Presidential Palace, the Joint General Staff Headquarters, Tan Son Nhut airport, the radio station, South Vietnamese Naval Headquarters, the Phu Tho race track and other places—did not occur until the morning of January 31. About a score of other major towns and cities, including Hué, were attacked that day and on succeeding days; many of the other seventy district towns and smaller places were hit by mortars and rockets but were not struck by ground forces. The Communists attacked some thirty cities and towns, and, as it turned out, this was more than they could handle. When the offensive was launched, a general Order of the Day was issued to all participants by the National Liberation Front. It began with a special Tet poem written by Ho Chi Minh. Then came a statement that the assault on South Vietnamese and American installations was designed "to restore power to the people, liberate the people of the South, and fulfill our revolutionary task of establishing democracy throughout the country." The order added: "This will be the greatest battle ever fought throughout the history of our country. It will bring forth world-wide changes, but will also require many sacrifices. It will decide the fate and the survival of our Fatherland and will . . . cause the most bitter failure to the Imperialist Ringleaders. . . . ." An additional order, which referred to "the confused Americans who are bogged down and hurting badly" and to the "expected disintegration of the Puppet Army," called on the troops to punish drastically all "high-level traitors and all tyrants" and to "establish a people's revolutionary government at all levels." The attacking commando units were told that there would be a popular uprising, and that large elements of the South Vietnamese forces would desert and join them.

Although the attacks that took place were astonishingly well-coordinated, the synchronization was not perfect. For instance, there was evidence that the assault on Saigon was originally scheduled to take place on the morning of January 30, following by only a matter of hours the highlands assaults. If there was a delay, it was probably due to the fact that the Communists had not yet succeeded in infiltrating all the desired units into the city. Some eleven Communist battalions were in or around the Capital Military District when the attack occurred, and seven of them were composed entirely of local forces, which therefore did not have to come from any great distances. The fact that the Communists were able to infiltrate so many men and weapons into the city without being detected revealed an astonishing amount of successful covert planning and organization, and it also showed that an effective underground was in existence in the city. A distinction must be made between the commando units and the four thousand Vietcong soldiers who attacked the city in two waves from the north and the south. The commandos, who wore civilian clothes, were given orders to infiltrate into town by motor scooter, by boat, by truck, by taxi, on bicycles, or on foot, and to smuggle their weapons and ammunition in by hiding them in carts bringing watermelons, charcoal, wood, or other supplies into the city for the Tet celebration. The attackers were told where and how to meet certain guides who would conduct them to safe houses, where they would get their specific instructions and, if they did not already have them, their weapons. In some cases they were given red armbands or other identifying markers, or were told to roll up their shirt sleeves. Once the commandos had received their orders to attack designated targets—and some were not assigned their objectives until the last moment—they became, in effect, suicide squads, since most of them had no contingency or withdrawal plans and were carrying out their orders in the expectation that they would be reinforced by main-force units and by the promised uprisings, which of course failed to materialize. As it turned out, the commandos simply kept on fighting until in a day or two they ran out of ammunition and food, but the other local-force elements that took part in the attack fought on until February 7 or 8, mostly in Cholon, around the airport and the race track, which was supposed to be a sort of invasion headquarters. It became apparent that the Communists' decision to use local forces was predicated on their desire to retain the element of surprise, but they paid the price of not having a sufficient number of such troops to prosecute the offensive once the initial stunning impact was over. If they did intend to bring North Vietnamese elements in as reinforcements— and there is some doubt as to how serious they were about this— such troops would have had great difficulty finding their way through strange country and into the strange city without proper and sufficient guides.

The most sensational attack in Saigon was the one on the American Embassy, a recently completed modern building on Thong Nhut Boulevard. Five Americans and at least nineteen Vietcong, all but a few of the attackers, were killed. They were members of the C-10 Sapper Battalion that normally conducted terrorist activity in Saigon. The assault on the embassy began at 2:50 A.M. on January 31 and lasted about eight hours. The members of the unit that took part moved into Saigon by truck or car from Binh Duong and Hau Nghia provinces on January 28 and 29; some of them were guided by Nguyen Van Ba, a driver in the embassy motor pool, who was a key "inside man." According to one prisoner, Nguyen Van Sau, he and six others were picked up in Hau Nghia in a truck on the twenty-ninth, and upon arrival in Saigon at 7 P.M., each man was dropped off at a different house. On the evening of the thirtieth, most of the attacking force met at the home of a woman named Nguyen Thi Phe, who had been a secret Vietcong agent since 1955. They left her garage in a truck and a small Renault taxi at two o'clock on the morning of the thirty-first. The men were wearing slacks, open-necked shirts, and sandals, and red neckerchiefs and red armbands. Arriving at the embassy, they quickly unloaded their weapons, including bazookas and rockets. Two American military policemen were on duty at the side gate, which was open when the attack started but which they quickly locked. The sappers blew a hole in the front cement wall, however, and entered the compound, wounding the two M.P.'s but not before the latter had killed two of the commandos. In addition to the pair of M.P.'s, there were five Marine security guards in the embassy or in the annex alongside. One of them managed to lock the large teakwood front embassy door, which the Vietcong tried unsuccessfully to break open with rockets. Within ten minutes after the start of the attack Marine and M.P. reinforcements began to arrive, and the fighting went on all through the dark hours until elements of the 101st Airborne Division landed by helicopter on the embassy roof at 8 A.M., by which time virtually all the attackers had been killed.

One of the most harrowing experiences was that of George D. Jacobson, a former Army colonel who was serving as Mission Coordinator for the embassy and was living in a two-story house inside the compound. Jacobson's only weapon was an M-26 fragmentation grenade. He stayed on the second floor of his house throughout the night, looking out at the fighting, trying to inform Ambassador Ellsworth Bunker and other embassy officials on the phone about what was happening, and at the same time guarding his stairwell in case one of the sappers came up, in which event, as he later said, "I intended to use my grenade to the best advantage." Between seven and eight o'clock, when it was light, a severe fire fight took place on the ground floor of the house. Jacobson was temporarily deafened by two grenade blasts and momentarily blinded by some riot gas. Realizing any Vietcong still in the house would not risk the withering fire outside, he managed to have a gas mask, a pistol, and some ammunition thrown up to him by some of the security guards. He tossed a gas canister downstairs, and waited. Moments later, a Vietcong came up and began firing his AK-47 in the direction of Jacobson, who was half-hiding behind a plywood partition. The shots missed, and Jacobson then killed the man with his pistol. "Fortunately, there were no others and the incident was closed," he afterward reported.

It seems unlikely that the Vietcong intended to do anything more than create a psychological shock by attacking the embassy, and in that they succeeded—many Americans back home found it hard to believe that, in a war which General Westmoreland maintained was on the verge of being won, the enemy should have been able so brazenly to enter the embassy grounds. With the exception of the radio station, which was destroyed, none of the other major targets, including the palace, the race track, and the prison (where they had hoped to set free 2,500 inmates), was successfully attacked by the Communist commandos. The fourteen-man team that struck the palace was guided around town by a girl cadre and, as was the case with several other commando groups, gathered at a house on Le Van Duyet Street just before the assault. Repulsed almost at once by the palace garrison, the team took refuge on the roofs of two nearby buildings, where its surviving members surrendered on the morning of February 1. The team had received no support from local people, as it had been led to expect by its instructors. Some members of the attacking unit had been shown a sand-table model of the palace only a half-hour in advance of the attack, when they were told for the first time of their specific objective. They were not told anything else about the offensive, except that they were to hold out as long as they could, and, in their case, not to expect any help. In some other instances, such as in the abortive attack on the prison, careful training and indoctrination sessions were held over a three weeks' period; but this unit, which was promised quick relief, got lost on the way into town, and after failing even to come close to its objective, was mauled by American and South Vietnamese troops near the race track.

An interrogation report on a twelve-man commando squad that attacked the Naval Headquarters, along the Saigon River, threw further light on the detailed plans the Communists had drawn up. One of the survivors said that he and two other members of the team had come to Saigon together from Ben Tre, in the delta, a day and a half in advance, carrying false identification papers; they had been told to go to a downtown movie theater and, when they came out, to look for a man with a distinctive mark on his shirt. They did so and met the man, who took them to another house on Le Van Duyet Street, where they were told what their mission was. None of the four groups of three men each who met in the house had known each other until late on the evening of January 29—in fact, they all came from different parts of the delta. The attack, one of the boldest that had been conceived, was designed to capture the headquarters building, to employ three machine guns on

VIETNAM [409]

its roof to neutralize the guns aboard several small Navy vessels in the river, and then to capture these ships and use them as ferries to bring two Vietcong battalions into the city from the far shore. If the plan had succeeded, it could have altered the entire situation in Saigon. When the attack began, early in the morning, the commandos quickly killed three Navy guards and managed to blow a hole in the side of the headquarters building, but, thanks to the general alert that had gone out six hours earlier, all twelve commandos were soon killed or caught.

Among the real heroes of the attack on Saigon were the white-shirted National Police, under the command of General Loan, a tough, erratic leader who received considerable notoriety when he shot a Vietcong prisoner in the head with his pistol near the An Quang pagoda, a principal rebel objective. Loan's personal bravery, if not his personal behavior and his political judgment, was never questioned, and he hardly slept for several days as he took charge of the main counterattack (he was later severely wounded in action). In several of the city's nine precincts, especially those in Cholon, which is lined with canals, small groups of police fought off Vietcong attackers who made as many as seven assaults on individual police stations. Eighty-seven police were killed during the week-long fighting, but they probably killed ten times as many Vietcong and were mostly responsible for wiping out an estimated half of the cell members who were serving as guides in the city, and whose loss, during the first two days, was a crippling one for the Communists. In addition to the police, the South Vietnamese Rangers and A.R.V.N. units that later supported them fought extremely well, even though undermanned because of the Tet furloughs. These government units completely disproved one of the main Communist assumptions—that the South Vietnamese forces would fall apart and either quit or join the rebel ranks. At the time of the Saigon attack, mixed elements of some ten South Vietnamese battalions were in the city, in addition to the police. There was little cohesion among them, though, and the danger was at its greatest when the major attacking elements from the direction of the airfield first moved into Saigon. The Communists were trying to cut the city in half with their two main attack forces, from the north and the south, and not until the second or third day were the government troops in a sufficiently strong position to keep the enemy from overrunning the town from Cholon toward the center. Even then, had it not been for American and South Vietnamese air and artillery support, the attack might have succeeded. The Communists took full advantage of the fact that most of the damage was the result of Allied bombing and shelling—thousands of homes were destroyed, as I saw when I viewed the city from a helicopter on February 8—and this was duly stressed in Vietcong and Hanoi propaganda broadcasts to the world.

Although there were occasions when the government troops behaved toward the people with their traditional contempt and cruelty, by and large they conducted themselves a lot better than might have been expected in such a crisis. The police and intelligence agencies worked round the clock to keep up with the flow of information that gave them fresh clues to the Communists' plans. They employed a number of modern devices to check persons brought in for interrogation. For example, they used an ultraviolet machine on the hands of suspects to determine whether they had fired a gun within three days. By comparison, the Communists employed more terror tactics as they began to lose out. Initially, the infiltrating commandos carried out their tasks of sniping, attacking key government positions, and assassinating officials with precision in many parts of town. But, as the days passed, they became less discriminating. Men and women who were simply suspected of helping the government had their hands cut off or were otherwise maimed. On the other hand, the regular Vietcong battalions behaved quite well toward the population. Some of their members even went about helping people whose homes had been burned or bombed out. There were also dramatic displays of leniency here and there, if primarily for show purposes. For example, an impromptu people's court was set up on a wooden box at one street crossing, and a woman accused of being the mother of a government security officer was "pardoned" when the crowd shouted that she should be freed.

The Communists probably made their most serious attacks on Tan Son Nhut air base, which they hit at 3:20 A.M. January 31 with elements of three battalions. They managed to penetrate one of the main gates and move onto the airstrip area, but small American and South Vietnamese reaction forces blunted the force of the attack. When the commander of the Capital Military District asked for more help from the Americans, a cavalry squadron stationed eight miles away at Hoc Mon reached the air base in less than two hours, taking advantage of the fact that the Vietcong had amazingly failed to blow up a key bridge. The squadron moved through the darkest hours with the help of flares dropped by its unit commander, flying overhead. When it arrived in the city before daylight, it immediately counterattacked the strongest flank of the Vietcong invaders and averted what might have been the overrunning of the base. There was some subsequent criticism that the Americans had kept their forces too far out of town and that, if the Communists had blown the bridges sooner, the worst might have happened. General Weyand, however, having not expected the full force of the assault to hit Saigon, had plenty of helicopters at his command to ferry troops in case of emergencies. Furthermore, the fact that American troops were near Long Binh and the Bien Hoa air-base complex north of the city turned out to be a blessing, since the Communists attacked both places, blowing an ammunition dump at Long Binh, but by noon of January 1 both places had been resecured. Following the defeat of the attackers at Tan Son Nhut, the Vietcong put up a heavy fight within a textile mill alongside the air base. Allied gunships had to destroy the mill, in which were found 162 Vietcong bodies and a large cache of weapons. Throughout the city the Communists were unable to reach many of their weapons caches, which apparently they had also intended for arming the local population, and this proved one of their biggest handicaps.

The Allied capability to reinforce the Saigon area much more quickly than the Communists was probably the single most significant factor in turning the tide. At midnight on January 30, there were seven battalions in the Capital Military District, and twenty-four hours later there were thirteen—five American and eight A.R.V.N. outfits, plus three M.P. and two Regional Force units. Between February 2 and 5, though some fierce fighting was still going on in Cholon, the back of the Vietcong assault had been broken, and the Americans were then able to withdraw their troops in order to cut off the Communist reinforcements that belatedly had begun to move in, and at the same time to cut off the retreat of some of the defeated elements that had been in Saigon. By the fifth the Communists had suffered eight thousand killed, and by February 19 the figure was up to twelve thousand in the III Corps area alone, while the Allies in the area had lost one thousand. The Communists, on February 12, lost their top commander, General Tran Do, who was killed in a farmhouse outside of Cholon. Of the fifty-four battalions they had committed throughout the corps area, twenty-one were no longer rated combat-effective by the Americans, and twenty-six were considered marginal.

Elsewhere in the country, following their initial stunning success, the Communists also suffered heavily, and the nationwide total killed was somewhere between forty and fifty thousand. The most bitter, and the longest, fight took place in Hué, where the battle lasted nearly three weeks. After Saigon had quieted down, I went to Hué, and nothing I had seen during the Second World War in the Pacific, during the Korean War, and in Vietnam either during the Indochina War or since 1965 was as terrible, in point of destruction and despair, as what I witnessed in this historic northern capital, which has often been compared to Old Peking. Much of the city, particularly the old walled part known as the Citadel and including the Imperial Palace, on the northern side of the Perfume River, was in complete ruins. There were ninety thousand refugees receiving aid in Hué alone. Women and children wandered crying through the rubble, picking up the broken bits of their lives, gathering watercress from the ponds to eat, begging from strangers, collecting bricks and beseeching relief workers for some sort of roofing material to build shelters. I walked down Le Loi Street, on the south side of town, past a once-lovely waterfront park, now littered with broken telephone wires and garbage. The large hospital area, packed with refugees and wounded, was a disaster center. Nearly four thousand civilians were killed in Hué, out of an estimated seven or eight thousand killed throughout the country, and most of them were the victims of American air and artillery attacks employed to dislodge the stubborn North Vietnamese and Vietcong forces, who wanted to hold the city as long as they could. Once it became apparent they had to leave, they created an atmosphere of terror and encouraged the destruction by the Americans. If this was a revolutionary tactic, so to increase the misery of the people as to drive them into rebellion, the Americans fell into the trap, though the Communists fell in along with them.

Caught off guard in Hué, as they had been elsewhere, the American and government forces had reacted belatedly to the Communist assault, which had begun early on the morning of January 31, when the city was teeming with Tet celebrants. As the bitter fighting dragged on, ultimately costing some of the American Marine and Vietnamese battalions half their strength in killed and wounded, the Americans cursed the bad weather that helped the Communists and, when the clouds finally lifted, they called in their helicopter gunships and their heavy artillery. The inexperienced American Marines, unaccustomed to action in cities, fought as if they were taking hills instead of homes. They probed, as if ejecting the ballpoint of a pen, and then withdrew and summoned the heavy weaponry. If this saved some American lives, it added immeasurably to the number of Vietnamese corpses. Throughout the city, along the sidewalks, in the gardens of the houses that were still standing, and amid the rubble of those that weren't, crude graves, simple oblong mounds of earth marked by a stick and a name and perhaps a small twig or a plastic Tet flower, told the story of the death of Hué more poignantly than anything else.

None of this, and not even the looting that was done by the Americans and the government forces, excused what the North Vietnamese and the Vietcong had done to Hué. In the words of Robert Kelly, the former senior American adviser in the area, who was sent back to Hué after his successor became one of the thirty American civilians killed, captured, or missing during the battle, "Hué was like a naked woman. The people of the city just didn't believe the Communists would ever do this here." Kelly, who had had six years of experience in Vietnam and was about to be transferred to Thailand, was one of the relatively few Americans I had come to know in Vietnam who was not only deeply committed to the Vietnamese people but had also been highly critical of American failures, though he still believed firmly in the purpose of the American commitment. Married to a Vietnamese girl, his frustrations represented those of the handful of experienced Americans who had genuinely tried to improve the people's welfare and to instill a revolutionary awareness in them in the face of apathy, corruption, official Vietnamese obstructionism, and frequently confused and contradictory United States policies. His bitterness, on the eve of his departure, was directed chiefly against the citizens of Hué, who had always been the most complicated Vietnamese in the country. This was the result of their deep-seated sense of independence; they had been, in diminishing progression, antigovernment, anti-American, and anti-Communist.

What now upset Kelly most, as he surveyed the ruins of the city, was its citizens' lack of interest in anything but saving their own skins and either getting out or, in the case of officials in power, making money out of relief programs. "I walked through the refugee centers and was accosted by colonels out of uniform, high-society ladies, university professors and others who begged me to help them escape," he told me.. "No one ever really smiled at the United States here before, but I haven't met anyone who is mad at the Communists and what they did. I'm just as opposed to Communism as I ever was, but I am more than ever convinced that until the government is as committed to victory as the Vietcong is, it hasn't got a chance."

Hué's officials, and its officer corps, attached to the 1st A.R.V.N. Division, had always moved in a close-knit, almost incestuous atmosphere of local maneuver and intrigue—an atmosphere that had largely accounted for the success of the 1966 Struggle Movement in the city. After that movement was crushed, the American attitude of ostracism and condemnation helped encourage a xenophobia, which became deeper than ever, and this had undeniably enabled the Communists to make underground inroads in the city. It had also contributed to inefficiency, corruption, and intrigue. The Mayor, Lieutenant Colonel Phan Van Khoa, who was also Thua Thien Province Chief, was said to have had two days' warning from the Vietcong that the Tet attack was coming; the night it began, he was reported to have been playing poker in a friend's home. Told by two Vietcong agents to make himself scarce, he hid for six days in the rafters of the hospital, and when he finally came out, it was with a hangdog air. His subsequent unconvincing story was that he let the Communists enter the city so they could be trapped there. Khoa quickly surrounded himself with friends who had past histories of corrupt dealings and who lost no time making money out of the emergency shipments of rice sent into the stricken city. Finally, toward the end of February, President Thieu visited Hué and fired Khoa and most of the men around him, and the situation slowly began to improve. Except for the Citadel, most of the city has since been rebuilt.

The Continuing Communist Offensive

It was a matter of weeks before all the damage caused throughout the country by the Tet offensive could be thoroughly assessed. Generally, the Communists had tried to hit government military and civilian administrative headquarters and arsenals as well as American installations and operations centers in the cities and towns they attacked. While they were able only in rare cases to capture any of these objectives and hold them for even a few hours, they did a tremendous amount of over-all damage. Among the places that suffered the most, and where the Communists in turn suffered their greatest losses as a result of the fierce fighting, were Ban Me Thuot, Kontum, and Phan Thiet in the II Corps area (they destroyed two churches, some missionary buildings, and a leprosarium in Ban Me Thuot, which is a center for *montagnard—* tribal—activities, and in Phan Thiet they managed to free five hundred prisoners before being driven out of town); and the cities of My Tho, Can Tho, Ben Tre, and Vinh Long in the delta, where fighting went on for several days and many homes were burned. All in all, throughout Vietnam, some seventy thousand civilian homes were destroyed in the offensive. Approximately half a million persons became refugees, swelling the earlier nationwide total to more than two and a half million.

For at least a fortnight after the attacks, the Hanoi and National Liberation Front radios greatly exaggerated the success of the offensive, claiming tremendous popular enthusiasm around the country and accusing the Americans and the Saigon government of "enormous, savage and wicked crimes against innocent people." In the weeks and months that followed, however, in secret documents that were captured, the Communists were more critical of their failures, citing, among other things, insufficient proselyting activities, the lack of proper coordination and sustained efforts on the part of attacking elements, the absence of good combat plans for countering the Allied response, and, in general, the underestimation of the government's willingness and capacity to fight back.

In seeking to make a balanced appraisal of the offensive, I would say the following: The Communists suffered extremely heavy losses, probably at least twice as many killed as they had anticipated. While they lost some important commanders—in addition to Tran Do, at least one other general, Tran Van Tra, and a number of key battalion and company officers were killed—their basic infrastructure was not too badly damaged, though in some places, such as the seaport of Nha Trang, where the underground surfaced prematurely, they were shattered. In failing to rally a single government unit to their side, or to rouse the population in their behalf anywhere near to the degree they had expected, the Communists were made aware that cynicism, criticism of the government, and a longing for peace on the part of the people were not, in themselves, enough to create a willingness to join the Vietcong cause. The fact that the attackers violated the sacred Tet holiday was a great shock to many ordinary citizens, and a cause for resentment. The manner in which the government, with the help of the Americans, rallied initially to throw back the offensive, and then followed through with relief plans, was encouraging.

It could not be said, on the other hand, that the government demonstrated any subsequent political ability to react to the shock of the offensive by fostering a fresh unity. Attempts to create popular new political fronts and patriotic movements quickly foundered on the customary shoals of mutual recrimination and suspicion, including the continuing mistrust between Thieu and Ky and their respective followers. The pacification program in the countryside was set back at least three months, and the administrative apparatus of the government was badly jolted. The inability of officials to return to their posts for various reasons ranging from the lack of security to loss of spirit was one factor that enabled the Communists to move swiftly into the rural vacuum, and to strengthen their apparatus in the hamlets and villages, as well as to do some vital recruiting to make up for their heavy losses in manpower. The fact that the Communists had proved themselves able to carry off such a bold thrust, in the face of the awesome American power, was an undeniable psychological victory that had an effect not only in Vietnam but, even more, throughout the world. In Vietnam it added to the sense of fear, especially on the part of urban residents who had previously felt themselves fairly safe from Communist attacks. Abroad it added vastly to the growing sense of futility about the war, and was an important factor in provoking

President Johnson's decision, in the face of the mounting antiwar feeling in the United States, to announce the partial bombing suspension, and his own retirement, on March 31. Thus the Communists succeeded in what was certainly the aim of the predominant element in the Politburo in Hanoi: to begin in earnest the period of simultaneous fighting and negotiating.

It was apparent, soon after Tet and prior to Johnson's announcements, that the Communists would strike again. On February 17 and 18 they shelled Saigon and other cities in what at first seemed to be the anticipated "second wave," but the second major attack, on the ground, did not actually begin until May 5 and lasted ten days. While the basic plan of the new attack on Saigon was similar to the one used during Tet, there were some differences. Realizing that, this time, they would not enjoy the element of surprise, the Communists hoped to apply a larger number of forces and, instead of using the Vietcong regulars as the main striking element (though some of the refurbished and restrengthened Vietcong regiments and battalions did take part), they used North Vietnamese shock troops primarily. According to the subsequent testimony of a captured colonel who was the deputy commander of one of the six new subregions around Saigon, the planning for the attack began early in March. At approximately the same time the Americans and the Vietnamese launched a campaign they called "Resolute Victory," which, with its successor a month later, called "Complete Victory," was designed to seek out and destroy the Communist units that had withdrawn north and northwest from Saigon after Tet and were in the process of regrouping. These two drives had considerable success in inflicting further casualties on the Communists but did not keep them from mounting their new offensive, which, though aimed primarily at Saigon, was also directed at other places in the country; every province in the I Corps area was attacked, along with six provincial capitals in the II Corps area and twenty-six urban areas in the delta, though most of these attacks were limited to sporadic rocket and mortar barrages, followed in some instances by ground probes. General Weyand's forces in the III Corps area were able to intercept many of the infiltrating units on their way to Saigon, and engage them in battle. Even so, despite the intelligence of a Communist colonel who defected shortly before the attack and who gave important information on the

Communist battle plan for Saigon, the Communists managed to get elements of four battalions into the city and to inflict considerable fresh damage. Several precincts came under heavy fire and were then assaulted by Communist troops, who succeeded in capturing a number of police stations for short periods of time and even hoisting Vietcong flags. The race track was again a prime target and the Communists made their strongest penetration here, remaining in the area for three days despite intense allied artillery, air, and ground action. They also forced the Allies, especially the Americans, to call in their helicopter gunships, as at Tet, and this resulted in the destruction of another ten thousand homes in the city, which elicited a fresh amount of criticism of such tactics.

However, the Communists suffered heavy casualties—eleven thousand were killed in May in III Corps, and the countrywide total for the year rose to ninety thousand by the end of that month, which was as many as they had lost in all of 1967. This kept them from continuing their military offensive, as they had planned, into June and July, when the "third wave" of attacks was supposed to have begun. Instead, they retreated to the Cambodian border region, as before, where they were relentlessly pursued and suffered still more killed and wounded. They were losing in excess of the five or six thousand men a month they were infiltrating into South Vietnam from the North in mid-1968. This adverse ratio of losses over infiltratees undoubtedly was a factor in their subsequent decision to withdraw into Laos and Cambodia, and northward across the D.M.Z., for a respite. These withdrawals in turn led to their expressed willingness to start serious negotiations in Paris, and to accept the South Vietnamese as participants on a tacit if not openly admitted equal basis at the conference table—in return, of course, for having the National Liberation Front take part, too.

During the May attack in Saigon the Communists did not, as they had during Tet, overplay their propaganda hand. During Tet the city was flooded with armed proselyting teams which sought— unavailingly for the most part—to instigate demonstrations and whip up support for a new coalition movement that would pave the way for peace talks on the basis of Hanoi's "Four Points" and the "Five Points" of the National Liberation Front, issued in 1965; these included, most importantly, demands for the complete withdrawal of the Americans and for the determination of South Vietnam's political future and its ultimate reunification with the North without foreign interference and in accordance with the "popular will" as expressed by the Front. The Communists' serious preparation of the political battlefield for negotiations began in 1966, when they already envisaged the possibility of peace, or at least the start of talks by late 1967 or early 1968.

This was corroborated in several long talks I had after Tet with a top-level captured cadre named Le Ngoc Lan, alias Ba Tra. Ba Tra, who was arrested near Saigon in mid-1967, was the deputy chief of the Vietcong's intellectual proselyting organization in the Saigon area. A thin, soft-spoken, spectacled man, born in the South in 1918, he had attended school in My Tho, where Prime Minister Huong had been one of his teachers. He joined the resistance in 1945 and became a party member four years later. He never went to North Vietnam but always operated in the South, and after 1955 he worked steadily among intellectuals and bourgeoisie in Saigon, except for a brief period at the end of 1960 when he went to the jungle to help establish the National Liberation Front. From 1955 to 1958 he worked more or less in the open and then underground. Beginning in 1966, Ba Tra told me, he and the other cadres of his group convinced the Front that it had to make "a special appeal to people in the urban areas, particularly to bourgeois and intellectual elements who disapproved of the government, which had nothing but contempt for them, and who were sympathetic to our cause but believed the Front was 'too red.' " With the approval of Hanoi, Ba Tra received permission to establish a number of legal fronts that would come out in favor of national sovereignty, freedom and democracy, and peace—neutrality was not initially mentioned because it was felt to be too much of a Communist slogan.

The first group he helped promote was the Committee for the Protection of the National Culture. It functioned in the open and in January, 1967, published a magazine called *Voice of the Intellectuals*, which included a score of articles and poems that were xenophobic in tone and outlook and decried the destruction of Vietnamese culture as a result of foreign influences, particularly that of American troops. After the first issue, the censors forbade the publication of any others. Additional organizations and fronts that Ba Tra and his associates secretly helped create in 1966-67 included the Committee for a Self-Sufficient Economy, the Association for the Protection of the Personality of Vietnamese Women, the Association for Improved Relations Among Vietnamese Classes, and the Movement for Student Autonomy. They all operated nationally and, to some extent, internationally. By mid-1967 these organizations were gaining support among university professors and other intellectuals, as well as among members of the bourgeoisie, but when Ba Tra and some other top-level Front leaders were arrested in the summer and fall of last year, the various groups fell apart, and most of the unwitting members realized they had been used as Communist dupes.

Although they had suffered a setback, the Communists by no means gave up their Front tactics, and in the months before Tet they established a whole new series of political "alliances" designed to attract intellectuals and prominent professional persons; territorial "administrative organizations" in the provinces and cities; "insurrectionary committees," and proselyting "armed forces groups" which, among other things, were supposed to encourage military and civilian defectors from the government side. As the National Liberation Front itself pointed out, there was nothing new about these tactics, which had been applied successfully in North Vietnam in 1945, when the Vietminh Front was established, and later the Lienviet and Fatherland Fronts. "The more allies we can find, even precarious ones and temporary ones, the better," one document captured in mid-1967 said.

A sound Front policy is one of the decisive factors for a successful revolution. It is only when the Front has real strength that it can secure the participation of in-between forces and recruit in-between classes such as nationalist bourgeoisie who are opposed to imperialism in certain respects but are essentially reformers and compromisers. If more in-between forces participate in the Front, the prestige of the revolution will increase, the revolution will win approval from neutralist countries in the world, and the Americans and their lackeys will be isolated.

According to Ba Tra (and many independent analysts have agreed), the long-term strategic goal of Hanoi and the Front was to create a "Socialist" state in South Vietnam and then tie it *gradually* to the Communist North (other analysts, of course, have stressed Hanoi's desire to hurry reunification). The momentary tactic built around the various alliances and committees at Tet was to stress "peace and coalition government." All the bodies and groups established just before and during Tet had different names —at least seventeen were identified, and the Vietcong and Hanoi claimed that "hundreds" of others had been created throughout the country. This was an apparent effort by the Communists to emphasize the spontaneity of the uprising and its mass appeal. The principal urban alliances were not supposed to represent new revolutionary governments in themselves, at least not initially, nor were they to be overt Vietcong organizations. They were to act as independent "united front" groups and, after demanding the withdrawal of American troops and establishing their national and international *bona fides,* they were to portray themselves as the true representatives of the people in negotiating for a coalition government *not with Saigon but with the National Liberation Front.* Nevertheless, from the outset both the Front's Liberation Radio and Radio Hanoi acted as channels for disseminating the various communiqués and appeals of the "spontaneous" organizations, all of which, with the exception of two in Hué, the only city the Communists held until almost the end of February, were short-lived as the General Uprising failed to develop.

In Hué, the Front of National, Democratic, and Peace Alliance (*sic*) and the Thua Thien–Hué People's Revolutionary Committee were both headed by Le Van Hao, a professor of anthropology at the Universities of Saigon and Hué. The first appeal of the Front, read over the captured Hué radio on February 1 and later rebroadcast by Hanoi, declared: "Dear compatriots: We cannot stand with folded arms and see our country fall into the hands of the U.S. aggressors and the Thieu-Ky clique of traitors. We can no longer endure slavery, exploitation, poverty, and misery. We cannot let the U.S. aggressors and their lackeys prolong a war which only serves their selfish interests. We only want independence, sovereignty, freedom, democracy, peace, neutrality, food, clothes, and land." In the ensuing weeks, as the battle raged in the city, Le Van Hao issued several more communiqués and open letters to U Thant, Secretary General of the United Nations, and to the heads of various nations, denouncing American policy and acclaiming the deeds of the revolutionary forces. When the Americans and the South Vietnamese finally recaptured Hué, the revolutionary groups, led by Le Van Hao, left the city with the Communist troops and set up new headquarters in the nearby jungle.

The failure of the Communists to sustain their Tet drive and to obtain more popular support in the cities did not weaken their political or military resolve. The post-Tet political activity, specifically the further preparation of the political battlefield locally as well as nationally to pave the way for possible coalition government, must here be placed in historical context. In 1964, at the hamlet and village level in the Communist areas, there theoretically existed a three-ply organization: the local chapter of the People's Revolutionary Party, the National Liberation Front, plus its several member groups, and the so-called Autonomous Administrative Committees, or Liberation Committees, which were supposed to be modeled on the local People's Councils in North Vietnam. These committees were ostensibly chosen by election, but in point of fact they were selected by the local P.R.P. cadres who headed the party's sections on finance and economy, security and propaganda, and so on. The P.R.P. also increasingly tightened its control over all the branches of the N.L.F. Late in 1966 the selection of these administrative and liberation committees was postponed, and the idea of creating local "resistance governments," rising up hierarchically through the districts and provinces, as in North Vietnam, was replaced by the broader "peace and coalition" tactic referred to by Ba Tra. Toward the end of 1967, however, when the Tet offensive was already being prepared, the Communists ordered the establishment of the Village Liberation Committees resumed and said they should be completed by January, 1968. Specifically, for coalition purposes, they were to form a Vietcong structure parallel to that of the government.

By the time the Tet offensive took place an unknown number of these committees had been set up in several provinces. The announcements by the Front and Hanoi immediately afterward of "hundreds" of such committees was apparently an effort to stimulate this development, and to make more obscure the lines previously drawn between Vietcong and government authority in these villages, particularly those in contested areas. The Alliance and the Thua Thien Revolutionary Committee in Hué quickly recognized the new "revolutionary committees at the district, village, and city-quarter levels as the only legitimate people's representatives." An important directive from the Central Office for South Vietnam, dated March 5, which was captured in Saigon, spelled out the political plan further. It made clear that, in the wake of the limited achievements of the Tet offensive, the plan was a flexible one, designed to meet the demands of continued fighting while the approach to local accommodation and coalition government continued. The cadres were told that the fight would go on for at least "several more months" but that victory, it was hoped, would be achieved sometime in 1968 or early in 1969. The emphasis in this important document—which projected the subsequent discussions in Paris—was on consolidating local strength in order to achieve either of the three options that lay ahead: total victory, coalition, or a return, if necessary, to protracted war. There was less specific reference to the General Uprising as such. The March directive thus spoke of the need to create "a fighting machinery" that would be locally elected and based among the people. "We should build up the revolutionary government in order to enlarge the coalition government of higher echelons," it said. Village People's Liberation Councils were now to be set up in Communist areas, on top of the functioning Liberation Committees. There were to be fifteen members in villages with a population of three thousand or less; from twenty to twenty-five members in villages of from three to five thousand population, and from thirty to thirty-five in those with more than five thousand people. Below these councils, the Village Liberation Committees of from five to seven members were to carry out the orders of the councils and supervise military and security matters, food production, finance, information and cultural affairs, education, and health. Actually, the committees remained more important, and the new councils were window dressing.

Having tested their new political apparatus, the Communists at this point established their principal new Front organization to deal with the coalition question when it arose. This was the Alliance of National, Democratic, and Peace Forces of Vietnam, formed at a meeting on April 20-21 "at a locality near the Saigon-Cholon area," according to Liberation Radio. The meeting was attended by "many notables, intellectuals, scholars, teachers, students, writers, influential businessmen, civil servants, private enterprise employees, and officers of all sections representing different political and religious organizations in southern cities." A few days later the Communist radio network and press agencies made public a communiqué and a manifesto issued by the new Alliance and the names of a ten-man Central Committee, headed by a well-known Saigon lawyer named Trinh Dinh Thao. Thao and his fellow committee members had apparently left Saigon for secret headquarters, believed to be somewhere in the delta, during the previous month. They subsequently moved to the Cambodian border.

The communiqué excoriated the United States for having "sabotaged the Geneva agreements on Vietnam" and having "rigged up a series of puppet governments, from Ngo Dinh Diem to Nguyen Van Thieu and Nguyen Cao Ky, launched a war of aggression against the South Vietnamese people and turned South Vietnam into a new-type colony of the U.S." This war of "unheard-of barbarity," the communiqué went on, "is becoming ever fiercer, causing untold mourning and destruction, seriously affecting the whole material and spiritual life of our compatriots from the countryside to the towns. The national sovereignty is trampled underfoot, democratic liberties are being throttled, the economy has been brought to a standstill, and cultural and social activities are deteriorating." The Alliance had "gradually emerged" with the aim of "uniting all patriotic forces and individuals determined to resist foreign aggression, overthrow the Thieu-Ky puppet regime, establish a national coalition administration and achieve independence, democracy, and peace" as a preliminary to "the reunification of the country through consultations and negotiations between the North and the South on an equal footing." Significantly, the communiqué made only one mention of the National Liberation Front, almost patronizingly, as a "patriotic force that has made worthy contributions to the cause of national liberation" and that "cannot be absent in the settlement of any problem in the South." In creating the Alliance, Hanoi had obviously sought, at least initially, to give the appearance that a new independent force for coalition could operate separately from the National Liberation Front. Unlike the earlier attempts to create urban committees that would negotiate with the Front, this new umbrella group declared itself "prepared to enter into discussions with the United States government" to end the war, obtain the withdrawal of American troops and the dismantling of bases, and secure recognition of South Vietnam's "national independence and sovereignty."

Hanoi no doubt felt that the Front had become compromised by its obvious dependence on North Vietnam. It was not that the Front had no identity of its own, nor that it did not include some non-Communist elements; it was simply that, for tactical purposes, Hanoi deemed it wise to create another organization that it could control more easily and that could act as a bridge between the urban intellectuals and the Front's rather remote, jungle-bound membership. Moreover, by setting up the Alliance the Communists had a new instrumentality that they could use in various other ways; its initial advantage was its ability to bring the other alliances, fronts, and revolutionary committees around the country under one banner, and it was significant that the Hué Alliance and the Thua Thien Revolutionary Committee lost no time in accepting the "leadership" of the new Alliance—Thich Don Hau, an aged Buddhist bonze who had become vice chairman of the Hué group, also became a vice chairman of the national alliance. Similarly, a Saigon–Cholon–Gia Dinh Alliance of National, Democratic, and Peace Forces, formed early in May, expressed its full support for the new national group and recognized its "authority," while simultaneously summoning the citizens of Saigon "to crush the reactionary administration in the city." Late in May, it was announced by Radio Hanoi and the Liberation Radio that 170 new "uprising committees" had been formed in South Vietnam, mostly in the delta, and it was presumed that they, too, would support the Alliance. These rural committees, it should be noted, were apart from the new Village Liberation Committees ordered in March, the number of which the Communists claimed had grown to more than twelve hundred by the end of 1968. Hanoi obviously hoped the Alliance would spread its wings and in time gather in workers and peasants as well as intellectuals and urban bourgeoisie. But, if it failed, either as a surface or an underground organization once negotiations were seriously under way, it could be torpedoed, in classic Communist style, without jeopardizing the vital rural and urban infrastructure existing separately.

The Alliance, in fact, got off to a bad start, and its efforts to distinguish itself from the Front were not persuasive. As a result, late in 1968 and early in 1969, it drew perceptibly closer to the Front, and the two groups began issuing joint communiqués, with the Alliance dropping its pseudo-separatist line and declaring that the Front must play the "decisive" role in negotiations. (There may have been more than met the eye here, since the real leader of the Alliance was said to be Ton That Duang Ky, a former history professor at the University of Saigon who was deported to North Vietnam in 1965 for peace activities; he returned to the South sometime in 1967. The Front may have "asserted" itself with Hanoi and demanded that it be fully re-established as the governing body in the South, with the Alliance, as Hanoi's new instrument, relegated to a secondary role.) Nevertheless, American and Vietnamese intelligence officers, as well as observers in Paris who were close to the Front and to Hanoi, believed that the Alliance would still play an important role at the conference table or in the background. The fact that both Vice President Ky, as overseer of the Saigon delegation, and Prime Minister Huong made oblique references late in 1968 to the possibility of some political discussions being held with "insurgent" elements in South Vietnam, while Hanoi and Washington discussed a cease-fire and troop withdrawals, lent credence to this new theory.

In November, 1968, a new idea was floated by the Vietcong in Saigon: a "Peace Cabinet" was suggested, in keeping with the line that the "Thieu-Ky-Huong clique" had to be got rid of and that, before any serious negotiations could be carried on with Saigon, a more representative group containing acceptable persons who could carry on negotiations with the Front had to be chosen. Both the Front and the Alliance voiced this idea, and it was quickly picked up and repeated almost daily by the Hanoi and Liberation Front radios. The militant Buddhists, significantly, adopted the same line. Thich Don Hau, still in hiding somewhere in the country, called for the replacement of "the Cabinet of War" with "a Cabinet of Peace qualified to attend the Paris peace talks," and the An Quang pagoda group in Saigon made the same sort of plea. All of this was well orchestrated and coincided with a Buddhist motorcade through the delta, during which religious speeches were well sprinkled with fresh calls for peace. At the same time, in Saigon, the Vietcong organized a new Movement to Struggle for Peace, which held its first meeting at the An Quang pagoda in October and then summoned a large rally in Saigon in mid-November. The rally was attended by a number of liberal young Catholic priests and by a wide representation of Buddhist clerical and lay leaders, as well as by members of a dozen or so left-wing labor unions and

by intellectuals, lawyers, doctors, teachers, and journalists; a large
number of women also attended and spoke. The Vietcong cadremen who organized the meeting were there but stayed quietly in
the background. The rally was reminiscent of one summoned early
in 1954 by Nguyen Huu Tho, the current chairman of the National
Liberation Front, who was then in the vanguard of the peace
movement to end the Indochina War.

A number of other moves coincided with this new peace ploy.
Buddhist chaplains in the field, representing the An Quang group,
privately urged their soldiers, mostly recent draftees, not to sacrifice themselves any longer to the cause of war and to lay down
their arms, prompting about fifty men to desert and to return to
Saigon, where they hid out in several pagodas. In the countryside
the Communists continued to push the development of Village
Liberation Committees and to refer to the "democratic process" by
which they were chosen, though it was becoming more apparent
that trusted party members were moving in and taking over control of as many new hamlet and village administrations as possible
before negotiations in Paris came to a head and political solutions,
including new local elections on a one-man, one-vote basis, were debated. The government's response to this, the so-called Accelerated
Pacification Program, under which a presence, if only a platoon of
Popular Forces, was set up in about a thousand hamlets in contested areas, seemed insufficient. Among other things, the fifty-nine-
man Revolutionary Development Teams were divided into two
sections and then broken down into ten-man units, and while this
put more "bodies" into some hamlets, it weakened the relative
impact these teams had established elsewhere. The Communists,
while they stepped up their terror in the hamlets, aiming particularly at assassinating more local officials, including Revolutionary
Development workers, proffered a "soft glove" to go with the "hard
fist." In certain areas, including the III Corps region around Saigon
and parts of the delta, an increasing number of families and individuals in out-of-the-way places were visited clandestinely by Vietcong agents. Some of these agents were local friends or old ac-
quaintances who suddenly reappeared after years of absence,
while others were newcomers; these men, and sometimes women,
stressed the approach of peace, the imminent withdrawal of the
Americans, the continued corruption and failures of government

officials, and, in essence, sought to build up the tenuous but never-theless vital bridges between themselves and the peasant families that could prove decisive in the future. A survey in the III Corps area by an American psychological warfare expert, a Vietnamese-language officer with many years of experience in the country, elicited a surprisingly large number of admissions from villagers who spoke nonchalantly of having been visited by Vietcong rep-resentatives, of spending two or three congenial hours with them, and then seeing to it that they left safely.

Paris and Afterward

If these various political moves were part of the emerging fight-and-talk strategy, the Communists were by no means neglecting the first part of the equation as the Paris sessions finally ap-proached the serious phase early in 1969, when the "table-setting" maneuvers were completed. In South Vietnam, the North Vietna-mese and the Vietcong retained a number of options, but their principal effort still seemed to be concentrated in the III Corps area, west, northwest, and north of Saigon. During September and October, 1968, elements of four divisions withdrew into Cambodia, two other divisions farther north moved into Laos, and another two withdrew northward across the D.M.Z. By early December, however, there was mounting evidence that the divisions in Cam-bodia had started to move back into South Vietnam toward the infiltration routes to Saigon, as before. It seemed unlikely that another serious effort would be made to attack Saigon, but the intention at least was to infiltrate the capital with as many sapper and special-action squads as possible—and, if feasible, a battalion or two. The principal Communist objective, Allied intelligence maintained, was the seizure of as many district capitals in III Corps as possible, and perhaps a provincial capital or two; these places would then be held for however long they could be in order to "show the flag" and demonstrate to the negotiators in Paris the strength the Communists still maintained. In the II Corps area activity was slight, while to the north, in I Corps, there was some indication of renewed Communist activity, in the A Shau Valley stretching eastward from Laos and in the area southeast of Danang, a traditional Communist stronghold.

In many respects, the biggest change had taken place in the delta, which had for so long remained the heartland of the Vietcong and where the North Vietnamese had intervened only slightly. It was here that, in the fall months of 1968 and at the beginning of 1969, the Americans and the South Vietnamese made the greatest progress. Much of the heavy rate of attrition the Vietcong was suffering was due to a new aggressive naval patrol instituted by Vice Admiral Elmo Russell Zumwalt, Jr., whose aggressive attacks by new amphibious craft along the canals as well as the rivers that laced the whole delta area were reaching into Vietcong sanctuaries near the Cambodian border north of the Gulf of Siam, and into the swampy enemy base areas south and southwest of Saigon. The improvement in the delta reflected in part the more zealous reaction of the Regional Forces throughout the country, which was due to their receiving new M-16 rifles from the Americans, a long overdue step. The total government strength had now reached about a million armed men. In contrast, the Communists had perhaps 80,000 North Vietnamese troops in the country or just across its borders, but the strength of the Vietcong main force was probably below 40,000, while the regional and local guerrillas had dropped to under 100,000. North Vietnamese soldiers were increasingly moving in on top of the Vietcong and the guerrillas, while the guerrillas were also being used as fillers in the main-force units. If this blending process was primarily due to manpower and recruiting problems, there was also another reason: the Communists wanted to come up with as thorough a blend as possible so that, when troop withdrawals were agreed upon at the peace conference, they could claim as few "pure" North Vietnamese units as possible.

In analyzing the Communists' position both in Paris and in Vietnam, considerable weight had to be given to a speech made to party workers in June, 1968, by Truong Chinh, in which the policy of "reverting to protracted war" was set forth. The speech, which was only made public in September, was undeniably an answer to the Le Duan policy of seeking a quick solution to the war, a strategy that had proved a failure at Tet and in May. The fact that Truong Chinh's report was formally adopted by the Laodang and was used as a political study document proved, further, that he was in full ascendancy again, after several years of having given way to Le Duan, and that he and Le Duan might end fighting to inherit Ho Chi Minh's crown. After warning party workers to "overcome pacifist ideas" and "grasp the motto of the long-drawn-out fight," Truong Chinh said, "We must attack the enemy with a determination to fight and win. But at times, under certain circumstances, we must shift to the defensive to gain time, dishearten the enemy, and build up our forces for a new offensive. . . . A truly profound and broad revolution of the masses of people to seize power must naturally coordinate political struggle—including general strikes, market strikes, school strikes, office strikes, political meetings and demonstrations, show-of-force demonstrations, and so forth—with armed combat." He exhorted the cadres in the South to continue their attacks against the American imperialists and their South Vietnamese puppets and to "insure that the more we fight, the stronger we become." Stressing the fact that "the Vietnamese people are one," he made it clear that the Communists would continue to dominate their activities, despite window-dressing maneuvers like the creation of the Alliance of National, Democratic, and Peace Forces. He said it was theoretically sound to build "a united front with a broad basis," but "to insure the success of the revolution the Front has to base itself on a solid worker-peasant alliance and be led closely by a Marxist-Leninist party." Such a party, "with a maximum platform," Truong Chinh added significantly, must never share its "right" to exert complete revolutionary leadership "with any party whatever, and must absolutely not allow the national bourgeoisie to lead the national unified front."

In the Saigon government, increasing thought was being given to the problem of how to deal with the Communists both during the period of negotiations and after some sort of settlement had been reached. Privately, from President Thieu down, most officials and political leaders admitted that a compromise of one kind or another with the Front was inevitable. Despite public protestations, it was conceded that the Front would probably either become part of a new coalition or be allowed to function as a political party—one suggestion heard was that it be permitted to operate openly *if* it admitted it was a Communist organization. Most

Vietnamese continued to fear, however, that even if it was forced into the open, the Front might gradually succeed in taking over the country. Under such circumstances, they predicted, the first stage might be a liberal democracy, like the Third or Fourth French Republic. A period of instability marked by political party conflict would then lead to a Communist-dominated mixed administration. Such a coalition would be neutralist in its foreign policy, while internal policy would remain non-Communist on the surface, but would in fact be carefully controlled by the Communists. American disengagement would be followed by rising anti-American feeling, and only unconditional foreign aid, mostly from the Communist bloc, would be accepted, unless the United States altered its aid policies. Finally, as the government depended more and more on Communist assistance, a military-political coup, such as had taken place in Czechoslovakia, would solidify Communist rule.

The only way to avoid having this happen, on the basis of what might begin with a compromise in Paris, according to some of the tougher-minded Vietnamese, was to devise a counterstrategy of entrapment. "We should not deceive ourselves," one Vietnamese with many years of experience in dealing with the Communists said. "We remain politically and organizationally weak and they are strong. They will obviously try to sabotage the peace, and our job will not be made easier by the fact that, after a cease-fire, some government troops are likely to go over to the other side, while many common people will fall victim to Communist propaganda or will make their own accommodations. Our best course might be to allow the Communists to operate openly for two or three months, and then simply crack down on them. We may have no other choice, since with a divided and disintegrated population we will not be ready to engage them in an open political fight. But even if we do arrest their top leaders, they would retain their tight organization, underground, and that's the problem we must face."

It was when this problem was debated privately among Vietnamese and Americans that the discussion increasingly gravitated toward the central issue of creating and administering an altogether new government mechanism that would be both strong and effective. What was needed, many observers felt, was an altogether new rationale and approach based on a combination of Communist and early Diemist methods and tactics. Though this sounded like sacrilege, such a plan, carefully conceived and implemented, might alone be able to withstand the Communist political offensive by fashioning a strong nationalist base that could both hold off the Communists and prevent another dictatorship or more disintegration. The question was, could the mistakes of misconstrued purpose and organization that Diem made be avoided under the even more difficult circumstances that would obtain in the postwar period? Could a tightly coordinated system be devised that would adjust itself to Vietnamese institutions and traditions and retain popular support and enthusiasm even though the government manipulated it for political purposes? Despite the desire for political parties, many Vietnamese had come to believe that the elected government had to have enough freedom of maneuver to guide and control mass movements and to consolidate and direct its own motivated and trained cadre. The feeling was that the present cadres were too diffuse and lacked a proper rationale—"We don't need an ideology right now; we need a clear strategy and a reasonable explanation for implementing it," is the way one friend of mine put it. Under Diem a scientific approach to the problem was made, but it was too rigid and self-serving, and ultimately so complex in doctrine that, as guided by Ngo Dinh Nhu, it became metaphysical. In the pseudo-democratic context of 1969, with the more than ever divided and war-weary Vietnamese trying only halfheartedly to implement a Western-style political system foisted on them by the Americans, the critics maintained that a better-ordered and more revolutionary plan could still be instituted—but it would require American patience and assistance over the next several years. If properly executed and worked out on a brain-trust basis between the Americans and the Vietnamese, such a plan would actually enable the Americans to withdraw their armed forces from Vietnam more rapidly than might otherwise be possible without risking the quick loss of the country to the Communists. An obvious first step was to initiate the long-postponed reorganization of the armed forces.

"In all underdeveloped countries there is an essential contradiction between centralization and decentralization," one Vietnamese told me—a man who played a prominent role under Diem and later helped mount the coup against him. "Too much central control creates problems and delays, and if you decentralize power too

9

The United States after Vietnam

☙

Lessons Learned or Not Learned

Any adventure, or misadventure, in foreign policy should be
carefully analyzed and placed in its proper historical context if we
are to benefit at all from past experience. The real tragedy of Vietnam, it seems to me, is that we are likely to learn very little from
our guilt-ridden, misconstrued involvement there. It may be, as
Professor Samuel Huntington of Harvard has suggested, in citing
Santayana's famous warning that if we do not remember the past
we shall be condemned to repeat it, that in this case our future
policy-makers might be well advised to "blot out of their minds any
recollection" of Vietnam and regard the experience as an "unlesson." A great deal can actually be learned from Vietnam, but
Professor Huntington is afraid that we are "prisoners of the moment" and might do ourselves, and others, more harm than good
by trying too hard and too soon to judge what really happened
there. The dangers of a hasty appraisal in our present overheated
and fatigued condition are apparent, and when we do end or

ameliorate the Vietnam entanglement, we might indeed do well to forget the millions of words and TV action shots and debates that were devoted to it and go on to more urgent things, including, above all, our dreadful domestic problems.

On the other hand, one psychological and political risk of re-garding Vietnam as an "unlesson" would be to a reversion to isola-tionism—a kind of "shock withdrawal" that only the application of a nuclear drug—the misuse of the bomb in a future crisis—could "cure." However, if we become too preoccupied with our *mea culpas*, as we have shown an alarming tendency to do, we will do further injury to ourselves and probably to others, and preclude the basic re-evaluation of how we make and implement foreign policy that is so patently required. One does not have to be a con-firmed internationalist to reject even the temporary adoption of a Fortress America policy as that most calculated to defeat our national purpose—to subvert the expression of our very ethos—at home as well as abroad. However one allocates the degrees of at-tention we should devote to Europe, Asia, and the Middle East, we will ignore these areas separately and collectively at our own peril. But we do desperately need not only new estimates of their relative importance, but also new determinations of how, in today's politico-nuclear atmosphere, we can deal with individual nations in ways more rational and more productive for our mutual benefit.

In the case of Vietnam, as in all complicated episodes or chap-ters of American involvement, time will undoubtedly yield further evidence and testimony for the historians to debate. Certainly, one hopes, this will be true on the Communist side, for while we have captured many tons of documents and interrogated hundreds of low-level and high-level prisoners, we still do not know much about what motivated the men at the top in Hanoi and in the National Liberation Front in South Vietnam. We know, of course, of their burning desire to get rid of the Americans, as they got rid of the French before us, and to achieve independence and unity on their terms. But we know comparatively little of what really prompted the various changes in strategy and tactics, and of what took place in North Vietnam during the long years of the struggle. We know very little, too, of what the relationship of the North Vietnamese was and is to Moscow and Peking, and of how they envisage their "independent" role vis-à-vis the rest of the Communist world in the future—and in relation to Laos and Cambodia more immediately. However, we already know a great deal about *our* role and participation in the war, and about that of the South Vietnamese, going back to 1945-46.

As far as policy-making and waging war are concerned, we have come as close to "instant history" in Vietnam as we ever have, although there are blank spots. One major blank, for example, is what really *did* happen in the Gulf of Tonkin in August, 1964, when our planes attacked and badly damaged the North Vietnamese PT-boat bases in alleged reprisal for a surface attack on the American destroyer *Maddox*. There is evidence, partially aired at Congressional hearings, that we *did* decoy the North Vietnamese and provoke their attack on the *Maddox* by previously firing on offshore enemy radar stations from our own torpedo boats. (Without passing judgment as to whether this was justified as part of our long-range strategy, I believe we did entrap the North Vietnamese, who may have had their reasons for wanting to test us in a confrontation. At any rate, although the bombing of North Vietnam did not begin steadily until the spring of 1965, the *Maddox* incident led to the first air attack on the North and is therefore historically important.) There are other gaps. We know relatively little of the planning, campaign by campaign, of the American high command, based on its capability and intelligence, or of the effectiveness of the astonishing new scientific weapons of detection and destruction we used in the jungle. And, though a good part of the story of the American role in the 1963 coup that overthrew Ngo Dinh Diem has been told, not all of our involvement has been disclosed, and the full story of how the Army officers planned and carried out the coup has not been told either. Nevertheless, for the most part, particularly in the general area of policy-making and its enforcement, the evidence is in on Vietnam, and there are certain fundamental judgments and conclusions that should be made sooner rather than later.

Perhaps the most important one—because it has to do not only with Vietnam but with possible future contingencies—concerns what is loosely called "limited war." What does this really mean, and what specifically did it mean in Vietnam?

There are, unavoidably because of its subjective premises, many definitions of limited war. The very phrase itself, however, seems to me a contradiction in terms—war is war, and there is not much that can be done semantically or otherwise to treat it any differently. You can bomb or not bomb a country completely, or just bomb some of its factories and its trails of infiltration into another country, but if you are engaged in killing to prove a point, and if you commit half a million men to that cause, you are at war, whether you like to admit it or not, or whether or not you obtain Congressional approval of a Presidential act, as was the case with the Gulf of Tonkin Resolution. To paraphrase Thomas Wolfe, in his famous letter to Scott Fitzgerald about Ernest Hemingway, "Gulf me no Gulf of Tonkin Resolutions." What I am essentially saying is that limited war, as we have defined it in Vietnam—something supposedly aimed at something else called "limited objectives"—is an anomaly. No war, no killing, and no playing serious or semiserious revolutionary games, certainly not with the Communists, has anything "limited" about it. We may think it's limited, but they don't. They are after one thing— total revolutionary victory, in one or two or ten stages—and anything "limited" will never be acceptable to them. They may, in their peculiar but effective jargon of "Protracted War" versus the "General Uprising" and so on, adjust themselves, strategically and tactically, to the situation as they see it, in military and political terms, and then, if necessary, *readjust* themselves over and over again. But they will not lose sight of their goals, and they will simply wait, if necessary, for us to tire of limited views of ours. In revolutions, as in football, touchdowns count for more than field goals.

Mistakes and Misunderstandings

What, then, did we do or fail to do in Vietnam—or, rather, how did the various levels, echelons, and centers of power that constitute the American policy-making Establishment confound our purpose?

We began, unfortunately, by having no clear and positive objective. Our posture from the start was defensive, preventive. If, having for various reasons failed to "save" China from Communism—and I am among those who believe this was an impossible task, given the social and political disintegration in China after the Second World War—we thought we might be able to deal more effectively with a seemingly small and clear-cut revolutionary situation in Indochina, we failed miserably to meet the challenge. During the war we had made clear our opposition to any postwar continuance of colonialism, yet by supporting the French between 1946 and 1954 we did just about everything we could to re-establish colonialism in the lower part of Indochina (in contrast, one should add in all fairness, to what we did in Indonesia). At the outset we had a limited objective, too. We thought we could make do with a policy of encouraging the French to give the Vietnamese their independence but not pushing them so hard that we would lose their support for the new defense community being formed in Europe. We ended halfway between the two goal lines. We failed to persuade the die-hard French in Indochina politically, we supported their bootless war militarily and almost got into it ourselves as early as 1954, and the French ultimately ceased to back us in Europe. After 1954 we supported Diem, a strayed nationalist dogged by his own mandarin mentality and by the metaphysical conceits of his brother, Ngo Dinh Nhu. We got into a love-hate relationship with Diem that made us lose what degree of leverage we had at the outset with him, and we ended by helping to get rid of him. It was, in its own weird way, a kind of American political soap opera.

With Diem gone, and in the absence of any plans of our own to reinforce the fragmented clique of South Vietnamese who took over from him—another sad result of having a "limited objective" —we floundered, they floundered, and the real limited war began for us. I will modify what I have said about goals and objectives to this extent: there is such a thing as a flexible response to a situation, as we sought to have in Vietnam. But as John Roche has written, defending such an approach in Vietnam, we were in trouble from the beginning because we were fighting for what was essentially "an abstraction—American national interest in a nontotalitarian Asian future."* Ho Chi Minh was quick to realize this, and set out to prove to the American people that the war, politically and otherwise, but especially politically, was *not* in their national interest. In short, what Ho sought to do was to demonstrate that, whatever limits we wanted to set on the war militarily,

* *The New Leader,* October 21, 1968.

there were no possible limits politically, in Vietnam or in the United States. And he did just that. In fact, he achieved even more than he had hoped, for, as Richard Rovere has pointed out, this became the first war of the century "in which opposition was not only widespread but fashionable."

I do not want here, having done so elsewhere, to repeat the litany of our political failures in Vietnam—missed opportunities, contradictory and self-defeating decisions, and other lapses. What I am saying is that flexibility may be a virtue, in war and diplomacy and in ordinary daily life, but if it is pursued too long, if it fails to create a design and to achieve a sure purpose, it is little more, in the final analysis, than vacillation.

Should we therefore have gone whole hog or got out? Either choice is too simplistic. But one can bear with the considerable number of sensitive and sensible members of the military who don't belong to what Arthur Schlesinger, Jr., summarily dismisses as the "warrior caste" but who became convinced we were putting ourselves into a military strait jacket in Vietnam; and with those sensitive and sensible liberals such as Rovere who believed in our Vietnam commitment until 1965, but who came to feel the war was "intolerable" because of what it was doing to American society. I sympathize with both those views, though I was not for all-out war (regarding the bombing of the North initially with skepticism), and my cut-off point of intolerability came later. Nor do I feel that, in 1969, we can just pull up stakes and get out quickly. (This would seem to put me in the limited-war category, but I reject that—categorically; I suppose I am a disillusioned "flexibilist," who believes we suffered from an abysmal hardening of the political arteries in Vietnam, and lost, or surrendered, our flexibility and leverage unnecessarily. Which is to say that, among other things, we should have been much firmer than we were in dealing sooner with such matters as the reorganization and improvement of the South Vietnamese armed forces, and in insisting on political and administrative reforms, especially after the coup against Diem. And if these things failed, we should not have put a large ground force of our own into the country. Once it was there, the manner of its withdrawal necessarily became *vital*.)

What I want to examine further, are the reasons within ourselves—the American system, and the American character and personality—for our shortcomings or failures in Vietnam.

There are a number of objective and subjective observations that can be made. For instance, I believe that President Johnson misunderstood the internal political situation in Vietnam, or allowed his preoccupation with the military side of the war to subsume his political concern, and this probably led to his failure to explain the conflict, in all its complications, to the American people. (One always had the feeling, seeing him in pictures with President Thieu or Vice President Ky at Honolulu, Guam, Manila, or elsewhere, that he was wondering what irony of fate had taken him out of Washington and brought him there.) I have always been among those who have believed that if the American people are told the truth about something, even something complex and unsavory, they will invariably be ahead of the State Department in their comprehension and in their willingness to come to grips with the problem. For whatever reasons—his own confusion of purpose, his frustrations resulting from the collapse of his Great Society dreams, the limitations of his international outlook—Johnson did not take the American people sufficiently or consistently into his confidence. He failed to explain, except on such rare occasions as his Johns Hopkins speech about postwar development and some political speeches toward the end of his tenure, *why* we were in Vietnam and *why* our presence there was important to the rest of Southeast Asia, *why*, in fact, Southeast Asia is important to us. At least, he did not do so convincingly, and it was no wonder that the American people were confused and bewildered.

Certainly it is also true that Johnson was a victim of "outrageous fortune." There *was* an undeniable "patriotism gap" between the Korean War and the Vietnam war. At the time the Korean War started we were still willing and eager to oppose aggression and to fight evil; but by the time the Vietnam conflict began in earnest we had lowered our emotional sights toward the rest of the world. Our deep domestic cleavages and problems over civil rights, urbanization, affluence versus poverty, and other issues had by 1965 assumed a priority of concern. However, I think that both challenges, domestic and foreign, including Vietnam, could have been dealt with far more subtly and successfully if Johnson had not had to endure at the same time one of those peculiar social and intellectual aberrations that periodically take place in American life. He was incapable of dealing with the explosive social phenomenon because, among other things, he was both its target and its victim.

Much has been written about the alienation of intellectuals and the rebellion of youth during the Johnson period. Both used Vietnam as a kind of catalyst of their discontent, but both reactions had far deeper roots, it seems to me, and would have taken place with or without Johnson, and with or without Vietnam. If Johnson hadn't existed, they would have found it necessary to invent someone or something like him—a scourge, an instrument of self-flagellation. I doubt that Vietnam by itself would have been enough to spark the discontent, and if President Kennedy had lived to handle the problem with more grace and restraint, as I suspect he would have, its catalytic function would have been even less. But Johnson + Vietnam = LSD (long-smoldering dementia). People did seem to go out of their minds in their vilification of the President over Vietnam ("Hey, hey, LBJ, how many kids did you kill today?" etc.). Contempt and shame bred irrationality. There was, both in the reaction of intellectuals and in the mindlessness of much of the hysterical response of youth, a quality of self-hatred, which was also reflected in the attitude of whites and blacks as the racial conflict reached its perhaps inevitable historical crescendo.

In many cases, zeal turned into zaniness. "The land is filling up with cranks and zanies—some well intentioned, some vicious," Rovere wrote in *The New Yorker* in the fall of 1967. "It can be contended that Vietnam is not the only cause of goofing off, of alienation. Of course it isn't. But it provides the occasion, and it heightens the degree." I agree with that, though I think a calm, reasoned voice or two at the top could have diminished the hysteria, which Johnson was scarcely able to do because the war was all but driving him out of his mind, too. The intellectuals, as a group, were perhaps more to blame, and their role is more difficult to analyze. Aside from a certain hangover of anti-anti-Communism, plus the "folk herofication" of the Vietcong and the North Vietnamese—their long struggle in the jungle against all odds, their stoicism in the face of inexcusable bombings, etc.—a good deal of the violently expressed opposition of the intellectuals to the war stemmed from their own malaise due just as much to other causes, and perhaps above all to a growing sense of frustration and futility about their place in American life. In a perceptive essay in *Foreign Affairs*, in July, 1967, on "American Intellectuals and Foreign Policy," Irving Kristol spoke of the phenomenon of intellectual confusion and discontent as involving "the highly problematic relationship of the modern intellectual to foreign affairs, the basic self-definition of the American intellectual, the tortured connections between American liberal ideology and the American imperial republic, and the role of the newly established academic classes in an affluent society." Kristol pointed out, further, that ideology has traditionally in Western thought played a subsidiary role in the realm of foreign affairs to "contingency, fortune and fate." This factor of expediency, with its implications of immorality, has heightened the intellectuals' sense of indignation and misdirected moral condemnation. Belief in the common man, sympathy for the wretched of the earth (i.e., the beleaguered Vietnamese on the Communist side), support of a revolutionary thrust almost anywhere as something better than gradualism, and a disrespect of traditionalism and authority, are all part of the average American intellectual's makeup. Collectively, these qualities have created an intellectual attitude described by Kristol in historical terms as "transcendentalist populism," or "protestantism." The result, as he said, is that "the isolationist ideal is experiencing its final, convulsive agony" among American intellectuals more than in any other group, and their dissent, particularly on an issue as volatile and debatable as Vietnam, has made them strongly anti-Establishment and against anything that implies or presupposes an imperial role for the United States. Ergo, United States military intervention in Southeast Asia has nothing to do with American national security, and assuredly not with any justifiable moral purpose.

There is no doubt that, even within the government Establishment, and among those specifically dealing with foreign policy and Vietnam, intellectual disaffection increased during the Johnson administration. The Bay of Pigs was at least "intellectualized" by Kennedy and those around him; they did extract some lessons from the fiasco. (Kennedy's own comment, about never again trusting the "experts" was one manifestation.) Vietnam, however, simply put people through a wringer. Perhaps the best expression of this came from James C. Thomson, Jr., who worked in the White House and in the Department of State from 1961 to 1966 under both Presidents Kennedy and Johnson, and who subsequently, in *The Atlantic*, sought to analyze, in intellectual terms, his traumatic experience. After pointing out, quite correctly, the lack of earlier expertise in the State Department on Indochina, and the obvious conscious or subconscious impact the "loss" of China had on official reporting from Vietnam, he cited a number of things in his combined testament and autopsy. They included what he described as "the domestication of the dissenters," including himself; "the curator mentality" in the State Department; confusion over the nature of the war and how it could be ended, which in turn created both "bureaucratic detachment" and "oversell"— "a preoccupation with Vietnam public relations as opposed to Vietnam policy-making." Other factors such as plain fatigue and "human ego investment"—probably Walt Rostow was the outstanding exemplar of that—contributed to the internal frustration and malaise. It is worth noting here that the man in the Johnson administration who finally demonstrated the most spunk and forthrightness in challenging the precepts and guidelines on Vietnam was Secretary of Defense Robert McNamara, who was less of an intellectual than a top-level technician or technocrat, and who questioned the efficacy of the bombing of North Vietnam simply because, as he said, it wasn't *working* as well as had been expected. It was far more difficult, in Washington or Saigon, as I myself repeatedly discovered in both places, to get anyone to admit the inefficacy or even the imperfections of our *political* policy in Vietnam.

Faults in the Structure

This brings us directly to the question of how foreign policy is made and implemented, and to problems of leadership and organization. The American character has a deep expiatory streak, which is also part of the Protestant ethic, and it has its bureaucratic manifestations. We have had governmental committees galore, composed of countless experts, insiders and outsiders, who hear evidence and take testimony on what is wrong with the State Department or with the whole national administrative apparatus; then, when the long process is over, all the recommendations are in, and the volumes are neatly printed and leather-bound, everyone concerned beams on the product, as upon a newborn child, and wishes it well in the harsh world. We have atoned for our sins, we have confessed—and life goes on just as before. I'm afraid, as I said at the outset, that this may happen with Vietnam unless we take a much more careful look not only at what was right or wrong about our policy and its implementation there, but at the whole procedural and structural apparatus of policy-making. Some of the "think tanks" have done and are doing this, but they have their own tendency to become part of the "Parkinsonized" Establishment —in fact, most of them are under government contract, and a number were engaged, early in 1969, in figuring out schedules of withdrawal from Vietnam.

I am not an expert on administration, only a long-time critical observer of the foreign and domestic scene. So I can simply offer some random observations on what appears to me to be wrong or ineffective. I am also aware that it is easier to criticize than to participate, but one of the functions of a journalist, after all, is to offer just such criticism, and he is often in a better position than those on the inside because he is not as involved (though he may be more concerned). He is able to see and hear things that the members of the Establishment cannot, because he is a freer agent and has more time to move about. Also, he is apt to stay longer in a country, or at least to be in and out of it over a longer period of time, and to have the chance to obtain a larger perspective.

This matter of perspective is as good a starting point as any. There are advantages to having "fresh eyes" and "new ears" in a complex situation, especially one of long duration, but these can be outweighed by the disadvantages of losing continuity of experience. The main reason morale remained high among the military in Vietnam was that the average soldier only had a one-year tour of duty there. The Foreign Service and its adjunct branches (U.S.I.S., A.I.D., etc.), however, consist of professional career people. Their average length of stay in Vietnam, as is customary in any foreign post, was eighteen months. This was demonstrably an insufficient time for anyone to learn and understand enough about the place and its people and to come to grips either with Vietnam as a country or with the American engagement there, in its multifarious aspects. A number of men who became personally committed extended their tours of duty, as did a considerable number of military officers, especially those in the middle and higher ranks, but the turnover among the great majority of civilians was constant. This was as deeply disturbing to the Vietnamese as it was disenchanting to anyone who, like myself, sought to build "bridges" between Vietnamese friends and the ever-rotating Americans. As the inevitable friction between the Americans and the Vietnamese increased the longer the frustrating war went on, more and more Vietnamese simply made it clear that, unless they had official business to conduct, they saw no point to getting to know their American counterparts on a more personal basis. The diminishment of dialogues except for necessary business was scarcely conducive to the creation of real understanding. The customary social schedules of lunches and dinners and cocktail parties brought Vietnamese and Americans together, but such occasions were seldom productive in the sense that I mean, and if the Americans thought they were getting to know the Vietnamese, the Vietnamese I know, and with whom I was accustomed to spend hours at a time "just talking," did not. In fact, most of the time at social gatherings they felt out of touch and were bored, and the fact that many of them had learned some English did little to improve the level of meaningful discourse, especially in a crowd or even in a small group. Furthermore, even in the earlier years when there was more rapport, the Americans invariably operated on what can be described as a "crisis schedule" —that is, too often they saw the Vietnamese they knew only when "something was happening." Again, there were obvious exceptions to this, but it was the general rule.

This whole concept of swinging-door diplomacy was in sharp contrast to what the British did in Malaya during the Emergency of the late nineteen-forties and -fifties. Many if not most British military and civilian officials who took part in that ultimately successful counterinsurgency stayed several years at a time, and some of them stayed for the whole decade of its duration. If their families were not with them, they were nearby, and leaves were regular. (Many of the Americans actually had their families in Bangkok or Hong Kong during their short tours of duty, but the fact that American dependents were sent out of Vietnam in a moment of panic early in 1965 was another error of judgment; there were many top-flight Foreign Service officers who would have been glad to stay on for added tours if their wives had been permitted to stay with them.) Certainly, in a subtle counterinsurgency and complex political contest such as Vietnam, the need to establish a continuum of effort is, or should be, apparent. There would seem to be little reason why the outmoded eighteen-month-tour-of-duty system should have been continued in Vietnam. I once asked President Johnson about this, but he indicated there wasn't much he could do about it. I still wonder why not. Was this part of the "limited war" concept?

The perspective of the average Foreign Service officer was always further limited by the unbelievable amount of paper work he had to do. This kept him chained to his desk a good part of the time. A "provincial reporting" system was instituted by the Political Section in the American Mission some years ago, and this did enable some of the younger officers, particularly those who spoke Vietnamese, to move around the country and to furnish reports to their superiors. Invariably, however, the reports heaped up and simply added to the monumental paper work, to the extent that anyone back in Washington seeking *his* perspective on what was happening in Vietnam would have required not a single pair of glasses but a many-sided spectrum and a month off to read what was sent back in a week. When one also takes into account the plethora of agencies and bureaus and departments and what not that make up the American bureaucracy, both at home and in a busy foreign post, the confusion is compounded to the point of madness.

The doom of modern diplomacy may well be modern communications, as has often been said. I have heard more than one ambassador or section chief curse the cables with all their special mumbo jumbo, beginning with "eyes only" messages down to those "for limited distribution." Policy-making on the ground, under such circumstances, even when an ambassador and his staff are effective, is virtually impossible. Instead of being "the representative of the President of the United States," as an ambassador is supposed to be, he becomes the local head of an international message-control center, and a crisis provokes more panic and possibility of error than policy of any kind. An excellent example of this is the crisis that occurred between the Americans and the Vietnamese in Saigon before the Paris peace talks got seriously under way. Ambassador Ellsworth Bunker's instructions were to deal only with "heads of state" in transmitting President Johnson's decision to call off the bombing and in obtaining President Thieu's agreement. It was apparent to Bunker that this would cause trouble when, at the last moment, Thieu would have to bring others into his confidence, and, Vietnamese being Vietnamese, this would unavoidably lead to debate and opposition about the tacit pledges made by the Communists in Paris and other matters. This is just what happened. Had Bunker, a highly astute diplomat of long experience, been permitted to handle the matter alone in the way that he saw fit, the chances are the crisis would either not have occurred or it would have been resolved much sooner and with far fewer ruffled feelings.

Part of the difficulty in recent years, of course, has resulted from the usurpation of the conduct of foreign affairs by the White House, and this was especially true in the Vietnam war under Johnson. If Johnson was God, Walt Rostow was the Holy Ghost, down in the White House basement, and the various apostles all over Washington—in the State Department, in the Central Intelligence Agency, in the Pentagon, in A.I.D., in the United States Information Agency, and in a flock of lesser bodies—all played their clearly defined, or not so clearly defined, roles. All of them were in separate contact with Saigon, and all of them were trying to run the war in their own way, or at least trying to protect what they thought was their rightful part of it. Top-level meetings of "interdepartmental boards" in Washington became sounding boards for the expression and defense of individual and departmental positions, and Mission Council meetings in Saigon were often compared to unsuccessful group therapy sessions. The more complicated it all got, the more visiting firemen from Washington, "special representatives," high-level brass, Congressmen and Senators, "think-tank" consultants, and agents and experts in everything from land mines to floating docks streamed in and out of Saigon, so that the poor officials on the scene in Vietnam didn't even have time to get to their paper work. Added to that was the ever-swelling press corps, which reached a total of more than five hundred correspondents, each with his own demands and problems. It has become fashionable, among some of the more ardent defenders of the American position in Vietnam, to blame the press for much of the disaffection at home. It may have been true that TV did play an unseemly role, consciously or unconsciously, in showing all the worst features of the American effort and few of the good ones, and that the press was sometimes prone to be overcritical and oversuspicious—a result largely of the early Vietnam days when the truth was not always told officially. But it is my impression that, by and large, the correspondents over the years did a creditable job in covering one of the most difficult and incomprehensible of conflicts. It may be said, though, that there was a tendency to overstress the military aspects and a little too much gung ho spirit on the part of the younger correspondents, and that relatively few reporters had the patience or capacity to understand the politics.

The Responsibilities of Response

During the Adlai Stevenson Institute of Public Affairs symposium in June, 1968, in Chicago, on "No More Vietnams?" Professor Stanley Hoffman, of Harvard, suggested that the handling of the whole Vietnam problem "reveals flaws that come from the very depths of our political style and machinery" and that, in fact, "Vietnam is like a blow-up of many of our flaws." Professor Hoffman is more interested in the "national style" than in "administrative reforms" or "a romantic revolt against the national security bureaucracy." He feels, as I do, that the Vietnam tragedy was primarily the result of "our refusal to come to grips with realities in South Vietnam . . . that happened to be decisive from the viewpoint of politics," and that our *hubris* led us into an overoptimistic and simplistic trap in which "we saw our task hopefully as saving [South Vietnam] from its enemies instead of from itself." If the machinery sometimes makes the "style," the "style" also determines how the machinery functions—a Secretary of State with grace, wisdom, and forcefulness, and with a competent Under Secretary at his side, can do a lot better with the cumbersome bureaucracy at Foggy Bottom than one who lacks those qualities. Nevertheless, in keeping with the *hubris* Professor Hoffman decries, I think that in consistently criticizing Vietnamese institutions, and doing little to help improve them, we also made it clear that our ineptitude was at least in part due to the inadequacy of our *own* institutions. And part of this failure to cope *had* to be bureaucratic—the tremendous overlap, the competition among departments and individuals in the American "Vietnam empire," etc.—all of which would seem to call for re-evaluation and fresh appraisal.

It may be too much to expect that American Presidents, weighed down with so many immense burdens nowadays, *can* successfully be their own Secretaries of State—there may just not be time in the modern world. By the same token, no Secretary of State with imagination and the desire to *make* policy can allow himself to be bogged down by administrative detail in running the world-wide apparatus of the State Department. Some rationalization, beyond the scope of personalities in power and the inescapable fact that the President does make the final decisions, seems to be in order in defining the roles and responsibilities of the Secretary of State and of his assistants. There has been some reorganization in the State Department in recent years and some elimination of unnecessary channels and echelons, but more is needed—the place is still more of a Foreign Factory than a Foreign Office. The liaison between the White House and the State Department should become a main and not a secondary artery of government, as it has been in the past, with the staff in the White House basement functioning as a schizoid substitute for, and not an alter ego of, the Department.

The amount of leeway ambassadors in the field have should be reclarified, and they should actually and not symbolically function once more as representatives of the President, in however many directions the cables flow—and the flow is ridiculously high. A reorganization of our whole system of representation abroad is overdue. United States embassies, especially in critical and busy places, are far larger than they need be, and this leads to waste of time on endless meetings as well as on the volume of paper work. It simply clogs the whole operation, delaying and precluding swift decisions in dealing with emergencies, and affording no time for quiet reflection and analysis. The roles of the Defense Department, of the National Security Council and the Joint Chiefs of Staff, of A.I.D., and of the C.I.A. in the making and direction of foreign policy remain unclear and competitive. This results, as when the Vietnam war was known as "McNamara's War," in a fuzzy focus and in all sorts of hierarchical confusion. (I remember an incident during one of McNamara's many visits to Saigon when a military adviser in the delta was specially summoned by Ambassador Henry Cabot Lodge to give McNamara "the real lowdown" on why things were not going as well as the Defense Secretary thought; looking at the man's charts and listening to him, McNamara said he was "very impressed," though the briefer told him absolutely nothing that correspondents, let alone Lodge, had not known for months. Somehow, though, what the man said had never got through to Washington, perhaps because the matter at hand was not essentially the prerogative of the Defense Department.)

These are just some of the bureaucratic-institutional problems. Their irresolution surely inhibited, throughout the Vietnam crisis, the formulation of a sound counterinsurgency strategy that would have reduced or eliminated the constant experimentation with the pacification program which for so long held progress to a snail's pace. Men knowledgeable on this subject, such as Edward G. Lansdale, who was attached to the Mission in Saigon over a three-year period, became victims of the bureaucratic struggle and were all but wasted—in Lansdale's case his additional intimate knowledge of the Vietnamese political situation and his special gifts for obtaining the confidence of Vietnamese political and religious leaders were only briefly put to use toward the end of his frustrating and fretful stay. Something is obviously wrong when our best brains, including some of our maverick ones, are not used. For whatever historical reasons, dissent and innovation in the Establishment continue to be frowned upon. (I can't count the times when important members of the American Mission in Saigon, who were, like Lansdale, friends of mine, said of him, "Ed would be O.K. if he would just be a member of the *team*.") When there are voices in opposition who are respected—George Ball and Jim Thomson during the Johnson period in Washington were other examples—they too readily come to be regarded simply as foils or conscience-salving protagonists of a minority or unpopular viewpoint.

The larger problem of bringing outside critics and dissenters

back into the orbit of policy-making and action is obviously a
more complicated one, and this, of course, is a two-way street.
Such a phenomenon has not occurred in American life since the
period of Franklin D. Roosevelt, though Kennedy, had he lived,
might have achieved it. There has to be an ardor and a fervor
to serve, and what we seem to need most in America today, and
what must somehow be contrived, is a widening of our options,
an increase of scope. I disagree with most of the views expressed
by those who took part in the Adlai Stevenson symposium on Vietnam, and I agree with most of the academic experts who belong
to the quasi-official Far Eastern policy advisory group, but I would
like to see a new body created composed of half of each. We need
dialogues and disagreements, not just meetings of the board. The
best consensus is dialectic. It is obvious that most of our ills today,
in all areas of national endeavor and conflict, are societal—they
are caused by many things that range from apathy to affluence,
from passion to pride, and to plain fear and confusion. Our
educational system is full of traditional, outmoded, stodgy forms
that preclude legitimate exchanges between those who teach and
those who learn, just as our bureaucracy is full of similar strictures
that make it hard for new ideas to burgeon. What we certainly
cannot afford, either in foreign affairs or in domestic politics, is
to "coast," to "take a breather." A great many people, including
some intellectuals, now hope that the Nixon administration will
provide just that. There may be some things to calm down about—
above all, the still unresolved racial problem—but there are far
more matters that require our arousal and our rededication.

Our role in the world has been seriously questioned in recent
years. Whatever we think of de Gaulle, he has recreated a sense
of European identity, self-sufficiency, and independence. The Atlantic Community, if it is to be salvaged, will be a more equitable
one, or at least it will no longer be as thoroughly dominated by
the two senior partners, the United States and Great Britain. We
are in a dilemma in the Middle East. In Asia we are in the odd
position of having made blunders in Vietnam and yet of having
gained friends by the simple act of having maintained a worthwhile if misconstrued commitment. If Ho Chi Minh has outlasted
us, in political patience, most of the rest of Southeast Asia is
grateful for what degree of patience and fortitude we have

demonstrated. One reason Southeast Asia will remain important is that new ideas—about political organization, about the relationship between authoritarianism and democracy, about the meaning and value of religion both in and out of politics, about social and economic experimentation, and about the possibilities of regional cooperation—have been brought to life there, and are now beginning to find mature expression. We cannot afford to ignore these ideas, even if we think that our national security is not always directly affected. In fact, important as our national security is, we cannot afford as a great power to make that always our paramount consideration. It is, as Wendell Willkie said a long time ago, "One World," whether we like it or not.

At the moment, partly but not particularly as a result of our failure to achieve what many of us hoped to achieve in Vietnam, it is undoubtedly true that we should devote our principal attention to domestic matters. But that does not mean we can forget Southeast Asia, if for no other reason than that neither the Soviet Union nor China will forget it. If time has been "out of hand," in Southeast Asia as elsewhere, and if events have taken place at such a dizzying pace that it has been all but impossible to keep up with them, then at least we can try to get them back "in hand" again. We can try to readjust ourselves to what is still a revolutionary condition in Vietnam and seems bound to remain so indefinitely. This is true of other countries in Southeast Asia, above all of Indonesia, and of much of the rest of the world, too. The process of adapting or readapting ourselves to an era of continuing change must, of necessity, be both subjective and objective. Abroad as well as at home, *hubris* must give way to humility. But even that is not enough. In a nuclear-powered world, older forms of power are still important, including the power to give assistance and the power to protect. I don't see how we can escape that dual responsibility, whether there are any more Vietnams or not. Inevitably, there will be comparable crises, calling for different kinds of response. If Vietnam has taught us how to be more careful and moderate, perhaps more selective, in our basic approach, it should also have demonstrated the difficulties of being overinvolved without being sufficiently committed to specific, attainable goals. If we have learned that much in Vietnam, we will at least have learned something about responsibility and response.

Index

About the Author

Robert Shaplen was born in Philadelphia in 1917 and has degrees from the University of Wisconsin and Columbia University. He was a Nieman Fellow at Harvard in 1947-1948. After six years as a reporter for the New York *Herald Tribune*, he went to the Pacific in 1943 as war correspondent for *Newsweek*, where he took part in fourteen amphibious landings. From 1945 to 1947 Mr. Shaplen was head of *Newsweek*'s Far East bureau, covering China, Manchuria and Southeast Asia. Out of his Far East experience came two works of fiction, *A Corner of the World* (1949) and *A Forest of Tigers* (1956). A regular contributor to *The New Yorker*, his examinations of Henry Ward Beecher, the McKesson and Robbins case, and Ivar Kreuger the Match King have been particularly memorable. But his speciality has been foreign reporting and his last seven years have been given to covering the Far East, with emphasis on Vietnam.

Mr. Shaplen is now *The New Yorker*'s Asian correspondent and lives in Hong Kong. He is married to the former June Herman and has three children.

His book about the Vietnam crisis, *The Lost Revolution* (1965), won awards from the Overseas Press Club and the Columbia School of Journalism and was nominated for the National Book Award.